LONGMAN STUDY GUIDES

GCSE
Biology

Chris Millican
Martin Barker

LONGMAN

LONGMAN STUDY GUIDES

SERIES EDITORS: **Geoff Black and Stuart Wall**

Titles Available

Biology
Business Studies
Chemistry
Design and Technology
Economics
English
English Literature
French
Geography
German
Information Technology

Mathematics
Mathematics: Higher Level
Music
Physics
Psychology
Religious Studies
Science
Sociology
Spanish
World History

Addison Wesley Longman Limited
Edinburgh Gate, Harlow,
Essex CM20 2JE, UK
and Associated Companies throughout the World

First published 1997

ISBN 0582-30481-4

British Library Cataloguing-in-Publication Data
A catalogue record for this book is
available from the British Library

Set by 30 in 9.75/12pt Sabon
Produced by Longman Singapore Publishers Pte
Printed in Singapore

CONTENTS

Longman Study Guides have been written by people who set and mark the exams – the examiners. Examiners are aware that due to lack of practice and poor preparation, some students achieve only the lowest grades: they are not able to effectively show the examiner what they know. These books give excellent advice about exam practice and preparation, and organising a structured revision programme, all of which are essential for examination success. Remember: the examiners are looking for opportunities to *give* you marks, not take them away!

Longman Study Guides are designed to be used throughout the course. The self-contained chapters can be read in any order appropriate to the stage you have reached in your course. The examiner guides you through the essential parts of each topic, making helpful comments throughout.

We believe that this book, and the series as a whole, will help you establish and build your basic knowledge and examination technique skills. For additional help with exam practice and revision techniques, we have published a series called **Longman Exam Practice Kits**, which are available from all good bookshops, or direct from Addison Wesley Longman.

GEOFF BLACK AND STUART WALL

ACKNOWLEDGEMENTS

We are indebted to the following Examination Groups for permission to reproduce questions which have appeared in the examination papers. Whilst permission has been granted to reproduce their questions, the answers, or hints on answers, are solely the responsibility of the authors and have not been provided by a Group.

EDEXCEL Foundation (London)
Midland Examining Group (MEG)
Northern Examinations and Assessment Board (NEAB)
Southern Examining Group (SEG)
Welsh Joint Committee (WJEC)
Northern Ireland Council for Curriculum, Examinations and Assessment (NICCEA)

We record our thanks to Stuart Wall and Geoff Black, from whom we have received a great deal of help and guidance and whose comments have led to improvements on the original manuscript.

Thanks to Clive and Meg, who kept me going when the going was tough.

Thanks to all my pupils, past and present, who make work so interesting and enjoyable.

CHRIS MILLICAN

This book has been written as a study aid for use throughout your GCSE course in Biology.

The first chapter gives advice about revision, examinations and coursework, with tips on:

▷ how to plan your revision;
▷ preparing for the examination;
▷ sitting the examination;
▷ coursework.

The second chapter gives important information about the National Curriculum assessment objectives, schemes of assessment and skill requirements for GCSE Biology. You should read these first two chapters carefully as they give invaluable advice which will be useful throughout your Biology course.

The book is then divided into the five key topic areas covered by the National Curriculum: Life processes and cell activity; humans as organisms; green plants as organisms; variation, inheritance and evolution; and living things in their environment. Note that Chapter 4, Humans as organisms, is a vast subject area so it has been split it into four sections (life processes, co-ordination, maintaining the internal environment and being healthy) to help you study it more easily. Chapter 8 looks at the extension topics covered by the various examination boards.

Each chapter includes six ingredients to help you do well:

1. **Getting started**: This page gives a short introduction to the chapter and includes a **Topic chart**, a table which at a glance, shows the breakdown of the topics covered by the chapter. The chart can be used to check your study and revision progress over the two years. A Topic Chart looks like this:

TOPIC	STUDY	REVISION 1	REVISION 2
Life processes			
Organs and systems in humans			
Organs and systems in plants			
Cell structure			
Specialised cells			
Movement in and out of cells			
Cell division			

Chapter 8 looks at the extension topics chosen by the different examination boards, so here the Topic Chart also gives a breakdown of the topic by examination board, so that you can easily identify which topics are covered by your board.

2. **What you need to know**: this is the core of the chapter and contains the information you are expected to know when you take your examination.

3. **Revision activities**: these are found within the 'What you need to know' section. You should use these to check your understanding as you are going through the course, or when you are revising. Answers are found at the end of the section.

4. **Examination questions**: to help you practise what you have learnt, up-to-date questions from all the major boards are included at the end of each chapter. This will give you vital practice in examination technique. Try not to look at the answers until you have attempted the questions to the best of your ability.

5. **Answers**: to all revision activities and examination questions are provided so that you can check your understanding. Questions have a mark breakdown with the answers so that you can see how to gain extra marks. In each chapter there is also an examination question with a typical student's answer, some of the answers are excellent A grade answers and some may have faults or weaknesses. These answers will help you

see what problems are identified by examiners and where you could improve your own examination answers.

6. **Topic summaries**: to help you learn the key points for the topics covered in the chapter. You should check that you know, and understand more fully, each of the key points listed.

The ideal way to use this book is to use it throughout your course as a **study guide**. When you are studying a topic at school you could:

▶ read the relevent chapter to reinforce your theory knowledge;
▶ fill in the revision activities to check your understanding;
▶ answer the examination questions, so you can see the level of knowledge which is needed;
▶ learn the topic summaries for your tests at school.

Alternatively, you could use this book as a quick **revision guide**, and work from it intensively in the period before your examination. For further practice of examination questions we also publish Longman Exam Practice Kit GCSE Biology which contains revision summaries, practice questions and practice timed papers. Quick revision will help you, but remember that there is no substitute for hard work during your course.

Good luck!

Revision, examinations and coursework

> **Introduction**

Everyone wants to do well in examinations, to get the best grades they possibly can; however it will require a lot of hard work and organisation from **you** to achieve this.

Every year I talk to students who say they have worked hard for examinations, but who are disappointed by their results. There are several possible reasons for this:

Reasons to fail
• put in effort

> **They have not worked hard enough.** Success demands a lot of time and effort from you; it is quite easy to fool other people into thinking you are working hard but, deep-down, you know how much effort you have really made.

• don't delay revision

> **They have left it too late to start revision.** Lots of people put off starting to revise; they feel as though tomorrow will be the ideal day but then they find reasons to delay again. When they finally do start, sometimes with only days to go before the actual examination, they feel rushed and panic. They try to read through all of their work, but have no time to concentrate properly on what they are doing.

• active not passive revision

> **They are spending time and effort on revision, but are using the wrong techniques.** If you are just reading through your notes, it is very easy to let your mind wander. You find yourself staring blankly at the page, or you are actually reading without thinking about the meaning of the words. To be effective, revision must be active, i.e. it must involve you in doing something.

• understand everything

> **They know the facts, but cannot apply them.** This happens if you learn something by rote, but do not understand it, e.g. you learn a list of labels for a diagram without learning to recognise the structures, or you learn an explanation 'parrot-fashion', but cannot relate it to a particular set of circumstances. Lots of questions ask for recall and understanding, i.e. they may want you to use your theory knowledge in a new context.

• read question properly

> **They do not know what the question wants.** Sometimes they cannot recognise which area of the syllabus is being tested, or have no idea what the question is asking. However, if the question is asked in a slightly different way, or if they are prompted (perhaps by an additional question), they are able to gain full marks. You probably recognise this feeling when your teacher goes over a test you have done in class; you can't believe it would be so easy to get it right!

There are three factors vital for success:

1. **Understand the work covered.**
2. **Learn it thoroughly.**
3. **Communicate it clearly in exams.**

From this you can see that passing examinations is not just a matter of whether you perform well for two hours in the examination itself. There are three routes to success:

1. **Throughout the course** you should be working hard to make sure you **understand** the topics covered. If you have tests in school, look carefully at where you lost marks, and why. If you don't understand a particular section, read about it in a textbook, or ask your teacher. Never just leave a section of the syllabus you don't understand.
2. **In the run-up to examinations** you should be revising the work covered in the course so that you really **know your facts.** First, get your files or books organised and make a list of everything you need to revise. Make a revision plan and stick to it. Use books

like this and past paper questions to get practice. If your school runs lunchtime or after school revision lessons, make sure that you go to them.

3. **In the examination** you should be concentrating hard to **show what you know**. This means reading the questions carefully, and writing clear, concise answers. Examination technique helps you to know how long an answer should be, and to recognise which key words to include for maximum marks. Too many people lose marks by being vague, or by writing long, waffly answers, which suggest that they do not understand the topic.

There is an element of luck in exams, but a successful student does not depend on being lucky – they work hard to make sure they will do well.

▷ Revision

Revision is not something that you do only on the night before an examination. You should have a planned programme of revision to make sure that you learn all topics thoroughly in the run-up to the examination.

Planning your revision

▶ **Start revising early**. You may think that you will forget the first things you revise, but this is not the case. Give yourself enough time to cover the whole syllabus at least twice.

▶ **Organise your books and files**. Make sure that your work is complete, and that it is in the right order. If you have bits missing you will need to photocopy work from a friend.

▶ **Make sure that you know what you have to revise.** Check with your teacher which syllabus you are studying, and to what level. Some topics will only be tested on higher level papers, so you may not have to learn all of it.

▶ **Make a revision plan using your topic list.** This breaks up the work into manageable chunks, and gives you a sense of achievement when you can see you are making progress.

▶ **Make sure you cover all the topics in your revision,** and don't try to predict which questions will come up. If you have studied a course for two years, you have probably had 100–150 hours of lessons, but your exams will last only two to three hours; you have to accept that some parts of the syllabus will not be tested, but it is not possible to guess which!

▶ **Revise actively**. This means do something, don't just read your notes! You could practise drawing and labelling, make up mnemonics to help you remember facts (like MRS GREN for life processes), write summary notes, write lists of key words onto summary cards, make spider diagrams ... the list is almost endless.

▶ **Learn definitions and equations properly,** so that you can recall them straight away. It is far easier to spend a bit of time learning them, than to try to make them up in the examination. It is worth practising writing key words as well, to make sure you get the spelling right. Spelling, punctuation and grammar are worth up to 5% of your total mark.

▶ **Test yourself frequently,** or get someone else to test you. It is easy to test recall with short, verbal answers to a friend or parent. You can find out how well you understand a topic by trying to explain it to someone else – it's even better if they know nothing about it before you start. Think about explaining mitosis, or osmosis, or how the heart beats, and you'll see what I mean. If you get stuck, or you can't explain it simply enough for someone else to follow, go back to your notes, read about it, then try again.

Using examination questions in revision

Once you have revised a topic, it is very useful to try out some practice questions. This will help you in several ways:

▶ It shows whether you really understand the topic. If not, go back to your notes.

▶ You will become familiar with the language used in questions (look at the list of command words' on page 4).

▶ You can check your answers against the outline answers, and see how to gain extra marks.

▶ You can attempt a whole examination paper and time your work, i.e. work under examination conditions.

Types of examination questions
In Biology GCSE there are eight main types of question:

1. **Short answer.** These are very common and often require a one word or phase answer. You are not expected to answer in a full sentence – there is usually not enough space, e.g. What form of energy is necessary for photosynthesis to occur?

_____

2. **Longer answer.** This is often part of a structured question, and requires a 3–4 line answer. The number of lines available and the number of marks give an indication of the length and detail required in the answer. You are expected to write in sentences, or to produce a well-organised list, but try to make your answer concise, e.g. Explain why it is useful for household rubbish to be made into compost? *(3)*

_____

_____

_____

3. **Extended answer.** This is usually an 'essay-type' question worth eight to ten marks, and you are expected to write between half a page and a whole page. This needs careful thought to decide which facts are relevant, to organise them into a coherent answer and to make sure you have answered the question fully.
   e.g. Explain how an increase in the human population can have a harmful effect on the environment. (10)
   You could write about:
   ▷ increased need for food (1), therefore more land needed for farming (1), possible over-use of pesticides and fertilizers to increase yield (1), possible over-fishing;
   ▷ increased need for living space, roads, etc (1), so natural habitats destroyed (1);
   ▷ increase need for resources, e.g. wood, metal stone, fuels (1), so natural habitats destroyed by mining, quarrying etc. (1), deforestation as wood is used for building/fuel (1), or land is cleared for grazing animals (1);
   ▷ increased pollution from homes, industry, cars (1) causes acid rain (sulphur dioxide and nitrogen oxides) (1), increased carbon dioxide linked to the greenhouse effect (1), CFCs (in aerosols, packaging) damages the ozone layer (1), sewage pollutes rivers and the sea (1), farm waste and chemicals leached from fields, e.g. pesticides, fertilisers, pollute rivers and the sea (1).

4. **Drawing and labelling diagrams.** Make sure you know which diagrams you must be able to draw **and** label, and which you must label only (your teacher will have a list). Look at diagrams carefully to make sure you can recognise the key features, and practise drawing and labelling them when you are revising.
   Make sure label lines point accurately at the required structures, and always make your diagrams big enough to be clear.

5. **Drawing of graphs and bar charts.** You may be given a set of axes which are already labelled, sometimes with a scale ready drawn. If not, the following rules apply:
   (a) The independent variable is plotted across the bottom of the graph (x-axis), and the dependent variable is plotted along the side of the graph (y-axis).
       e.g. If you were counting number of bubbles of oxygen produced by pondweed each minute, time in minutes would be the independent variable (this is the one where **you** choose the intervals, e.g. each minute), and number of bubbles would be the dependent variable.
   (b) Use the largest possible scale on the graph paper you are given.
   (c) Make sure that the scales are uniform, i.e. the numbers increase by the same amount across each square.
   (d) Label your axes clearly, including units.
   (e) Plot points carefully using pencil (you can rub it out if you make mistakes).
   (f) Join the points with a straight line or a smooth curve.
   (g) If it is a bar chart, use a ruler to draw the bars, and make sure they are labelled.

6. **Data analysis.** You may be given some data, e.g. in a table, in a graph, in a comprehension passage, and asked questions about it. It is likely that you will not have seen exactly the same material before, but it will relate to part of your syllabus.

(a) If it is a table: look carefully at the column headings and units, you may have to carry out calculations to answer some parts of the question.

(b) If it is a graph: look at the axis labels and units. What are the main trends shown by the graph?

(c) If it is a comprehension passage: read it through carefully at least twice, and underline key words.

7. **Simple calculations.** These are particularly common in Scottish Examination Board questions, although most examination boards set some calculations. You should be able to:

   (a) carry out simple addition, subtraction, multiplication and division

   (b) calculate ratios

   (c) calculate percentages

   (d) calculate averages.

   Remember, you must always show your working, and include units in your answer.

8. **Describing experiments.** You should be able to draw labelled diagrams of apparatus and explain the key features of common experiments,

   e.g. photosynthesis experiments (with pondweed)

   food tests (for sugar, starch, protein).

Command words used in examinations

Describe	Give an outline of the process or structure. Include key points.
Explain	Give biological reasons to account for what is happening.
State	Give a simple description/definition.
Suggest	Give possible reasons/explanations. You are not expected to recall an answer here, but should give reasonable suggestions.
Compare	Look for similarities and differences. Make sure your answer relates to both.
Define	Give a concise definition. Do not use the 'question word' in you answer.
Summarise	Write the key points.
Discuss	Give the points for and against. This word is normally used in longer or extended prose answers.
Give an account of	Describe the process which is occurring or methods used in the experiment. Make sure that your answer is written in a logical sequence.

▷ Examinations

At the end of your course you will have written examinations which count as 75% towards your final grade. Usually there are two examination papers, and you may be told which topics are covered in each paper (each examination board will have different arrangements for this, see p. 8).

Preparing for the examinations

▷ Make sure you know **when** your examinations will be, **how long** each examination is, and which **topics** are covered on a particular paper.

▷ Check with your teacher which tier of paper you will be sitting (foundation or higher), and which topics you must revise.

▷ Look at the **types** of examination questions and **command words** you are likely to meet (see pp. 3–4). Check that you understand how to answer them.

During the examination

▷ Make sure you have the right equipment with you, i.e. pencils, pens, rubber, ruler, calculator.

▷ Read the instructions on the front of the examination paper (there is normally no choice of questions in Biology GCSE).

▷ Look at the number of questions to be answered, and plan your time roughly.

When you are about to answer a question:

▷ Read the question carefully and underline key words.

▷ Decide which part of the syllabus is being tested. Remember, a question may require information from different parts of the syllabus.

e.g. a question on exercise may include information on muscles, heart rate, respiration and lactic acid,
a question on blood may include information on transport, immunity and genetics (blood groups or haemophilia).

▷ Look at the number of lines and number of marks available to decide the amount of detail needed.

▷ Keep an eye on the time, and check your progress through the paper after 30 minutes and after one hour.

▷ If you get stuck, mark the question (in pencil), leave it and get on with other questions. Return to it if you have time.

▷ If you finish early, go back and check that you have completed all the questions, and read over your answers.

▷ Coursework

During your course you will carry out science coursework which will count as 25% towards your final grade. Your coursework consists of science experiments and investigations which you do in school, and then write up at home or at school. You must do at least one full investigation in Biology, and will probably be assessed on several other occasions as well.

You are assessed in four different skill areas:

1. Planning experimental procedures (maximum 8 marks).
2. Obtaining evidence (maximum 8 marks).
3. Analysing evidence and drawing conclusions (maximum 8 marks).
4. Evaluating evidence (maximum 6 marks).

See pp. 7–12 for details of how your work will be assessed. It is very important to look at these mark descriptions carefully, so that you can see how to gain high marks.

Your total mark will then be doubled, and you will be given up to 3 marks for **spelling, punctuation and grammar** in your written reports. SPAG marks are allocated like this:

Threshold Performance (1 mark)	Candidates spell, punctuate and use the rules of grammar with reasonable accuracy; they use a limited range of specialist terms appropriately.
Intermediate Performance (2 marks)	Candidates spell, punctuate and use the rules of grammar with considerable accuracy; they use a good range of specialist terms with facility.
High Performance (3 marks)	Candidates spell, punctuate and use the rules of grammar with almost faultless accuracy, deploying a range of grammatical constructions; they use a wide range of specialist terms adeptly and with precision.

It is worth spending time on your coursework reports to make sure that you obtain as many marks as possible. Remember that your report should be a full record of your investigation: what you predicted would happen (and why), what you did, what you found out, and how you can explain your results.

(a) There should be a clear heading or title, and an introduction which describes the investigation, and shows that you understand what the investigation is about.

(b) You should have your name, the date and your form or set, clearly written on the work.

'Presentation is very important'

(c) Underline the headings and subheadings.

(d) All diagrams, charts, graphs, photos, etc. should have a heading and labels.

(e) When you make a prediction about what will happen, use scientific theory to explain it.

(f) List all relevant equipment and apparatus.

(g) Describe any safety precautions which you have taken, for example wearing safety goggles.

(h) Present your results as a chart or graph. Refer to, and make use of, your results when writing up your coursework.

(i) Give a short conclusion stating what your results tell you.

(j) Use scientific theory to explain your results.

(k) Describe any problems you had during the investigation and suggest possible solutions.

(l)   Identify possible sources of error and suggest further investigations.

(m) List any references which you may have used.

Students often lose marks because they start their write-ups very well, but then lose motivation so the later sections are shorter and less detailed. Check the criteria that will be used to mark your report (given on pp. 9–11) so that you can get as many marks as possible.

The courses

▷ **Introduction**

In England and Wales each examination board will set a slightly different course for Biology GCSE, because the syllabus consists of core topics (the same for all exam boards) and extension topics (which vary from board to board).

Marks are allocated as follows:

Core topics   50%
Extension topics   25%
Coursework   25%

The situation is different in Scotland and Northern Ireland, because pupils are not required to follow the National Curriculum, but broadly the same topics are studied.

▷ **Aims**

During the course, pupils should:

▸ acquire a systematic body of scientific knowledge and develop an understanding of science including its power and limitations;
▸ develop experimental and investigative abilities;
▸ develop an understanding of the nature of scientific ideas and activity and the basis for scientific claims;
▸ develop their understanding of the technological and environmental applications of science and of the economic, ethical and social implications of these.

▷ **Assessment objectives**

The examination will test your ability to:

1. carry out experimental and investigative work;
2. recall, understand, use and apply biological knowledge;
3. communicate biological observations, ideas and arguments (using appropriate vocabulary);
4. evaluate biological information.

The marks are allocated as follows:

Table 2.1

Assessment objectives	% of mark
1. experimental and investigative work	25%
2. knowledge, understanding, use and application of biological knowledge	60% (about one-third of this for recall)
3. and 4. communication and evaluation	15%

Important points:

▸ experimental and investigative work is assessed by coursework;
▸ the written examinations count for 75% of your total mark;
▸ 40% is for understanding, use and application of knowledge.

▷ **Scheme of assessment**

From 1998, examination boards will set papers at two different tiers, leading to different grades. The names for the tiers vary between boards, but the basic pattern is like this:

Foundation/Basic Tier – Grades C–G
Higher Tier – Grades A*–D

Most exam boards set two written papers, lasting a total of 2–3 hours, in addition to coursework.

You will be entered for one of the two tiers in your exam. The tier of entry will determine:

▶ which topics you need to learn (some topics are examined at higher tier only);
▶ the grade you can achieve.

It is **vital** that you know which tier you are likely to be entered for.

▷ **Core topics**

These are the same for all examination boards in England and Wales. They are divided into five main topic groups:

1. **Life processes and cell activity** (Chapter 3)
2. **Humans as organisms** (Chapter 4)
3. **Green plants as organisms** (Chapter 5)
4. **Variation, inheritance and evolution** (Chapter 6)
5. **Living things in their environment** (Chapter 7)

For details of what is involved in each topic, you should refer to the relevant chapter.
Remember, questions on core topics will account for 50% of your final mark.

▷ **Extension topics**

Each examination board selects its own extension topics, and these are as follows.

London	▶ Micro organisms and disease in humans
	▶ Biotechnology in food production
MEG Syllabus A	▶ Diversity and adaption
	▶ Micro–organisms and food
	▶ Infectious diseases
MEG Syllabus C (Salters)	▶ Off the blocks
	▶ Growing crops
	▶ Ploughman's lunch
	▶ Industrious microbes
MEG Syllabus D (Nuffield)	▶ Helpful organisms
	▶ Harmful organisms
	▶ Vaccines and antibiotics
	▶ Applied genetics
	▶ Genetic engineering
	▶ Conservation
	▶ Pollution
NEAB	▶ Using microbes to make useful substances
	▶ Enzymes in the home and industry
	▶ Biotechnology and disease
SEG	▶ Patterns of feeding
	▶ Patterns of support and movement
	▶ Micro-organisms
	▶ Controlling the spread of disease
WJEC	▶ Technology and life processes

Remember, questions on extension topics will account for 25% of your final mark. It is **vital** to know which syllabus you are studying, and which tier you will be entered for.

▷ **Coursework**

Coursework accounts for 25% of your final grade. In England and Wales, you are assessed on four skill areas:

1. planning experimental procedures;
2. obtaining evidence;
3. analysing evidence and drawing conclusions;
4. evaluating evidence.

Each examination board uses the same criteria to assess your coursework.

Criteria for assessing coursework

Skill area P: Planning experimental procedures
To satisfy the programme of study requirements, candidates should be taught:

(a) to use scientific knowledge and understanding, drawing on secondary sources where appropriate, to turn ideas suggested to them, and their own ideas, into a form that can be investigated;
(b) to carry out preliminary work where this helps to clarify what they have to do;
(c) to make predictions where it is appropriate to do so;
(d) to consider the key factors in contexts involving a number of factors;
(e) to plan how to vary or control key variables;
(f) to consider the number and range of observations or measurements to be made;
(g) to recognise contexts, e.g. **fieldwork**, where variables cannot readily be controlled and to make judgements about the amount of evidence needed in these contexts;
(h) to select apparatus, equipment and techniques, taking account of safety requirements.

All the mark descriptions are arranged to be hierarchical (see Table 2.2). All work should be assessed in the context of the syllabus.

Table 2.2 Skill area P mark descriptions

Marks		Candidates should:	Increasing demand of activity
2	P.2a	plan a simple safe procedure	
4	P.4a	plan a fair test or a practical procedure, making a prediction where appropriate	
	P.4b	select appropriate equipment	
6	P.6a	use scientific knowledge and understanding to plan a procedure, to identify key factors to vary, control or take into account, and to make a prediction where appropriate	
	P.6b	decide on a suitable number and range of observations or measurements to be made	
8	P.8a	use detailed scientific knowledge and understanding to plan an appropriate strategy, taking into account the need to produce precise and reliable evidence, and to justify a prediction where appropriate	
	P.8b	use, where appropriate, relevant information from secondary sources or preliminary work	

Skill area O: Obtaining evidence
To satisfy the programme of study requirements, candidates should be taught:

(a) to use a range of apparatus and equipment safely and with skill;
(b) to make observations and measurements to a degree of precision appropriate to the context;
(c) to make sufficient relevant observations and measurements for reliable evidence;
(d) to consider uncertainties in measurements and observations;
(e) to repeat measurements and observations when appropriate;
(f) to record evidence clearly and appropriately as they carry out the work.

All mark descriptions are arranged to be hierarchical (see Table 2.3). All work should be assessed in the context of the syllabus.

Table 2.3 Skill area O mark descriptions

Marks	Candidates should:		Increasing demand of activity
2	O.2a	use simple equipment safely to make some observations or measurements	
4	O.4a	make appropriate observations or measurements which are adequate for the activity	
	O.4b	record the observations or measurements	
6	O.6a	make sufficient systematic and accurate observations or measurements and repeat them when appropriate	
	O.6b	record clearly and accurately the observations or measurements	
8	O.8a	use equipment with precision and skill to obtain and record reliable evidence which involves an appropriate number and range of observations or measurements	

Skill area A: Analysing evidence and drawing conclusions
To satisfy the programme of study requirements, candidates should be taught:

(a) to present qualitative and quantitative data clearly;
(b) to present data as graphs, using lines of best fit where appropriate;
(c) to identify trends or patterns in results;
(d) to use graphs to identify relationships between variables;
(e) to present numerical results to an appropriate degree of accuracy;
(f) to check that conclusions drawn are consistent with the evidence;
(g) to explain how results support or underline the original prediction when one has been made;
(h) to try to explain conclusions in the light of their knowledge and understanding of science.

All the mark descriptions are arranged to be hierarchical (see Table 2.4). All work should be assessed in the context of the syllabus.

Table 2.4 Skill area A mark descriptions

Marks	Candidates should:		Increasing demand of activity
2	A.2a	explain simply what has been found out	
4	A.4a	present findings in the form of simple diagrams, charts or graphs	
	A.4b	identify trends and patterns in observations or measurements	
6	A.6a	construct and use appropriate diagrams, charts, graphs (with lines of best fit), or use numerical methods, to process evidence for a conclusion	
	A.6b	draw a conclusion consistent with their evidence and relate this to scientific knowledge and understanding	
8	A.8a	use detailed scientific knowledge and understanding to explain a conclusion drawn from processed evidence	
	A.8b	explain how results support or undermine the original prediction when one has been made	

Skill area E: Evaluating evidence

To satisfy the programme of study requirements, candidates should be taught:

(a) to consider whether the evidence collected is sufficient to enable firm conclusions to be drawn;
(b) to consider reasons for anomalous results and to reject such results where appropriate;
(c) to consider the reliability of results in terms of the uncertainty of measurements and observations;
(d) to propose improvements to the methods that have been used;
(e) to propose further investigation to test their conclusion.

All the mark descriptions are arranged to be hierarchical (see Table 2.5). All work should be assessed in the context of the syllabus.

Table 2.5 Skill area E mark descriptions

Marks		Candidates should:	Increasing demand of activity
2	E.2a	make a relevant comment about the procedure used or the evidence obtained	
4	E.4a	comment on the accuracy of the observations or measurements, recognising any anomalous results	
	E.4b	comment on the suitability of the procedure and, where appropriate, suggest changes to improve the reliability of the evidence	
6	E.6a	comment on the reliability of the evidence, accounting for any anomalous results or explain whether the evidence is sufficient to support a firm conclusion	
	E.6b	propose improvements, or further work, to provide additional evidence for the conclusion, or to extend the enquiry	

Remember to refer to these criteria when you are planning coursework, and writing up reports.

▷ Mathematical requirements

These are broadly the same for each examination board.

At **foundation level** you are expected to be able to do the following:

▷ Use the four rules applied to whole numbers and decimal fractions (add, subtract, multiply and divide).
▷ Use tables and charts.
▷ Interpret and use graphs.
▷ Draw graphs from given data.
▷ Read, interpret and draw simple inferences from tables.
▷ Use vulgar and decimal fractions and percentages.
▷ Use scales on graphs.
▷ Measure rates.
▷ Handle measurements of averages.
▷ Substitute numbers for words and letters in formulae (without transformation of simple formulae).

At **higher level** you are expected to be able to do the following:

▷ Square and square root numbers.
▷ Convert between vulgar and decimal fractions and percentages.
▷ Express one quantity as a percentage of another; percentage change.
▷ Draw and interpret related graphs.
▷ Understand the idea of gradient.
▷ Transform simple formulae.
▷ Make simple linear equations in one unknown.
▷ Handle elementary ideas and applications of direct and inverse proportion.

▷ **General requirements**   These are a basic part of the National Curriculum in England and Wales. During your course you should have the opportunity to acquire five skill areas:

1. Systematic enquiry
2. Application of science
3. The nature of scientific ideas
4. Communication
5. Health and Safety

1 Systematic enquiry

Pupils should be given opportunities to:

(a) use practical tasks and investigations to acquire scientific knowledge, understanding and skills;
(b) use and bring together information from a range of secondary sources;
(c) work quantitatively;
(d) judge when to use IT to collect, handle and investigate scientific information.

2 Application of science

Pupils should be given opportunities to:

(a) consider ways in which science is applied and used, and to evaluate the benefits and drawbacks of scientific and technological developments for individuals, communities and environments;
(b) use scientific knowledge and understanding to evaluate the effects of some applications of science on health and on the quality of life;
(c) relate scientific knowledge and understanding to the care of living things and of the environment;
(d) consider competing priorities and the decisions that have to be made about energy requirements, taking into account relevant social, economic and environmental factors;
(e) consider the power and limitations of science in addressing industrial, social and environmental issues and some of the ethical dilemmas involved.

3 The nature of scientific ideas

Pupils should be given opportunities to:

(a) develop their understanding of how scientific ideas are accepted and rejected on the basis of empirical evidence, and how scientific controversies can arise from different ways of interpreting such evidence;
(b) consider ways in which scientific ideas may be affected by the social and historical contexts in which they develop, and how these contexts may affect whether or not the ideas are accepted.

4 Communication

Pupils should be given opportunities to:

(a) use a wide range of scientific and technical vocabulary and conventions, and to use diagrams, graphs, tables and charts to communicate information and to develop an argument;
(b) use SI units;
(c) present scientific information in symbolic or mathematical form.

5 Health and safety

Pupils should be given opportunities to:

(a) take responsibility for recognising hazards in a range of materials, activities and environments, including the unfamiliar;
(b) use information sources in order to assess the risk of the unfamiliar;
(c) manage their working environment and justify the action taken to control risks.

Life processes and cell activity

▷ **GETTING STARTED**

| MEG | SEG | NEAB | LONDON | WJEC | NICCEA | SEB |

All living things are made up of basic units called cells. Some organisms are unicellular, e.g. bacteria, yeasts, some algae, but many organisms are multicellular, e.g. humans, insects, flowering plants. When an organism is multicellular, cells can be grouped to form organs, and organs can be grouped to form systems, i.e. there is a division of labour.

In this chapter, you will look at the structure of cells, and how cells are adapted to carry out a particular function. You will consider important organs and systems in humans and flowering plants. You will find out how substances move in and out of cells, and you will learn how cells divide.

TOPIC	STUDY	REVISION 1	REVISION 2
Life processes			
Organs and systems in humans			
Names and locations of the major organs			
Functions of the major organs			
Functions of the main systems			
Organs and systems in plants			
Names and locations of the major organs			
Functions of the major organs			
Cell structure			
Components of cells and their functions			
Specialised cells			
Types of cells			
How are cells organised within the body?			
Movement in and out of cells			
Diffusion			
Osmosis			
Active transport			
Cell division			
Mitosis			
Meiosis			

WHAT YOU NEED TO KNOW

▷ **Life processes**   All living things carry out these seven important processes (they are sometimes called the **characteristics of living things**):

Movement   they move all or part of themselves
Respiration   they make energy from food
Sensitivity   they detect and respond to changes in their surroundings
Growth   they increase in size
Reproduction   they produce offspring similar or identical to themselves
Excretion   they get rid of waste products which they have made
Nutrition   they obtain food (either by making it during photosynthesis, or by eating other organisms)

Some people use the mnemonic **MRS GREN** to remember these life processes.

REVISION ACTIVITY I ▨ Use the list of life processes above to explain why cars are not alive.

▷ **Organs and systems in humans**   Within the human body are millions of cells organised into groups called **organs**. Each organ has specific functions within the body, e.g. the **heart** pumps blood through the blood vessels. The organs work together so that the person is healthy and their body processes are carried out efficiently.

Key points

▷   humans have many different organs, each with their own specific functions;

▷   organs are grouped together to form systems;

▷   there are eight systems in the human body;

▷   if all the organs are working properly, the person will be healthy.

Names and locations of the major organs

Inside the human body there are lots of different **organs** (Fig. 3.1)

e.g.   heart   stomach   kidneys   ovaries
        lungs   intestines   bladder   testes
        brain   liver   bones   uterus.

'You must be able to label a diagram like this.'

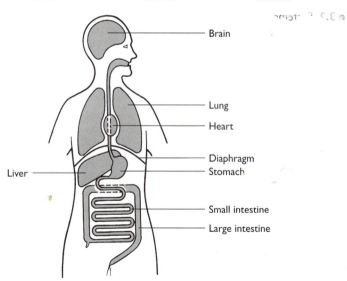

Fig. 3.1

Each organ has a particular **function** (job to do) within the body (Table 3.1), e.g. heart pumps blood around the body.

Functions of the major organs

Table 3.1 The major organs and their functions

Organ	Functions
Brain	1. to control all the processes of the body, e.g. heart rate, body temperature 2. to make decisions 3. to think and remember
Lungs	1. to transfer oxygen from air into blood ⎫ this is gas 2. to transfer carbon dioxide from blood into the air ⎭ exchange
Heart	to pump blood around the body
Diaphragm	to move up and down so that air moves in and out of the lungs
Stomach	to mix food with digestive juices (enzymes)
Liver	1. to destroy poisons in the body e.g. alcohol, drugs 2. to make bile (helps to digest fats) 3. to break down excess amino acids 4. to change glucose into glycogen or fat
Small intestine	1. to mix food with digestive juices (enzymes + bile) 2. to absorb digested food into the blood
Large intestine	1. to absorb water from faeces 2. to store faeces before they are egested
Kidneys	1. to remove urea from the blood 2. to remove excess salt from the blood 3. to remove excess water from the blood
Bladder	to store urine before it is excreted
Testes	1. to make sperm 2. to make the male sex hormone (testosterone)
Penis	to pass sperm into a woman's body during sex
Ovaries	1. to make ova (egg cells) 2. to make the female sex hormones (oestrogens)
Uterus	to provide a safe place for the foetus to develop
Bones, e.g. skull, vertebrae, limb	1. to protect soft organs e.g. brain, lungs 2. to help us to move

important

Functions of the main systems

In humans, organs work together to form **systems**. There are eight different systems (Table 3.2).

Table 3.2 Systems of the human body

System	Functions	Organs/Parts
circulatory	• to transport substances around the body, in blood	heart, blood vessels
respiratory	• to transfer oxygen into the body and remove carbon dioxide	lungs, trachea, diaphragm
urinary	• to remove urea, salts and water from the body, in urine	kidneys, bladder
nervous	• to control all the activities of the body • to link all parts of the body to the brain, and pass impulses (messages) between them • to find out about our surroundings	brain, sense organs, e.g. eyes nerves
digestive	• to digest the food we eat • to absorb digested food into the blood	stomach intestines, liver
reproductive	• to make sperm and egg cells • to provide a safe place for the foetus to develop	testes, penis – male ovaries, uterus – female
skeletal	• to move parts of the body • to protect soft organs, e.g. skull protects brain	bones muscles
endocrine	• to make hormones	endocrine glands, e.g. adrenal gland pituitary gland

REVISION ACTIVITY 2 The diagram (Fig 3.2) shows the human digestive system.

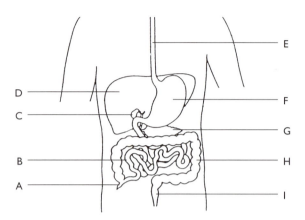

Fig. 3.2

Choose words from the box below to name the structures labelled **A, C, E, F, G** and **I**.

Salivary gland	Appendix	Liver	Oesophagus
Stomach	Gall bladder	Pancreas	Bile duct
Small intestine	Large intestine	Rectum	Anus

▷ Organs and systems in plants

Plants are a very important group of organisms to biologists. Animals rely on them for food, and for oxygen; in fact all life on Earth depends on plants. Biologists need to study plants to find out how their life processes work. Although they are very different to animals, they are just as successful.

Key points

▷ plants have a totally different lifestyle to animals;

▷ the structure and organisation of plants is suitable for their lifestyle;

▷ they have only four main organs;

▷ these organs are grouped into two systems.

Names and locations of the major organs

There are two **systems** in flowering plants:

1. **Shoot system** – all the parts of the plant which are above ground
2. **Root system** – all the parts of the plant which are below ground

There are four main **organs** in plants:

1. roots
2. stems
3. leaves
4. flowers

Functions of the major organs

Each organ has its own specific **function**, in the same way that animal organs do. However, plants have a different mode of life to animals so they have a simpler pattern of organisation (Table 3.3).

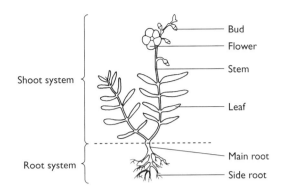

Fig. 3.3

Table 3.3 Functions of the major organs in a flowering plant

Organ	Functions
Root	1. to collect water from the soil 2. to collect minerals, e.g. nitrate, from the soil 3. to anchor the plant in the soil
Stem	1. to transport substances, e.g. water and sugars, around the plant 2. to support the shoot system
Leaf	to photosynthesise (make sugar)
Flower	to reproduce and make seeds, which will grow into new plants

▷ **Cell structure**

Key points

▷ cells are the basic **units of life** – all living things are made of them;

▷ all cells contain a **nucleus**, **cell membrane** and **cytoplasm**;

▷ plant cells are surrounded by a cellulose **cell wall**, and have a large sap-filled **vacuole**. Some will contain **chloroplasts**.

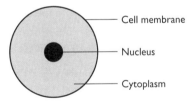

Fig. 3.4 Structure of animal cell e.g. human cheek cell

'You should be able to draw and label both of these diagrams.'

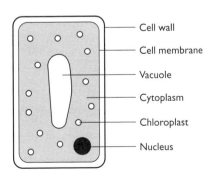

Fig. 3.5 Structure of plant cell e.g. palisade cell from leaf

These are the parts of the cell which can be seen using a light microscope which magnifies about 1,000 ×.

If you observe a cell with an electron microscope which magnifies 500,000 ×, it looks much more complicated, and you can see other cell components, e.g. ribosomes, (involved in protein synthesis) and mitochondria (involved in respiration).

REVISION ACTIVITY 3   Make a table to show at least three similarities and three differences between plant and animal cells.

Components of cells and their functions

Each part of the cell has a particular function to make sure that the whole cell works properly. These are the functions of the main parts of the cell (Table 3.5).

Table 3.5 Functions of the cell parts

Cell part	Functions
Nucleus	1. It controls all of the activities of the cell, e.g. dividing, making new proteins. 2. It contains chromosomes (made of DNA) which carry genetic information (genes).
Cytoplasm	1. This is a jelly-like substance where most of the chemical reactions occur in the cell. 2. It contains vacuoles and food stores, e.g. starch grains, oil droplets.
Cell membrane	1. It controls what enters and leaves the cell. It is semi-permeable (lets some substances through, but not others). 2. It protects the cytoplasm and nucleus.
Cell wall *	This is a tough, outer layer made of cellulose. It is rigid and it keeps the cell the right shape.
Chloroplast *	1. It contains a green chemical, chlorophyll, which traps light energy. 2. Photosynthesis occurs here.
Vacuole *	1. It stores water, sugar and minerals. 2. It is important in supporting the plant (stops wilting).

* found in plant cells only

▷ Specialised cells

Key points

▶ cells are adapted to the function they perform, e.g. palisade cells have lots of chloroplasts for photosynthesis, red blood cells have haemoglobin to carry oxygen;

▶ when cells carry out different functions, it is called **division of labour**.

Types of cells

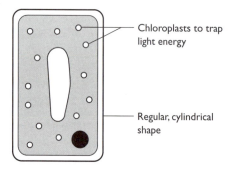

Chloroplasts to trap light energy

Regular, cylindrical shape

Palisade cell
Function: to make sugar by photosynthesis.
Adaptation: 1. has lots of chloroplasts to trap light energy
              2. cylindrical shape to pack together tightly.
Location: close to the upper surface of leaves.

Fig. 3.6 Palisade cell

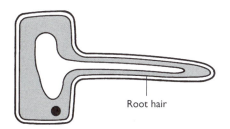

Fig. 3.7 Root hair cell

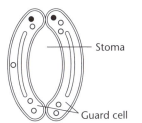

Fig. 3.8 Guard cells

Guard cells
Function: to open and close the stomata on
             the leaf.
Adaptation: can change shape.
Location: on the lower surface of leaves.

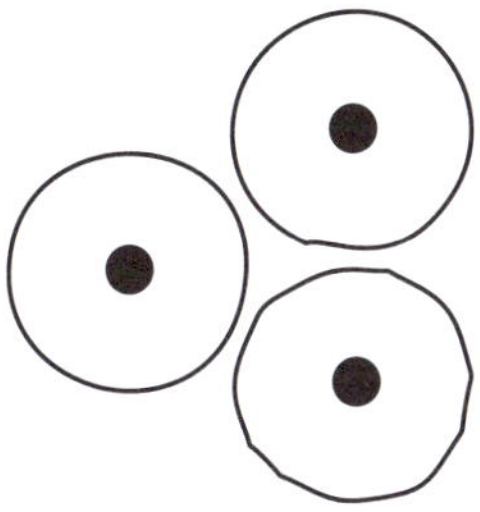

Fig. 3.9 Cheek cells

Cheek cells
Function: to line the inside of the mouth.
Adaptation: thin, flat shape so they can fit
             together closely.
Location: inside of mouth.

Cytoplasm contains haemoglobin

No nucleus   Biconcave disc shape

Fig. 3.10 Red blood cell

Red blood cells
Function: to carry oxygen.
Adaptations: 1. biconcave disc shape gives it
                 a large surface area so it can
                 absorb more oxygen,
              2. it contains a red chemical,
                 haemoglobin, which joins to
                 oxygen,
              3. it has no nucleus so it can
                 carry more oxygen.
Location: in the blood.

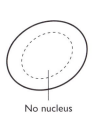

Large nucleus

Spherical shape

Fig. 3.11 Lymphocytle

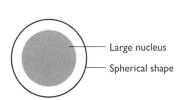

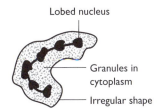

Lobed nucleus

Granules in
cytoplasm

Irregular shape

Fig. 3.12 Phagocyte

White blood cells
Function: to fight disease by destroying
             pathogens.
Adaptation: 1. lymphocytes (Fig. 3.11) make
                chemicals called antibodies
                which destroy pathogens.
             2. phagocytes (Fig. 3.12) can
                change shape to engulf and
                destroy pathogens.
Location: in the blood.

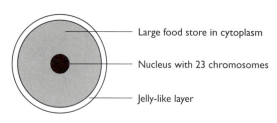

Fig. 3.13 Ovum

Ovum

Function: to develop into a baby when fertilized.

Adaptations: 1. large food store in cytoplasm (gives energy for the growth of the zygote),
2. jelly-like layer surrounds cell membrane (prevents entry of more than one sperm cell),
3. nucleus contains 23 chromosomes.

Location: produced in the ovary.

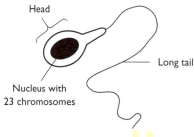

Fig. 3.14 Sperm cell

Sperm cell

Function: to fertilize an ovum.

Adaptations: 1. has a head with a nucleus containing 23 chromosomes,
2. has a tail which helps it to swim.

Location: produced in the testis.

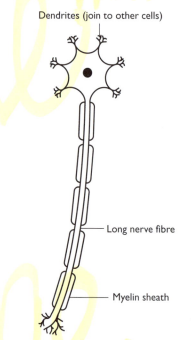

Fig. 3.15 Neurone

Neurone (nerve cell)

Function: to carry nerve impulses around the body.

Adaptations: 1. has a long nerve fibre to reach other cells,
2. nerve fibre has a covering made of myelin to speed up transmission of nerve impulses.

Location: all parts of the body.

How are cells organised within the body?

'This sections is often tested in exams.'

▷ A group of similar cells carrying out the same function is called a **tissue**, e.g. nerve cells make up nerve tissue.

▷ A group of tissues which work together to carry out a particular function is called an **organ**, e.g. heart contains muscle tissue, nerve tissue, epithelial tissue.

▷ A group of organs which work together to carry out a particular function is called a **system**, e.g. circulatory system is made up of heart and blood vessels.

REVISION ACTIVITY 4 The diagrams opposite (Fig. 3.16) show four cells, some from animals and some from plants.

Note: The diagrams are not all drawn to the same scale.

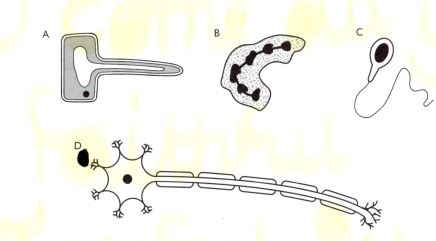

Fig. 3.16

(a)   The list below gives the functions (jobs) of each cell.
    (i) Carries nerve impulses
    (ii) Fertilises an ovum (egg)
    (iii) Kills bacteria
    (iv) Absorbs water

Name of cell	Letter A–D	Number of the function of the cell
White blood cell	B	3
Neurone (nerve cell)	D	1
Root hair cell	A	4
Sperm cell	C	2

Complete the table by matching the cells with letters from the diagrams and the number of their correct function.

(b)   Give **one** feature that is shown by all the four cells.

(c)   Give **one** feature, apart from shape, which is shown by cell A but not shown by the other three cells.

(d)   Name the **two** cells which can move by themselves.

> **Movement in and out of cells**

If the cell is to remain healthy, it is vital that it can exchange materials with its environment. Some substances must move in, e.g. nutrients, oxygen for respiration, while other substances move out, e.g. waste products.

Key points

▷ the cell membrane controls the movement of substances in and out of the cell;

▷ substances move in one of three ways: **diffusion**, **osmosis** or **active transport**.

Diffusion

'Learn this definition.'

> **This is the movement of a substance from a region where it is at a high concentration to a region of lower concentration down a concentration gradient.**

The rate of diffusion depends on how steep the concentration gradient is, i.e. the difference in concentration between the two regions. It is only effective over short distances, e.g. 1mm, but it is very important in all types of living things.

e.g. oxygen diffuses from the alveolus into red blood cells in humans
      carbon dioxide diffuses from muscle cells into blood in humans
      carbon dioxide diffuses into palisade cells for photosynthesis.
It does not require energy.

Osmosis

'Learn this definition.'

> **This is the movement of water molecules from a region of high concentration of water (a dilute solution) to a region of low concentration of water (a concentrated solution) through a semi-permeable membrane (Fig. 3.17)**

Here we have a high concentration of water molecules on the outside and a lower concentration of water molecules on the inside, so water would move IN by osmosis.

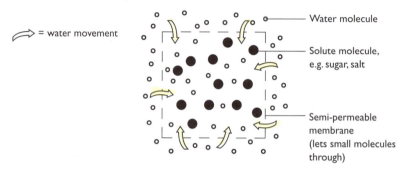

Fig. 3.17 Movement of water by osmosis

Osmosis in cells

The cell membrane is a **semi-permeable** (selectively permeable) membrane. This means that it lets small molecules, e.g. water, in so osmosis occurs as long as the cell membrane is not damaged. It does not require energy.

The cytoplasm of cells contains dissolved sugars and salts, so we could think of it as a weak solution. The direction of osmosis depends on the concentration of the fluid surrounding the cell.

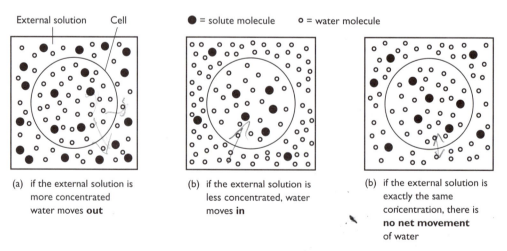

Fig. 3.18 Importance of external solution in osmosis

In plant cells the cell wall will limit the amount of water that enters by osmosis. When a cell is swollen with water, we say it is **turgid**; turgid cells are important in plant support (see Chapter 5). If water leaves the cell by osmosis, the cell will become squashy and flaccid, but the basic shape stays the same (due to the rigid cell wall). We say it is **plasmolysed** and if many cells are plasmolysed, the plant will wilt.

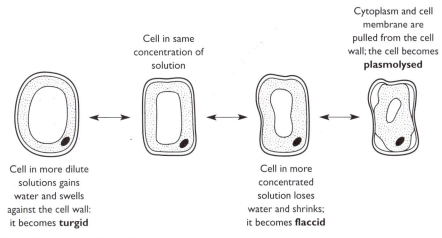

Fig. 3.19 Osmosis in plant cells

In animal cells there is no cell wall, so the amount of water entering the cell is not limited; the cell will swell until it bursts. If water leaves the cell by osmosis it will shrink and shrivel up.

Blood cells are particularly vulnerable to this problem, so it is important that the concentration of sugar and salt in blood plasma does not vary too much.

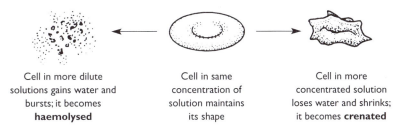

Fig. 3.20 Osmosis in red blood cells

Experiments with osmosis
There are three main types of experiments you may be expected to know.

1. **Visking tubing experiments**
Visking tubing is a semi-permeable membrane (so it acts like the cell membrane). It is sometimes used to make artificial cells, which can be placed in a variety of external solutions.

REVISION ACTIVITY 5

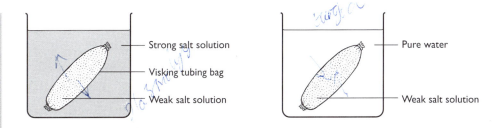

Fig. 3.21 Visking tubing experiment

Explain what will happen to each of the visking tubing bags.

2. **Thistle funnel experiments**
A piece of visking tubing is fastened over the neck of a thistle funnel and it is placed in an external solution. Fluid is poured into the thistle funnel and the level is marked. The level will change, depending on the concentrations of the external solution and the solution inside the funnel.

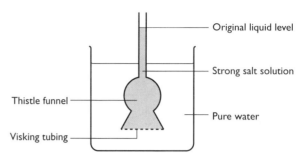

Fig. 3.22 Thistle funnel experiment

REVISION ACTIVITY 6 What will happen to the liquid level in Fig. 3.22?

3.   Potato stick experiments
Potato sticks are cut carefully (usually using a cork borer) and their exact length, diameter and mass is measured. They are left in a variety of external solutions for a few hours, then re-measured.

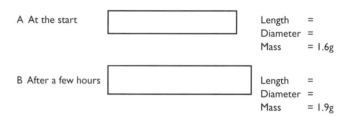

A At the start

Length   =
Diameter =
Mass   = 1.6g

B After a few hours

Length   =
Diameter =
Mass   = 1.9g

Fig. 3.23 Potato sticks experiment

REVISION ACTIVITY 7 What can you say about the strength of the external solution in Fig. 3.23?

Active transport

'Learn this definition.'

> **This is the movement of a substance across a cell membrane against a concentration gradient, using energy.**

This process can only occur in **living** cells, and is thought to involve carrier proteins which can transport the substance across the membrane. It is important because it allows large concentrations of a substance to accumulate inside cells, e.g. movement of minerals into root cells from soil.

▷ **Cell division**   Cell division is necessary for growth, development, repair and reproduction. There are two types of cell division, **mitosis** and **meiosis**, which produce different types of daughter cells.

Key points

▷   there are two types of cell division, mitosis and meiosis;

▷   mitosis is a type of cell division occurring in body cells. During mitosis, exact copies of all the genetic material in the cell nucleus are made. The genetic material then divides, resulting in two nuclei. Each nucleus contains a full set of chromosomes;

▷   **mitosis** can most easily be seen in parts of an organisation where rapid growth is occurring, e.g. root tips in plants;

▷   **meiosis** is the type of cell division which occurs during gamete formation. The gametes (sex cells) have half the normal number of chromosomes, so meiosis is sometimes called reduction division.

Mitosis

The **chromosomes** inside a cell (long threads of DNA) carry all the genetic information in the form of genes. When a cell divides by mitosis, each daughter cell receives an exact copy of the chromosome from the original cell, i.e. the chromosome number is the same and the genetic information is exactly the same.

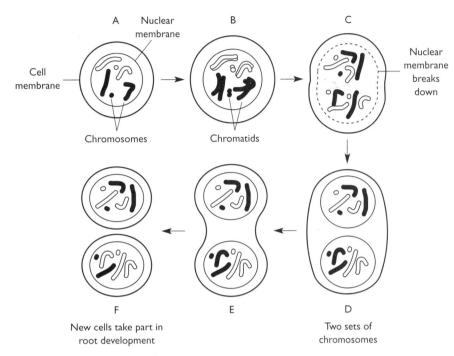

Fig. 3.24 Mitosis in a root tip cell

Summary of events in mitosis
(A) Cell before cell division. It contains six chromosomes (diploid number).
(B) Each chromosome makes a copy of itself so it is made up of two chromatids.
(C) The chromatids separate and move to opposite ends (poles) of the cell.
(D) A nuclear membrane forms around each group of chromosomes.
(E) The cell begins to divide.
(F) Cell division has occurred. There are two daughter cells, and each contains six chromosomes (diploid number).

Mitosis is important in growth, development, repair and asexual reproduction.

▷   **Growth** Mitosis increases the number of cells so organisms can increase in size.
▷   **Development** Mitosis allows cells to become specialised for different functions. This is division of labour.
▷   **Repair** Mitosis provides new cells to replace damaged or old cells, so organisms can continue to function efficiently.
▷   **Asexual reproduction** Bacteria, yeasts, simple animals and many plants can reproduce like this. Only one parent is involved, and the offspring are genetically identical to the parent. Examples include: binary fission, budding, spore formation.

Meiosis

When a cell divides by meiosis, each daughter cell obtains half the number of chromosomes in the parent cell.

Chromosomes normally exist as matching (homologous) pairs, i.e. a cell with 46 chromosomes will contain 23 homologous pairs. During meiosis, each daughter cell obtains one chromosome from each pair. This means that the chromosome number is halved, and the genetic material differs from the parent cell.

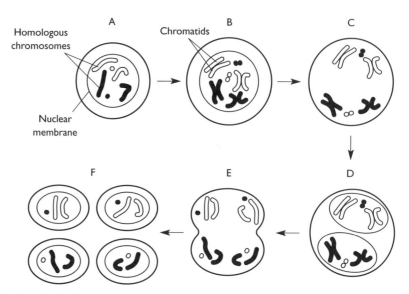

Fig. 3.25 Simplified diagram showing the main stages in meiosis

Summary of events in meiosis
(A) Cell before cell division. It contains six chromosomes (diploid number).
(B) Each chromosome makes a copy of itself so it is made up of two chromatids.
(C) Homologous chromosomes separate. One of each pair moves to opposite poles of the cell.
(D) A nuclear membrane forms around each set of chromosomes (this is temporary).
(E) Chromatids are pulled apart to opposite poles of the cells.
(F) New nuclear membranes form around the four sets of chromatids. The cell divides to form four daughter cells. Each contain three chromosomes (haploid number).

Meiosis only occurs in gamete formation,
i.e. formation of ova and sperm in animals;
    formation of egg cell nucleus and pollen in plants.

The daughter cells are haploid (have half the normal chromosomes numbers) so that when fertilization occurs, the correct chromosomes number will be obtained. In other words, meiosis is vital for successful sexual reproduction.

Table 3.6 Comparison of mitosis and meiosis

Mitosis	Meiosis
Two daughter cells are formed.	Four daughter cells are formed.
Daughter cells are diploid.	Daughter cells are haploid.
Daughter cells are identical to original cell.	Daughter cells are not identical to original cell.
Occurs as part of growth and asexual reproduction in simple organisms.	Occurs in gamete formation (sexual reproduction) in plants and animals.

REVISION ACTIVITY 8

The drawings (Fig. 3.26) show stages in cell division (mitosis).

(a) Using the letters A–E, put these stages in the correct order.
     (first) ____C____ ____B____ ____A____ ____A____ ____D____ (last)

(b) A human skin cell contains 46 chromosomes.
     If the cell divides once, how many chromosomes would each daughter skin cell contain? *(1)*
     23

(c) Each body cell of a mouse contains 40 chromosomes.
     How many chromosomes would you expect to find in a mouse sperm cell?   40   *(1)*

(d) A sperm cell with one chromosome missing fertilises an egg.   *(1)*
     Suggest one reason why the embryo is unlikely to develop in the normal way when some genes are absent.
     (1)

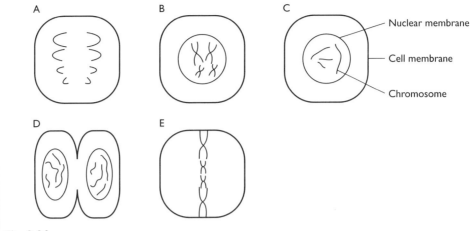

Fig. 3.26

SOLUTIONS TO REVISION ACTIVITIES

S1   Although cars do show **some** of the 'life processes', they do not carry out the majority of them, so they cannot be alive,

e.g.   movement – yes
      respiration – no, but they do get energy from fuel
      sensitivity – no
      growth – no
      reproduction – no
      excretion – yes, they get rid of exhaust gases
      nutrition – no, but they need fuel to move

S2   A = appendix   F = stomach
      C = gall bladder   G = pancreas
      E = oesophagus   I = rectum

S3   Similarities
      1.   They both have a nucleus.
      2.   They both have cytoplasm.
      3.   They both have a cell membrane.

Differences

Plant cells	Animal cells
Always have a cell wall	Do not have a cell wall
Usually have one large vacuole	Do not have a large vacuole
Often contain chloroplasts	Never contain chloroplasts
Often contain starch granules	Never contain starch granules

S4   (a)   B (iii), D (i), A (iv), C (ii)

      (b)   All contain a cell membrane, all contain a nucleus.

      (c)   A has a cellulose cell wall, large vacuole

      (d)   1. White Blood Cell   2. Sperm Cell

S5   (a)   Water will move **out** of the bag by osmosis.
      (b)   Water will move **into** the bag by osmosis.

S6   The liquid level in the tube will **rise** because water moves into the funnel by osmosis.

S7   The external solution is **water** or a **very weak** salt or sugar solution, because water has moved into the potato sticks by osmosis.

S8   (a) C B E A D
        (b) 46, because the daughter cells are identical to the parent cell.
        (c) 20, because gametes are always haploid.
        (d) The missing chromosome would have carried thousands of important genes. Each gene is an instruction about how to make a particular protein. An embryo which has lots of missing genes will not be able to make all the proteins it needs to survive.

EXAMINATION QUESTIONS

▷ **Question 1**   The drawing shows a young plant.

(a) Plants make their own food. Which part of the plant does this?   *(1)*
     leaf

(b) Give **one** function of the root hairs.   *(1)*
     absorb water

(c) Roots grow downwards and sideways.
     Give **two** advantages of sideways growth.   *(2)*

     1. it allows it to gather water over area

     2. anchor the plant

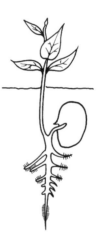

Fig. 3.27

▷ **Question 2**   The diagram below shows a leaf cell

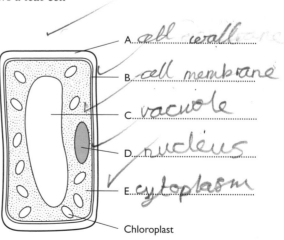

A. cell wall

B. cell membrane

C. vacuole

D. nucleus

E. cytoplasm

Chloroplast

Fig. 3.28

(a)   Name the structures labelled **A** to **E** on the lines provided   *(5)*

(b)   Which part
    (i)   contains cell sap? vacuole
    (ii)   contains genes? nucleus
    (iii)   contains chlorophyll? chloroplasts   *(3)*

▷ **Question 3**   Three strips of plant epidermal cells were placed on microscope slides. Each was covered by one drop of a solution, as shown in the table below.

Strip 1	Strip 2	Strip 3
Distilled water	Dilute sugar solution	Concentrated sugar solution

The diagrams below show the appearance of some of the cells after one hour. Two of the strips had cells as shown in diagram **A**. One strip had cells as shown in diagram **B**.

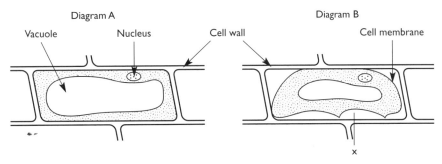

Fig. 3.29

(a)   (i)   Which **one** of the strips 1, 2 or 3 would have cells that look like diagram **B**? 3 *(1)*
    (ii)   Explain what happens to a cell to make it look like diagram **B**. lost water via osmosis *(1)*

(b)   Which one of the following would be found at the position labelled **X** in cell **B**? Tick the correct answer.

Water alone ☐   Sugar solution ☐   Cell sap ☐

Air ☑   Cytoplasm ☐

(c)   What would happen to a leaf if most of its cell became like diagram **B**? wilt   *(1)*

▷ **Question 4**   Here are steps taken by Farah to prepare a slide of an onion cell. They are not in the correct order.

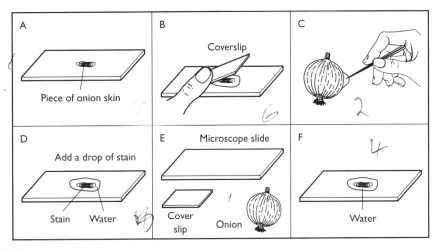

Fig. 3.30

(a) Fill in the blanks to complete the correct order of steps to be taken.   *(6)*

<u>E</u>   <u>C</u>   <u>A</u>   <u>F</u>   <u>D</u>   <u>B</u>

(b) Give a reason why you should be careful when carrying out step **B**.   *(1)*

no air bubbles

(c) Farah made a drawing of a single onion cell. It looked like this:

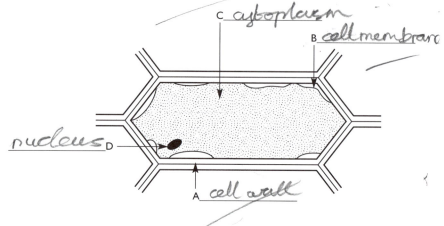

Fig. 3.31

(i) Label **A – D**.
(ii) What structure **can you see** which tells you it is a plant cell?   *(3)*

cell wall

(WJEC)

▷ **Question 5**   The diagram shows some stages in mitosis.

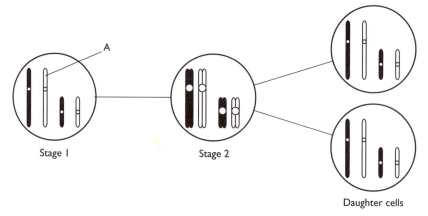

Stage 1   Stage 2   Daughter cells

Fig. 3.32

(a) Name the structure labelled **A**.   chromosome   *(1)*

(b) What important process has taken place between Stage 1 and Stage 2?   *(1)*
mitosis – replication of chromosome

(c) Compare the contents of the two daughter cells.   *(1)*
the same.

(NICCEA)

▷ **ANSWERS TO EXAMINATION QUESTIONS**

▷ **Question 1**   (a) leaves make food

(b) absorb water
absorb minerals

(c) 1. holds plant more firmly in soil
2. allows it to collect water and minerals over a large area

▷ **Question 2**   (a)   A = cell wall
                            B = cell membrane
                            C = vacuole (sap)
                            D = nucleus
                            E = cytoplasm

                (b)   (i) C (vacuole)
                       (ii) D (nucleus)
                       (iii) chloroplast

▷ **Question 3**   (a)   (i) Strip 3
                       (ii) Water moves out of cell; from a region of high concentration of water to a region
                             of lower concentration of water; by osmosis.

                (b)   Air is found in region X.

                (c)   It would wilt.

▷ **Question 4**   (a)   E C A F D B

                (b)   to avoid trapping air bubbles under the coverslip,
                       to avoid getting fingermarks on the coverslip

                (c)   (i) A = cell wall
                            B = cell membrane
                            C = cytoplasm
                            D = nucleus
                       (ii) cell wall

▷ **Question 5**   (a)   chromosome

                (b)   replication; each chromosome has made a copy of itself (so it is made of 2 chromatids).

                (c)   they are identical

▷ **STUDENT'S ANSWER WITH EXAMINER'S COMMENT**

An investigator used a cork borer to cut five cylinders of potato, each 20mm in
length and of equal diameter as shown below.

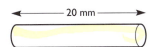

Fig. 3.33

The cylinders were placed in sugar solutions of different strengths as recorded in
the table below. After one hour they were removed, measured, and the length
again recorded in the table.

Potato cylinder	Concentration of sugar solution (Molar)	Starting length (mm)	Final length (mm)
A	0.5	20	17
B	0.4	20	18
C	0.3	20	20
D	0.2	20	22
E	0.1	20	23

(continued)

'Correct'

(a)   Name the process being investigated.

Osmosis   *(1)*

'This student is confused about osmosis – water is moving, not sugar. The answers should be

(i)   The potato gets shorter, because water is moving out

(ii)   Water is not moving in or out

(iii)   The potato gets longer, because water is moving in from the sugar solution.'

(b)   Explain concisely the results in

(i)   A and B   *The potato gets shorter*   *(1)*

Sugar is moving out.

(ii)   C   *Nothing happens*

(iii)   D and E   *The potato gets longer. Sugar is moving in.*

(6)

(c)   State one example where this process occurs in living plants

When sugar moves   *(1)*

(d)   What prevents plant cells bursting when placed in pure water?

The cell wall stops the cell getting any bigger   *(1)*

(WJEC)

'This is completely wrong. Osmosis occurs when water moves into plant cells e.g. into the root hair cells.'

'Correct'

SUMMARY

▷   there are seven important life processes shown by all living things. Remember MRS GREN!

▷   multicellular organisms often show division of labour. Cells are grouped into organs, and organs are grouped into systems so that the organism can function efficiently;

▷   you must be able to label and state the function of important organs in humans and flowering plants;

▷   the basic unit of all living things is the cell;

▷   all cells consist of a cell membrane, cytoplasm and nucleus (containing genes). Plant cells also have a cell wall and a sap vacuole, and some have chloroplasts (for photosynthesis);

▷   cells are specialised so that they can carry out particular functions efficiently: e.g. red blood cells have haemoglobin to carry oxygen, root hair cells have a long root hair to increase the surface area for absorption of water and minerals;

▷   substances can move in and out of cells in three ways: diffusion, osmosis and active transport;

▷   you must be able to define diffusion, osmosis and active transport;

▷   there are two types of cell division: mitosis and meiosis;

▷   mitosis occurs in body cells, and it makes two daughter cells which are identical to the parent cell;

▷   meiosis occurs during gamete formation, and it makes four daughter cells which have half as many chromosomes as the parent cell;

▷   genes are units of inherited information, they are part of chromosomes inside the nucleus.

Humans as organisms
Life processes

▷ **GETTING STARTED**

| MEG | SEG | NEAB | LONDON | WJEC | NICCEA | SEB |

Humans are complex, multi-cellular organisms, and it is very important that all parts of the body are working properly so that the whole organism can function efficiently.

In this section you will study five of the systems of the human body, and the vital functions they carry out.

TOPIC	STUDY	REVISION I	REVISION 2
Nutrition			
A balanced diet			
Enzymes			
Digestive system and digestion			
Absorption and assimilation			
Circulation			
Blood			
The heart			
Blood vessels and circulation			
Gas exchange			
The respiratory system			
Breathing			
Gas exchange in the alveoli			
Aerobic respiration			
Exercise and anaerobic respiration			
Movement			
The skeleton			
Joints			
Muscles and movement			
Reproduction			
The reproductive system			
The menstrual cycle			
Fertilization and implantation			
Birth			
Contraception			

WHAT YOU NEED TO KNOW

▷ **Nutrition**   Humans need food for three main reasons:

1.   as a **fuel** to make energy, in the process of respiration;
2.   as a source of **raw materials** for growth;
3.   to remain **healthy** and keep the body functioning efficiently.

Humans get their food by eating plants or other animals.

A balanced diet

To stay healthy, we must make sure that we eat the correct **nutrients** (sometimes called food groups), in the correct **proportions**. This is known as a balanced diet.

Key points

  ▷   there are **seven food groups** – carbohydrates, lipids, proteins, vitamins, minerals, fibre and water;
  ▷   we must have nutrients from each group, in the correct proportions, to stay healthy;
  ▷   if we are short of a particular nutrient it may cause a **deficiency disease;**
  ▷   excessive amounts of some foods can cause health problems.

Food groups
For each food group you should know:

  ▷   examples of foods containing it;
  ▷   what it is needed for in the body;
  ▷   health problems associated with deficiency or excess.

Table 4(1).1

Food group	Foods containing it	Role in the body	Health problems
Carbohydrate Sugary foods	Sweets, cakes, jam, fizzy drinks, chocolate	provides energy	too much causes tooth decay and obesity
Starchy foods	bread, rice, pasta, potatoes, flour	provides energy	too much causes obesity
Lipid (fat)	red meat, butter, cheese, nuts, crisps, anything fried	• provides energy • to make cell membranes • for insulation and protection of body organs	too much causes obesity
Protein	meat, fish, nuts, beans, cheese, soya, eggs	• provides raw materials for growth and repair • needed to make hormones and enzymes	deficiency causes kwashiorkor
Vitamins e.g. Vitamin C	citrus fruits, potatoes, blackcurrants	healthy skin, gums and bones	deficiency causes scurvy
e.g. Vitamin D	fish, egg yolk, butter, cream; also made in the skin in sunlight	healthy teeth and bones (needed for absorption of calcium)	deficiency causes rickets (weak bones)
Minerals e.g. calcium	milk, cheese, yoghurt	healthy teeth and bones	deficiency causes brittle bones, teeth decay easily
e.g. iron	red meat, green vegetables, chocolate	to make red blood cells	deficiency causes anaemia
Fibre	fruits and vegetables, wholemeal bread and pasta, brown rice	to encourage peristalsis and keep the gut healthy	deficiency causes constipation
Water	most food and drinks, especially fruits and vegetables	vital for a wide range of processes e.g. chemical reactions, transport	deficiency causes dehydration, and can lead to death

REVISION ACTIVITY I   The table below shows the food value of a school lunch eaten by a 16-year-old girl.

Table 4(1).2

Food eaten	Protein (g)	Carbohydrate (g)	Fat (g)	Iron (mg)	Vitamin C (mg)
Sausages	9	5	24	1	0
Chips	8	70	20	2	20
Baked beans	10	20	1	3	4
Apple pie	5	60	25	1	1
Ice cream	2	20	12	0	0
Fizzy drink	0	30	0	0	0

(a)   (i)   In this meal, which food gave the girl most protein?
      (ii) Name **one** other food not eaten in this meal which is rich in protein?
      (iii) Why does the girl need protein?

(b)   (i)   The total energy value of this meal in 6600 kJ.
            In one day the girl needs 9600 kJ.
            If she ate this meal, how many **more** kJ would she need in that day?
      (ii) What would happen if she eats much more than 9600 kJ of food every day?
      (iii) A lot of energy comes from fat.
            Name the **two** foods in this meal which gave her most energy.

(c)   The girl needs 14 mg of iron and 25 mg of Vitamin C each day to keep healthy.
      (i)   How much of her daily iron did this meal give her?
      (ii) How much of her daily Vitamin C needs did this meal give her?
      (iii) What will happen if she does not have enough iron and Vitamin C?

(d)   Why should she eat fibre (roughage) every day?

Food and health
An individual who does not receive a balanced diet – especially over a long period – may be in a state of **malnutrition**. There are two main types of malnutrition:

▶   **Undernutrition.** Approximately two-thirds of the world's human population are suffering from undernutrition. These people, mainly living in developing countries, are 'malnourished' in the sense that they do not receive enough food, or they do not receive a suitable range of foods.
      If specific nutrients are missing from the diet, they may suffer from deficiency diseases.

Table 4(1).3

Disease	What is missing from the diet	Symptoms
Anaemia	Iron	Not enough red blood cells, so the person is pale, weak and tired.
Scurvy	Vitamin C	Skin and gums are weak and bleed easily. Wounds take a long time to heal.
Rickets	Vitamin D	Children's bones do not grow properly, and they bend under pressure.
Kwashiorkor	Protein	Children do not grow properly, and they feel very weak and tired.

▶   **Overnutrition.** People living in parts of the world where food is more readily available may consume more food than they need in a balanced diet. If this continues, an individual may become **obese** (overweight).
      If particular nutrients are eaten to excess, they may suffer from specific health problems, e.g. too much sugar causes tooth decay (dental caries), too much saturated fat causes blockage of the arteries leading to heart disease.

Food and energy
It is important that the energy taken in in food balances the energy used up by an individual.

Energy in food: 1g of lipid contains 38 kJ of energy,
1g of carbohydrate contains 17 kJ of energy,
1g of protein contains 17 kJ of energy.

We can see from this that lipids are high-energy foods. Although protein can be used to provide energy, it is normally used as a source of raw materials for growth, not energy.

Energy requirements: Energy is normally needed for four roles
1. growth;
2. moving around;
3. keeping warm;
4. vital body processes.

The exact amount of energy needed by an individual depends on his or her age, activity level, body mass and the climate he or she lives in. Pregnant and breast-feeding women need large amounts of energy to supply the energy needs of their baby.

Measuring energy in food: The easiest way to find out about the energy content of foods is to look at the nutrition label on processed foods.

INGREDIENTS	NUTRITION INFORMATION		
Water, Carrots, Potatoes Concentrated Tomato Puree Peas, Onions, Pasta (made from Wheat), Modified Cornflour Sugar, Salt, Haricot beans Green Beans, Vegetable Oil Flour, Flavour Enhancer – Monosodium Glutamate Hydrolysed Vegatable Protein Herbs	Typical Values	Amount per 100g	Amount per Serving (202g)
	Energy	205kJ/48kcal	414kJ/97kcal
	Protein	1.5g	3.0g
	Carbohydrate (of which sugars)	8.7g (3.4g)	17.6g (6.9g)
	Fats (of which saturates)	0.9g (0.1g)	1.8g (0.2g)
	Fibre	1.1g	2.2g
	Sodium	0.5g	1.0g

Fig. 4(1).1 Nutrition label – can you guess what type of food it is from?

In school, experiments are often done to find the approximate energy content of food by burning it under a tube of water. To do the calculation, you must know:

1. mass of the peanut;
2. volume of the water;
3. original temperature of the water;
4. final temperature of the water.

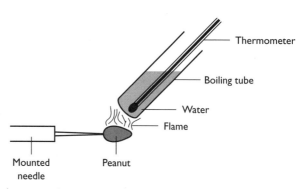

Fig. 4(1).2 Finding the energy in a peanut

Amount of energy in one peanut (kJ)
$$= \frac{\text{temperature rise (°C)} \times \text{volume of water (ml)}}{1000} \times 4.2$$

Amount of energy in 100g of peanut (kJ)
$$= \frac{\text{energy in one peanut (kJ)}}{\text{mass of peanut (g)}} \times 100$$

REVISION ACTIVITY 2 If you carry out this experiment, the value you calculate will be far less than the value for energy given in the nutrition panel on a packet of peanuts. Explain why.

Food tests
You should know how to test foods to find out if they contain starch, reducing sugars and protein.

Table 4(1).4

Type of food	Food test	Positive result
Starch	Add iodine solution to the food.	Colour change: orange → black
Reducing sugar	Add Benedicts solution to the food and heat in the waterbath at 80°C for five minutes.	Colour change: blue → green → orange
Protein	Add Biuret solution to the food and leave to stand for five minutes.	Colour change: blue → violet

Enzymes

Key points

▷ enzymes are biological catalysts;
▷ they control the rate of all chemical reactions in the body, including digestion;
▷ there are thousands of different types of enzymes;
▷ they work best at a particular temperature and pH (optimum conditions).

Enzymes are biological **catalysts** which alter the rate of a reaction without themselves being changed. They are globular proteins.

Enzymes are believed to work by forming a temporary 'complex' with the chemical they are acting upon, the **substrate**, before forming the **product** or products. The way in which this could occur is called the 'lock and key' model, shown in Fig. 4(1).3.

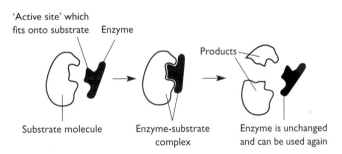

Fig. 4(1).3 The role of the active site in enzyme activity

Characteristics of enzymes
Enzymes have certain **characteristics** which can be explained in terms of the 'lock and key' model:

1. **Enzymes are specific for a particular substrate:**
   The active site on the enzyme has to 'fit' the substrate.
2. **Enzymes work within a narrow range of temperature** (Fig. 4(1).4):
   At high temperatures, enzymes are **denatured**; the shape of the molecule, including the active site, is distorted. At low temperatures, enzyme and substrate molecules are less liable to react together.
3. **Enzymes work within a narrow range of pH** (Fig. 4(1).5):
   Extremes of pH may denature the enzyme; some enzymes are very sensitive to this. Acid or alkaline conditions may affect the other substances involved in the reaction.

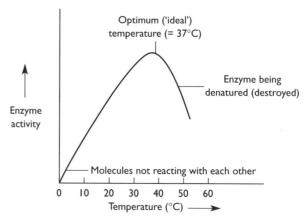

Fig. 4(1).4 The effect of temperature on enzyme activity

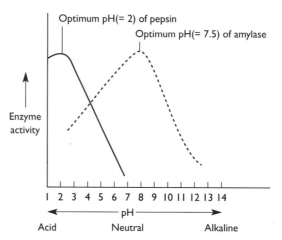

Fig. 4(1).5 The effect of pH on enzyme activity. Pepsin and amylase are found in acid and in alkaline regions of the gut, respectively

Role of enzymes in the body

Enzymes control the rate of **all** chemical reactions within the body. Enzymes are specific, i.e. they only catalyse one type of reaction, so there are thousands of different enzymes in the body. **Extracellular enzymes** are secreted outside the cell where they have their effect, e.g. digestion in the gut cavity. **Intracellular enzymes** are retained within the cell and catalyse reactions there, e.g. respiration within mitochondria.

Figure 4(1).3 shows a breaking down (catabolic) reaction like digestion; the 'lock and key' model can also explain building-up (anabolic) reactions, in which two substrate molecules are combined into a single product.

Digestive system and digestion

Key points

▷ the digestive system is specialised for the digestion and absorption of food;
▷ food is chewed by teeth and mixed by muscular contractions of the gut wall;
▷ enzymes are secreted onto the food to digest it.

Digestive system

The digestive system consists of the gut (alimentary canal), a tube about 8m long running from the mouth to the anus, and the organs joined to it, e.g. pancreas, gall bladder.

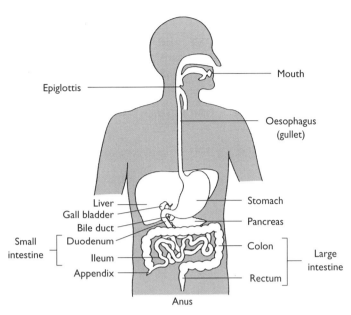

Fig. 4(1).6 Structure of the human gut

What happens in the different regions of the gut?
Each region of the gut is specialised for a particular function.

Table 4(1).5

Region	What happens	Reason
Mouth	Food is chewed by teeth. Food is mixed with saliva.	It is broken into smaller pieces and moistened so it is easier to swallow. Digestion of starch begins.
Stomach	Food is mixed with acid and enzymes. Gut muscles contract to mix food properly.	Acid kills bacteria and helps enzymes to work properly. Digestion of protein begins.
Small intestine (duodenum and ileum)	Food is mixed with bile. Food is mixed with enzymes from pancreas and gut wall. Digested food is absorbed from the ileum into the blood.	Bile emulsifies fats. Digestion of protein and starch continues, digestion of sugars and lipids begins. It can travel to all parts of the body.
Large intestine (colon and rectum)	Water is absorbed into the blood. Faeces are stored.	To prevent large amounts of water being lost from the body in faeces.
Anus	The sphincter muscle relaxes to allow faeces to pass out of the body.	This is egestion.

Teeth
The four main types of teeth in humans are **incisors** (for cutting), **canines** (for piercing and grasping), **premolars** and **molars** (for crushing and slicing). These teeth all have the same basic structure, though their shape and position in the jaw vary according to their function (Fig. 4(1).7).

REVISION ACTIVITY 3   Complete this table.

Table 4(1).6

Part of tooth	Description
	contains nerves and blood vessels
	very hard, resistant material
	holds the tooth in the jaw-bone
	brings oxygen and food to living cells in the tooth
	causes you to feel pain in the tooth
	a layer of living material

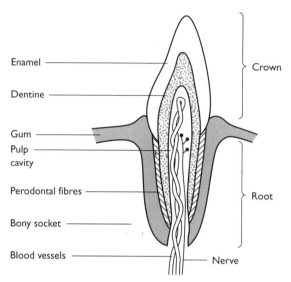

Fig. 4(1).7 Structure of a 'typical' tooth; canine (vertical section)

There are two main types of dental disease; both are caused by **plaque**, an accumulation of food (especially sugar) and bacteria on the exposed surfaces of teeth:

1. **Dental caries (tooth decay)**
   Acid produced as a waste product by bacteria in plaque dissolves through the enamel layer of teeth. Decay can spread more rapidly through the softer dentine and then into the pulp cavity. Infection of the pulp may cause an inflammation (abscess) of the gum.
2. **Periodontal disease**
   Spread of plaque between teeth and gums may cause an inflammation (gingivitis) around the roots. Periodontal fibres become destroyed as the gums recede, resulting in teeth becoming loose and possibly being lost.

The prevention of both diseases may be achieved by increased oral hygiene. For instance, by regular brushing, the avoidance of sugary foods and regular dental checks. Enamel can be made more resistant by the presence of fluoride; this is naturally present in the drinking water in some areas. Many water authorities in the UK add fluoride to drinking water and this fluoridation seems to be associated with a significant reduction in dental caries. However, some people object to being given fluoride without choice. Fluoride is present in many toothpastes.

How is food moved through the gut?
Muscles in the gut wall contract to move food by peristalsis. Peristalsis is caused by the alternate contraction of the circular and longitudinal muscles contained in the gut wall (Fig. 4(1).8).

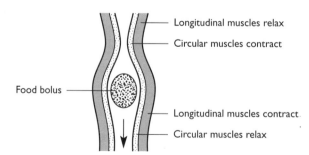

Fig. 4(1).8 Peristalsis in the gut

Muscle contraction helps to mix food with digestive juices, e.g. enzymes, bile, acids, and to physically break it down into smaller pieces.

Muscles are also used to control the movement of food through the gut. For instance the **epiglottis** is a muscular flap which closes during **swallowing** to prevent solid and liquid food from entering the trachea; **sphincters** are circular muscles which, when contracted, prevent food moving in the wrong direction or at the wrong time, for example, at the entrance and exit of the stomach and at the anus.

Processes occurring in the digestive system

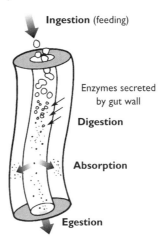

Fig. 4(1).9 Key processes in the digestive system

Digestion

> **Digestion is the breakdown of large, insoluble food molecules to form smaller, soluble food molecules.**

Many foods (proteins, lipids and some carbohydrates) must be digested, otherwise they are too big to be absorbed into the blood.

Digestive enzymes made in the pancreas and the gut wall are mixed with the food to digest it. Enzymes can be grouped according to the type of food they digest:

Carbohydrases, e.g. amylase and maltase, break down carbohydrates to simple sugars.
Proteases, e.g. pepsin and trypsin, break down proteins to amino acids.
Lipases digest fats to fatty acids and glycerol.

The gut provides optimum conditions for enzyme activity by maintaining a favourable temperature and pH. The pH (acidity or alkalinity) in each region of the gut is kept fairly constant by additions of acid or alkali.

Table 4(1).7 Summary of the main stages of digestion in humans

Region of gut	Secretions	Examples of chemical digestion
Mouth	Saliva (from three pairs of salivary glands) contains mucus and the enzyme salivary amylase.	$\text{Starch} \xrightarrow{\text{amylase}} \text{maltose (sugar)}$ (pH 7)
Stomach	Gastric juice (from stomach wall) contains hydrochloric acid and enzymes including pepsin.	$\text{Protein} \xrightarrow{\text{pepsin}} \text{amino acids}$ (pH 2)
Duodenum	Intestinal juice (from duodenum wall) contains enzymes, including maltase and amylase.	$\text{Maltose} \xrightarrow{\text{maltase}} \text{glucose}$ (pH 8.5) $\text{Starch} \xrightarrow{\text{amylase}} \text{maltose}$ (pH 7)
	Pancreatic juice (from pancreas) contains alkaline secretions and also enzymes including amylase, trypsin, lipase.	$\text{Fats} \xrightarrow{\text{lipase}} \text{fatty acids + glycerol}$ (pH 7)
	Bile (from liver) contains bile salts.	Bile salts emulsify lipids; they reduce lipids into small droplets, increasing the surface area for digestion.

Food is mixed with enzymes by muscular movements of the gut, which also cause physical digestion to take place. Food remains briefly in the mouth before being swallowed; conditions in the stomach are very acid (pH 2) and any digestion of starch by amylase is temporarily prevented. Food is held (by sphincter muscles) in the stomach for about four hours. This allows protein to be digested. A mucus lining prevents the lining of the stomach (which contains protein) from being digested, or damaged by the acid conditions. The acidic mixture in the stomach is called chyme. This is later neutralised in the duodenum by alkaline secretions from the pancreas. Digestion is mostly completed in the duodenum.

Absorption and assimilation

Once the food has been digested, it can travel all parts of the body to be used by body cells.

Key points

▷ absorption is the movement of food from the gut to the blood;
▷ absorption occurs in the ileum;
▷ assimilation means that body cells use the digested food.

Absorption

Absorption of digested food occurs in the ileum. It is adapted for absorption in four main ways.

1. It is about 5m long, so it has a **large surface area**.
2. It has **villi** to increase the surface area. Each villus is a tiny spike sticking into the lumen of the ileum, and there are hundreds of villi on each mm². The walls of the villi are only **one cell thick** so digested foods can pass through them easily.

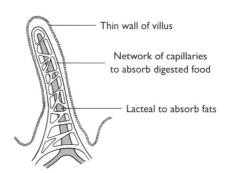

Thin wall of villus

Network of capillaries to absorb digested food

Lacteal to absorb fats

Fig. 4(1).10

3. It has a very good **blood supply** to carry away digested food. Each villus contains a network of capillaries.
4. It has branches of the **lymphatic system** to carry away fats. Each villus contains a lacteal.
    Nutrients are absorbed through the lining of the ileum by **diffusion** or **active transport** depending on the size of the molecules and concentration gradients. Digested lipids are absorbed into the lymphatic system; all other nutrients, which are now water soluble, enter the blood system.

Assimilation

Assimilation occurs when nutrients are used, or modified by body cells. Absorbed food substances travel to the **liver** in the hepatic portal vein; many substances are modified while they are in the liver.

▷ **Sugars** (from digestion of carbohydrates) are used to provide energy for all body cells, in the process of respiration; excess sugar is changed to glycogen, and stored in the liver and muscles, or converted to fat and stored under the skin and around body organs.
▷ **Amino acids** (from digestion of proteins) are used inside body cells for growth and repair; excess amino acids are broken down in the liver. This process is called deamination, and it produces the highly toxic product urea which must be excreted from the body.

▷ **Fatty acids and glycerol** (from digestion of lipids) are used to provide energy for all body cells in the process of respiration; excess fats are stored under the skin and around body organs.

Egestion

After most water has been absorbed, the contents of the gut are known as faeces. These consist of any undigested material, mainly cellulose, combined with microbes, mucus and dead cells from the lining of the gut. This is passed out of the body through the anus during the process of egestion, or defecation. This should not be confused with excretion which involves getting rid of the waste products of metabolism. Faeces are temporarily stored in the rectum and then egested at intervals.

REVISION ACTIVITY 4   Define these terms: ingestion, digestion, absorption, assimilation, egestion.

▷ **Circulation**   Humans (like other vertebrates) need a transport system to move substances around the body. In humans there are three components of the circulation system:

1. blood (the transport fluid);
2. heart (a pump to keep the blood moving);
3. blood vessels (to carry blood around the body).

Blood

Key points
▷ blood is made up of four components: plasma, red blood cells, white blood cells, and platelets; ▷ blood carries materials around the body, e.g. oxygen, food, carbon dioxide, urea, hormones, and heat; ▷ blood is important in defence against disease.

Structure of the blood

If we look at blood with a powerful microscope, we can see there are four components:

1. plasma;
2. red blood cells;
3. white blood cells;
4. platelets.

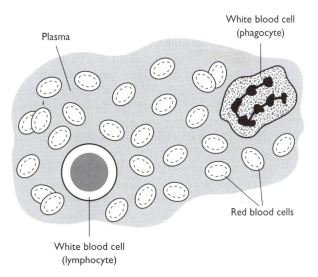

White blood cell (phagocyte)

Plasma

Red blood cells

White blood cell (lymphocyte)

Platelets are too small to be seen with most microscopes

Fig. 4(1).11 Looking at blood under the microscope

Plasma is a pale watery liquid. Most of the substances transported in the blood are carried dissolved in plasma. It is about 90% water, but also contains blood proteins, which are important in blood clotting.

Red blood cells are small, biconcave disc-shaped cells. They are adapted to carry oxygen in the following ways:

▷   they contain a red chemical, haemoglobin, which combines with oxygen;
▷   they have no nucleus, so they contain more haemoglobin;
▷   haemoglobin contains iron, so a lack of iron in the diet leads to anaemia (shortage of red blood cells);
▷   the biconcave disc shape gives them a large surface area, so they can absorb more oxygen.

Red blood cells are made in the bone marrow, and there are about 5 million per ml of blood.

White blood cells are involved in defence against disease. They do not have any role in transport. There are two main types:

1.   phagocytes: these can change shape to engulf and destroy pathogens;
2.   lymphocytes: these make antibodies to destroy pathogens.

There are about 7,000 white blood cells per ml of blood (the number increases when we are ill), and they are made in the bone marrow and lymphatic system.

Platelets are tiny cell fragments made in the bone marrow. They are important in the blood clotting process.

Blood and transport
The following materials are carried round the body in the blood:

▷   **oxygen** from the lungs to all body cells;
▷   **carbon dioxide** from body cells to the lungs;
▷   **digested food** from the ileum to all body cells;
▷   **urea** from the liver to the kidneys;
▷   **hormones** from endocrine glands to all body cells;
▷   **heat** from the liver and muscles to all body cells.

Oxygen is carried inside red blood cells, combined with haemoglobin.
     All other materials are carried dissolved in plasma.

Blood and defence against disease
Blood helps to protect the body from infection in three main ways:

1.   phagocytes engulf pathogens;
2.   lymphocytes produce antibodies;
3.   platelets are involved in blood clotting.

Phagocytes engulf pathogens: Phagocytes can change shape to squeeze out of capillaries and into the spaces between cells. They are attracted by the chemicals produced by pathogens and move towards them (this is chemotaxis). They surround and engulf pathogens, then produce enzymes to destroy them.
     Lymphocytes produce antibodies: When lymphocytes make contact with pathogens in the body, they produce antibodies. Antibodies are not alive, they are chemicals which travel in the blood and attach themselves to pathogens. They destroy the pathogens by making them clump together, or by making them burst (see section on Immunity on pp. 121–124).
     Platelets are involved in blood clotting: When a blood vessel is damaged, or when blood comes into contact with air, platelets release a chemical which starts the blood clotting process. This is a complex series of reactions which results in soluble blood proteins becoming insoluble and forming a network of fibres. Red blood cells get trapped in this network and form a clot.
     Blood clotting is important because:

▷   it prevents pathogens getting into an open wound;
▷   it prevents excess blood loss.

However, it is important that blood only clots at the appropriate time. If blood clots in undamaged vessels it can have very serious consequences, e.g. heart attack, stroke.

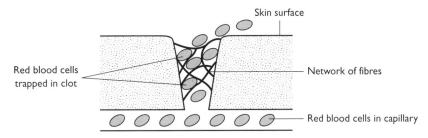

Fig. 4(1).12 Blood clotting

The heart

> ### Key points
>
> ▷ the heart is a pump which circulates blood around the body;
> ▷ the right side of the heart pumps deoxygenated blood to the lungs;
> ▷ the left side of the heart pumps oxygenated blood around the body;
> ▷ valves keep blood flowing in the right direction;
> ▷ coronary vessels bring food and oxygen to the heart muscle, and if these become blocked the person may have a heart attack;
> ▷ at rest, the heart beats about **70** times per minute, but it speeds up when we exercise.

Structure of the heart
The heart is a muscular pump which keeps blood moving through the circulatory system. The heart in humans consist of two fused pumps, which pump either **oxygenated blood (left side)** or **deoxygenated blood (right side)**. Each side of the heart is further divided into two compartments (Fig. 4(1).13) the **atria** and **ventricles**, which allow blood to be pumped in two stages.

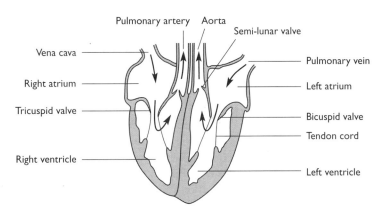

Fig. 4(1).13 Section through the heart

REVISION ACTIVITY 5

(a) What are the functions of the following?

    (i) vena cava
    (ii) pulmonary artery
    (iii) pulmonary vein
    (iv) aorta
    (v) left atrium

    (vi) left ventricle
    (vii) bicuspid valve
    (viii) tendon cord
    (ix) semi-lunar valve

(b) Why is the wall of the left ventricle thicker than the wall of the right ventricle?

How does the heart pump blood?
The heart beats in a continuous series of rhythmic muscular contractions; each repeating sequence is called a **cardiac cycle**. The frequency of cardiac cycles and the power of each contraction depends on the body's need for blood, and is regulated by the brain, by nerves

and hormones. The heart can also regulate its own activity by a small patch of tissue, called the **pacemaker**, embedded in the wall of the right atrium. The average adult rate of the cardiac cycle is about 70 beats per minute. This can be increased dramatically, for instance to supply and remove more materials to exercising muscle.

Blood from all the veins in the body drains into the two atria of the heart at the beginning of each heart beat. Both atria contract together (Fig. 4(1).14), forcing blood into the ventricles. These then contract, pumping blood into arteries leading to the lungs or the rest of the body. The ventricles have thicker muscular walls than the atria because they need to push blood over greater distances; the left ventricle has particularly thick walls because it pumps blood around most of the body.

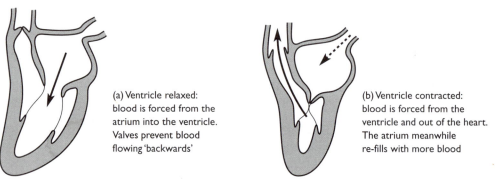

(a) Ventricle relaxed: blood is forced from the atrium into the ventricle. Valves prevent blood flowing 'backwards'

(b) Ventricle contracted: blood is forced from the ventricle and out of the heart. The atrium meanwhile re-fills with more blood

Fig. 4(1).14 The cardiac cycle (left side of the heart shown)

REVISION ACTIVITY 6   Put these statements about the cardiac cycle into the right order

A   Blood moves from the veins into the atria.
B   The ventricles contract.
C   Blood moves into the arteries.
D   The bicuspid and tricuspid valves open.
E   The semi lunar valves open.
F   The atria contract.
G   Blood moves into the ventricles.

| A | | | | | | |

Coronary vessels

Running over the surface of the heart are small blood vessels called coronary vessels. These supply the heart muscle with food and oxygen and take away waste products.

If the coronary vessels are blocked, e.g. by cholesterol, or by a blood clot, a patch of heart muscle does not get the nutrients it needs and may die. This is a **heart attack**, and its severity depends on the amount of heart muscle affected.

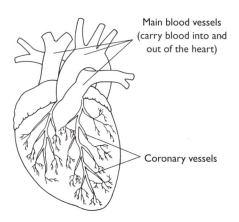

Main blood vessels (carry blood into and out of the heart)

Coronary vessels

Fig. 4(1).15 Surface of the heart, showing some coronary vessels

Narrowing or blockage of a coronary vessel can be treated in one of two ways

1. angioplasty: a small balloon is passed through the vessel to unblock it;
2. coronary bypass: another blood vessel is grafted onto the heart to provide an alternative route for blood.

Pulse rate

An average resting heart rate is about 70 beats per minute. It increases when we exercise so that:

▷   food and oxygen can be delivered to muscle cells more quickly (these are the raw materials for respiration);
▷   waste products, e.g. carbon dioxide made in respiration, can be removed more efficiently.

After exercise, the time taken for the pulse rate to return to normal is known as the **recovery time** – this is relatively short in fit people.

Other factors influencing pulse rate are stress, excitement and illness.

Blood vessels and circulation

Key points

▷   there are three types of blood vessels: arteries, veins and capillaries;

▷   exchanges between blood and body cells occurs in the capillaries;

▷   humans have a double circulation, where blood travels twice through the heart on each complete circuit of the body.

Structure of blood vessels

Blood vessels are tubes which form the circulatory system and which carry blood around the body in a particular direction. There are three main types of blood vessel; the **artery**, **capillary** and **vein**. These are compared in Fig. 4(1).16.

Comparison	Artery	Vein	Capillary
Function	to carry blood away from the heart.	to carry blood towards the heart.	to carry blood through body organs and to allow exchange between body cells and the blood.
Cross-section (not to scale)	outer coat / muscle layer	outer coat	wall one cell thick
Internal (lumen) diameter	Fairly narrow; can expand (= pulse)	Fairly wide.	Very narrow; red blood cells squeeze through.
Wall structure	The wall is relatively thick and also elastic, to withstand pressure.	The wall is relatively thin; there are **valves** to keep blood moving in one direction.	Wall is composed of a single cell layer; gaps between cells allow exchange of materials with surrounding tissues.
Blood direction	Blood flows away from the heart.	Blood flows towards the heart.	Blood flows from arteries to veins.
Blood pressure	High.	Low.	Falling.
Blood flow rate	Rapid, irregular.	Slow, regular.	Very slow.

Fig. 4(1).16 Comparison of the main types of blood vessel

Exchanges between blood and body cells

As blood flows through the capillaries it slows down. Capillary walls are thin and permeable, and high blood pressure forces some of the plasma out through the capillary walls into the spaces between body cells – now it is called **tissue fluid**. When plasma leaves the blood it carries dissolved food and oxygen with it, and these materials diffuse into the body cells.

Most tissue fluid returns to the capillaries, carrying waste materials, e.g. carbon dioxide which it has picked up from the body cells. Some tissue fluid passes into lymph vessels (now it is called **lymph**) and travels through the lymphatic system before it rejoins the blood.

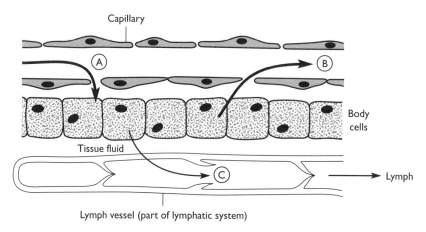

Fig. 4(1).17 Exchange of materials between capillaries and surrounding tissues

A – plasma is moving from the capillary into the spaces between cells (now it is called tissue fluid). It carries food and oxygen to the body cells

B – tissue fluid is moving back into the capillary (now it is called plasma). It carries waste products, e.g. carbon dioxide from the body cells.

C – excess tissue fluid moves into the lymph vessel (now it is called lymph), and is eventually returned to the blood.

REVISION ACTIVITY 7   Examine Fig. 4(1).18 which shows the relationship between part of the blood system and some cells in the body.

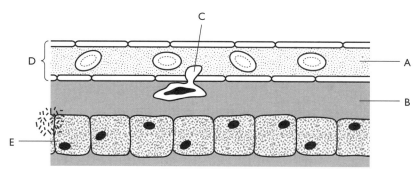

Fig. 4(1).18

(a)   (i)   Name the liquid found in Area **A**.
      (ii) Name the liquid found in Area **B**.
      (iii) What does the shaded part of cell **C** represent?_____
      (iv) Name the structure labelled **D**.

(b)   State two observations from Fig. 4(1).18 which helped you to name the structure labelled **D**.

(c)   Cell **E** is being invaded by bacteria. Describe how the blood might help to control the infection.

Circulation

Humans have a double circulation: this means that the blood passes twice through the heart on each complete circuit of the body. This system is very efficient and transports materials to and from body cells quickly.

REVISION ACTIVITY 8   What are the names of blood vessels. A, B, C and D?

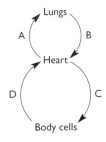

Fig. 4(1).19

Deoxygenated blood travels to the lungs in the pulmonary artery. It is oxygenated in the lungs.

Oxygenated blood travels back to the heart in the pulmonary vein. When the left ventricle contracts, blood is forced into the aorta. Branches of the aorta carry blood to all body organs (except lungs). Exchange between blood and body cells occurs in the capillaries as blood travels through body organs.

Deoxygenated blood flows out of body organs in veins. Veins join together to form the vena cava. The vena cava returns deoxygenated blood to the right atrium.

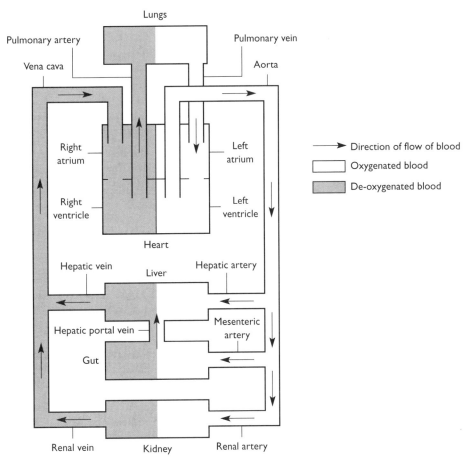

Fig. 4(1).20 Circulatory system

REVISION ACTIVITY 9

(a)   How is the pulmonary artery different to all other arteries?
(b)   Name the blood vessel carrying blood away from the kidneys.
(c)   What is the biggest vein in the body?
(d)   Which blood vessel has the highest blood pressure?
(e)   Where does the hepatic portal vein carry blood to; is it oxygenated or deoxygenated blood?

▷ Gas exchange

Humans need to obtain oxygen in order to carry out respiration. Respiration is a chemical reaction occurring in all cells of the body to make **energy**.

Oxygen + sugar ⟶ energy + carbon dioxide + water

The carbon dioxide made in respiration is removed via the lungs.

The respiratory system

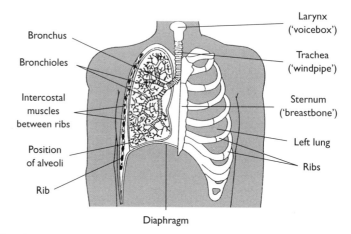

Fig. 4(1).21 Respiratory system

Table 4(1).8 Summary of the main components of the respiratory system

Component	Description
Lungs	Consist of **alveoli** and **bronchioles.** Each lung is covered by a double **pleural membrane**, enclosing **pleural fluid**; these membranes protect the lungs.
Alveoli	Alveoli are the sites of gaseous exchange. The total number of alveoli in the lungs is about 700 million, giving a combined surface area of 80 m².
Bronchioles	Bronchioles consist of a branching network of tubes, carrying air to and from the alveoli.
Bronchi	Bronchi connect the bronchiole network with the trachea. Each **bronchus** is strengthened by **cartilage**.
Trachea	The trachea (windpipe) connects the lungs to the mouth and nose cavities. **Cilia** (very fine hairs) cover the lining of the trachea; these beat rhythmically and move particles away from the lungs. **Mucus** secreted by the trachea, traps particles including microbes. The trachea is kept open by rings of cartilage.
Ribs	The ribs protect the lungs (and heart) and are important in breathing movements.
Intercostal muscles	There are two sets of **antagonistic muscles** between the ribs. **External** intercostal muscles are used for inhalation; **internal** intercostal muscles contract during exhalation. The muscles raise and lower the rib 'cage'.
Diaphragm	The diaphragm consists of a muscle sheet which, when relaxed, becomes **domed** in shape. Contraction of the diaphragm muscles causes it to flatten, increasing the chest volume.
Nasal cavity	Air that is breathed through the nose is **filtered** by hairs, moistened by **mucus** and warmed by blood capillaries lining the nasal cavity. Breathing can continue whilst chewing occurs in the mouth cavity, but is temporarily interrupted by swallowing.

Breathing

> ### Key points
>
> ▷ breathing (ventilation of the lungs) makes gas exchange more efficient;
>
> ▷ the ribs and diaphragm are involved in breathing;
>
> ▷ pressure changes inside the thorax draw air into, or force air out of the lungs.

When resting, a person normally breathes in about 16 times per minute. The steps involved are:

1. the diaphragm contracts and becomes flatter;
2. the external intercostal muscles contract so the ribs move upwards and outwards;
3. the volume of the thorax increases;
4. the pressure inside the thorax decreases;
5. air is drawn into the lungs.

When breathing out, the opposite of these processes occurs. Natural elasticity also helps the lungs to deflate.

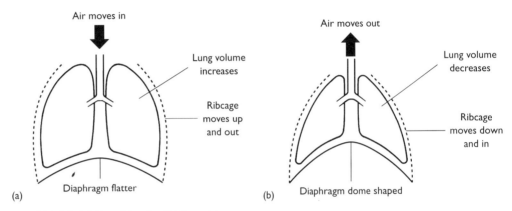

Fig. 4(1).22 (a) Breathing in (b) Breathing out

Table 4(1).9 Summary of inhalation and exhalation

Change	Inhalation	Exhalation
Intercostal muscles	**External** muscles contract, causing the ribs to move upwards and outwards.	**Internal** muscles contract, causing the ribs to move downwards and inwards; gravity may assist this.
Diaphragm	Contracts and flattens, pushing down on the contents of the abdomen below.	Relaxes and becomes doomed; displaced contents of abdomen push from below.
Volume of thorax	Increases	Decreases
Pressure of throax	Decreases	Increases
Lungs	Become inflated.	Elasticity of lungs causes them to become deflated.

REVISION ACTIVITY 10

(a) What do the following, seen in Fig. 4(1).23, represent?
　　(i) bell jar　　　　　　(iii) balloons
　　(ii) rubber sheet　　　　(iv) plastic tubing

(b) What would happen to the balloons if you pushed the rubber sheet up (to the dotted line)?
　　Explain why.

(c) How is this model different to the real breathing system?

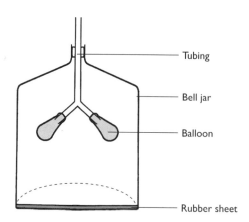

Fig. 4(1).23

Gas exchange in the alveoli

Key points
▷ the alveoli are well adapted for gas exchange;
▷ gases move by diffusion;
▷ oxygen diffuses out of the alveoli into the blood;
▷ carbon dioxide diffuses out of the blood into the alveoli.

Structure of the alveolus

Each lung contains about 350 million alveoli. They are well adapted for gas exchange because:

▷ they have a **large surface area** (total for both lungs is about 80m²);
▷ the alveolus walls are **thin** (they are only one cell thick), so gases can pass through them easily;
▷ the alveolus walls are **permeable** (let gases through easily);
▷ the alveolus walls are **moist** (so gases can dissolve and diffuse more easily);
▷ each alveolus is close to a **capillary** (so gases do not have far to diffuse).

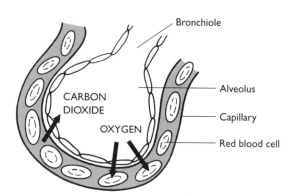

Fig. 4(1).24 Gas exchange in humans

Movement of gases

Oxygen. The air we breath in contains about 21% oxygen. The blood in the capillaries contains less oxygen than this, so oxygen diffuses from the alveoli into the blood. It quickly combines with haemoglobin inside red blood cells, and is carried round the body as oxyhaemoglobin.

Carbon dioxide. Carbon dioxide is mainly carried in the blood plasma in the form of sodium hydrogen carbonate. When blood reaches the lungs, the concentration of carbon dioxide is much higher in the blood than the alveoli, so carbon dioxide diffuses into the alveoli and is breathed out.

Comparison of inhaled and exhaled air

Table 4(1).10 Relative composition of inhaled and exhaled air

Component	Inhaled air	Exhaled air
Oxygen	21%	17%
Carbon dioxide	0.04%	4%
Nitrogen	78%	78%
Water vapour	Variable, depends on humidity; average = 1.3%	Saturated = 6.2%
Temperature	Variable	37°C
Dust particles	Varies	Very few

REVISION ACTIVITY 11

(a) Why is there less oxygen in the air we breathe out than in the air we breathe in?
(b) Why is there more carbon dioxide in the air we breathe out than in the air we breathe in?
(c) What do the figures for nitrogen tell you?
(d) Why is there less dust in the air we breathe out than the air we breathe in?

Experiment to compare the amount of carbon dioxide in inhaled and exhaled air
The experiment is set up as shown in Fig. 4(1).25. Each of the two test-tubes contain a **carbon dioxide indicator** solution such as bicarbonate indicator (or limewater). The arrangement of delivery tubes causes inhaled air to bubble through tube A whilst exhaled air bubbles through tube B.

After a few seconds, tube B will show the presence of carbon dioxide; bicarbonate indicator will change colour from red to yellow; limewater will go 'milky'. Tube A will take much longer to give a positive result. This demonstrates that relatively more carbon dioxide is contained in exhaled air (the actual amounts are given in Table 4(1).10).

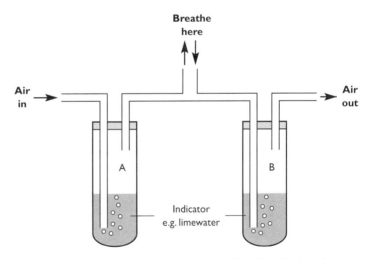

Fig. 4(1).25 Experiment to compare carbon dioxide in inhaled and exhaled air

Aerobic respiration

> **Key points**
>
> ▷ aerobic respiration requires oxygen;
> ▷ the purpose of respiration is to make energy.

Respiration is occurring in all cells of the human body at all times to make energy. Normally enough oxygen is available for the following reaction to occur:

Glucose + oxygen ⟶ energy + carbon dioxide + water

This is aerobic respiration, because oxygen is involved.

The oxygen for respiration is breathed in through the lungs. The glucose for respiration is absorbed from the ileum after digestion. Both oxygen and glucose are transported to body cells in the blood.

The energy is needed to:

▷ carry out vital processes, e.g. muscle contraction;
▷ synthesise new materials for growth, e.g. protein synthesis;
▷ keep the body temperature constant at 37°C.

Exercise and anaerobic respiration

> **Key points**
>
> ▷ when we exercise, respiration rate increases;
> ▷ heart rate and breathing rate increase to deliver more oxygen to muscles;
> ▷ if oxygen is in short supply, muscle cells can respire without oxygen. This is anaerobic respiration.

Effect of exercise on the body

Muscle cells use a lot of energy when they contract, and this energy is made during respiration. When we exercise, muscle contraction increases, so the rate of respiration must increase to provide the energy needed.

Look at the respiration equation:

$$\text{Glucose + oxygen} \longrightarrow \text{energy + carbon dioxide + water}$$

If respiration increases:

▷ more **glucose** is needed – glycogen stored in the liver and muscles is changed into glucose;
▷ more **oxygen** is needed – so breathing rate and depth increase, and heart rate increases to deliver oxygen to the muscles;
▷ more **carbon dioxide** is produced – this is carried by the blood to the lungs and breathed out. The increased heart rate and breathing rate help to get rid of it more quickly.

Anaerobic respiration

If exercise is heavy or prolonged, the amount of oxygen supplied to muscle cells may not be enough, and anaerobic respiration may occur.

$$\text{Glucose} \longrightarrow \text{energy + lactic acid}$$

This is less efficient than aerobic respiration for two reasons:

1. less energy is produced;
2. lactic acid builds up in muscle and causes pain and cramp.

Recovery after exercise

When a person stops exercising vigorously, the body takes some time to get back to normal. The following processes must occur:

▷ **Lactic acid is broken down.** Extra oxygen is breathed in to combine with the lactic acid, and convert it to carbon dioxide and water. The amount of extra oxygen needed is called the oxygen debt.
▷ **Pulse rate goes back to normal.**
▷ **Breathing rate goes back to normal.**

The time it takes the body to return to its pre-exercise state is called the **recovery time**. This is shorter for fit people, and can be reduced by taking regular exercise.

▷ **Movement**

This topic is not part of the National Curriculum for England and Wales at Key Stage 4.

Humans have a complex skeletal and muscular system which allows a wide range of movements. Locomotion involves moving the whole body from one place to another, e.g. walking, and is useful when looking for food or escaping from danger.

Humans can also move part of the body, and can carry out a variety of intricate co-ordinated movements, e.g. when playing a musical instrument.

The skeleton

Key points

▷ the skeleton protects some internal organs, e.g. heart, lungs;

▷ the skeleton supports the body, and holds it upright;

▷ the bones of the skeleton act as levers for movement.

The human skeleton consists of 206 bones.

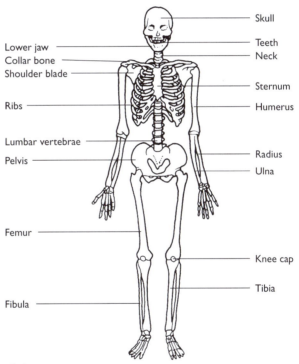

Fig. 4(1).26 Human skeleton

Joints

Key points

▷ joints occur wherever two or more bones meet;

▷ there are different types of joint, with different ranges of movement;

▷ joints contain cartilage and synovial fluid to reduce friction.

Types of joints
There are three main types of joint:

(a) **Immovable joints.** Bones are fused, or held together by a protein called collagen, e.g. the bones of the skull.

(b) **Partially movable joints.** Bones slide or glide over each other. The articulating ('rubbing') surfaces are covered by a layer of cartilage, e.g. wrist, ankle.

(c) **Movable (synovial) joints.** There are two types, each allowing a different amount of movement:

▶ **ball-and-socket joint**, which allows movement in most directions. Several pairs of muscles are attached to each of the bones of the joint, e.g. hip, shoulder.

▶ **hinge joint**, allows movement in one plane only, e.g. elbow, knee, finger joints.

Structure of a synovial joint, e.g. hip joint.

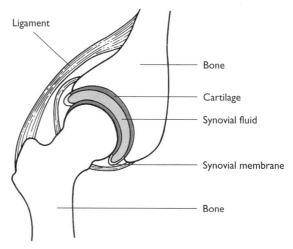

Fig. 4(1).27 Inside a movable joint

Table 4(1).11

Part	Description
Cartilage	Smooth material which covers ends of bones to reduce friction.
Synovial membrane	Produces synovial fluid to lubricate the joint.
Ligaments	Form a 'joint capsule' to enclose the joint and hold the bones in place. Ligaments can stretch slightly to allow movement.

Artificial joints

Natural joints are capable of withstanding massive strains. For example, a knee is subjected to approximately five times the body weight during mild activities such as jogging or climbing stairs. Certain sports impose even higher forces on the body's joints. Recovery from injuries to joints in young people can often be achieved by natural processes, although in some cases surgery may be needed.

Damaged joints in older people often do not heal naturally or by surgery, and may need to be replaced by **artificial joints**. These are commonly fitted in elderly people suffering from **arthritis**, or 'joint inflammation'. Examples of artificial joints are knees and hips. Hip replacements tend to be more successful than knee joints. This is because hips are ball-and-socket joints, and are more stable and better protected by surrounding tissues than the more exposed hinge joint of the knee.

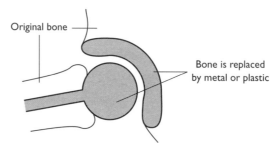

Fig. 4(1).28 Inside an artificial joint

Replacement joints consist of materials such as stainless steel, alloys and plastics. These materials are not usually 'rejected' by the body as part of the immune reaction. The joint is designed so that surfaces are smooth, to decrease friction, and do not produce fragments of 'debris'. The artificial joint is attached directly to the limb bones, using special glues and steel pins.

Muscles and movement

> ### Key points
>
> ▷ muscles are joined to bones by tendons;
> ▷ muscles can contract to pull bones closer together;
> ▷ muscles always operate as part of an antagonistic pair – they have opposite effects, and when one is contracted, the other is relaxed.

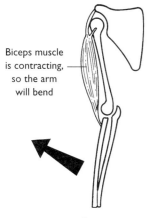

Biceps muscle is contracting, so the arm will bend

Fig. 4(1).29 When a muscle contracts, bones are pulled closer together

Muscle cells can contract, using energy from respiration. When they do this, they become shorter and thicker, and they pull bones closer together.

When a muscle relaxes, it cannot push the bones back to their original position. For this reason, muscles always operate as part of an antagonistic muscle pair: one muscle will bend (flex) the joint and the other will straighten (extend) the joint.

Movement of the elbow joint

Two muscles are involved in moving the elbow joint:

1. Biceps is a flexor muscle. When it contracts, the joint bends (flexes).
2. Triceps is an extensor muscle. When it contracts, the joint straightens (extends).

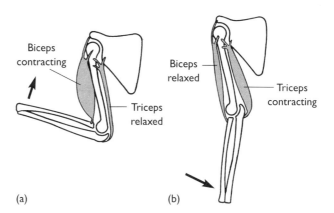

Fig. 4(1).30 Antagonistic muscles (a) biceps is contracting, so the arm will bend (b) triceps is contracting, so the arm will straighten

▷ Reproduction

> This topic is not part of the National Curriculum for England and Wales at Key Stage 4.

Once humans reach puberty, they start to produce gametes (eggs and sperm), and become fertile. After sexual intercourse sperm cells swim up through the female reproductive system and can fertilize an ovum inside the fallopian tube. The zygote divides to form an embryo which implants in the uterus lining and continues to develop. After nine months of pregnancy, the baby is ready to be born, although it will need a lot of parental care for several years.

The reproductive system

Key points

▶ the male and female reproductive systems are completely different;

▶ the male reproductive system is adapted to make sperm, and to get the sperm inside the woman's body, close to the egg cell;

▶ the female reproductive system is adapted to make eggs, and to provide a safe place for the foetus to develop.

Male reproductive system

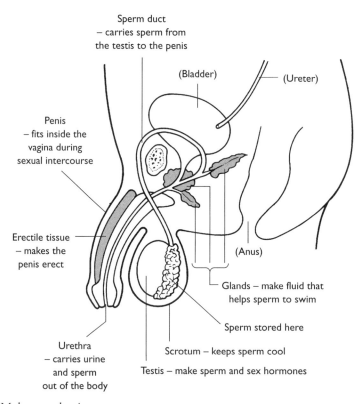

Sperm duct
– carries sperm from
the testis to the penis

(Bladder)   (Ureter)

Penis
– fits inside the
vagina during
sexual intercourse

Erectile tissue
– makes the
penis erect

(Anus)

Glands – make fluid that
helps sperm to swim

Sperm stored here

Urethra
– carries urine
and sperm
out of the body

Scrotum – keeps sperm cool

Testis – make sperm and sex hormones

Fig. 4(1).31 Male reproductive system

Table 4(1).12

Part	Function
Testis	makes sperm, makes male sex hormone (testosterone)
Epididymis	stores sperm
Sperm duct (vas deferens)	carries sperm from the epididymis to the urethra
Glands (seminal vesicle, prostate gland, Cowpers gland)	make fluid which is mixed with sperm to form semen. This fluid has two main functions: 1. to activate sperm, and help them to swim; 2. to neutralise traces of acid on the inside of the urethra (left by urine)
Urethra	carries semen out of the body
Penis	contains erectile tissue which expands when filled with blood. This allows sexual intercourse to take place.
Scrotum	holds the testes outside the abdomen to keep them cool (sperm do not develop properly if they are too hot)

Female reproductive system

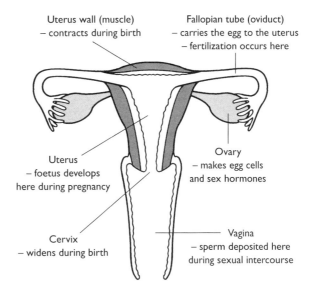

Uterus wall (muscle)
– contracts during birth

Fallopian tube (oviduct)
– carries the egg to the uterus
– fertilization occurs here

Uterus
– foetus develops
here during pregnancy

Ovary
– makes egg cells
and sex hormones

Cervix
– widens during birth

Vagina
– sperm deposited here
during sexual intercourse

Fig. 4(1).32 Female reproductive system

Table 4(1).13

Part	Function
Ovary	releases ova (eggs), makes female sex hormones (oestrogen and progesterone).
Oviduct (fallopian tube)	carries ova from the ovaries to the uterus. Fertilization occurs here.
Uterus	foetus develops here during pregnancy. It has a thick, blood-filled lining where implantation occurs, and strong, muscular walls which contract during birth.
Cervix	narrow section where the uterus joins the vagina (sometimes called the 'neck of the womb'). This opens wide (dilates) during birth.
Vagina	passage linking the uterus to the outside of the body. Sperm are released here during sexual intercourse, and the baby travels out through the vagina when it is born.

Production of gametes

Once a person reaches puberty, gametes start to be produced.

In females one ovum ripens and is released from an ovary each month (this is ovulation). This process continues until the woman reaches the menopause (40–55 years old).

In males sperm are made continuously, at a very rapid rate (about 100 million sperm per day). This process continues throughout life.

The menstrual cycle

These are all the changes occurring in a woman's reproductive system each month. Two main processes are happening:

1. the ovary releases an egg;
2. the lining of the uterus gets ready to receive the egg if it is fertilized. If the egg is not fertilized, the lining breaks up and the woman has a period (menstruation).

The menstrual cycle is controlled by female sex hormones (see p. 88 for more details of this). The whole menstrual cycle lasts for about 28 days, then it is repeated. It is important to know when the main events occur.

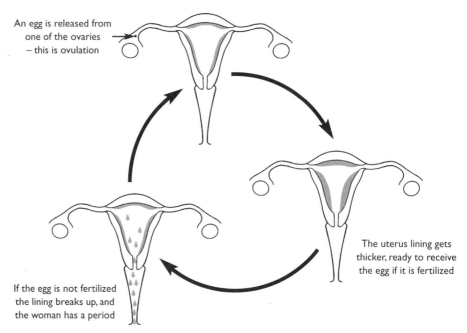

Fig. 4(1).33 The menstrual cycle

Days 1–5	Menstruation (uterus lining breaks up).
Days 1–13	Ovum developing in ovary.
Day 14	Ovum released (ovulation).
Days 5–14	Uterus lining getting thicker.
Days 15–27	Uterus lining stays thick.

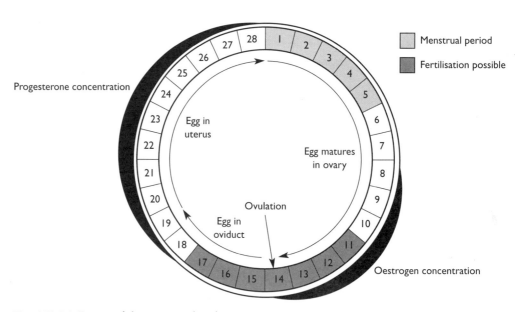

Fig. 4(1).34 Events of the menstrual cycle

REVISION ACTIVITY 12 When is fertilization most likely to occur? Explain why.

Fertilization and implantation

> ## Key points
>
> ▷   during sexual intercourse, sperm are released from the penis inside the vagina, and swim through the uterus to reach the fallopian tube;
>
> ▷   if an ovum is in the fallopian tube it can be fertilized;
>
> ▷   fertilization means that the male and female gametes (sperm and ovum) join to make a zygote;
>
> ▷   the zygote divides repeatedly to form an embryo, and the embryo implants in the uterus lining.

Sexual intercourse

The penis of a sexually excited male becomes erect as blood under pressure fills the spongy 'erectile tissue'. The vagina of a sexually excited female widens and becomes lubricated by the secretion of mucus. During sexual intercourse the erect penis is inserted into the vagina. Movements of the penis may result in increasing physical excitement in the male and the female and can lead to a peak of excitement, called orgasm. Orgasm in the male is a reflex process which results in the ejaculation of about 5 ml of semen by rhythmic contractions of the sperm duct. Orgasm in the female results in contractions of the vagina and uterus, which draws sperm towards the uterus.

Only a small proportion (i.e. several hundreds) of the 400 million sperm deposited at the cervix actually reach the site of fertilization in the oviduct. Some will be unable to swim properly, and some will run out of energy; others will swim into the 'wrong' fallopian tube, i.e. the tube without an ovum.

Only one sperm is actually needed to fertilize an ovum, but large numbers are produced to increase the probability of fertilization occurring.

Fertilization

When the sperm reach the ovum they will try to penetrate the jelly-like layer surrounding it. Eventually one sperm will do this, and the sperm head passes through the ovum's cell membrane (the tail remains outside). The sperm's nucleus fuses with the ovum's nucleus, and the cell is now known as a **zygote**. Once a sperm has broken through the cell membrane, the membrane changes so that no more sperm cells can enter.

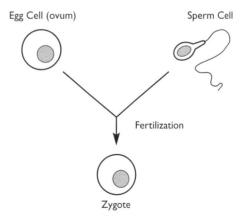

Fig. 4(1).35 Fertilization

Implantation

The zygote is moved through the fallopian tube towards the uterus, and it begins to divide by **mitosis**. By the time it reaches the uterus, it is a ball of about 32 cells, and is known as an **embryo**. The embryo sinks into the soft, blood-filled lining of the uterus – this is **implantation**. Here it will continue to grow and develop during pregnancy.

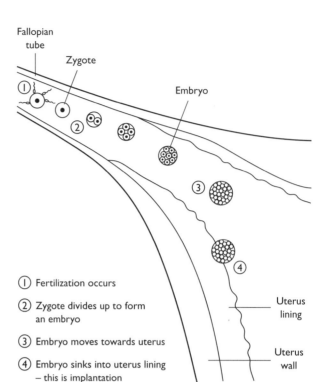

Fig. 4(1).36 Events after fertilization

Development of the foetus

> ## Key points
>
> ▷ the cells of the embryo continue to divide, so it will grow and develop. After about eight weeks it looks recognisably human, and is known as a foetus;
>
> ▷ the placenta develops to provide the foetus with nutrients and oxygen and to take away waste products;
>
> ▷ the foetus is surrounded by amniotic fluid which acts as a shock-absorber to cushion bumps.

In humans, pregnancy lasts for nine months. At first, the embryo looks like a ball of cells, but gradually it grows and develops, and looks more human. After eight weeks, it is about 25mm long, but it looks like a miniature human baby, and it is known as a **foetus**. It has a beating heart, and can move its arms and legs, but it is too small for the mother to feel it. As pregnancy continues, the foetus gets bigger and becomes ready for life outside the uterus. By the time it is born, it will weigh around 3kg, and be about 60cm long. Its lungs will be able to cope with breathing air, and it will be able to see and hear its surroundings.

The placenta
This is a very important organ which develops during pregnancy; it is made from cells from the embryo. It can be thought of as a 'life-support' system for the foetus. It is a large disc of tissue attached to the uterus lining, with lots of villi, which stick into spaces in the uterus lining. The mother's blood fills up these spaces. In the villi are blood vessels containing foetal blood. The villi have very thin walls, so substances can pass between the foetal blood and the mother's blood, but the two types of blood never mix.

The main substances transferred are:

1. **To the foetus**
   ▷ oxygen;
   ▷ nutrients (sugars, amino acids, fatty acids, glycerol, vitamins and minerals);
   ▷ harmful substances, e.g. viruses and drugs, may also be transferred across the placenta.
2. **From the foetus**
   ▷ carbon dioxide;
   ▷ urea.

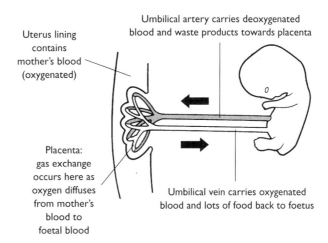

Fig. 4(1).37 The placenta

The foetus is joined to the placenta by the umbilical cord.

REVISION ACTIVITY 13 Why should the mother:

(a)   eat plenty of calcium and protein during pregnancy?
(b)   avoid smoking during pregnancy?
(c)   be vaccinated against German measles (Rubella) before she plans to become pregnant?

Amniotic fluid
During pregnancy, the foetus floats in amniotic fluid inside the amnion. It helps to protect the foetus from being harmed as the mother moves around (cushions it from bumps).

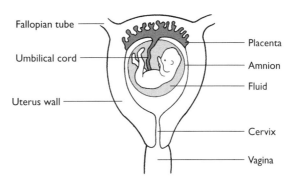

Fig. 4(1).38 Foetus inside the uterus

Birth

Key points
▷   pregnancy lasts for about 40 weeks;
▷   there are three stages to birth: labour, delivery and afterbirth.

Birth normally commences after about 40 weeks with the baby in a head-down position; less usually the baby may be born feet first (breech birth). The baby is expelled by muscular contractions of the uterus wall, which increase in intensity and frequency during labour.

The cervix, vagina and even the hips expand to allow the baby through. The separate bones of the baby's skull, which are not yet fused, allow the head to be compressed. Amniotic fluid is released as the baby is born, and the placenta (afterbirth) is delivered shortly afterwards. The umbilical cord is then tied and cut.

The sudden temperature drop at birth causes a reflex response in the baby, which begins to breathe. This involves an inflation of the lungs as the pulmonary circulation comes into use.

Although the baby is now completely separate from the mother, it is unable to focus its eyes, or to co-ordinate its muscles, and is completely dependent on parental care for several years.

Contraception

> ## Key points
>
> ▷   this means avoiding pregnancy;
>
> ▷   it allows couples to decide when to have children, and how many to have, i.e. to plan their families;
>
> ▷   some people are opposed to contraception on religious or moral grounds.

Sexual partners may want to remove the possibility of conception (fertilization) from sexual intercourse. This is called **contraception** (birth control, family planning). It is achieved by preventing the egg and sperm from meeting, or by preventing implantation. There are various ways in which this can be done, but all have their advantages and disadvantages. No method of contraception is 100% effective, and couples must choose the method which suits them best.

Table 4(1).14

Method	How it works	Advantages	Disadvantages
Contraceptive pill	Contains hormones which prevent ovulation.	Very effective.	Possible side effects (including thrombosis); possible to forget.
Cap (diaphragm)	Blocks path of sperm at cervix.	Simple, effective if used with spermicidal cream.	May be incorrectly fitted.
Intra-uterine device (IUD)(coil)	Fitted in uterus; prevents implantation (remains in place for months/years).	Once fitted, does not require frequent attention.	May cause pain or heavy bleeding.
Condom	Rubber sleeve, fits over erect penis or inside vagina; retains semen.	Simple, effective, may prevent sexually transmitted diseases, e.g. AIDS.	May be damaged; may not be carefully removed.
Withdrawal	Penis withdrawn from vagina before ejaculation.	Does not require any preparation.	Semen may be released before ejaculation (therefore, unreliable method).
Rhythm method (safe period)	Intercourse avoided during 'high risk' time around ovulation.	Relatively 'natural'; acceptable to Roman Catholic church.	Menstrual cycles may be irregular (therefore, unreliable method).
Sterilization	Male: sperm ducts surgically cut (vasectomy). Female: oviducts surgically cut.	Totally effective.	Permanent, irreversible.

▷ ## SOLUTIONS TO REVISION ACTIVITIES

S1   (a)   (i)   baked beans
         (ii)   cheese, nuts, eggs
         (iii)   for growth and repair (to make new cells)

     (b)   (i)   3000 kJ (don't forget the units!)
         (ii)   She would become overweight (would store the excess nutrients as fat).
         (iii)   sausages and apple pie

(c) (i) half of it (7mg)
(ii) all of it (25mg)
(iii) a lack of iron causes anaemia, a lack of Vitamin C causes scurvy

(d) to prevent constipation, and keep her gut working efficiently.

S2 Not all of the energy in the peanut is used to heat the water, e.g.

▶ some escapes in the air;
▶ some heats the pyrex of the boiling tube;
▶ some heats the mounted needle;
▶ some remains in the peanut.

S3 **Table 4(1).15**

Part of tooth	Description
pulp cavity	contains nerves and blood vessels
enamel	very hard, resistant material
cement and fibres	holds the tooth in the jaw-bone
blood vessel	brings oxygen and food to living cells in the tooth
nerve	causes you to feel pain in the tooth
dentine	a layer of living material

S4 ▶ **Ingestion** movement of food into the gut through the mouth.
▶ **Digestion** breakdown of large, insoluble food molecules to give small, soluble food molecules.
▶ **Absorption** movement of food from the gut into the blood.
▶ **Assimilation** food molecules are used by cells all over the body.
▶ **Egestion** movement of faeces (undigested food) out of the gut through the anus.

S5 (a) (i) **vena cava** brings deoxygenated blood into the heart
(ii) **pulmonary artery** takes blood to the lungs
(iii) **pulmonary vein** bring oxygenated blood back to the heart
(iv) **aorta** carries oxygenated blood around the body
(v) **left atrium** contracts to move blood into the left ventricle
(vi) **left ventricle** contracts to move blood into the aorta and all around the body
(vii) **biscuspid valve** stops backflow of blood when the ventricle contracts
(viii) **tendon cord** stops bicuspid valve turning inside out (stops valve flaps being distorted)
(ix) **semi-lunar valve** stops backflow of blood when the ventricle relaxes

(b) The left ventricle needs a thick wall because it must contract hard to pump blood all around the body

S6 | A | F | D | G | B | E | C |

S7 (a) (i) plasma
(b) (ii) tissue fluid
(c) (iii) nucleus of phagocyte
(iv) capillary
(b) Narrow lumen (compared to size of red blood cell), wall is one cell thick, it is very close to body cells.
(c) A phagocyte (**c**) will move out of the capillary, and will change shape to surround the bacteria; it will then destroy them.

S8 A = pulmonary artery
B = pulmonary vein
C = aorta
D = vena cava

S9 (a) It contains deoxygenated blood (all the rest carry oxygenated blood).
(b) renal vein

(c)   vena cava

(d)   aorta

(e)   It carries deoxygenated blood to the liver.

S10   (a)   (i)   bell jar = rib cage
  (ii)   rubber sheet = diaphragm
  (iii)   balloons = lungs
  (iv)   tubing = trachea and bronchi

(b)   If you push the sheet up, the balloon will deflate because the volume in the bell jar is smaller, so the pressure in the bell jar increases, and air is forced out.

(c)   In several ways, e.g.
  ▷   the rib cage (bell jar) cannot move;
  ▷   the lungs (balloons) are too small;
  ▷   the lungs (balloons) are not attached to the rib cage (bell jar).

S11   (a)   Some is used in the body in the process of respiration.
(b)   It is made during respiration.
(c)   Nitrogen is not made in the body or used in the body.
(d)   Because some is trapped by the mucus in the air passages of the respiratory system.

S12   Fertilization is most likely if intercourse occurs on days 11–17.

11 ─────────────────────────→ 14 ─────────────────────────→ 17

Sperm can swim into   Ovulation   Sperm can fertilize
fallopian tube and fertilize   occurs.   egg in fallopian tube.
egg as soon as it is
released from ovary.

S13   (a)   The foetus needs calcium for bone development and protein for making new cells.

(b)   Carbon monoxide in cigarettes stops the mother's blood carrying oxygen so efficiently, so the foetus gets less oxygen. It is likely to be smaller, and to be born early.

(c)   If the Rubella virus passes across the placenta and infects the baby, it can cause deafness, blindness and heart disease. If the mother has been vaccinated before pregnancy, this will not happen.

▷ **EXAMINATION QUESTIONS**

▷ **Question 1**   We can compare the amount of energy stored in a peanut and in a pea by burning them and using the heat they give off to heat water. The drawings (Fig. 4(1).39) show some of the apparatus you would need to carry out this experiment. They are not to the same scale.

(a)   Describe, in detail, how you would put together and use the apparatus to carry out the experiment. **Do not draw a diagram.**   *(9)*

_____

_____

_____

_____

_____

_____

_____

_____

_____

(b)   Suggest a safety precaution which should be taken when carrying out this experiment.   *(1)*

_____

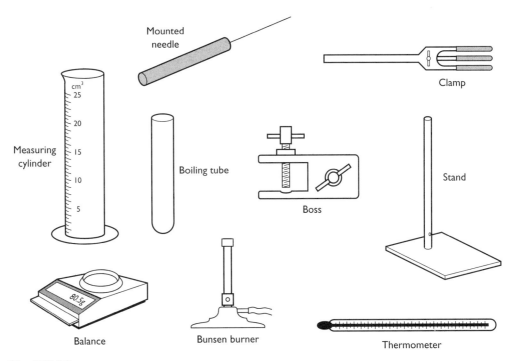

Fig. 4(1).39

(c) The drawings below (Fig. 4(1).40) show the temperature of the water at the start and at the end of the experiments.

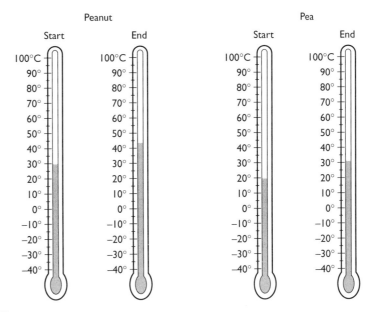

Fig. 4(1).40

(i) Complete Table 4(1).17 below: *(2)*

Table 4(1).16

	Temp. at start (°C)	Temp. at end (°C)	Rise in temp. (°C)
Peanut			
Pea			

(ii) State **one** conclusion from these results and explain your reasoning.
Conclusion   *(2)*
Reason   *(2)*
(WJEC)

▷ **Question 2**   Lengths of visking tubing were set up as follows:

A contained 1% starch and amylase;
B contained 1% starch and boiled amylase;

Both were left in water at 30°C for one hour. They were then placed in beakers of dilute iodine solution and left for five minutes as shown below. Iodine solution can pass through visking tubing.

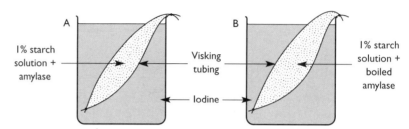

Fig. 4(1).41

(a)   What colour would you expect to see inside

    (i)   **A** _____

    (ii)   **B?** _____   *(2)*

(b)   Explain what has happened inside **A**   *(2)*

(c)   (i)   Describe a test to prove your explanation.   *(2)*
    (ii)   State the expected results.   *(1)*

(d)   What appears to be the effect of boiling the amylase?   *(1)*

(e)   The drawing shows a section through some villi.

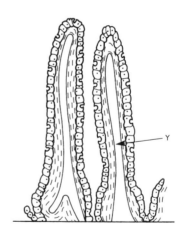

Fig. 4(1).42

    (i)   In which part of the alimentary canal would they be found?   *(1)*
    (ii)   Label with an arrow and an **X** the part of the villus which is represented by the visking tubing.   *(1)*
    (iii)   What is the function of part **Y**?   *(1)*
                                                     (WJEC)

▷ **Question 3**   A pupil set up an investigation into the activity of amylase extracted from barley seeds. Starch discs were placed in amylase solution in a test-tube and every five minutes one of the discs was removed and tested for the presence of starch, using iodine solution as shown in the diagram (Fig. 4(1).43).

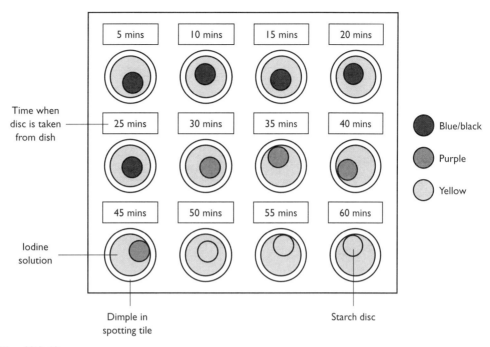

Fig. 4(1).43

(a) What is produced by the action of amylase on starch?   *(1)*

(b) How long does it take for amylase to digest all the starch discs?   *(1)*

(c) Explain why the temperature of the amylase in the test-tubes was kept at 25°C during the investigation and suggest how this was done.

(2)

(d) The investigation was extended by repeating the experiment with solutions of amylase extracted from other plants. The results are shown in Table 4(1).18.

Table 4(1).17 Time for amylase to digest starch/min

Potato	Maize	Oats	Pea
25	35	30	20

Suggest **two** conditions which must be kept constant to ensure a fair comparison.

1. _____

2. _____   *(2)*

(NICCEA)

▷ **Question 4**   (a) The diagram below shows part of the human thorax.

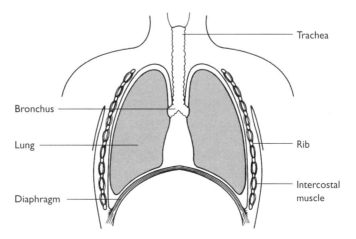

Fig. 4(1).44

Describe in detail, the changes which take place in the thorax during inhalation.   *(5)*

(b) (i) Give **two** changes that occur to inhaled air as it passes through the nasal passages.

1. _____

2. _____   *(2)*

(ii) List **two** features of the lung's respiratory surface which aid the efficient absorption of oxygen.

1. _____

2. _____   *(2)*

(c) Asthmatics have sensitive airways. The diagrams below show a section through a normal bronchiole and a bronchiole during an asthmatic attack.

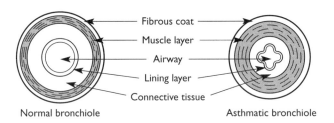

Fibrous coat
Muscle layer
Airway
Lining layer
Connective tissue

Normal bronchiole   Asthmatic bronchiole

Fig. 4(1).45

(i) Using the information in the diagrams, describe **three** changes which occur in the bronchiole during an asthmatic attack.

1. _____

2. _____

3. _____   *(3)*

(ii) What effect would all these changes have on breathing?   *(1)*

(d) The apparatus shown below can be used to investigate the respiration of yeast cells.

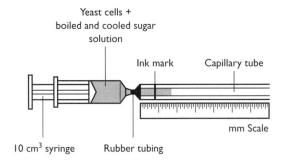

Yeast cells +
boiled and cooled sugar
solution

Ink mark   Capillary tube

mm Scale

10 cm³ syringe   Rubber tubing

Fig. 4(1).46

(i) Explain why the respiration of the yeast cells in the syringe is mainly anaerobic.   *(2)*

(ii) Sucrose and glucose are both sugars. Explain how the apparatus could be used to compare the rate of respiration of yeast in sucrose and in glucose solutions.   *(5)*

(NICCEA)

▷ **Question 5**   (a)   Look at Fig. 4(1).49 and name

    (i) Gas **A** _____ *(1)*

    (ii) Gas **B** _____ *(1)*

    (iii) Cell **C** _____ *(1)*

    (iv) Fluid **D** _____ *(1)*

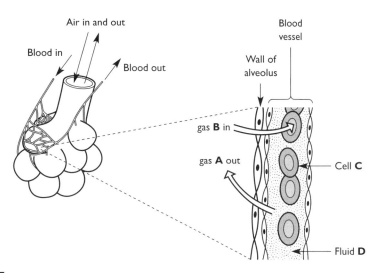

Fig. 4(1).47

    (b) Name

    (i)   the process by which gases **A** and **B** move.   *(1)*

    (ii) the blood vessel that would carry cell **C** to the heart.   *(1)*

    (WJEC)

ANSWERS TO EXAMINATION QUESTIONS

▷ **Question 1**   (a)   Use the measuring cylinder to measure a known volume of water, e.g. 15ml, 20ml. (1)
                  ▶ Place it in the boiling tube. (1)
                  ▶ Use the boss, clamp and stand to hold the boiling tube about 20cm above the bench. (1)
                  ▶ Position the boiling tube at an angle (not vertical). (1)
                  ▶ Place the thermometer in the boiling tube and take the temperature of the water. (1)
                  ▶ Find the mass of the peanut using the balance. (1)
                  ▶ Impale it on the mounted needle. (1)
                  ▶ Use the Bunsen burner to set fire to the peanut. (1)
                  ▶ Hold it under the tube of water so it heats the water as it burns. (1)
                  ▶ Wait until the peanut has burned completely, then take the temperature of the water again. (1)

          (b) Wear goggles, tie long hair back.

          (c) (i)

Table 4(1).16

	Temp. at start (°C)	Temp. at end (°C)	Rise in temp. (°C)
Peanut	30	44	14
Pea	20	31	11

          (ii) Conclusion: the peanut contained more energy than the pea.
                Reason: because the temperature rise was greater when the peanut was burned.

▷ **Question 2**   (a)   (i)   **A** yellow-brown
                              (ii)   **B** black

(b)   Amylase has digested starch (1),
       to form maltose (1),
       so starch is no longer present (1).

(c)   (i)   Test the liquid in the beaker or inside the visking tubing for sugar,
              add Benedicts solution (1),
              heat to 80°C for 10 minutes (1).
       (ii)   The colour changes from blue to orange (1).

(d)   The enzyme is denatured (no longer works).

(e)   (i)   ileum
       (ii)

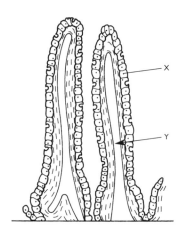

Fig. 4(1).48

(iii) It absorbs fats (it is the lacteal).

▷ **Question 3**   (a)   maltose (sugar)

(b)   50 minutes

(c)   The temperature was kept at 25°C because the enzyme works well at this temperature
       (it is the optimum temperature). (1)
       Temperature would be controlled by keeping the tubes in a waterbath at 25°C. (1)

Answer with two of the following:

(d)   1.   temperature;
       2.   amount of starch in starch discs;
       3.   amount of amylase solution.

▷ **Question 4**   (a)   diaphragm contracts and flattens (1)
                          intercostal muscles contract, rib cage moves up and out (1)
                          volume of thorax increases (1)
                          pressure inside thorax decreases (1)
                          so air moves into the lungs (1)

(b)   (i)   Any two of the following:

              the air is warmed
              the air is moistened
              the air is cleaned

              Any two of the following:

              alveoli are thin
              alveoli are moist
              alveoli are permeable
              alveoli have a large surface area

(c) (i) Any three of the following:
    1. muscle layer contracts (becomes thicker)
    2. airway is narrower
    3. lining layer is folded
    4. whole bronchiole narrows
 (iii) it would be more difficult to breathe

(d) (i) there is no air in the syringe (1)
    the sugar solution does not contain oxygen (it has been boiled and cooled) (1)
 (ii) Set up apparatus with glucose solution (1)
    use the plunger to move the liquid to the ink mark as a starting point (1)
    leave it for a set time, e.g. 30 minutes (1)
    observe how far the liquid level has moved along the capillary tube (1)
    repeat the experiment with sucrose solution (1)
    make sure it is a fair test, e.g. carried out at the same temperature, for the same length of time, with the same amount of sugar and yeast.

▷ **Question 5** (a) (i) Gas A = carbon dioxide
              Gas B = oxygen
              Cell C = red blood cell
              Fluid D = plasma

        (b) (i) diffusion
          (ii) pulmonary vein.

▷ **STUDENT'S ANSWER WITH EXAMINER'S COMMENT**

Question 1

You are provided with 1% starch solution, distilled water, and a solution of an enzyme X which breaks down starch. You also have test tubes and a temperature controlled water bath.

    You are told to set up four test tubes containing the various mixtures of substances shown in the table and to leave each for 10 minutes at the stated temperature, 1cm³ of iodine solution is then added to each test tube.

(a) Complete the table to show the colours you would expect after adding iodine and the conclusions you can make. *(4)*

Table 4(1).16

Substances	Colour with iodine solution	Conclusions
1cm³X + 10cm³ starch solution at 38°C	*brown* (1)	*All the starch has been digested* (1)
1cm³X + 10cm³ starch solution at 10°C	✗ *brown*	*All the starch has been digested*
1cm³X which has been boiled and cooled + 10cm³ starch solution at 38°C	*black* (1)	*the heat has killed the enzyme*
1cm³ distilled water + 10cm³ starch solution at 38°C	*black* (1)	*there is no enzyme to digest starch* (1)

'No. the enzyme works more slowly at 10°C, so some starch will be left.'

'No. The heat has denatured the enzyme, not killed it.'

(b) What substance is produced when starch is broken down? *Sugar* *(1)*

'This is not detailed enough. The answer required is glucose.'

(c) Suggest a name for the enzyme. *Amylase* (1) *(1)*

'Correct.'

(d) (i) Describe, **with full experimental details**, how you would test for the presence of the substance produced in part (b).

(continued)

'This answer is not detailed enough; you should:
▶ mix your sample with Benedicts solution
▶ heat it to about 80°C
▶ for 10 minutes'

(1)
mix it with Benedicts solution and heat it. If sugar is there you would see a

blue colour.   (3)

'No, the colour changes **from** blue (1) to orange (1)'

(ii) State your expected results. *It would go blue*   (2)
                                                                                               (WJEC)

Question 2

(a) The diagram (Fig. 4(1).49) represents the heart, some of the major blood vessels of the human circulatory system and the organs they supply.

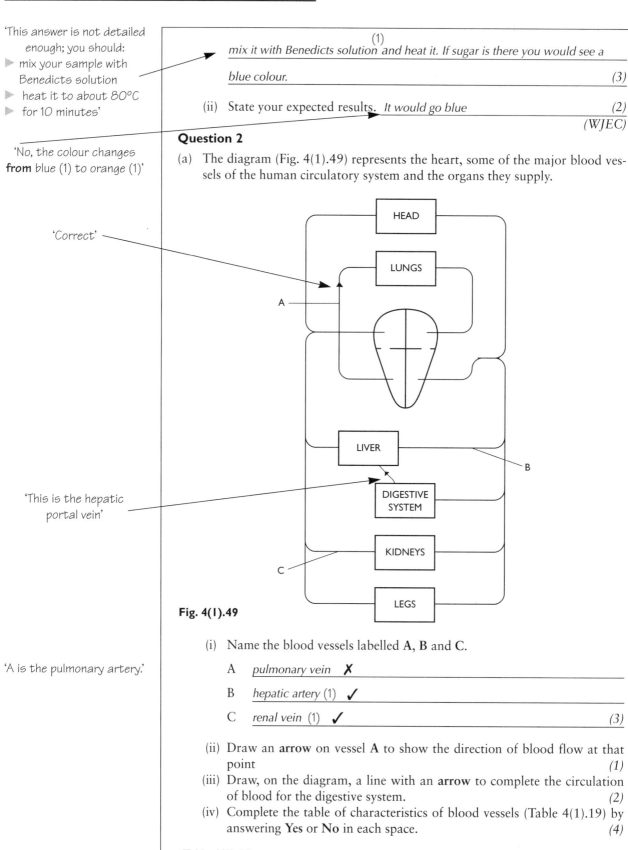

'Correct'

'This is the hepatic portal vein'

Fig. 4(1).49

(i) Name the blood vessels labelled **A**, **B** and **C**.

'A is the pulmonary artery.'

A   *pulmonary vein* ✗

B   *hepatic artery* (1) ✓

C   *renal vein* (1) ✓   (3)

(ii) Draw an **arrow** on vessel **A** to show the direction of blood flow at that point   (1)

(iii) Draw, on the diagram, a line with an **arrow** to complete the circulation of blood for the digestive system.   (2)

(iv) Complete the table of characteristics of blood vessels (Table 4(1).19) by answering **Yes** or **No** in each space.   (4)

Table 4(1).18

'This student has a good understanding of blood vessels. It is all correct except line 3, glucose cannot pass out of the aorta.'

| | | Blood vessel | | |
Characteristic	Aorta	Capillary	Vena cava	
Thick muscular wall	Yes	No	No	(1)
Valves present along length	No	No	Yes	(1)
Glucose passes through walls	Yes	Yes	No	
May transport oxygenated blood	Yes	Yes	No	(1)

                                                                                               (continued)

(b) The diagram shows the heart of a person who has suffered a mild heart attack.

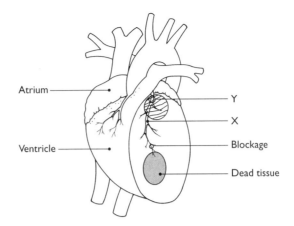

Atrium

Y

X

Ventricle

Blockage

Dead tissue

Fig. 4(1).50

'Good.'

(i) Name the blood vessel labelled **X**.

Coronary artery   (1)   *(1)*

'No. It would be a blood **clot** or cholesterol'

(ii) What could cause the blockage in blood vessel **X**?

blood ✗   *(1)*

'No. The area of dead tissue would be much bigger. The whole of the left ventricle would die because its blood supply stops'

(iii) On the diagram shade the expected area of dead tissue if the blockage was at **Y**.   *(1)*

(iv) Explain why the heart would stop beating if the blockage had occurred at **Y**.

The heart muscle dies.   (1)   *(2)*

'More detail is needed. The student should say that the whole ventricle will stop working, so blood cannot be pumped around the body.'

(c) Table 4(1).19 shows three diseases linked to smoking and the numbers of smokers who died from these causes.

Table 4(1).19

Cause of death	Number of smokers/100 deaths	
	Men	Women
Heart disease	25	20
Lung cancer	90	80
Bronchitis	72	23

'Correct.'

(i) which disease caused the greatest number of deaths among smokers?

lung cancer   (1)   *(1)*

'This does not **explain** the link. The student should have said that smoking damages arteries, so heart disease is more likely, and smoke contains chemicals which cause lung cancer.'

(ii) Explain the link between

smoking and heart disease *smokers get heart disease* ✗

smoking and lung cancer *smokers get lung cancer* ✗   *(4)*

(iii) Explain why there is a difference in the number of deaths due to bronchitis in men and women.

men smoke more than women. ✗   *(2)*

(NICCEA)

'This is not likely to be true, because the death rates from other diseases are similar for men and women. Perhaps men are more at risk of bronchitis due to dangers in their jobs, e.g. in mining (coal dust, etc.), building, working with chemicals, etc.'

SUMMARY

▷   Humans need a balanced diet to remain healthy.

▷   There are seven food groups in a balanced diet (carbohydrates, proteins, lipids, vitamins, minerals, fibre and water).

▷   Enzymes are chemicals produced by the body to speed up digestion.

▷   Each enzyme has a specific function (e.g. proteases digest protein) and works best at its optimum temperature and pH.

▷   Digestion involves breakdown of large insoluble food molecules to form small, soluble food molecules.

▷   Digested food is absorbed by the blood, then used by body cells.

▷   Blood is the transport fluid of the body, and it is also important in defence against disease.

▷   The heart beats (contracts) to move blood around the body.

▷   Veins carry blood towards the heart and arteries carry blood away from the heart. Capillaries carry blood through body organs.

▷   Substances are exchanged between blood and body cells in the capillaries.

▷   Humans have a double circulation (blood travels through the heart twice on each complete circuit of the body).

▷   Gas exchange occurs in the alveoli, which are very well adapted (large surface area, thin permeable wall, moist, good blood supply).

▷   The ribs and diaphragm move to force air in and out of the lungs.

▷   Respiration is an important chemical reaction occurring in all cells to make energy.

▷   When oxygen is available, aerobic respiration occurs: oxygen + glucose → energy + carbon dioxide + water.

▷   During exercise, when insufficient oxygen is available, anaerobic respiration can occur in muscle cells: glucose → lactic acid.

▷   This is less efficient than aerobic respiration, and produces less energy.

▷   When muscles contract, they pull bones of the skeleton closer together.

▷   Muscles always work in antagonistic pairs, e.g. biceps and triceps. An antagonistic pair of muscles have opposite effects to each other.

▷   Human reproduction involves the joining of male and female gametes (sperm and ovum). This happens inside the fallopian tube, after sexual intercourse, and a zygote is formed.

▷   The zygote divides by mitosis to form an embryo, and the embryo implants in the uterus lining. It will grow and develop in the uterus throughout pregnancy (which lasts about nine months).

▷   The placenta is a very important organ in pregnancy. It acts as a life-support system for the foetus, delivering food and oxygen and removing waste products.

▷   After nine months of pregnancy, the foetus is fully developed and is ready to be born. The muscles of the uterus wall contract, and the cervix widens so the baby is forced out through the vagina. The umbilical cord is then clamped and cut, and the placenta and remains of the umbilical cord (afterbirth) are pushed out of the uterus.

Humans as organisms
Co-ordination

> GETTING STARTED

| MEG | SEG | NEAB | LONDON | WJEC | NICCEA | SEB |

Co-ordination is the process by which an organism's activities are organised to increase its chances of survival. This is especially important in large, complex organisms which are capable of carrying out many simultaneous processes in organised cells and tissues. An individual process in one part of the organism cannot occur independently of other processes in the same body.

In humans, two systems of the body are responsible for co-ordination: the nervous system and the endocrine system.

TOPIC	STUDY	REVISION 1	REVISION 2
The nervous system			
Structure of the nervous system			
Reflexes			
The eye			
The endocrine system			
Structure of the endocrine system			
Insulin and blood sugar			
Sex hormones			
Adrenaline			
Comparison of the nervous and endocrine systems			

WHAT YOU NEED TO KNOW

▷ **The nervous system**

The nervous system responds rapidly to the stimuli it detects. It has three main functions:

1. to collect information about conditions inside and outside the body;
2. to process and analyse this information;
3. to co-ordinate an appropriate response.

Structure of the nervous system

Key points

▷   the nervous system consists of the brain, spinal cord, nerves and sense organs;

▷   the nervous system contains millions of nerve cells (neurones). These are adapted to carry nerve impulses. A synapse is a junction between nerve cells;

▷   sense organs can detect external stimuli, and pass on information to the brain where it is analysed;

▷   there are two types of nerve pathway; voluntary actions and reflexes.

The central nervous system (CNS)

This is made up of the brain and spinal cord.

The brain weighs about 1.5 kg and is protected by the bones of the skull. It has four main functions:

1. to receive information from our sense organs about our surroundings;
2. to think, decide and remember (a lot of our actions are based on previous experience);
3. to send nerve impulses to our muscles, so we can move;
4. to control other body organs, and vital processes, e.g. heart and heart rate, blood flow and body temperature, diaphragm and breathing rate.

The brain is a very complex organ, and doctors do not fully understand how it works. However, they have identified key areas of the brain and the functions for which they are responsible.

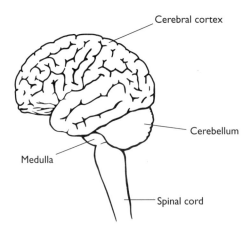

Fig. 4(2).1 Brain

Table 4(2).1

Part	Functions
Cerebral cortex	receives information from sense organs; sends out instructions to effectors, e.g. muscles and glands; interprets and analyses information; memory, learning and emotions
Cerebellum	co-ordinates balance and movement
Medulla	co-ordinates automatic processes, e.g. heart rate, breathing rate, swallowing

REVISION ACTIVITY I Which part of the brain would you use to:

(a)   decide what to eat for lunch?
(b)   regulate your blood pressure?
(c)   balance when riding a bicycle?
(d)   remember your telephone number?

The spinal cord is the main route for information into and out of the brain. It is a cylinder of nervous tissue surrounded by membranes, protected by the vertebrae (it runs up through the middle of the vertebral column). It contains sensory neurones and motor neurones.

Nerves

The body contains thousands of nerves. Each one is a bundle of neurones, surrounded by an insulating layer.

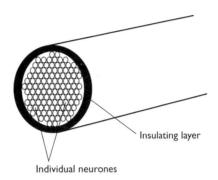

Fig. 4(2).2 Section through a nerve

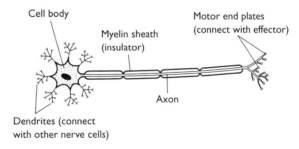

Fig. 4(2).3 A motor neurone

There are three main types of neurones:

1.   **Sensory neurones** carry impulses from a receptor (in a sense organ) to the central nervous system.
2.   **Relay neurones** connect sensory and motor neurones within the CNS. They are also known as intermediate neurones, connector neurones and associate neurones.
3.   **Motor neurones** carry nerve impulses from the CNS to a muscle or gland (called an effector).

Nerve cells are adapted to their function because:

▶   they have a long nerve fibre (axon) to connect to other structures in the body (other nerves, or muscles/glands);
▶   they have dendrites, so they can form complex nerve networks with other nerve cells;
▶   they have a myelin sheath which speeds up the transmission of nerve impulses.

How do nerve impulses travel?

A nerve impulse is an electrical charge passing through a nerve. It begins at a sense organ, then travels through neurones to the CNS, rather like a current passing from a battery around a circuit.

Neurones are not connected directly to each other but are separated by very small gaps called **synapses**. Nerve impulses arriving at one side of the synapse cause the secretion of a chemical transmitter (**neurotransmitter**) substance, which diffuses across the gap and restarts the nerve impulse in the next neurone. Synapses ensure that nerve impulses travel in one direction only.

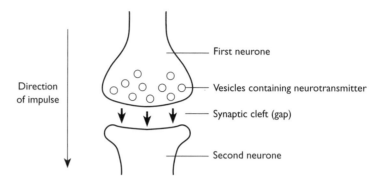

Fig. 4(2).4 Events at a synapse

Sense organs
Sense organs contain groups of sensory cells which detect a particular stimulus. This allows organisms to detect changes in their environment. Most sense organs are arranged near the outer surface of the body (where they are most likely to detect stimuli), particularly in the head region.

Table 4(2).2

Sense organ and sensory structure	Stimulus
Eye (retina)	Light
Ear	Sound
Tongue (taste buds)	Chemicals in food
Nose (olfactory tissue)	Chemicals in air
Skin (various receptors)	Heat, cold, touch, pressure, pain

Nerve pathways
There are two main types of nerve pathway in the body:

1. voluntary actions;
2. reflex actions.

Voluntary actions involve the brain making a decision about how to respond to a particular stimulus

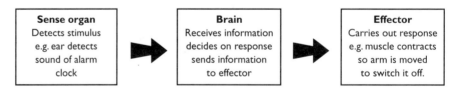

Fig. 4(2).5 A voluntary action

Reflex actions do not involve the brain in making decisions. They are automatic responses to a stimulus, e.g. if you put your hand onto a hot object, you will move it.

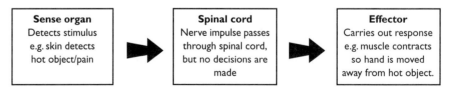

Fig. 4(2).6 A reflex action

Reflexes

> ## Key points
>
> ▷ a reflex is an immediate, unlearned response to a stimulus;
>
> ▷ a simple reflex arc involves three neurones;
>
> ▷ many reflexes help to protect the body from danger.

A reflex is a special type of nerve pathway; it does not involve the brain in making decisions. A reflex is defined as:

> **an immediate, unlearned response to a stimulus.**

Immediate = very rapid, because only three neurones are involved.

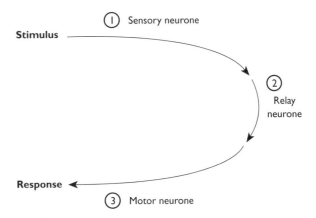

Fig. 4(2).7 Neurones in a reflex arc

Unlearned = a reflex is an automatic process we are born with. Reflexes are very important in the survival of young babies.

Many reflexes help humans to avoid danger, or increase their chances of survival; a rapid response helps to do this.

REVISION ACTIVITY 2 | Complete this table about reflexes.

Table 4(2).3

Name of reflex	Stimulus	Response	Reason for reflex
Withdrawal reflex	pain due to hot/sharp object	to move the body away from stimulus	to prevent damage to the body
Pupil reflex	bright light in eyes		to prevent too much light entering the eye
Choke reflex	if food enters the trachea	coughing/choking to expel food	
Blink reflex		rapid lowering of eyelid	to prevent foreign objects entering the eye
Suckle reflex	touching a baby's face (near mouth)	it will turn towards the object touching it, and close its lips around it	

The reflex arc

The route taken by nerve impulses in a relex is called a relex arc. There are five key events:

1. receptor cells in a sense organ detect a stimulus;
2. nerve impulses travel through a sensory neurone to the spinal cord;

3.   nerve impulses travel through a relay neurone inside the spinal cord;
4.   nerve impulses travel through a motor neurone to reach an effector, e.g. muscle;
5.   the effector responds, e.g. muscle contracts.

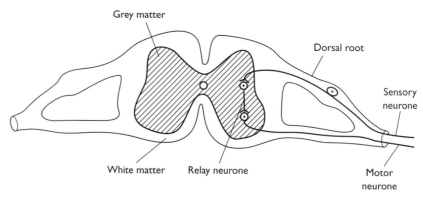

Fig. 4(2).8 The reflex arc

In the withdrawal reflex:

the **stimulus** would be a hot object;
the **receptor cells** would be pain/temperature detectors in skin;
the **effector** would be a muscle, e.g. biceps in arm;
the **response** would be to move the arm.

REVISION ACTIVITY 3   Fig. 4(2).9 below shows a transverse section of the spinal cord of a mammal.

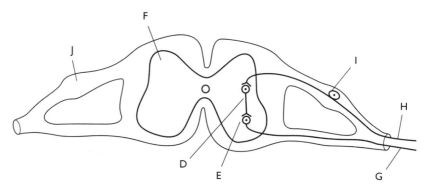

Fig. 4(2).9

By referring to the letters used in the labelling of Fig. 4(2).9 answer the following questions:

(a)   Give the name of cell **D**.
(b)   What name is given to **E**, where nerve cells meet?
(c)   What is region **F** called?
(d)   What is the destination of fibre **G**?
(e)   What type of neurone is **H**?
(f)   What is **I**?
(g)   Name the structure **J**.

The eye

Key points

▶   the eye is the sense organ responsible for detecting light;

▶   the size of the pupil depends on the amount of light entering the eye;

▶   the lens can change shape to focus light onto the retina. This is called accommodation;

▶   the retina contains two types of sensory cells, rods and cones.

Structure of the eye
Humans have two eyes, partially protected by bony ridges of the skull. Each eye is roughly spherical with layers of important cells making up the wall. The space inside the eyeball is filled with a jelly-like substance called vitreous humour.

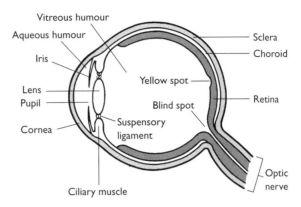

Fig. 4(2).10 Structure of the eye

Table 4(2).4

Structure	Function
Eyelid	Protects eye by blinking (a reflex action).
	Blinking washes eye surface with tears (which contain a mild antiseptic).
	Prevents the contact of harmful substances with the eye surface.
	Protects the retina against bright light.
Conjunctiva	Protects part of the cornea.
Cornea	Refracts (bends) light entering the eye.
Aqueous humour	Supplies nutrients to the lens and cornea (it is a watery fluid).
Iris	Controls the amount of light entering the eye by adjusting the size of the pupil.
Pupil	Hole which allows light into the eye.
Lens	Allows fine focusing by changing shape.
Suspensory ligament	Attaches lens to ciliary muscle
Ciliary muscle	Changes the shape of the lens by altering the tension on the suspensory ligaments.
Vitreous humour	Maintains the shape of the eye (it is a jelly-like substance).
Retina	Contains light-sensitive rod and cone cells which convert light energy into a nerve impulse.
Yellow spot	Very sensitive region where most light is focused.
Optic nerve	Carries nerve impulses to the brain, where they are interpreted.
Choroid	Supplies retina with nutrients.
	Contains pigments which absorb the light not absorbed by the retina (this stops light being reflected inside the eye).
Sclera (sclerotic coat)	Protects and maintains the shape of the eye.

The pupil and light intensity
The amount of light entering the eye can be controlled by changing the size of the pupil, e.g. in dim light the pupil is large, whereas in bright light it is smaller.

Opening and closing the pupil is a reflex action brought about by contraction of muscles in the iris. There are two types of antagonistic muscles in the iris:

1. **radial** muscles, contract to widen the pupil;
2. **circular** muscles, contract to narrow the pupil.

This helps to protect the retina from damage by too much bright light.

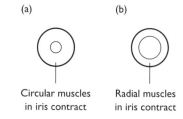

Fig. 4(2).11 Pupil size (a) in bright light (b) in dim light

Other factors which influence pupil size include:

▶ fear;
▶ sexual attraction;
▶ some drugs.

The lens and accommodation
Light entering the eye is bent (refracted) by two structures:

▶ the cornea;
▶ the lens.

The lens can change shape so that light rays are focused onto the retina – it is vital that the image is properly focused if we are to see properly.

If we are looking at **near objects**, e.g. the page of a book, the lens must be short and fat to focus the light properly.

If we are looking at **distant objects**, e.g. an approaching bus, the lens must be long and thin to focus the light properly.

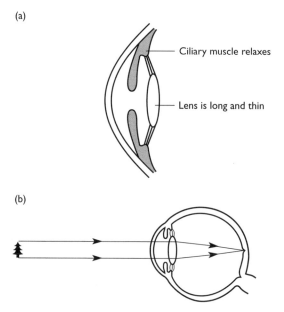

Fig. 4(2).12 Focusing on a distant object (a) lens is long and thin (b) path of light rays

The lens changes shape because it is attached to a ring of ciliary muscles by the suspensory ligaments.

If the ciliary muscles contract, the lens become short and fat; if the ciliary muscles relax, the lens becomes long and thin.

The ability to focus properly depends on two factors:

1. the shape of the eyeball
2. the elasticity of the lens (this decreases with age).

If a person is unable to focus properly they may have to use spectacles or contact lenses: these are simply additional lenses placed in front of the eye to refract light rays.

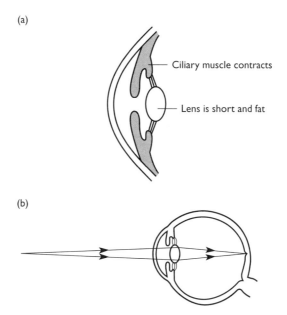

(a)

— Ciliary muscle contracts

— Lens is short and fat

(b)

Fig. 4(2).13 Focusing on a near object (a) lens is short and fat (b) path of light rays

REVISION ACTIVITY 4 Would your ciliary muscles be contracted or relaxed if you were:

(a)   reading a book?
(b)   watching a kite being flown?

The retina
The retina is the part of the eye which is sensitive to light, because it contains two types of light sensitive cells called rods and cones. The function of the retina is to convert the information carried by light into nerve impulses, which are transmitted to the brain.

The lens focuses light rays onto the retina to form an inverted (upside-down) image. The rods and cones contain light-sensitive pigments which are 'bleached' in the light, generating a nerve impulse. The impulses travel through the optic nerve to the brain, where the information is interpreted.

Table 4(2).5

Comparison	Rods	Cones
Distribution	120 million cells spread throughout retina; much less in yellow spot.	Six million cells concentrated in the yellow spot.
Sensitivity: light intensity	Sensitive to low light intensities	Sensitive to bright light intensities only.
Sensitivity: colour	Not sensitive to different colours (gives 'black and white' vision); used mainly in dim light.	Sensitive to colour. Different types of cones respond to the primary colours red, green and blue; the relative amounts of each type of colour allows humans to detect about 200 different colours.
Nerve connections	Rods share common nerve connections. This increases sensitivity to dim light and decreases acuity ('visual accuracy')	Cones have individual nerve connections. This decreases sensitivity to dim light, and increases acuity.

▷ **The endocrine system**   The endocrine system produces chemicals called hormones which act on target organs in the body. They are usually (but not always) responsible for co-ordinating long-term changes, and have a slower effect than the nervous system.

Structure of the endocrine system

Key points
▷ glands which produce hormones are called endocrine glands;
▷ hormones are chemicals which are released directly into the blood;
▷ they have an effect on target organs in the body;
▷ there is a wide range of hormones, each with an effect on specific target organs.

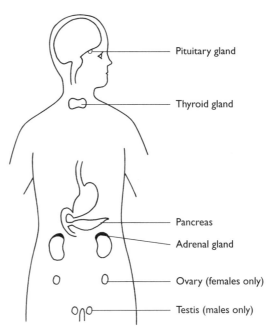

Fig. 4(2).14 Endocrine glands

Most of the endocrine glands produce more than one hormone. They secrete their hormones directly into the blood, so they are called 'ductless glands'.

Hormones
Hormones are chemicals released by endocrine glands. Many are made of protein, e.g. insulin and ADH, while others are described as steroid hormones (modified lipids).

They travel around the body in the blood until they reach target organs. Receptors on the surface of target cells are the right shape to fit hormone molecules, so hormones

Table 4(2).6
Summary of some of the main hormones in humans

Gland	Hormone	Effects
Pituitary	ADH	Increases water reabsorption in nephrons of the kidney.
	Oxytocin	Causes contraction of the uterus during birth.
	Prolactin	Stimulates milk production from breasts after birth.
Thyroid	Thyroxine	Increases the general rate of metabolism (chemical reactions in the body) and stimulates growth.
Adrenal gland	Adrenaline	Sometimes call the fight, flight or fright hormone; prepares the body for potentially difficult or dangerous situations, for instance by increasing hear rate, efficiency of muscles and breathing rate. Adrenaline also raises the blood glucose level.
Pancreas (islets of Langerhans)	Insulin	Causes the conversion of glucose to glycogen.
	Glucagon	Causes the conversion of glycogen to glucose.
Gonads: – Ovary	Oestrogen	Promotes the development of female secondary sexual characteristics; cause ovulation.
	Progesterone	Maintains the uterus lining during pregnancy.
– Testes	Testosterone	Promotes the development of male secondary sexual characteristics.

'These are examples of human hormones. You would not be expected to learn all of them.'

become attached to target cells and have an effect. The effect depends on the hormone involved. Hormones have no effect on other cells, e.g. cells without the correct receptors on their surface.

Insulin and blood sugar

> ## Key points
>
> ▷ blood sugar level is controlled by two hormones, insulin and glucagon (both made by the pancreas);
>
> ▷ regulation of blood sugar levels is an example of homeostasis;
>
> ▷ some people cannot produce enough insulin, they are diabetic.

The amount of sugar in the blood must be very carefully controlled because most body cells need a supply of sugar to respire and make energy. When carbohydrate is eaten, it is digested and absorbed through the walls of the ileum into the blood. The amount of sugar in the blood is regulated by two hormones, insulin and glucagon.

Insulin
Insulin is made in the **pancreas** and travels all round the body in the blood. It affects cells in the **liver** and **muscle** (these are the target organs), causing them to absorb glucose from the blood and convert it to glycogen. The glycogen is then stored in liver and muscle cells.

Insulin is produced whenever blood sugar levels are too high, e.g. after a meal containing carbohydrate, and it **lowers** the blood sugar level.

Glucagon
Glucagon is made in the **pancreas** and travels all round the body in the blood. It affects cells in the **liver** (this is the target organ) causing them to convert glycogen into glucose. This glucose then enters the blood and can be used by cells all over the body for respiration.

'Do not get glycogen and glucagon mixed up.'

Glucagon is produced whenever blood sugar levels are too low, e.g. after a long period without food, and it **raises** the blood sugar level.

Regulation of blood sugar levels
Most body cells need a regular supply of glucose for respiration. If there is not enough glucose in the blood, cells cannot function properly and the person may go into a coma. If there is too much glucose in the blood, some will be lost in urine. There is an efficient

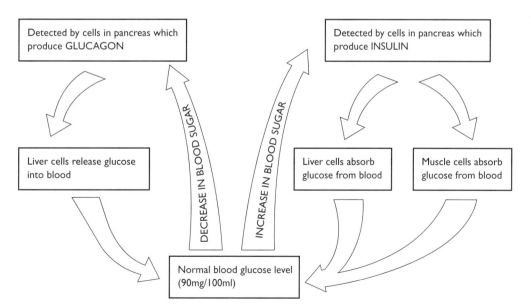

Fig. 4(2).15 Regulation of blood sugar level

homeostatic mechanism which regulates blood sugar levels, involving two hormones made by the pancreas, **glucagon** and **insulin** (Fig. 4(2).15).

Optimum value: 90 mg of glucose per 100 ml blood
Sensor: cells in pancreas
Effector: cells in liver and muscle

Diabetes
Some people cannot produce enough insulin and are **diabetic**. They are likely to have the following problems:

▶ they do not have glycogen stores in their liver so must eat small amounts of food regularly to keep blood sugar levels up;
▶ they cannot store excess sugar (by converting it to glycogen) so this excess sugar is lost in urine;
▶ blood sugar level fluctuates (changes) much more than in a non-diabetic person.

Most diabetics can overcome these problems by regulating their diet or by having insulin injections, and can live normal, healthy lives.

REVISION ACTIVITY 5 ▮ Why must diabetics inject their insulin rather than take insulin tablets?

Sex hormones

Key points

▶ sex hormones start to be produced just before puberty begins;

▶ sex hormones control gamete production;

▶ female sex hormones control the menstrual cycle;

▶ sex hormones can be used to increase or decrease fertility in humans.

Production of sex hormones
The main sex hormones are:

▶ oestrogen ⎫
▶ progesterone ⎬ in females
▶ testosterone in males

Other sex hormones exist, e.g. FSH and LH (made by the pituitary gland), but you do not have to study these at GCSE.

Oestrogen and progesterone are made in the ovary. Production starts just before puberty, and continues until the menopause. Progesterone is also made in the placenta during pregnancy.

Testosterone is made in the testes. Production starts just before puberty and continues throughout life.

Sex hormones and gamete production
Before puberty, the reproductive systems of males and females are inactive. Once puberty begins (under the influence of sex hormones), the body begins to change to its adult form. These changes are called the **secondary sexual characteristics**; some of them are listed in Table 4(2).7.

Table 4(2).7
Changes at puberty

Female	Male
breasts develop	voice deepens
vagina and uterus enlarge	testes and penis enlarge
hips widen	shoulders broaden
menstrual cycle begins	facial hair grows
body hair grows (pubic and underarm hair)	body hair grows (pubic hair, underarm hair and hair on chest)
grows taller	grows taller

Production of ova: When a baby girl is born, she already has hundreds of ova inside her ovaries. These remain inactive until puberty when sex hormones are produced. Usually one ovum ripens each month and is released from an ovary. As the ovum is ripening, it is surrounded by a layer of cells and a bubble of fluid: the whole structure is called a **follicle**. It is the follicle cells which make oestrogen, and which bring about ovulation.

This process continues, with one ovum being released from the ovary each month, until the woman reaches the menopause. After this oestrogen is no longer produced, and ovulation stops so the woman is no longer fertile.

Production of sperm: When a boy reaches puberty, his testes start to produce sperm cells. Inside each testis are many metres of very narrow tubes. The walls of these tiny tubes are lined with sperm producing cells and with cells which make testosterone. Testosterone causes the sperm-producing cells to divide by meiosis and make huge numbers of sperm – up to 100 million per day. The new sperm cells are stored in the epididymis. This process continues throughout life, so the man remains fertile until he dies.

Sex hormones and the menstrual cycle

The menstrual cycle is a complex series of events occurring each month in a woman's reproductive system. It lasts for about 28 days, and is co-ordinated by oestrogen and progesterone, and by two other sex hormones made by the pituitary gland. Two main things are happening:

1. One ovum develops inside the ovary, and is released.
2. The lining of the uterus gets ready to receive a fertilized ovum (zygote). If this happens, the lining of the uterus remains thick during pregnancy. If it does not happen, the lining of the uterus breaks up and passes out of the body through the vagina. This is menstruation (a period).

Oestrogen:

▷   is made by the developing follicle;
▷   it peaks at day 12–13;
▷   it causes repair of the uterus lining after menstruation;
▷   it causes ovulation.

Progesterone:

▷   is made by the yellow body;
▷   it peaks at day 25–26;
▷   it maintains the thickness of the uterus lining (stops it breaking up);
▷   it prevents development of a new follicle in the ovary.

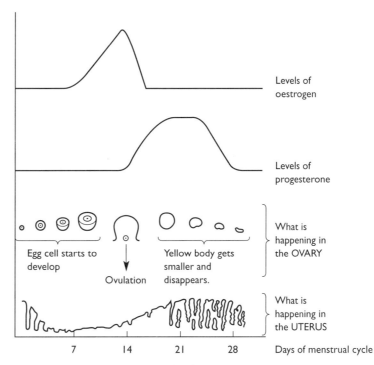

Fig. 4(2).16 Sex hormones and the menstrual cycle

If the ovum is not fertilized, the yellow body gradually gets smaller and stops producing progesterone. A fall in progesterone levels has two effects:

1. it allows menstruation to start;
2. it allows a new follicle to start developing in the the ovary.

If the ovum is fertilized, it will implant in the uterus, and the developing embryo will secrete chemicals which stop the yellow body shrinking. It continues to make progesterone so that the uterus lining remains thick and new follicles do not start to develop in the ovary. Later in the pregnancy, the placenta takes over production of progesterone.

REVISION ACTIVITY 6   During pregnancy, why is it important that:

(a)   the uterus lining remains thick?
(b)   new follicles do not develop in the ovary?

Sex hormones and fertility
Sex hormones can be used to increase or decrease fertility in humans.

Increasing fertility: One reason for infertility is irregular or absent ovulation. Women with this problem can be given injections of sex hormones (usually FSH and LH which are made by the pituitary gland) to cause ovulation of mature ova.

This technique is relatively simple and successful, but it can cause ovulation of large numbers of ova (up to 10) and if all of these are fertilized it may cause several problems, e.g.

▶   each foetus will be much smaller than usual;
▶   they are likely to be born prematurely, and are less likely to survive;
▶   there are considerable health risks to the mother;
▶   if they do survive, it is very difficult for parents to care for so many children of the same age.

Hormone injections are also used as part of the *in-vitro fertilization* process, sometimes called **test-tube babies**. This was first successfully carried out in 1978, and involves six main steps:

1. The woman is given injections of FSH and LH to make her ovulate.
2. She has an operation to remove the ova, and they are placed in a sterile glass dish.
3. They are mixed with sperm collected from the man, and fertilization will occur in the dish to form zygotes.
4. The zygotes will be monitored carefully, until they have started to divide to form embryos.
5. Two or three of the embryos will be put inside the woman's uterus so that they can implant, and the rest will be frozen (in storage).
6. If an embryo does implant, the woman is pregnant, and the pregnancy will continue as normal. If the embryos do not implant, the couple will be able to try again with the embryos they have in storage.

Decreasing fertility: When a woman is pregnant, levels of sex hormones in her body prevent any new follicles developing in the uterus. It is possible to prevent pregnancy by giving artificial doses of these hormones (mainly oestrogen and progesterone, in the right proportions).

The usual way to do this is by the contraceptive pill. One tablet containing sex hormones is taken each day for 21 days to keep hormone levels constant (mimics pregnancy). When the woman stops taking the pills (for seven days) hormone levels drop and she has a period.

Alternatively, the hormones may be delivered by implants (slow release) or by injection.

If fertilization has already occurred, a woman can take the **morning after pill** to prevent implantation. This is a large dose of sex hormones (mainly oestrogen), and it can be taken up to 72 hours after intercourse. This is not suitable as a regular form of contraception, because it can have unpleasant side effects, but it is an effective form of emergency contraception.

Adrenaline

Key points
▷ adrenaline is produced by the adrenal glands at times of stress or danger;
▷ it is sometimes called the fight or flight hormone because it prepares the body to respond to danger;
▷ adrenaline is different from most other hormones, because its effects are short-lived.

When we are in a stressful or dangerous situation, nerve impulses from the brain cause the adrenal glands to release adrenaline. This travels round the body in the blood and has an effect on several target organs (Table 4(2).8).

Table 4(2).8

Target tissue	Effect	Purpose
Brain	causes 'instructions' to be sent out to increase breathing rate and depth	increased supply of oxygen, and removal of carbon dioxide
Heart	pacemaker makes heart beat faster	more rapid delivery of essential substances to muscles, e.g. glucose and oxygen
Blood supply to skin	reduced	blood to skin is not urgently needed, so can be diverted
Blood supply to gut	reduced	blood to gut is not urgently needed, so can be diverted
Gut muscles	causes muscles to relax	digestion is not urgent, and can be temporarily stopped
Liver	increased conversion of glycogen to glucose	glucose is needed for respiration in body muscles
Fat deposits	increased conversion of fats to fatty acids	fatty acids are need for body muscle contraction
Iris of eye	pupil increases in size	more light enters the eye to improve vision

Examples of situation when adrenaline might be produced are:

▷ being confronted by a violent person;
▷ watching an exciting film;
▷ being on a first date;
▷ performing in public, e.g. playing a musical instrument;
▷ entering an examination room;
▷ going to the dentist.

The feeling of 'butterflies in your stomach' and a pounding heart are due to adrenaline!

▷ **Comparison of the nervous and endocrine systems**

The two systems work together to co-ordinate the activities of the body, but they act in quite different ways. Exam questions often ask for a comparison like this:

Table 4(2).9

Comparison	Nervous system	Endocrine system
Message	Nerve impulse	Hormones
Route	Nervous system	Blood system
Method of transmission	Electrical impulses and chemicals (neurotransmitters)	Chemicals (hormones)
Transmission rate	Rapid	Slower, depends on circulation
Origin of message	Receptor (sense organ)	Endocrine gland
Destination of message	Effector (muscle)	Target organ or organs
Speed and duration of effect	Immediate, brief	Delayed, prolonged

▷ SOLUTIONS TO REVISION ACTIVITIES

S1 (a) cerebral cortex
(b) medulla
(c) cerebellum
(d) cerebral cortex

S2
Table 4(2).10

Name of reflex	Stimulus	Response	Reason for reflex
Withdrawal reflex	pain due to hot/sharp object	to move the body away from stimulus	to prevent damage to the body
Pupil reflex	bright light in eyes	pupil gets smaller	to prevent too much light entering the eye
Choke reflex	if food enters the trachea	coughing/choking to expel food	to prevent food entering the trachea
Blink reflex	an object close to the eye	rapid lowering of eyelid	to prevent foreign objects entering the eye
Suckle reflex	touching a baby's face (near mouth)	it will turn towards the object touching it, and close its lips around it	to get food

S3 (a) connector neurone/relay neurone/intermediate neurone
(b) synapse
(c) grey matter
(d) a muscle or gland
(e) sensory neurone
(f) cell body
(g) dorsal root ganglion

S4 (a) contracted (to focus on a near object)
(b) relaxed (to focus on a distant object)

S5 Insulin is a hormone made of protein. If insulin tablets were taken, the hormone would be digested by protease enzymes in the gut, so it would not work.

S6 (a) If the lining broke up (menstruation), the implanted embryo would become dislodged, or the placenta would become detached from the lining. Both of these would result in miscarriage.
(b) If a new follicle developed and was released from the ovary, it could be fertilized after sexual intercourse. The woman would then have two embryos at different stages of development. It would be impossible for both to develop and be born safely.

▷ EXAMINATION QUESTIONS

▷ **Question 1**   Figures 4(2).17 (a) and (b) show the reproductive organs of a man and a woman.

(a) Write down the correct labelling letter of the following parts.

(i) The structure which produces sperms. _____ *(1)*

(ii) The sperm duct. _____ *(1)*

(iii) The ovary. _____ *(1)*

(b) Figure 4(2).18 shows a human female menstrual cycle.

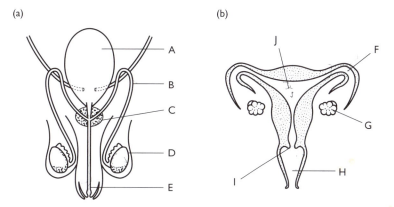

(a)   (b)

Fig. 4(2).17

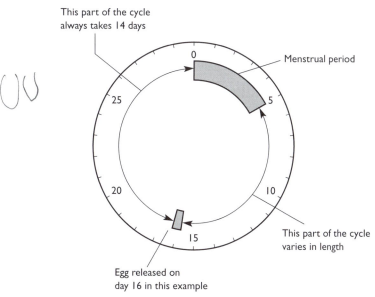

This part of the cycle always takes 14 days

Menstrual period

This part of the cycle varies in length

Egg released on day 16 in this example

Fig. 4(2).18

(i)   What is the length of the complete cycle for this particular woman?

_(1)_

(ii) What was the length of the menstrual period?

_(1)_

(iii) On what day did ovulation take place?

_(1)_

(iv) Although the length of the menstrual cycle can vary, one part is always the same length. Which part is this?

_(1)_

(v)   If the interval between the start of the period and the release of the egg in **another woman** is twelve days, how long will her cycle be? Show your working.

_(2)_

(MEG)

▷ **Question 2**   (a)   Which gland produces adrenaline? _____   _(1)_

(b) Underline the correct alternatives in each sentence.
   (i) Adrenaline increases/decreases the heart rate.
   (ii) Adrenaline narrows/widens the bronchioles in the lungs.
   (iii) Adrenaline narrows/widens the arteries carrying blood to muscles.
   (iv) Adrenaline raises/lowers the blood sugar level by causing the liver to absorb/release glucose.
   (v) Adrenaline increases/decreases the size of the pupil of the eye.   *(6)*

(c) For each effect, explain how it helps the body to cope with stress or danger.
   (i) **Heart rate**
   (ii) **Bronchioles**
   (iii) **Arteries**
   (iv) **Blood sugar level**
   (v) **Pupil size**   *(5)*

▷ **Question 3** (a) Describe as fully as you can how a human foetus gets rid of the carbon dioxide produced during respiration.   *(3)*

(b) The menstrual cycle is controlled by a number of hormones. The graph shows the concentrations of four of these hormones at different times during the menstrual cycle.

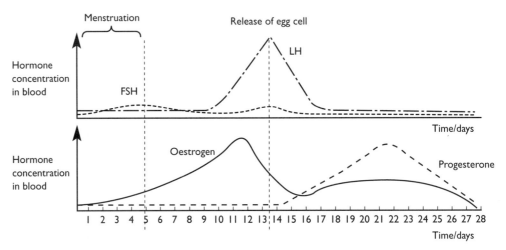

Fig. 4(2).19

The functions of the four hormones include:
FSH – stimulates the development of immature cells into eggs in the ovary;
LH – stimulates the release of the mature egg cell;
oestrogen – stimulates production of LH, but inhibits FSH production;
progesterone – inhibits production of both LH and FSH.

Use this information to explain as fully as you can

   (i) how the concentration of oestrogen can affect and control the release of an egg during the monthly cycle.   *(3)*
   (ii) how one or more of these hormones could be used to treat infertility.   *(3)*

(c) Progesterone continues to be produced throughout pregnancy.
   Explain as fully as you can why this is so.   *(3)*

(d) A hormone called mifepristone is used in low doses as a female contraceptive. Higher doses can be used to induce an abortion. As a consequence mifepristone is often referred to as 'the morning-after pill'. The use of mifepristone is currently tightly controlled by the medical profession.

   Evaluate the benefits and problems which might arise from making this hormone more freely available.   *(4)*
   (NEAB)

▷ **Question 4**

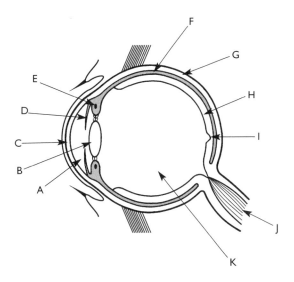

Fig. 4(2).20

(a) Which **labelled** part of the eye

   (i) controls the amount of light entering the eye _____

   (ii) contains rods and cones _____

   (iii) connects with the brain _____

   (iv) is most colour sensitive _____

   (v) stops light reflecting inside the eye? _____ *(5)*

(b) Which **two** letters show parts involved in focusing (accommodation)?

   (i) _____ (ii) _____ *(2)*

   (WJEC)

▷ ANSWERS TO EXAMINATION QUESTIONS

▷ **Question 1**   (a) (i) D   (ii) B   (iii) G

(b) (i) 30 days   (ii) 5 days   (iii) day 16
   (iv) between ovulation and menstruation (14 days)
   (v) 26 days: start of period to ovulation = 12 days
   ovulation to menstruation = 14 days

▷ **Question 2**   (a)   adrenal gland

(b) (i) Adrenaline **increases** the heart rate.
   (ii) Adrenaline **widens** the bronchioles in the lungs.
   (iii) Adrenaline **widens** the arteries carrying blood to muscles.
   (iv) Adrenaline **raises** the blood sugar level by causing the liver to release glucose.
   (v) Adrenaline **increases** the size of the pupil of the eye.

(c) (i) **Heart rate:** blood travels more quickly, so it can deliver glucose and oxygen to muscles more quickly (1) and carry waste products, e.g. CO_2, away more quickly (1). Blood does **not** carry energy to muscles.
   (ii) **Bronchioles:** more air enters the lungs with each breath, so more oxygen can be absorbed. (1) Oxygen is needed for respiration. (1)
   (iii) **Arteries:** more blood is delivered to the muscles, so more glucose and oxygen is brought to them for respiration. (1) Blood is diverted away from other organs, e.g. gut. (1)
   (iv) **Blood sugar level:** stored glucose is released from the liver so more is available for respiration. (1)
   (v) **Pupil size:** increases, so more light enters the eye. This increases detailed vision. (1)

▷ **Question 3**   (a) Carbon dioxide travels through the umbilical cord in foetal blood. (1) When it reaches the placenta, it diffuses into the mother's blood. (1) It travels in her blood to her lungs, and is breathed out. (1)

(b) (i) When levels of oestrogen rise, levels of LH rise; (1) high levels of LH cause ovulation; (1) high levels of oestrogen stop FSH being produced; (1) this stops more eggs developing in the ovary. (1)

(ii) **FSH** could be used to make large numbers of eggs develop in the ovary in one month. (1) LH could be used to increase the number of eggs released from the ovary, (1) and to control **when** they are released. (1)

Both of these would increase the chances of pregnancy.

(c) Progesterone keeps the uterus lining thick (prevents menstruation), (1) so the growing embryo is not dislodged after implantation. (1) It prevents more eggs developing and being released from the ovary, (1) so a second embryo cannot start to develop. (1)

(d) You are not expected to 'know' the answer to this question. Look carefully at the information you have been given, and think about what you already know. Any sensible points would be given credit, e.g.

Benefits

▶   Would reduce the number of unwanted pregnancies.
▶   Allows abortion to occur at a very early stage of pregnancy (within 72 hours).
▶   Women would not have to wait to see doctors in order to get the hormone.

Problems

▶   Higher doses may make women ill, i.e. have side-effects.
▶   Women might rely on this as a regular form of contraception.
▶   It is not 100% effective, so the woman may remain pregnant.
▶   If pregnancy continued, the foetus may be harmed by the high doses of hormone.

▷ **Question 4**   (a) (i) D   (ii) H   (iii) J   (iv) I   (v) F

(b) B and E

▷ **STUDENT'S ANSWER WITH EXAMINER'S COMMENTS**

The diagram below shows a simple reflex arc.

'Correct'

Sensory neurone Y

Z

X Motor neurone

Fig. 4(2).21

(a) Label structures X and Y on the lines provided.   (2)

(continued)

(b) The diagram below shows some of the details of region Z.

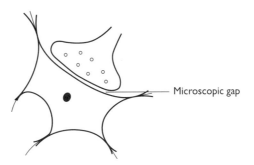

Microscopic gap

Fig. 4(2).22

(i) Name the microscopic gap shown in the diagram above.

Synapse ✓ *(1)*

'Yes, or synaptic cleft.'

(ii) Describe how nerve impulse are transmitted across this gap.

chemicals are released

(4)

'This answer does not give enough detail: there are 4 marks available. The chemicals are **neurotransmitters**; they **diffuse** across the gap and **restart the impulse** in the second neurone.'

(c) The charts below show the heartbeat and breathing of a person who was suddenly frightened by a fierce dog.

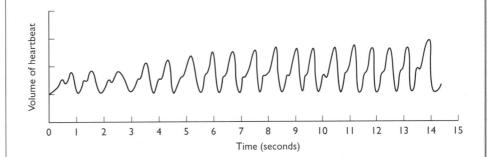

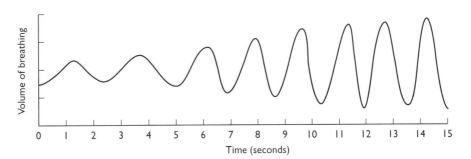

Fig. 4(2).23

(i) Describe the changes shown in both breathing and heartbeat.

Breathing becomes faster. ✓

Heartbeat become faster. ✓

(2)

'Yes, and they both increase in volume as well.'

(continued)

'No, the blood is not carrying energy to the muscles. It is carrying extra food and oxygen. The muscles use food and oxygen to make energy by respiration. Breathing more deeply means that extra oxygen enters the body, and you can get rid of extra carbon dioxide.'

(ii) Explain why these changes are important during times of stress.

You might need to run away or fight, so your muscles need extra energy. If

more blood travels to the muscles, it carries more energy.

_____

_____

(4)

(LONDON)

SUMMARY

▷ Complex, multi-cellular organisms like humans need co-ordination systems to regulate body activities. Humans have two co-ordination systems: the nervous system and the endocrine system.

▷ The nervous system is made up of the brain, spinal cord, nerves and sense organs.

▷ The brain is a complex organ controlling the majority of body functions.

▷ Nerve cells are adapted to carry nerve impulses around the body. They have a long nerve fibre (axon), and a myelin sheath to speed up transmission of impulses. The junction between nerves is called a synapse, and neurotransmitter chemicals are released to diffuse across the small gap between nerve cells.

▷ A reflex is an immediate, unlearned response to a stimulus. Reflexes are very rapid responses, and often protect the individual from danger, or increase its chances of survival.

▷ A reflex arc involves only three neurones, and does not involve the brain in making decisions.

▷ Sense organs contain receptor cells to detect stimuli.

▷ The retina of the eye contains light-sensitive rod and cone cells which send nerve impulses through the optic nerve to the brain.

▷ The size of the pupil changes, altering the amount of light entering the eye, when muscles in the iris contract and relax.

▷ The ciliary muscle can contract or relax to change the shape of the lens. This is necessary so that the lens can focus light rays effectively on the retina (it is called accommodation).

▷ The endocrine system is made up of glands which release hormones directly into the blood.

▷ Hormones are chemicals which have an effect on target organs in the body.

▷ Insulin and glucagon (made by the pancreas) control blood sugar levels in the body. Diabetics do not make enough insulin, and may need to be given injections.

▷ Sex hormones (oestrogen, progesterone and testosterone) control puberty, gamete production and the menstrual cycle.

▷ Female sex hormones can be given artificially to increase or decrease fertility.

▷ Adrenaline is produced by the adrenal glands at times of stress or danger (fight or flight hormone). It has an effect on many target organs of the body.

4.3

Humans as organisms
Maintaining the internal environment

> **GETTING STARTED**

| MEG | SEG | NEAB | LONDON | WJEC | NICCEA | SEB |

One of the reasons that humans are successful organisms is their ability to control conditions inside the body (the internal environment). This includes levels of waste products, e.g. carbon dioxide and urea, levels of water, and body temperature. If these factors are controlled so that they stay constant, the whole body can function more efficiently.

TOPIC	STUDY	REVISION I	REVISION 2
Excretion			
The kidney and urea			
Kidney failure			
The lungs and carbon dioxide			
Homeostasis			
The skin and temperature control			
ADH and water balance (osmoregulation)			
The foetus during pregnancy			

WHAT YOU NEED TO KNOW

▷ **Excretion**   Excretion means removal of waste products made inside the body e.g. carbon dioxide made in all cells by respiration, urea made in the liver by deamination (breakdown of amino acids). It is vital that these waste products are removed, because they will cause damage if they accumulate in the body.

The kidney and urea

> ## Key points
>
> ▷   the kidney has three main functions:
>   1.   removal of urea from blood
>   2.   production of urine
>   3.   osmoregulation (regulating the amount of water in the body);
>
> ▷   urea is a poisonous waste product made when amino acids are broken down in the liver;
>
> ▷   urine is mainly water, with urea, minerals and vitamins dissolved in it;
>
> ▷   the kidney is composed of thousands of tiny 'filtration units' called **nephrons**. Each nephron 'cleans' the blood flowing through in two main processes; **filtration** of small molecules, and **reabsorption** of useful molecules. The remainder are waste molecules, mainly urea, which leave the body as a solution called **urine**.

Production of urea
Urea is a poisonous chemical made in the liver. If we have too much protein in our diet, or when proteins in the body are being broken down, amino acids are deaminated in the liver. This reaction produces ammonia, which is quickly converted to urea:

amino acids $\longrightarrow$ ammonia $\longrightarrow$ urea

Urea is released into the blood, and travels around the body until it is removed by the kidneys.

Structure of the kidneys
Humans have two kidneys, situated in the abdomen. Each kidney is connected to two blood vessels (the renal artery and vein), and has a tube called the ureter leading to the bladder. The cortex and medulla are the main regions inside the kidney.

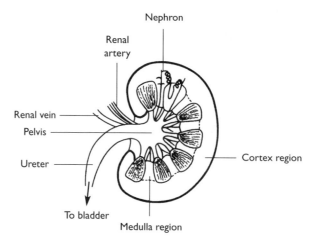

Fig. 4(3).1 Section through the kidney

Each kidney contains about one million nephrons (kidney tubules). The nephron is a narrow tubule about 3cm long, and the combined length of the nephrons in each kidney is about 30km: this provides a very large surface area for cleaning blood.

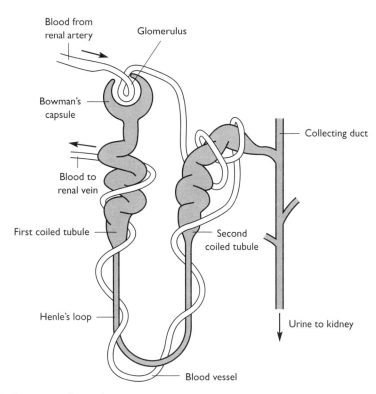

Fig. 4(3).2 Structure of a nephron

Each nephron is made up of four main parts:

▷ Bowman's capsule;
▷ first coiled tubule;
▷ loop of Henlé;
▷ second coiled tubule.

Each nephron is joined to wider tube called the collecting duct, which carries urine to the ureter.

Each nephron is very close to a blood vessel which carries substances to and from the nephron.

The kidney cleans the blood using two main processes:

1. **Ultrafiltration**
   Blood from a narrow branch of the renal artery enters the glomerulus (capillary knot). Blood pressure in the glomerulus is very high, so small molecules, e.g. water, sugar, urea, amino acids, vitamins and minerals, are forced out of the glomerulus into Bowman's capsule. Large molecules, e.g. proteins, and cells, e.g. red blood cells and white blood cells, stay inside the glomerulus. (See Fig. 4(3).3.)

2. **Selective reabsorption**
   As the molecules (called the filtrate) travel along the nephron, useful molecules are reabsorbed back into the blood.
   Sugar, amino acids, minerals and some water are reabsorbed in the first coiled tubule.
   Water is also reabsorbed in the second coiled tubule and collecting ducts.
   Altogether 99% of the filtrate is reabsorbed. (See Fig. 4(3).3.)

Production of urine
About 1% of the filtrate is not reabsorbed into the blood. This contains water, urea, excess minerals and vitamins. These materials pass down the collecting ducts and travel through the ureter to the bladder – they are now known as urine.

Humans produce about 1.5 litres of urine each day. It contains water, urea, vitamins, minerals and hormones; the exact composition depends on the individual's diet and surroundings, e.g. temperature.

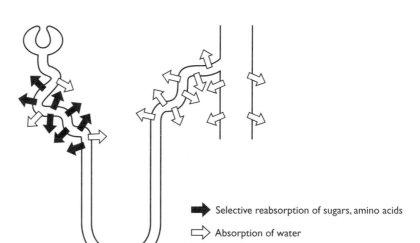

Fig. 4(3).3 Absorption of water and useful materials from the nephron

REVISION ACTIVITY 1

(a)   How would the composition of urine be changed if the person:
   (i)   ate a high protein diet?
   (ii)   ate a lot of crisps?
   (iii)   played tennis on a hot day?
   (iv)   drank lots of coffee on a cold day?

(b)   Urine should never contain sugar. Which disease would you suspect if you found sugar in the urine?

(c)   Urine should never contain protein. What problem would you suspect if you found protein in the urine?

REVISION ACTIVITY 2

(a)   Put these statements about urine production into the right order.
   A   Small molecules are forced out of the capillary knot into the capsule (due to high blood pressure).
   B   Fluid containing urea and salt trickles down the ureter to the bladder.
   C   Water is absorbed back into the blood from the second coiled tubule.
   D   Blood containing lots of urea enters the kidney in the renal artery.
   E   Useful substances, e.g. sugars, amino acids and some water are reabsorbed back into the blood from the first coiled tubule.
   F   Small molecules pass from the capsule into the first coiled tubule.

(b)   Which step is   (i)   ultrafiltration?
                      (ii)   selective reabsorption?

Kidney failure

Kidneys may fail because of disease or because blood pressure drops too low to maintain filtration. If this happens, urea and excess water can accumulate in the body, causing damage.

> **Key points**
>
> ▷   if the kidneys fail, the blood is no longer filtered efficiently, and urea and excess water accumulate in the body;
>
> ▷   kidney failure can be treated by dialysis (use of a kidney machine). This process must be repeated regularly to remove urea and excess salts and water;
>
> ▷   kidney failure can be treated by transplanting a healthy kidney from a donor. This is a long-term solution, but rejection of the donor kidney is possible.

Kidney dialysis

Blood from the patient is temporarily diverted from an artery in the arm through a machine and is then returned to a vein in the arm. Blood in the machine is passed over a **dialysis membrane**, which is **selectively permeable**. This membrane is surrounded by a solution containing the 'ideal' concentrations of substances, e.g. glucose, amino acids, minerals, water.

Some substances, e.g. glucose and amino acids, stay in the blood: this happens because the concentrations of these substances in the dialysis fluid is high.

Some substances, e.g. urea, water and salt, pass through the dialysis membrane into the dialysis fluid: this happens because the concentration of these substances in the dialysis fluid is low.

i.e. water ⎫
     urea   ⎬ are removed from the blood, so the dialysis machine is acting as an
     salt   ⎭ 'artificial kidney'

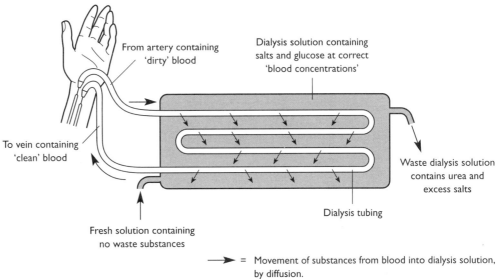

Fig. 4(3).4 Kidney dialysis machine

A person who needs dialysis will usually require treatment every 2–3 days. Between treatments, urea and excess water will build up, so they may feel ill. They must also carefully control their diet, avoiding foods high in protein and salt, and limit their fluid intake.

Dialysis is expensive, and there is a waiting list for treatment, so some people who need dialysis are not able to have it.

REVISION ACTIVITY 3 ▌ Why must dialysis patients avoid high protein foods?

Kidney transplants

A kidney from a suitable donor can be transplanted into the patient, usually in the lower abdomen. It is connected to blood vessels (so blood can enter and leave the kidney), and is joined to the bladder so that the urine it makes can be removed.

The donor of the kidney is usually dead, e.g. a previously healthy person who has been killed in an accident and who was carrying an organ donor card. Unfortunately many people do not carry donor cards, so there is a long waiting list of people who need transplants.

The tissues of the donor kidney must be similar to the patient's own tissues (tissue-matched) or an immune reaction may occur, leading to rejection of the transplant organ.

Occasionally the kidney donor is alive, e.g. a close relative of the patient. The donor will remain healthy with one kidney as long as it is working efficiently.

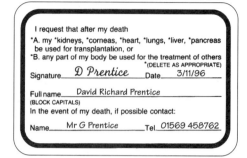

Fig. 4(3).5

The lungs and carbon dioxide

> ## Key points
>
> ▷ carbon dioxide is made in all cells by the process of respiration;
>
> ▷ carbon dioxide travels in the blood to the lungs;
>
> ▷ it is breathed out when we exhale; this is an example of excretion.

How is carbon dioxide produced?
All cells respire constantly to make energy. During this process, they also make a waste product, carbon dioxide.

glucose + oxygen $\longrightarrow$ energy + carbon dioxide + water

This carbon dioxide must be removed from the body, because it will cause harm if it accumulates. It diffuses from body cells into the blood, where it reacts with water and salt to form sodium hydrogen carbonate. This is carried to the lungs in blood plasma.

How is carbon dioxide excreted?
When blood reaches the lungs, sodium hydrogen carbonate breaks down (dissociates) to release carbon dioxide. This diffuses out of the capillaries and into the alveoli, and is breathed out when we exhale. The air we exhale contains about 4% carbon dioxide.

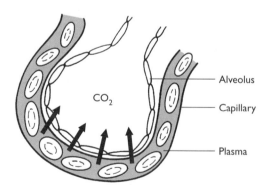

Fig. 4(3).6 Excretion of carbon dioxide

▷ **Homeostasis**   Homeostasis is the process by which an organism controls its internal environment. This is necessary if it is to be independent of its surroundings, and if its body processes are to function efficiently. Most homeostatic mechanisms work by **negative feedback**, i.e. if there is a change away from the optimum value, a process which will reverse this change automatically occurs. There must be a **sensor** to detect the change, and an effector to reverse the change.

Control of **body temperature, blood sugar levels** and **water balance** are all examples of homeostasis.

The skin and temperature control

> ## Key points
>
> ▷ humans are **endothermic**, i.e. maintain a constant body temperature;
>
> ▷ skin is responsible for maintaining body temperature at 37°C;
>
> ▷ **blood flow** through the skin is regulated as the diameter of capillaries changes. This is **vasodilation** (when they become wider) or **vasoconstriction** (when they become narrower);
>
> ▷ **sweat** is produced in hot conditions;
>
> ▷ skin **hairs** move to trap a layer of air close to the skin in cold conditions.

Structure of the skin

The skin is a large organ covering the entire body surface. It has two main functions:

1. regulation of body temperature;
2. detection of stimuli (i.e. it is a sense organ and can detect touch, pressure, pain and temperature).

It consists of two layers, called the **epidermis** and **dermis** (Fig. 4(3).7).

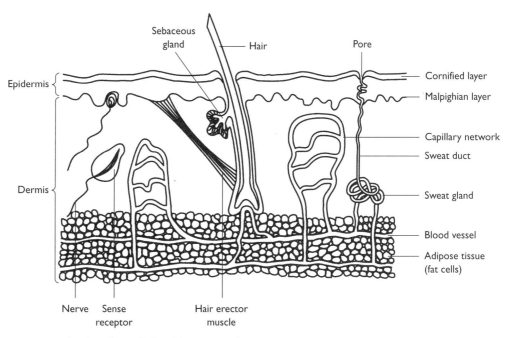

Fig. 4(3).7 Section through the skin

1. **Epidermis**

   The function of the epidermis is to protect the dermis. In some parts of the body, e.g. soles of feet, palms of hands, it is very thick. The top layer of cells (**cornified layer**) is tough and dead. These cells are continually worn off and replaced from beneath. The **Malpighian layer** is constantly dividing to make new cells, which move towards the top of the epidermis to replace the cells which have been worn off.

   Cells in the Malpighian layer contain a chemical called **melanin** which protects the skin from ultra-violet rays (in sunlight). If you are exposed to UV rays you make more melanin (get a tan), but in extreme cases the dermis may still be damaged.

2.   **Dermis**
This contains many different structures:

▷   hairs with sebaceous glands (make oil) and hair erector muscles;
▷   sweat glands with pores on the skin surface;
▷   sense receptors, e.g. for touch, pain, pressure, etc, and nerves;
▷   blood vessels;
▷   adipose tissue, made up of fat cells;
▷   connective tissue, made up of packing cells (this is not shown in Fig. 4(3).7).

How does the skin control body temperature?

The skin controls body temperature in three ways:

'Capillaries do not move. Their diameter changes to alter blood flow.'

1.   **Changes in skin capillaries**
There are millions of capillaries in the dermis layer of the skin. These can change in size to alter the volume of blood flowing through them.

In hot conditions **vasodilation** occurs:

▷   capillaries close to skin surface widen;
▷   more blood flows close to surface of skin;
▷   heat is lost through skin surface;
▷   skin feels warmer and looks redder.

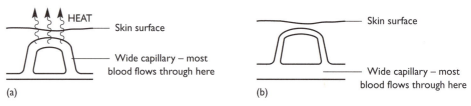

Fig. 4(3).8 Change in diameter of capillaries alters blood flow through the skin.
(a) Hot conditions (b) cool conditions

In cool conditions **vasoconstriction** occurs:

▷   capillaries close to skin surface narrow;
▷   less blood flows close to surface of skin;
▷   less heat is lost through skin surface;
▷   skin feels cold and looks pale.

2.   **Sweating**
Sweat glands in the dermis produce a liquid (mainly water and salt) called sweat. This moves up the sweat duct and onto the surface of the skin. It evaporates (changes into a vapour) and cools the skin, because it takes away some of the body heat when it evaporates. (Fig. 4(3).9). In very hot conditions a person may lose up to 30 litres of water per day as sweat.

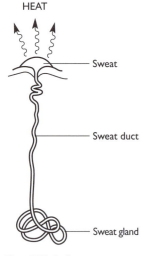

Fig. 4(3).9 Sweat evaporates from the skin surface

3.   **Movement of skin hairs**
This is not very important in humans as they have relatively few hairs on their skin, but it is important in other mammals, e.g. dogs. In warm conditions the hair erector muscles are relaxed, and hairs lie flat against the skin (Fig. 4(3).10).

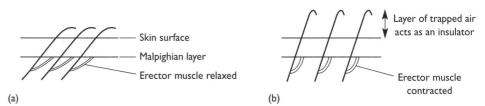

Fig. 4(3).10 Position of skin hairs (a) in warm conditions (b) in cool conditions

In cold conditions the hair erector muscles contract and hairs move upright, trapping a layer of air close to the skin. This makes an insulation layer which prevents heat loss (similar to the effects of wearing clothes).

> *Remember:* heat loss is also affected by:
> (a)   surface area : volume ratio (small animals lose heat faster);
> (b)   thickness of fat layer under skin.

Why is body temperature important?

'Do not get these terms mixed up.'

Mammals and birds are **endothermic** (warm blooded): this means that they have a relatively constant body temperature which does not depend on the temperature of their environment. This is an advantage because they can operate effectively in fairly low temperatures so they can live in cold regions. Animals which cannot maintain their body temperature are described as **ectothermic** (cold blooded), e.g. fish, amphibians, reptiles. Humans have a constant body temperature of 37°C, even when the external temperature varies widely. Ectotherms have a body temperature which varies with the external temperature (Fig. 4(3).11).

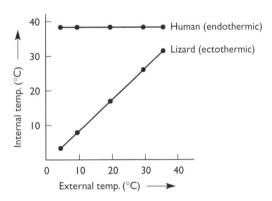

Fig. 4(3).11 The relationship between internal and external temperature in ectothermic and endothermic animals

If human body temperature falls too far the person suffers from hypothermia, and may die.

REVISION ACTIVITY 4

The diagram below (Fig. 4(3).12) shows the structure of human skin.

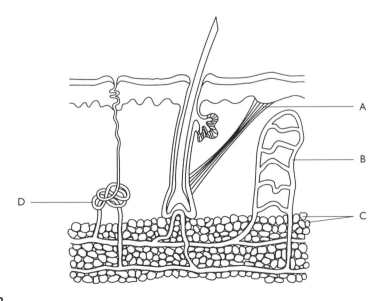

Fig. 4(3).12

(a)   (i)   Complete Table 4(3).1 by naming the parts A, B and C and then say how each part helps keep us warm in cold conditions.

Table 4(3).1

	Name of part	How it helps to keep us warm
A		
B		
C		

   (ii) Name part D.
   (iii) How does part D react to a fall in body temperature.
(b)   (i) What is normal body temperature?
   (ii) What is hypothermia?
   (iii) Give one biological reason why hypothermia mainly affects old people.
   (iv) How would you treat a person with hypothermia?

How is body temperature regulated?

Humans are endothermic, i.e. they maintain a constant body temperature of 37°C, irrespective of the surrounding temperature. This is very important because body temperature affects **metabolic rate**, i.e. the rate of chemical reactions within the body. There is an efficient homeostatic mechanism which regulates body temperature by causing changes in the skin (Fig. 4(3).13).

Optimum value: 37°C
Sensor: cells in hypothalamus of brain
Effectors: capillaries in skin, hair erector muscles in skin, sweat glands in skin.

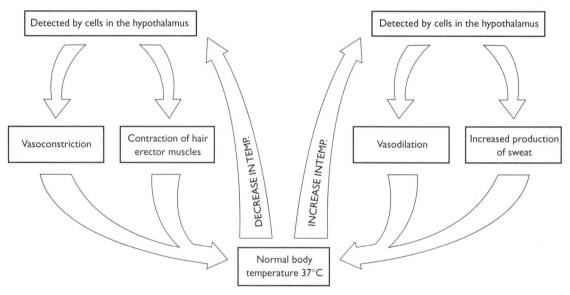

Fig. 4(3).13 Maintenance of body temperature

REVISION ACTIVITY 5 This diagram shows an example of negative feedback. Define negative feedback.

ADH and water balance (osmoregulation)

> **Key points**
>
> ▶ water balance in the body is achieved by regulating the amount of water in the **urine**;
>
> ▶ water balance is controlled by **ADH**;
>
> ▶ ADH is a hormone released by the pituitary gland;
>
> ▶ it affects the nephron (kidney tubule) so more water enters the blood, i.e. it reduces the amount of urine.

Why is water balance important?

Water is gained by the body in drinks and food, and made within the body by respiration. It is lost in urine, faeces, sweat and in the water vapour we breathe out.

It is vital that there is a **balance** between the water gained and lost. If this balance breaks down, then body cells will either gain or lose water by the process of **osmosis**, and they would no longer function properly.

Table 4(3).2 Typical daily water gain and loss (adult human male)

Gain (cm³)		Loss (cm³)	
ingested in drinks	1500	lost in urine	1500
ingested in food	700	lost in faeces	100
made inside cells	300	lost as sweat	500
(by respiration)		breathed out	400
Total	2500	Total	2500

The kidney regulates the amount of water present in the body by varying the amount of urine produced.

What does ADH do?

ADH (anti-diuretic hormone) is very important in osmoregulation. It is released by the **pituitary gland** (at the base of the brain). It travels all around the body in the blood and affects cells in the second convoluted tubule and collecting duct of the **nephron** (these are the target organs). It makes these cells more permeable to water, so more water is absorbed from the nephron into the blood and there is less water in the urine (Fig. 4(3).14).

The pituitary gland produces ADH if a person has ingested very little water, or if they have lost a lot in sweat or in faeces.

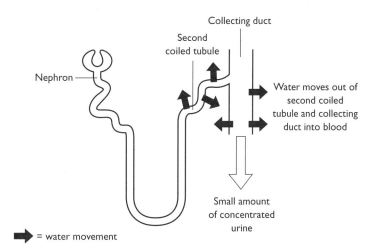

Fig. 4(3).14 Effect of ADH on the Nephron

How is water balance regulated?

There is an efficient homeostatic mechanism which regulates water in the body, involving ADH (Fig. 4(3).15). This hormone is made in the hypothalamus but stored in the pituitary gland.

Optimum value: variable, depending on circumstances
Sensor: cells in hypothalamus
Effector: cells in second coiled tubule of nephron and collecting ducts of kidney.

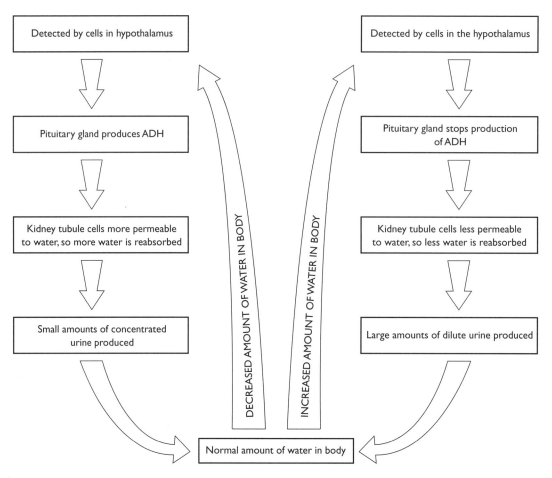

Fig. 4(3).15 Osmoregulation

REVISION ACTIVITY 6

When the amount of water in the blood is low, e.g. after _____ _____ , the pituitary gland produces ADH. This makes the second coiled tubule and _____ duct of the nephron _____ permeable to water, so _____ urine is produced. If the amount of water in the blood is high, e.g. after _____ , ADH is not produced, so the urine volume _____ .

Remember: regulation of blood sugar is also an example of homeostasis: see p. 87.

▷ **The foetus during pregnancy**

Key points

▷ materials passing between the foetus and the mother must pass through the **placenta**;

▷ the foetus needs oxygen for respiration, and **nutrients** so that it can develop properly – it gets these from the mother;

▷ the foetus makes waste products, e.g. **urea** and **carbon dioxide** which would harm it if they built up – it passes these substances to the mother;

▷ the foetus is protected by **amniotic fluid**, and by **antibodies** (chemicals which fight diseases).

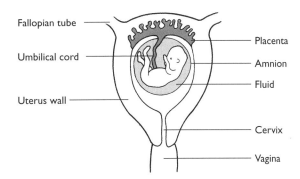

Fig. 4(3).16 Foetus inside the uterus

While the foetus is developing inside the uterus, it is dependent on its mother for all the things it needs to stay alive.

The foetus is connected to the mother through an organ called the **placenta**; here the mother's blood and the foetal blood are very close together (although they do not mix) and substances can be exchanged between them (see Fig. 4(3).16).

Importance of the placenta

This very important organ develops in the uterus early in pregnancy. It contains cells from the embryo and has villi which are embedded in the uterus lining. Blood from the foetus passes through the umbilical cord and into the villi. The mother's blood circulates through blood spaces in the uterus lining. The two types of blood are very close together, but they do not mix.

The placenta acts as a life-support machine for the foetus:

▷   oxygen and nutrients pass through the placenta **to** the foetus;
▷   foetal waste products, e.g. urea and carbon dioxide, pass through the placenta **away from** the foetus;
▷   it makes progesterone (a female sex hormone) which prevents miscarriage by stopping the woman from having a period while she is pregnant.

Respiration in the foetus

Respiration is a chemical reaction occurring in all cells of all living organisms to produce energy.

$$glucose + oxygen \longrightarrow energy + carbon\ dioxide + water$$

The foetus has a high respiration rate as it needs a lot of energy for growth.

Oxygen passes from the mother's blood to the foetal blood for two reasons:

1.   there is a very low concentration of oxygen in blood in the umbilical artery, so oxygen diffuses into the foetal blood;
2.   the foetal blood contains a different type of haemoglobin which combines more readily with oxygen than the mother's haemoglobin does.

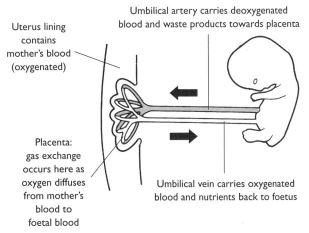

Fig. 4(3).17 Exchange of materials in the placenta

Nourishment of the foetus

The foetus needs nutrients in order to grow and to develop properly. All of the following will diffuse from the mother's blood to the foetal blood via the placenta: **sugars**, **amino acids** (needed to make foetal proteins for growth), **fatty acids**, **glycerol**, **vitamins**, **minerals** (including iron to make red blood cells and calcium needed for formation of bones) and **water**. There is evidence that a deficiency of nutrients prevents proper development of the foetus, e.g. a lack of folic acid (vitamin) is linked to spina bifida (when the vertebrae do not develop properly and the spinal cord is exposed and damaged).

Removal of waste products

Chemical reactions inside the foetus produce toxic waste products which must be removed, otherwise the foetus would be poisoned. The main waste products are carbon dioxide (made by respiration) and urea, (made by breakdown of amino acids). These travel in the umbilical artery to the placenta, where they diffuse into the mother's blood, and are excreted from her body.

Protection of the foetus

The foetus is protected in two main ways:

1. it floats inside a bag of fluid (**amniotic fluid**) and is protected from bumps as the mother moves around;
2. **antibodies** can pass across the placenta from the mother's blood into the foetal blood. These are chemicals made by the mother's lymphocytes which can protect the foetus from diseases while it is developing and for a few months after it is born.

▷ ## SOLUTIONS TO REVISION ACTIVITIES

S1 (a) (i)   contains a lot of urea
(ii) contains a lot of salt
(iii) contains less water and less salt than normal
(iv) contains more water than normal

(b) diabetes

(c) kidney damage or kidney infection.

S2 (a) | D | A | F | E | C | B |

(b) (i) A   (ii) E

S3 Because when protein is digested, amino acids are formed. Excess amino acids are deaminated (broken down) in the liver to form urea. Urea is very poisonous. People with kidney failure cannot remove urea from the blood efficiently, so it accumulates in the body.

S4 (a) (i)

Table 4(3).3

	Name of part	How it helps to keep us warm
A	Hair erector muscle	Contracts to raise the hair; this traps a layer of air close to the skin.
B	Capillary	Narrows (vasoconstriction) to reduce the amount of blood near the skin surface.
C	Fat cells (adipose tissue)	Acts as an insulator to reduce heat loss.

(ii) D = sweat gland
(iii) It stops producing sweat.

(b) (i)   37°C
(ii) When body temperature falls below 35°C.

(iii) They tend to be less active than younger people, and they may be less aware of the cold.

(iv) Wrap in a blanket, and give them a warm drink. Get medical help.

S5 **Negative feedback** means that when a change away from the correct level occurs, a process which reverses this change happens automatically.

S6 When the amount of water in the blood is low, e.g. after **sweating a lot, not drinking much fluid,** the pituary gland produces ADH. This makes the second coiled tubule and **collecting duct** of the nephron **more** permeable to water, so **less** urine is produced. If the amount of water in the blood is high, e.g. after **drinking a lot of fluid,** ADH is not produced, so the urine volume **increases.**

EXAMINATION QUESTIONS

▷ **Question 1** (a) The diagram below shows a single kidney tubule.

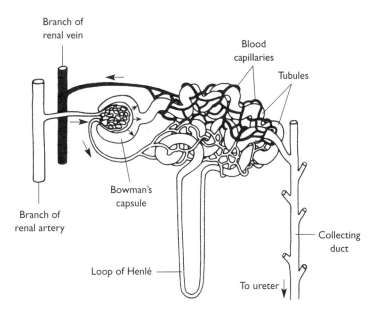

Fig. 4(3).18

(i) In which region of the kidney are the Bowman's capsules situated? *(1)*

(ii) Explain why the liquid trickles down the loop of Henlé does **not** contain glucose even though the Bowman's capsule does. *(1)*

(iii) Name the liquid in the collecting duct. *(1)*

(b) Desert rats can live on diets without water for long periods but normal rats cannot. Figure 4(3).19 shows the concentration of urea in urine produced by both types of rats when given the same diets.

(i) State the concentration of urea produced in the urine of the normal rats at eight days. *(1)*

(ii) Calculate the difference in concentration of urea produced by both rats when they have had no water for eight days. *(1)*

(iii) What change is seen in the working of the kidneys of normal rats after nine days? *(1)*

(iv) Urea contains nitrogen. Name the class of food which should be reduced in the diet for a smaller amount of urea to be produced. *(1)*

(v) On a sheet of graph paper draw the expected shape of the graph to show the volume of water excreted against diet per day for the normal rat. *(3)*

(WJEC)

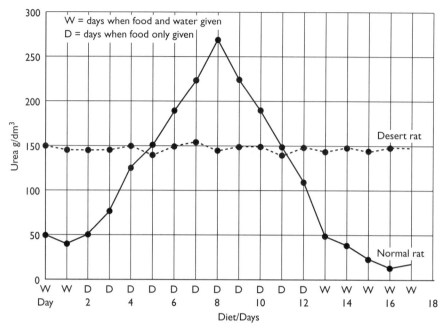

Fig. 4(3).19

▷ **Question 2**   (a)   The diagram shows a human foetus inside a uterus.

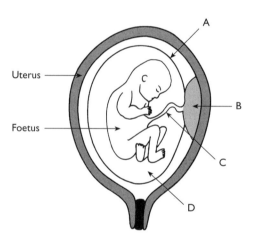

Fig. 4(3).20

(i) Name parts A and B.

A _____

B _____   *(2)*

(ii) Give **one** function for each of parts C and D.

C _____

D _____   *(2)*

(iii) Give **two** reasons which suggest that the foetus shown in the diagram is not about to be born.

1. _____

2. _____   *(2)*

(b)   Table 4(3).4 shows some substances that are exchanged between a mother and her foetus.

Table 4(3).4

Substance	Direction of exchange	Function
Carbon dioxide	Mother to foetus	For foetus to make red blood cells
		Excretion
	Mother to foetus	For respiration
	Foetus to mother	Excretion

(i)   Use some of the following words or phrases to complete the table.
Calcium; Foetus to mother; Haemoglobin; Iron; Mother to foetus;
Oxygen; Urea   *(4)*

(ii) Explain why a women should drink extra milk during pregnancy.   *(2)*

(ii) Suggest why a pregnant women might want to urinate more often in late
pregnancy.   *(1)*

(NICCEA)

▷ **Question 3**   (a)   The diagram shows a section through the mammal's kidney. Name the parts 1, 2 and 3.

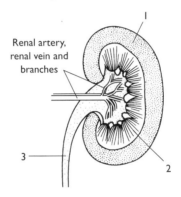

Renal artery,
renal vein and
branches

Fig. 4(3).21

Table 4(3).5

Rate of blood flow in kidneys	Rate of filtration into kidney tubules (nephrons)	Rate of urine passing out of kidneys
1.2dm³ per minute	0.12dm³ per minute	1.5dm³ per minute

(b)   The table gives information about the human kidney.

(i)   What percentage of blood passing into the kidney is filtered into the kidney
tubules?   *(1)*

(ii) Where in the kidney (part 1, 2 or 3 in the diagram) does filtration take place? *(1)*

(iii) About 17.2dm³ are filtered from the blood into the kidney tubules per day, yet
only 1.5dm³ of urine are excreted. What happens to the other 15.7dm³?   *(2)*

Table 4(3).6

	Urine lost per day (dm³)	Sweat lost per day (dm³)	Salt (sodium chloride) lost per day	
			In urine (g)	In sweat (g)
Normal day	1.5	0.5	18.0	1.5
Cold day	2.0	0.0	19.5	0.0
Hot day	0.375	2.0	13.5	6.0

(c)   The table shows the average amounts of urine, sweat and salt (sodium chloride) lost
on a normal day, a cold day and a hot day. (Assume that food and drink are the same
on all days.)

(i)   Why is more urine lost on a cold day than on a normal day?   *(2)*

(ii) Why do you think the total amount of salt lost on each of the three days is the
same?   *(2)*

(iii) The minimum amount of urine excreted in a day is 0.375 dm³. Why do you think the kidneys always produced some urine?   *(2)*

(iv) What **must** someone losing more than 7dm³ of sweat in a day do in order to remain healthy?   *(2)*

(SEG)

 ANSWERS TO EXAMINATION QUESTIONS

▷ **Question 1**   (a)   (i)   cortex
                            (ii) glucose has been reabsorbed back into the blood
                            (iii) urine

                     (b)   (i)   270g/dm³
                            (ii) No water for 8 days = day 10 of the experiment.
                                  Concentration of urea for normal rats = 190g/dm³
                                  Concentration of urea for desert rats = 150g/dm³
                                  ∴ difference in concentration = 40g/dm³
                            (iii) There is a lower concentration of urea in the urine than there is for desert rats.
                            (iv) protein
                            (v)

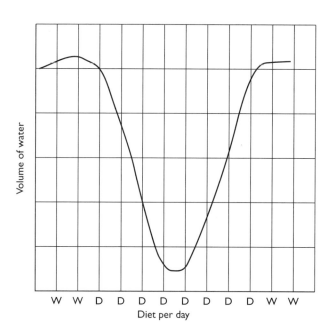

Fig. 4(3).22

▷ **Question 2**   (a)   (i)   A = amnion (amniotic sac)
                                  B = placenta
                            (ii) C – carries food and oxygen to the foetus; carries waste away from the foetus
                                  D – cushions the foetus from bumps
                            (iii) 1.   Babies are usually born head first.
                                  2.   There is a plug of mucus in the cervix.
                                  3.   It is not fully grown (there is a lot of space around it inside the uterus).

                     (b)   (i)

Table 4(3).7

Substance	Direction of exchange	Function
Iron	Mother to foetus	For the foetus to make red blood cells
Carbon dioxide	**Foetus to mother**	Excretion
Oxygen	Mother to foetus	For respiration
Urea	Foetus to mother	Excretion

(ii) The foetus needs calcium for its bones to develop properly. It needs protein for growth. Milk contains calcium and protein.

(iii) The foetus has grown quite big and is pushing down on the bladder, so it cannot fill properly.

▷ **Question 3**   (a) 1 = cortex; 2 = medulla; 3 = ureter

(b) (i) 10 per cent

(ii) part 1

(iii) It is reabsorbed from the nephron into the blood.

(c) (i) Less water is lost through sweating on a cold day; the water is lost instead in urine.

(ii) The salt content of the body is maintained at a constant level to avoid problems of osmosis; if a constant amount of salt is present in the diet, a constant total amount will be lost.

(iii) Urine is a solution of the waste urea and other toxins, which must be removed at intervals from the body.

(iv) Consume enough water and salts to maintain minimum amounts in the body.

▷ **STUDENT'S ANSWER WITH EXAMINER'S COMMENTS**

The pituitary gland is attached to the base of the brain. One of the hormones produced by this gland is the antidiuretic hormone (ADH). The amount of this hormone in the blood controls the amount of water excreted by the kidneys.

(a) You drink a very large quantity of water in a very short time. Your body has to control the amount of water in the blood. Describe how ADH achieves this.

*'This is an excellent answer. It is logical and well-structured and contains important **key words**, e.g. target organ, nephron, permeable. This student obviously understands how ADH works.'*

ADH is transported in the plasma all round the body. ✓ *It has an effect in the kidney –*

this is the target organ. ✓ *It makes part of the nephron more permeable* ✓ *to water*

(second coiled tubule and collecting duct), ✓ *so more water is reabsorbed into the the*

blood, and less urine is produced. ✓   (5)

(b) The action of ADH, in controlling the amount of water excreted by the kidneys, is an example of homeostasis. Explain why.

'A good definition and explanation of a complex process.'

Homeostasis means keeping conditions inside the body constant, at an ideal level.

ADH helps to keep the amount of water in the body constant – this is

osmoregulation.   (2)

                                                                                                                    (SEG)

SUMMARY

▷   homeostasis means keeping conditions inside the body constant at an optimum level. This is necessary so the body can work efficiently;

▷   regulation of body temperature, blood sugar levels, water balance and removal of waste products are all example of homeostasis;

▷   body temperature is regulated by the skin. The main mechanism involves vasodilation (widening) of capillaries if temperature increases, and vasoconstriction if temperature decreases. Sweating, shivering and erection of skin hairs also occurs to regulate temperature;

▷   the kidney is responsible for excretion of urea, a poisonous substance made in the liver, and for water balance;

▷   the nephrons (kidney tubules) are the site of ultrafiltration and reabsorption of useful materials;

▷   waste products (water, urea, salts) pass through the ureters to the bladder and are removed in urine;

▷   the amount of urine produced depends on the levels of excess water in the body;

▷   ADH is a hormone which regulates the amount of water in the urine;

▷   if the kidneys fail, harmful waste products and waste accumulate in the body and cause illness. This can be avoided by kidney dialysis or a kidney transplant;

▷   the placenta maintains constant conditions for the foetus during pregnancy.

4.4

Humans as organisms
Being healthy

GETTING STARTED

| MEG | SEG | NEAB | LONDON | WJEC | NICCEA | SEB |

Good health is quite difficult to define: it is more than just the absence of disease. When we are healthy, the systems of our body are working efficiently, and we have a positive attitude to life. Ill-health can be caused by a variety of factors: genetic problems, pathogens causing infection, unsuitable life-style, abuse of drugs, etc.

TOPIC	STUDY	REVISION I	REVISION 2
Health and disease			
Factors contributing to good health			
Factors contributing to disease			
Defences against disease			
Natural defences			
Artificial defences			
Drugs and the body			
Benefits and risks of drug use			
Types of drugs			

WHAT YOU NEED TO KNOW

▷ **Health and disease**

> ### Key points
>
> ▷ when we are healthy, the systems of the body work efficiently, and we have a positive outlook on life;
>
> ▷ it is impossible to guarantee good health, but all of use can make life choices which increase the probability of being healthy;
>
> ▷ there are many causes of disease, e.g. genetic problems, pathogens, lifestyle factors, etc. Some of these are outside our control, but many of them can be reduced or eliminated by careful lifestyle choices.

The World Health Organisation has defined health as:

'a state of complete mental, physical and social well-being, and not merely the absence of disease.'

In order to be healthy, we must:

▷ have a body that is working efficiently;
▷ have a positive mental attitude to our lives, and be able to relax and enjoy ourselves, and cope with stress;
▷ look after ourselves properly, by eating a balanced diet and exercising, and not abusing drugs.

Factors contributing to good health

It is impossible to guarantee good health, but there are many things we can all do to increase the probability of our being healthy, e.g.

▷ eat a balanced diet, with the right energy value for our needs;
▷ exercise regularly to keep fit;
▷ get enough sleep;
▷ make sure we have food and water which is free from infection;
▷ make time for relaxation and things we enjoy,
▷ avoid drugs;
▷ keep ourselves safe to avoid accidents;
▷ have health problems checked promptly;
▷ be vaccinated against common diseases.

Factors contributing to disease

There are many different causes of disease: some of them are within our control, and others are not. Some diseases may have more than one factor causing them, e.g. a person may have a high cholesterol level (leading to heart disease) caused by a faulty gene, and made worse by a poor diet.

The main causes of disease are:

▷ **Genetic**: the person inherits a faulty gene from his or her parents. Examples of genetic diseases include cystic fibrosis, haemophilia, Huntingdon's disease, sickle-cell anaemia.
▷ **Pathogens**: these are micro-organisms (bacteria, viruses, fungi) which cause infectious diseases. They can be caught from other people, or from contaminated food or water. Examples of diseases caused by pathogens include measles, TB, flu, AIDS, food poisoning.
▷ **Poor diet**: this may be due to a shortage of a particular nutrient (in which case it is called a deficiency disease), shortage of all nutrients, or excess of some nutrients. Examples of diseases caused by poor diet include scurvy (lack of Vitamin C), anaemia (lack of iron), tooth decay (excess sugar), and heart disease (excess saturated fats).

- **Degenerative diseases**: these are due to wear and tear on the body as we get older, or the accumulation of waste products or toxins in the body. Examples of degenerative conditions include osteoarthritis (damage to joints), Alzheimer's disease, deteriorating sight and hearing.
- **Environmental diseases**: these are due to factors in our lifestyle or surroundings. Examples of risk factors include smoking, pollution, drugs and stress. Some types of cancer are linked to environmental factors, e.g. lung cancer is linked to smoking.

Some diseases do not seem to have a single obvious cause; asthma may be due to both genetic and environmental factors.

▷ Defences against disease

These are the ways that the body can fight infectious diseases. These diseases are caused by pathogens (bacteria, viruses and fungi) which enter the body and reproduce there, causing harm. Pathogens can be transferred by direct contact with an infected person, through wounds in the skin, through swallowing contaminated food or water, or by being breathed in.

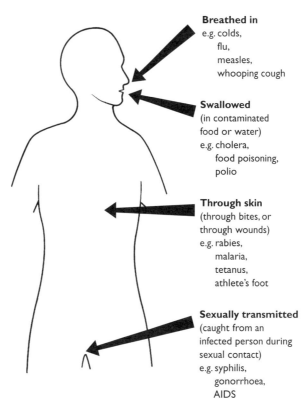

Breathed in
e.g. colds,
  flu,
  measles,
  whooping cough

Swallowed
(in contaminated
food or water)
e.g. cholera,
  food poisoning,
  polio

Through skin
(through bites, or
through wounds)
e.g. rabies,
  malaria,
  tetanus,
  athlete's foot

Sexually transmitted
(caught from an
infected person during
sexual contact)
e.g. syphilis,
  gonorrhoea,
  AIDS

Fig. 4(4). 1 Transmission of diseases

Natural defences

Key points
▷ these are mechanisms which are always in place to prevent entry of pathogens or to destroy them once they are inside the body;
▷ the skin and mucous membranes act as a barrier against pathogens;
▷ acid in the stomach may kill pathogens ingested through the gut;
▷ white blood cells destroy pathogens which have entered the body;
▷ immunity (due to antibodies made by lymphocytes) may last for many years.

Role of skin

The skin is a tough, waterproof barrier to the entry of pathogens. The outer layer (the epidermis) is made of dead cells which are resistant to infection. If the skin is broken, e.g. by a cut, or by an animal bite, pathogens may enter: several diseases are transmitted in this way, e.g. malaria by mosquito bites, rabies by mammal bites.

Role of the mucous membranes in the respiratory system

The air passages in the respiratory system (nasal passages, trachea, bronchi) are lined with ciliated cells and goblet cells. The goblet cells produce mucus which traps dust particles and pathogens, and the cilia beat to move the mucus away from the lungs.

Cilia are damaged by chemicals in cigarette smoke, so this system does not work properly in smokers.

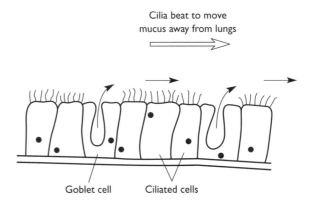

Fig. 4(4).2 Production of mucus by goblet cells

Role of chemicals in killing pathogens

It is relatively easy for pathogens to enter some parts of the body, but bacteriocidal chemicals prevent them from colonising these areas. For example:

▶ Pathogens may enter the gut in food or water. The stomach contains a strong acid which will kill them. However, if large numbers of pathogens enter the gut, the person may still become ill, because not all pathogens were killed or because of the toxins (poisons) they produced.
▶ Pathogens may get under the eyelids or into the ear-canal. They cannot colonise these areas because natural body secretions, e.g. tears and ear wax, contain chemicals which kill pathogens.

Role of the blood

There are two main types of white blood cell, and both are very important in destroying pathogens which have entered the body:

1. phagocytes;
2. lymphocytes.

Phagocytes

Phagocytes can change shape to squeeze out of capillaries (through tiny gaps in the capillary walls). They can detect and move towards pathogens by a process called chemotaxis. When they reach pathogens, they can change shape to surround them. Chemicals made inside the phagocyte then destroy the pathogens.

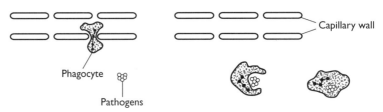

Fig. 4(4).3 Phagocytosis

Lymphocytes

When lymphocytes encounter pathogens inside the body they produce chemicals called antibodies. Antibodies are carried in the blood, and they stick to pathogens, causing them to clump together in large groups, or to burst.

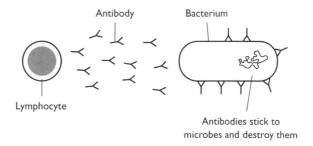

Fig. 4(4).4 Lymphocytes (white blood cells) make antibodies

The production of antibodies is called the immune response.

Antibodies:

- are specific to a particular type of pathogen, e.g. antibodies made to attack the measles virus would have no effect on the common cold virus;
- are made in very large amounts if we are suffering from an infection;
- can be made whenever that pathogen enters the body in the future, because lymphocytes can 'remember' how to do this. This is called **immunological memory**.

See p. 307 for more details about how antibodies are made.

In addition to this, **platelets** cause blood clotting when blood vessels are damaged. This helps to seal wounds and prevent the entry of pathogens (see p. 44 for further details of this process).

Artificial defences

Key points

- these are ways that the natural defence system of the body can be improved;
- vaccination (immunisation) causes antibody production which helps to defend the body against future attack by pathogens;
- ready-made antibodies can be injected into a person to give immediate protection against pathogens.

Immunisation (vaccination)

The purpose of immunisation is to cause antibody production without causing the symptoms of a disease.

Material from a pathogen (called the **antigen**) is injected into the patient. This material may be:

- dead pathogens;
- live weak pathogens which will not cause disease;
- parts of pathogens which will not cause disease.

Lymphocytes recognise that there is a pathogen in the body, and produce **antibodies** to destroy it. This is called the **primary response**.

It is an advantage to be immunised because the lympocytes can now 'remember' how to make antibodies to that particular pathogen. If at some point in the future the same pathogens enter the body again, lymphocytes will be able to make antibodies to destroy them immediately. This is the **secondary response**, and it will kill the pathogens before they can make the person ill.

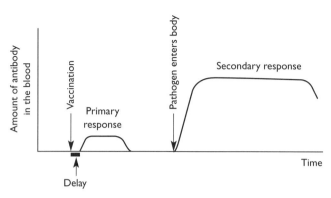

Fig. 4(4).5 Vaccination and the immune response

There are three main differences between the primary and secondary responses:

1. there is delay before antibodies are produced in the primary response, but in the secondary response they are produced immediately;
2. larger amounts of antibody are made in the secondary response;
3. the antibodies remain in the blood for longer in the secondary response.

See pp. 307–9 for more details about immunisation.

Injections of anti-sera
If a person is at serious risk of infection and needs to be protected from pathogens immediately, they can be given injections of an **anti-serum**. This is purified from animal blood and contains antibodies. The animal antibodies circulate in the person's blood, and stick to pathogens, destroying them. This is very useful if there is no time for the person to build up their own supply of antibodies, e.g. if they have been infected (by an animal bite or wound) and are at risk of rabies or tetanus.

The antibodies will kill the pathogen on this occasion but the person is not protected in future because their own lymphocytes have not 'learned' to make antibodies.

Injections of anti-sera are useful in an emergency, but should not replace a proper vaccination programme

REVISION ACTIVITY 1   Match the words in the box to the correct definitions.

antigen	vaccination	genetic disease
antibody	deficiency disease	degenerative disease
pathogen	infectious disease	environmental disease
toxins	immunity	anti-serum
bacteriocidal	chemotaxis	immune response

(a) _____   an organism which causes disease

(b) _____   purified animal blood containing ready-made antibodies

(c) _____   a disease caused by lack of a necessary substance

(d) _____   a disease caused by faulty genes

(e) _____   a disease caused by a pathogen

(f) _____   a disease caused by wear and tear on the body

(g) _____   a disease caused by lifestyle factors

(h) _____   poisons

(i) _____   chemicals made by lymphocytes to kill pathogens in the body

(j) _____   white blood cells can detect and move towards pathogens

(k) _____   white blood cells produce antibodies

(l) _____   the part of a pathogen which is recognised by lymphocytes, and causes antibodies to be produced.

(m)_____   a substance which kills bacteria

(n) _____   deliberately injecting harmless antigens into a person

(o) _____   when a person is protected from a disease because they can make antibodies, we say they have this.

REVISION ACTIVITY 2   Sort out the following diseases to show their main cause.

measles	heart disease	Alzheimer's disease
cystic fibrosis	haemophilia	AIDS
lung cancer	flu	rickets
scurvy	asthma	asbestosis
osteoarthritis	anaemia	Huntingdon's disease

Table 4(4).1

Type of disease	Examples
degenerative diseases	
deficiency diseases	
genetic diseases	
infectious diseases	
environmental diseases	

Two of these diseases do not have **one** clear cause. Which are they?

▷ **Drugs and the body**

Drugs are chemicals which change the way the body works.

In Britain, some drugs are **legal**: they can be bought at a chemist, or prescribed by a doctor, or they can be bought by adults. Examples of legal drugs include:

alcohol
antibiotics
aspirin
caffeine (in tea, coffee, coke)
nicotine
paracetamol
tranquilizers

Other drugs are **illegal**: it is against the law to sell them or to possess them. Some of these are legal drugs being used by the wrong people, i.e. not the people for whom they were prescribed.

Examples of illegal drugs include:

amphetamines
cannabis
cocaine
ecstasy
heroin
LSD
steroids*
solvents
tranquilizers*

* = can be prescribed legally, but it is illegal to sell them to others.

The laws about legal and illegal drugs vary from country to country.

Benefits and risks of drug use

> **Key points**
>
> ▷ drug use **always** involves a risk to the user;
>
> ▷ medical drugs are prescribed if there is likely to be a clear benefit to the patient;
>
> ▷ medical drugs may cure a disease, e.g. antibiotics, or may mask the symptoms, e.g. painkillers;
>
> ▷ non-medical drugs are normally taken because the person likes the way it makes them feel;
>
> ▷ some legal drugs are high risk, and are associated with thousands of deaths each year, e.g. cigarette smoking;
>
> ▷ illegal drugs are often high-risk because the actual dose is unknown.

Important terms

Tolerance:	this is the way that the body gets used to some types of drugs. The person then needs to take more of the drug to get the same effect.
Dependence:	this means that the person gets used to taking the drug, and feels that they cannot do without it. There are two types of dependence: 1. physical dependence, where the person becomes physically ill if they do not get the drug; 2. psychological dependence, where the person feels that they want or need the drug so much that they could not do without it.
Addiction:	this means that the person is so dependent on a drug that they are doing serious harm to themselves, or to society.
Withdrawal symptoms:	this is how the body reacts if a drug it has been used to is no longer available. The effects can be serious, and may last two or three weeks.

Benefits of drug use

The benefits depend on the **type** of drug taken, the **amount** which is taken, and the length of **time** it is taken for. Possible benefits include the following:

▷ to kill pathogens, and fight infection within the body (antibiotics);
▷ to lessen the symptoms of disease, so the person is less uncomfortable (painkillers);
▷ to calm people down and help them to sleep if they are anxious (tranquilizers, sleeping tablets);
▷ to lessen depression (anti-depressants);
▷ to help people relax with friends in social situations.

Risk of drug use

There are six main risks associated with drug use:

1. People **react** to drugs in different ways. Some people are allergic to some drugs, or particularly sensitive to them, so a drug that is safe for one person may be a danger to another.
2. If too much of a drug is taken (an **overdose**), the person may be severely affected, and may even die.
3. If drugs are taken regularly over a **long period** of time, many systems of the body may be damaged. This can cause serious health problems.
4. If drugs are taken during **pregnancy**, the foetus may be affected, e.g. by becoming addicted to being the drug itself, or by being harmed by the drug. Some drugs increase the risk of premature birth and of stillbirth.
5. If drugs are **mixed**, the dangers increase significantly. Even relatively low doses of drugs taken together can cause serious health problems.

6. Many drugs affect **co-ordination and concentration**, so people are more likely to have accidents after taking them. They may also affect moods, making the person more aggressive or violent, or may make people more anxious or withdrawn.

There are more risks with illegal drugs than with legal drugs because:

▶ There is no guarantee that the drug is pure. Many drugs are cut (mixed) with cheaper substances, e.g. sugar or talc, or with other drugs.

▶ There is no way knowing what the dose is. The amount of Ecstasy in one tablet may be completely different to the amount in another tablet from a different batch, or even in the same batch. This means that it is easy to overdose.

▶ Some illegal drugs are injected. This is particularly dangerous for three reasons:
1. Dirty or shared needles can cause blood poisoning and infections. Some of these can be very serious, e.g. hepatitis, AIDS.
2. Blood vessels and muscles can be damaged by the injections, causing abscesses and gangrene.
3. The drug is injected straight into the bloodstream and it reaches the brain within seconds, so the effects are very sudden.

Types of drugs

Key points

▶ there are many different ways of classifying drugs. We will use the effect they have on the body to classify them into five main groups;

▶ anti-microbial drugs fight pathogens in the body;

▶ stimulants speed up the way the nervous system works;

▶ depressants slow down the way the nervous system works;

▶ hallucinogens alter perception;

▶ analgesics reduce pain.

Summary of types of drugs

Table 4(4).2

Type of drug	Effect on the body	Examples
Anti-microbial drugs	These drugs are given to kill microbes in the body, i.e. to fight infections. There are different types of drugs to kill bacteria, viruses, fungi and protoctists.	Antibiotics, e.g. penicillin Anti-viral drugs, e.g. AZT Anti-fungal drugs, e.g. Nystatin
Stimulants	These drugs speed up the way the nervous system works, so the person becomes more alert. Too much can cause anxiety and panic attacks.	Tobacco Amphetamines Ecstasy Cocaine Caffeine
Depressants	These drugs slow down the way the nervous system works, so the person becomes more sleepy. Overdose can cause unconsciousness.	Alcohol Solvents Tranquillisers Barbiturates
Hallucinogens	These drugs cause hallucinations – the person perceives something which is not really there.	LSD Cannabis
Analgesics	These drugs block the part of the brain responsible for feeling pain.	Aspirin Paracetamol Heroin Morphine

Anti-microbial drugs
See pp. 309–10 for details of the drugs used to kill pathogens inside the body.

Stimulants

These drugs speed up the way the nervous system works, so the person feels more awake and alert. Too much can cause anxiety and panic attacks.

Examples include tobacco, amphetamines, Ecstasy, cocaine and caffeine.

Tobacco

About 30% of adults in Britain smoke, and tobacco is one of the most widely used addictive substances in this country.

Cigarette smoke contains tar, nicotine, carbon monoxide and other gases. Over a long period of time these can seriously damage health because smokers are more likely to suffer from:

'Every year in Britain more than 100,000 people die from problems caused by smoking.'

▶ heart disease and circulatory problems, e.g. strokes, blood clots (nicotine causes arteries to narrow);
▶ cancer, particularly of the lungs, throat and mouth because tar is a carcinogen (chemical which increases the risk of cancer);
▶ bronchitis and chest infections, because chemicals in smoke kill cilia (tiny hairs which keep the lungs and airways clean);
▶ emphysema, where the alveoli swell and burst, making gas exchange more difficult;
▶ premature babies or stillborn babies are more common in women who smoke during pregnancy;
▶ it may increase the risk of cot-death.

Ecstasy

This is an illegal stimulant drug. It is sold as tablets, and is often associated with raves. The effects start about 20 minutes after taking it, and last for several hours. They include feelings of friendliness and extra energy, but when this wears off the person feels very down. Large amounts can cause anxiety and confusion. Ecstacy has been linked to several deaths in Britain, because:

▶ it has caused heatstroke when taken by people dancing at raves;
▶ if the person drinks **too much** water (to avoid heatstroke), this may make the brain swell and cause death.

Ecstacy should be avoided by anyone who has epilepsy or heart problems, because it can make these worse.

Depressants

These drugs slow down the way the nervous system works so the person feels sleepy, and may become unconscious if too much is taken.

Examples include alcohol, solvents, tranquillisers and barbiturates.

Alcohol

This is a legal depressant drug. It is made by yeasts feeding on sugar in anaerobic conditions; the process is called fermentation.

The amount of alcohol in drinks varies,

e.g. beer is about 5% alcohol,
wine is about 10% alcohol,
spirits are about 50% alcohol.

Alcohol is normally measured in units. One unit is the amount of alcohol in:

▶ half a pint of beer, lager or cider;
▶ one glass of wine; or
▶ one measure of spirits.

The effects of alcohol start about ten minutes after it is drunk and last for several hours. They include:

▶ feeling more relaxed, and losing your inhibitions;
▶ loss of judgement, i.e. you are less capable of making sensible decisions;
▶ loss of muscle co-ordination, e.g. slurred speech, double vision, staggering;
▶ sedative effect; the person feels sleepy and may become unconscious.

What are the dangers of alcohol?

These can be divided into two groups:

1. **Short-term dangers,** i.e. from drinking a lot of alcohol at one time, include:

   ▶ being sick (and the person may choke on their vomit);
   ▶ lack of co-ordination, so the person is more likely to have an accident and injure themself (particularly if they are driving);
   ▶ becoming unconscious.

2. **Long-term dangers,** i.e. from drinking alcohol regularly over months or years include:

   ▶ liver damage (cirrhosis);
   ▶ heart disease, because alcohol causes hardening of the arteries;
   ▶ brain damage (due to death of brain cells);
   ▶ stomach ulcers and damage to the pancreas;
   ▶ addiction.

In 1996, doctors recommended that men should drink less than 28 units of alcohol per week and women should drink less than 21 units of alcohol per week.

Solvents

These are found in products like aerosols, e.g. deodorant, furniture polish, glue, lighter fluid and petrol. They are **extremely dangerous** – they can kill a person the first time they are used.

Solvents are inhaled (breathed in) and the effects start immediately, lasting about half an hour. They include feeling 'drunk', but repeated inhaling can cause dizziness, loss of control and unconsciousness.

Why are solvents so dangerous?

▶ If they are squirted straight into the mouth, e.g. deodorant, they can cause immediate death because the air passages (bronchi and bronchioles) in the lungs close up.
▶ If the person is sniffing solvents in a plastic bag, they may suffocate.
▶ Some solvents (e.g. butane gas, aerosols) cause heart failure.
▶ If the person becomes unconscious and then is sick, they can choke on their own vomit.
▶ The person may become confused and have an accident, particularly if they are on their own, e.g. on a riverbank, near a railway line.
▶ If solvents are used over a long period of time, they can cause liver and kidney damage.

Analgesics

These are painkillers which work by blocking the part of the brain responsible for feeling pain.

Examples include aspirin, paracetamol, heroin and morphine.

Aspirin

This is a legal analgesic drug. It is widely available and is sold over the counter to treat minor pain, e.g. headaches. It is also important in reducing swelling, and in breaking down blood clots, so is sometimes used to reduce the risk of heart attacks in vulnerable people.

However, it can cause irritation of the stomach lining and ulcers in some people, so it is not suitable for all adults. It should never be given to children under the age of 12 years because it can cause liver damage.

Overdose can be fatal.

Heroin

Heroin is sometimes legally prescribed by doctors, but for most users it is an illegal drug. Heroin can be smoked, sniffed or injected.

When heroin is taken, the person feels warm and happy, and may become drowsy. However, they rapidly develop tolerance to the drug, and usually become physically and psychologically dependent on it. If they do not take the drug, they can have severe withdrawal symptoms.

An overdose of heroin causes unconsciousness, and can result in death.

SOLUTIONS TO REVISION ACTIVITIES

S1 (a) <u>pathogen</u>   an organism which causes disease

    (b) <u>anti-serum</u>   purified animal blood containing ready-made antibodies

    (c) <u>deficiency disease</u>   a disease caused by lack of necessary substance

    (d) <u>genetic disease</u>   a disease caused by faulty genes

    (e) <u>infectious disease</u>   a disease caused by a pathogen

    (f) <u>degenerative disease</u>   a disease caused by wear and tear on the body

    (g) <u>environmental disease</u>   a disease caused by lifestyle factors

    (h) <u>toxins</u>   poisons

    (i) <u>antibodies</u>   chemicals made by lymphocytes to kill pathogens in the body

    (j) <u>chemotaxis</u>   white blood cells can detect and move towards pathogens

    (k) <u>immune response</u>   white blood cells produce antibodies

    (l) <u>antigen</u>   the part of a pathogen which is recognised by lymphocytes, and causes antibodies to be produced.

    (m) <u>bacteriocidal</u>   a substance which kills bacteria

    (n) <u>vaccination</u>   deliberately injecting harmless antigens into a person

    (o) <u>immunity</u>   when a person is protected from a disease because they can make antibodies, we say they have this.

S2 Asthma, Alzheimer's disease and heart disease do not have one clear cause (genetic and environmental factors seem to be involved).

Table 4(4).3

Type of disease	Examples
degenerative diseases	osteoarthritis, Alzheimer's disease
deficiency diseases	rickets, scurvy, anaemia
genetic diseases	cystic fibrosis, haemophilia, Huntingdon's disease
infectious diseases	flu, measles, AIDS
environmental diseases	lung cancer, asbestosis

EXAMINATION QUESTIONS

▷ **Question 1**   This headline and table appeared in a newspaper article.

Table 4(4).4
How much schoolchildren
drink in a week

Schoolchildren risk health with heavy drinking

Amount drunk* (units of alcohol)	Aged 11 (%)	Aged 12 (%)	Aged 13 (%)	Aged 14 (%)	Aged 15 (%)
None	75.7	64.1	56.7	44.7	31.4
1–6 units	20.1	29	29.7	34.2	38.8
7–10 units	1.7	3.5	5.4	8.8	13.3
11–14 units	1.6	1.4	3.7	5.2	5.4
15–20 units	0.7	1	2.1	3.8	4.6
21+ units	0.3	1	2.4	3.3	7.5

(* one unit = half a pint beer/one glass of wine/one measure of spirit)

(a) (i) Calculate the percentage of 13-year-old children who drink more than 10 units of alcohol per week. Show your working.

Answer _____%   *(1)*

(ii) Calculate how many pupils this would be, on average, in a year group of 180 13-year-old pupils. Show your working.

Answer _____%   *(2)*

(b) Fourteen-year-old Elaine was asked why she drank alcohol. She said, 'I think it helps you to unwind when you get home from school, or if you've had a really bad day.'
Suggest how alcohol has this effect.

_____

_____

_____

_____ *(2)*

(NEAB)

▷ **Question 2** (a) Explain as fully as you can how the body's white blood cells respond to infections.   *(6)*

(b) In 1988 a 'one-shot' vaccine was introduced to protect children from three common virus diseases of childhood – measles, mumps and rubella. This one-shot vaccine is called MMR vaccine. The viruses used in MMR are all non-virulent strains.
(i) Describe how these non-virulent strains are produced.   *(2)*

In autumn 1992, two brands of MMR vaccine were withdrawn in Britain. There were fears of possible links with meningitis. Meningitis is a serious illness which is sometimes fatal. Read the following 'vaccine facts'.

In 1988, before the MMR was introduced in Britain, there were 86,000 cases of measles and 16 deaths. In 1991 there were 9680 cases and no deaths.

1 in 15 children develop pneumonia or middle ear infections following an attack of measles.

The only danger from rubella is to the unborn baby if a pregnant woman contracts the disease. Before MMR there were about 20 babies born each year with congenital rubella syndrome. The vaccine has reduced this to around four per year.

Measles is widely perceived as a trivial illness so the risks of even mild attacks of meningitis become substantial when set against the benefits of protection.

Early reports of children developing mild attacks of meningitis following MMR were discounted by the Department of Health when statistics were produced to show that the risks from other diseases were greater.

Following the whooping cough controversy during the 1970s, most parents nowadays probably suspect that the vaccine may, rarely, cause serious brain damage. But they are prepared to take the risk on their child's behalf because whooping cough is such a devastating illness in the very young.

Despite the Chief Medical Officer's strong assurance that risks are low, his decision to withdraw two out of three brands of measles vaccines is bound to raise doubts about the benefits of vaccination.

(ii) You have been asked to give advice to some parents on vaccination against child-hood illnesses.
Summarise the points for and against childhood vaccination.
You should always refer to the 'vaccine facts' in your answer, but you will not receive credit for simply repeating the information. *(8)*

(c) Hepatitis B vaccine is produced by using genetically engineered bacteria to produce proteins identical to the hepatitis antigen.

Use your knowledge of the structure of DNA to explain as fully as you can how the proteins are produced. *(6)*
(NEAB)

ANSWERS TO EXAMINATION QUESTIONS

▷ **Question 1** (a) (i) Total of 13-year-old pupils drinking more than 10 units per week = 3.7 + 2.1 + 2.4
= 8.2%

(ii) In a year group of 180 pupils this would be
$$180 \times \frac{8.2}{100} = 14.76$$

Around 15 pupils aged 13 drink more than 10 units of alcohol per week.

(b) Alcohol is a depressant drug (1);
it slows down the way the brain works, (1) so she feels relaxed.

▷ **Question 2** This is quite a difficult question, requiring well-organised answers to gain high marks. Look at the number of marks available for each part, and plan your answer carefully.

(a) There are two types of white blood cells which respond in different ways.
Phagocytes can detect and move towards pathogens. (1)
This is chemotaxis. (1)
They change shape to surround them. (1)
They then destroy the pathogens using enzymes. (1)
Lymphocytes recognise pathogens as foreign. (1)
They make chemicals called antibodies. (1)
Antibodies travel in the blood. (1)
They stick to pathogens and destroy them, (1) e.g. by making them burst.

(b) (i) They can be:
▷ developed by genetic engineering;
▷ developed by selective breeding over many years.
(ii) There are lots of ways to answer this question. It is probably best to write in two main paragraphs (for and against vaccination). Be careful that you use the infor-mation given, and do not just repeat it.
Credit would be given for points like:

'You should have read through all the facts carefully before beginning to write.'

For childhood vaccination

▷ Childhood vaccination reduces the **number** and **severity** of cases of measles: in 1991 there were no measles deaths.
▷ The number of cases fell by almost 90% between 1988 and 1991 (from 86,000 to 9680).
▷ Children infected by measles are at risk of developing other serious diseases, e.g. pneu-monia and ear infections. This happens to over 6% of children who catch measles.
▷ Children vaccinated against MMR are protected for life. This means that when a woman is pregnant she cannot be infected by measles, mumps or rubella, so her foetus is protected.
▷ The number of babies born handicapped due to rubella infection in the uterus has fallen by 80% per year (from 20 to 5). These babies could have had heart disease, or have been born deaf or blind.
▷ The risk from meningitis is very low. Few children are affected and the cases of menin-gitis are mild.

Against childhood vaccination

▷ Any vaccine carries a small risk, and if a healthy child becomes ill as a result of a vaccination, it is an unacceptable risk.

▷ Measles is not a serious disease. It is safer to risk having measles than to risk catching meningitis, which can be fatal.

▷ If two-thirds of the MMR vaccines previously used have been withdrawn as unsafe, is it reasonable to have confidence in any MMR vaccines? If they were unsafe, they should not have been used on any child.

▷ Boys do not need to be vaccinated against rubella. It is only dangerous if passed to the foetus during pregnancy.

(c) The hepatitis antigen is a protein (1) found on the coat or envelope of the hepatitis virus. (1) The virus contains a gene to make that protein.

The vaccine can be produced by:

▷ cutting the gene out of the virus DNA or RNA using enzymes (restriction enzymes); (1)

▷ transferring the gene to bacteria, e.g. *E. coli*; (1)

▷ using a vector to carry the gene; (1)

▷ growing large amounts of the bacteria in a fermenter; (1)

▷ collecting and purifying the protein. (1)

▷ STUDENT'S ANSWER WITH EXAMINER'S COMMENTS

The table below shows the amount of alcohol in the blood of a party-goer in the hours following a party.

Table 4(4).5

Time after end of party (hours)	Amount of alcohol in party-goer's blood (mg per 100 cm³)
0	230
2	190
4	150
6	110

(a) (i) Add the vertical axis then plot the figures on the grid below.

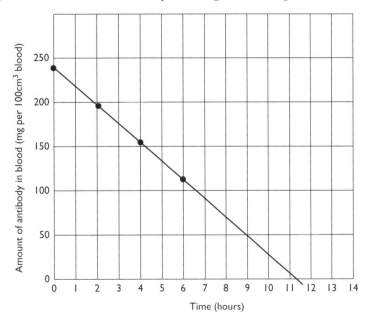

'Good. Points are plotted correctly and joined with a ruler.'

Fig. 4(4).6

(continued)

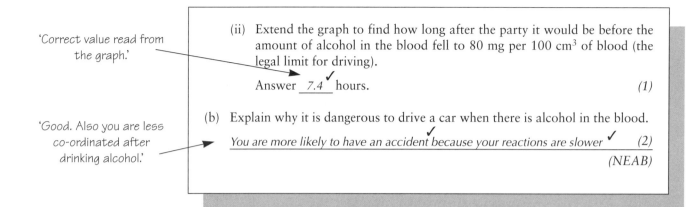

'Correct value read from the graph.'

(ii) Extend the graph to find how long after the party it would be before the amount of alcohol in the blood fell to 80 mg per 100 cm^3 of blood (the legal limit for driving).

Answer _7.4_ ✓ hours.   (1)

'Good. Also you are less co-ordinated after drinking alcohol.'

(b) Explain why it is dangerous to drive a car when there is alcohol in the blood.

You are more likely to have an accident ✓ because your reactions are slower ✓   (2)

(NEAB)

SUMMARY

▷   The body has several structures to prevent entry of pathogens, e.g. tough, waterproof skin; cilia and mucus to trap pathogens in the respiratory tract; acid in the stomach to kill pathogens.

▷   White blood cells attack pathogens which enter the body.

▷   Phagocytes engulf and destroy pathogens.

▷   Lymphocytes make antibodies to destroy pathogens – this is immunity.

▷   Vaccination (deliberate exposure to harmless antigens) makes a person immune to a particular pathogen.

▷   Drugs are chemicals which change the way the body works, and all drugs carry a risk for the person who uses them.

▷   Drugs are classified into groups, depending on their effects on the body. The five main groups are: anti-microbial drugs; stimulant drugs; depressant drugs; hallucinogenic drugs and analgesic drugs.

Green plants as organisms

▷ **GETTING STARTED**

| MEG | SEG | NEAB | LONDON | WJEC | NICCEA | SEB |

Plants are vitally important to all other living things for three reasons:

1. they make their own food by photosynthesis, i.e. they do not depend on other organisms for food;
2. they are at the start of every food chain;
3. they make oxygen during photosynthesis; this replaces the oxygen used by all organisms when they respire.

In this chapter you will study photosynthesis, and see how leaves are adapted for this process. You will find out about uptake of water and minerals, and how these are moved around the plant. You will consider the patterns of plant growth, and the importance of hormones in this process.

TOPIC	STUDY	REVISION 1	REVISION 2
Leaf structure			
Photosynthesis			
Experiments with photosynthesis			
Limiting factors in photosynthesis			
Measuring the rate of photosynthesis			
Products of photosynthesis			
Uses of glucose			
Importance of oxygen			
Respiration in plants			
Experiments with respiration			
Photosynthesis, respiration and the compensation point			
Importance of minerals			
Importance of nitrate			
Importance of magnesium			
Uptake of water and minerals			
How is water absorbed?			
How are minerals absorbed?			
Transport of water and minerals			
Transport of water			
Transport of minerals			
Transport of sugars			
How sugar is moved around			
Evidence for translocation			
Reproduction in flowering plants			
Asexual reproduction			
Sexual reproduction			
Germination and growth			
Germination			
Growth			
Plant hormones			
What do plant hormones do?			
Commercial applications of plant hormones			

WHAT YOU NEED TO KNOW

▷ **Leaf structure**   Leaves are very important plant organs. They provide a large surface area for photosynthesis and transpiration to occur.

Key points
▶ most plants have a large number of thin, flat, green leaves;
▶ leaves contain several types of cell, each adapted to a particular function;
▶ many cells have chloroplasts – these contain chlorophyll, which traps light for photosynthesis;
▶ the lower surface of the leaf has stomata (pores) to allow gas exchange and transpiration to occur.

Most leaves contain five types of cells, arranged in layers, and a network of veins (see Fig. 5.1. and Table 5.1).

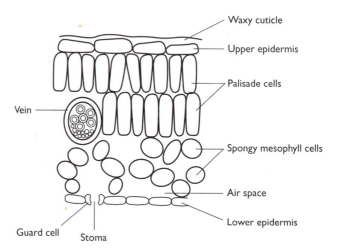

Fig. 5.1 Cells in a leaf

Table 5.1

Part of leaf	Structure	Function
Upper epidermins	A thin, flattened layer of cells at the top of the leaf.	Protect the other leaf cells and prevent excess water loss.
	They do not contain chloroplasts.	Allow light to pass through to the palisade cells.
	They make the waxy cuticle.	This protects and strengthens the leaf surface.
Palisade cells	Cylindrical cells packed tightly in one or two layers near the top of the leaf.	Close to the surface to obtain most light.
	They contain large numbers of chloroplasts (up to 100)	Chloroplasts contain chlorophyll to trap light energy for photosynthesis.
Spongy mesophyll cells	Loosely packed, rounded cells surrounded by air spaces.	Air spaces allow gases to diffuse to the palisade cells.
	They contain some chloroplasts.	Some photosynthesis occurs here (but less light is available).
Lower epidermis and guard cells	Edipermis cells are thin and flat.	They protect the lower surface of the leaf.
	Guard cells are found in pairs surrounding each stoma.	They can change shape to open and close the stomata, so they regulate gas exchange and transpiration.
Veins	They contain xylem and phloem tubes.	Xylem vessels carry water and minerals to the leaf.
		Phloem tubes carry sugars away from the leaf.
		The thick walls of xylem vessels help to support the leaf.

Leaves are usually arranged in a mosaic pattern around the stem so that they do not shade each other. Many plants can turn their leaves to face the sun, so that they get the maximum available light.

▷ **Photosynthesis**   This is the way that plants make their own food. It happens mainly in the palisade cells of leaves, and is a complex chemical reaction requiring energy from light.

Key points

▷ water from the soil, and carbon dioxide from the air are the raw materials;

▷ light energy is needed (light is trapped by chlorophyll);

▷ oxygen and glucose (sugar) are the products;

▷ most photosynthesis occurs in palisade cells of leaves.

Water from the soil travels up xylem vessels to the leaves and passes into palisade cells. Carbon dioxide diffuses into leaves through the stomata and moves through the air spaces to reach the palisade cells. Chlorophyll (inside chloroplasts) traps sunlight energy, and this powers the photosynthesis reaction.

$$\text{water + carbon dioxide} \xrightarrow{\text{light energy}} \text{glucose + oxygen}$$

The light energy splits water into the two elements hydrogen and oxygen (this is called photolysis).

The hydrogen combines with carbon dioxide to make glucose (a type of carbohydrate) and the oxygen is released through the stomata into the air.

When plants photosynthesise they use up carbon dioxide from the air. This is important because all living things make carbon dioxide when they respire, so plants stop the amount of carbon dioxide in the air from increasing.

An increase in atmospheric carbon dioxide is linked to the greenhouse effect.

Experiments with photosynthesis

1. Testing a leaf for starch

This simple test is used to show that photosynthesis has occurred (because the glucose made by photosynthesis is changed into starch and stored in leaves). There are five main steps:

Diagram	Step	Reason
1. 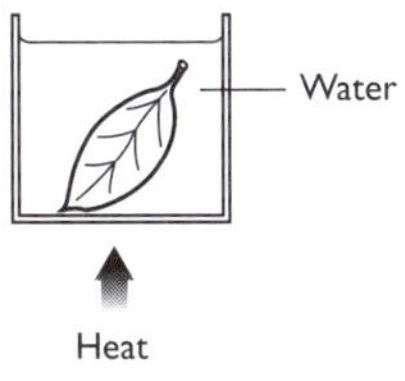 Water / Heat	Boil leaf in water for two minutes.	To kill leaf and make it permeable.
2. 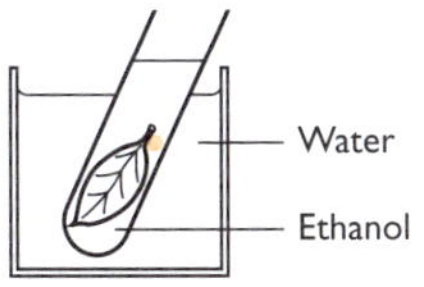 Water / Ethanol	Boil leaf in ethanol for five minutes.	To decolourise the leaf, i.e. to remove the chlorophyll.
3.  Water	Wash leaf in water.	To soften the leaf and remove traces of ethanol.
4. 	Lay leaf flat on a white tile and blot dry.	So that all parts of the leaf can be seen.
5. 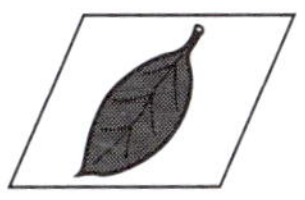	Cover the leaf in iodine solution.	To test for starch: black = starch present; orange/brown = no starch present.

Fig. 5.2 Testing a leaf for starch

REVISION ACTIVITY 1 ▓ State two safety precautions you would take when carrying out a starch test.

2. Is light necessary for photosynthesis?
Destarch a plant by leaving it in a dark place for 24 hours, then make a light-proof cover for part of one leaf. Leave the plant in a brightly lit area for 2–3 days, then test the leaf for starch.

3. Is carbon dioxide necessary for photosynthesis?
Destarch a plant by leaving it in a dark place for 24 hours. Place one leaf inside a conical flask containing sodium hydroxide or potassium hydroxide (this absorbs carbon dioxide), and leave it in a brightly lit place for 2–3 days. Test the leaf for starch.

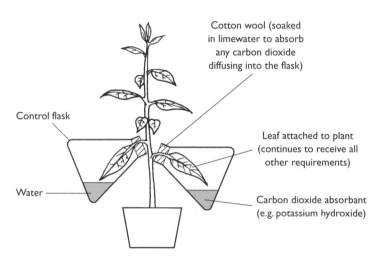

Fig. 5.3 Is carbon dioxide necessary for photosynthesis

4. Is chlorophyll necessary for photosynthesis?
Take a variegated leaf and carefully draw the leaf pattern. Test the leaf for starch, and compare with the green and white areas of the original leaf.

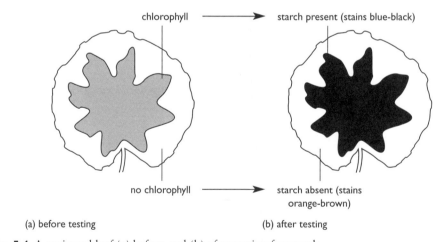

Fig. 5.4 A varigated leaf (a) before and (b) after testing for starch.

5. Pondweed experiment
This can be used to show that oxygen is made during photosynthesis, or to investigate the rate of photosynthesis. See p. 139 for details of the experiment.

▷ **Limiting factors in photosynthesis**
The rate of photosynthesis depends on the availability of raw materials, and the conditions at the time. If a material is in short supply, or conditions are wrong, we call this a limiting factor, and the rate will decrease.

Key points

▷ light, carbon dioxide, water and temperature can all act as limiting factors;

▷ the rate of photosynthesis is determined by the factor which is in short supply.

Imagine a plant in a dimly lit room. It will be photosynthesising slowly because there is not enough light energy available – light is acting as a limiting factor. If we increase the amount of light, the rate of photosynthesis will increase. Eventually the rate will stop increasing because another factor, e.g. carbon dioxide, is in short supply.

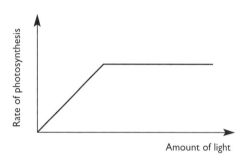

Fig. 5.5 Effect of light on photosynthesis

Measuring the rate of photosynthesis

This is usually done with pondweed, because it is easy to count the number of bubbles or measure the volumes of gas produced in a set time.

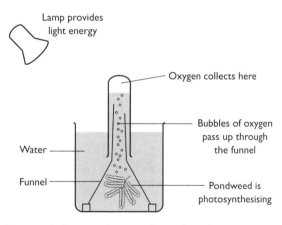

Fig. 5.6 Measuring the rate of photosynthesis with pondweed

Effect of light: this can be investigated by moving the lamp to different distances from the beaker.

'It is important to make sure it is a fair test.'

Effect of carbon dioxide: this can be investigated by adding sodium hydrogen carbonate to the beaker.

Effect of temperature: this can be investigated by adding ice or warm water to the beaker. As the temperature increases, the rate of photosynthesis will increase up to about 40°C, because enzymes are necessary for the photosynthesis reaction to occur efficiently. Above this temperature enzymes are denatured and the reaction stops.

Effect of water: this cannot be investigated using this apparatus because pondweed is an aquatic plant.

REVISION ACTIVITY 2   (a) Which factor is limiting in region A?
(b) Name one factor which could be limiting in region B.
(c) How could you find out if your answer to (b) was correct?

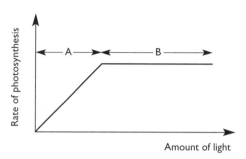

Fig. 5.7

▷ **Products of photosynthesis**   The two products of photosynthesis are glucose and oxygen.

Key points
▷ glucose is used to make energy, through respiration;
▷ glucose is changed into starch and stored;
▷ glucose is used to make cellular components, e.g. protein, cellulose, chlorophyll;
▷ oxygen is released into the air as a waste product.

Uses of glucose

The glucose made in photosynthesis can be transported to all parts of the plant by translocation. It can then be used in a variety of ways:

1. **To make energy by respiration**
    All plant cells need energy to stay alive and to carry out essential processes.

    glucose + oxygen ⟶ energy + carbon dioxide + water

2. **Changed into starch for storage**
    Plant cells cannot store large quantities of glucose because it affects their osmotic balance. The glucose is converted to starch, then stored in granules in the cytoplasm. Many plants store starch in their roots, leaves and seeds. It can then be converted back to glucose to provide energy for the plant.

3. **Changed to cellulose**
    Cellulose is a complicated molecule made up of lots of molecules of glucose joined together in a precise way. All plant cells have cell walls made of cellulose. They are strong and rigid, but they are permeable (let substances pass through). New cellulose is needed wherever plant cells are dividing, i.e. at the growing points of the roots and shoot.

4. **Changed to protein**
    Plants can make their own protein from glucose and minerals, especially nitrogen. Proteins are needed for many processes within the plant, e.g. to make cell membranes, to make enzymes to control chemical reactions inside cells. If plants can't make protein, e.g. if they are short of nitrogen, they cannot grow properly, and are very weak and unhealthy.

5. **Changed to chlorophyll**
    Plants make chlorophyll from glucose and minerals, especially magnesium. Chlorophyll is needed to trap light energy for photosynthesis. If plants can't make chlorophyll, they have a yellow appearance (chlorosis) and will not grow properly, because they cannot photosynthesise efficiently.

Importance of oxygen

All living things carry out respiration, and most use oxygen, yet the amount of oxygen in the air stays constant at about 21%. This is because plants make oxygen when they photosynthesise. If they did not do this, the Earth would soon run out of oxygen.

▷ **Respiration in plants**

Respiration is a chemical reaction occurring in all cells of all living organisms at all times. Its purpose is to make energy.

Key points

> glucose (from photosynthesis) and oxygen (from the air) are raw materials;

> water and carbon dioxide are waste products;

> energy is produced, and some of this is released as heat;

> in dim light, there is no gas exchange with the air, i.e. the amount of carbon dioxide made in respiration equals the amount needed for photosynthesis, and this is called the compensation point.

The process of respiration in plants is very similar to respiration in animals (see p. 50).

glucose + oxygen $\longrightarrow$ energy + carbon dioxide + water

Experiments with respiration

1. Is carbon dioxide produced?
Set up a potted plant in an air-tight bell jar with a dark cover as shown in Fig. 5.8. Use an air pump to draw air through the apparatus.

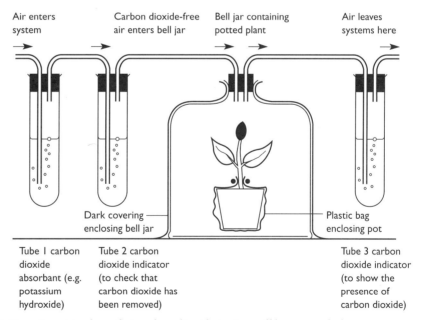

Fig. 5.8 Experiment to show that carbon dioxide is given off by a potted plant.

REVISION ACTIVITY 3 Why must the bell jar be covered in dark material?

2. Is heat produced?
Set up two vacuum flasks as shown in Fig 5.9; one containing live, germinating pea seeds and the other containing dead pea seeds (boiled then cooled) which have been soaked in an antiseptic solution, e.g. TCP. Leave the flasks for 4–5 days, taking the temperature regularly.

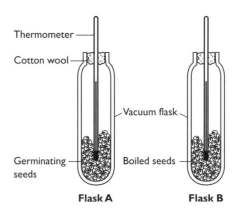

Fig. 5.9 Experiment to show that germinating pea seeds produce heat

REVISION ACTIVITY 4 (a) In which flask would you expect the temperature to be the highest, and why?
(b) Why do you use vacuum flasks instead of conical flasks?
(c) Why are the dead peas soaked in TCP?

Photosynthesis, respiration and the compensation point

If you look carefully at the equations for photosynthesis and respiration you can see that they are the opposite of each other:

$$\text{glucose + oxygen} \underset{\text{Photosynthesis}}{\overset{\text{Respiration}}{\rightleftarrows}} \text{carbon dioxide + water + energy}$$

If the average rates of photosynthesis and respiration were the same, the amount of carbon dioxide made in respiration would equal the amount used in photosynthesis, so there would be no gas exchange with the air. This is called the **compensation point**, and it occurs in dim light (see Fig. 5.10)

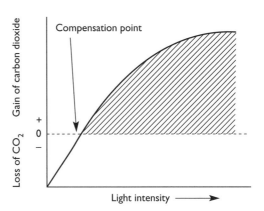

Fig. 5.10 Graph to show compensation point. The shaded part of the graph (beyond the compensation point) represents a net gain of glucose for the plant. This can be used for growth.

REVISION ACTIVITY 5 Underline the correct statement.

In bright light, the rate of photosynthesis is [more than, less than, equal to] the rate or respiration.

In dim light, the rate of photosynthesis is [more than, less than, equal to] the rate of respiration.

In the dark, the rate of photosynthesis is [more than, less than, equal to] the rate of respiration.

Experiment to show the compensation point

Changes in carbon dioxide concentration can be monitored by using bicarbonate indicator. This shows colour changes in the presence of different amounts of carbon dioxide. The gas dissolves in the indicator to form a weak acid (carbonic acid) which causes an alteration of acidity or alkalinity (Fig. 5.11):

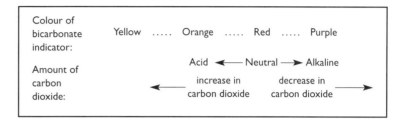

Fig. 5.11 Colour changes of bicarbonate indicator

The bicarbonate indicator is 'equilibrated' with normal atmospheric air before the experiment begins; air is bubbled through the solution, for instance by an aquarium pump. The solution should be **red** at the start of the experiment.

Leaves are placed in tubes containing bicarbonate indicator, as shown in Fig. 5.12. The lower surfaces of the leaves should face inwards, so that gas exchange with pores (stomata) on the underside of the leaves can occur more easily. One tube is set up in darkness one in bright light, and one in dim light. Two **control** tubes are set up without leaves, for comparison. All the tubes are left for about two hours.

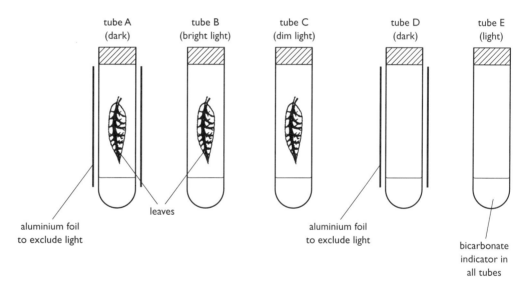

Fig. 5.12 Experiment to investigate respiration and photosynthesis

Table 5.2

Tube	Colour of indicator at end of experiment	Conclusion
A	Yellow	Carbon dioxide concentration is high; produced by respiration.
B	Purple	Carbon dioxide concentration is low; used in photosynthesis.
C	Red	Carbon dioxide concentration is constant. Rate of photosynthesis equals rate or respiration
D	Red	Carbon dioxide concentration remains constant; no respiration
E	Red	or photosynthesis is occurring because no living tissue is present.

Remember: respiration is occurring in tubes A, B, and C; photosynthesis is occurring in tubes B and C.

▷ Importance of minerals

Plants get the minerals they need from the soil. Minerals are released naturally when organic material rots, or they can be added to the soil in the form of fertilizers.

Key points

- ▷ plants get minerals from the soil;
- ▷ they need a variety of minerals to be healthy and grow properly;
- ▷ nitrate is needed to make protein;
- ▷ magnesium is needed to make chlorophyll.

When plants photosynthesise, they make glucose. They need minerals from the soil to combine with the glucose to make other important materials, e.g. protein, chlorophyll.

Importance of nitrate

Nitrate is formed in soil when proteins and nitrogenous waste, e.g. urea in urine, are broken down by bacteria. It is also made by nitrogen – fixing bacteria (see p.xxx on the nitrogen cycle).

If a plant does not get nitrate from the soil, it cannot make proteins. Proteins are an important component of cell membranes and enzymes, so without proteins the plant cannot grow properly and function efficiently.

Importance of magnesium

If a plant does not get magnesium, it cannot make chlorophyll. Chlorophyll is a very complex molecule containing magnesium and nitrogen, and its function is to trap light energy. A plant lacking in chlorophyll will look yellow (this is called chlorosis), and it will not be able to photosynthesise properly. This will lead to weakness and stunted growth.

Water culture experiments

It is possible to find out about the effects of mineral deficiency in plants by setting up a water culture experiment. Distilled water is placed in the culture vessells, and minerals added as shown. A seedling is placed in each vessel and air is bubbled through the mineral solution. A light-proof cover is placed around each vessel, and the growth of the seedlings is monitored for 2–3 weeks.

A   Solution with all minerals added
B   Solution without nitrate
C   Solution without phosphorus
D   Solution without potassium
E   Solution without magnesium

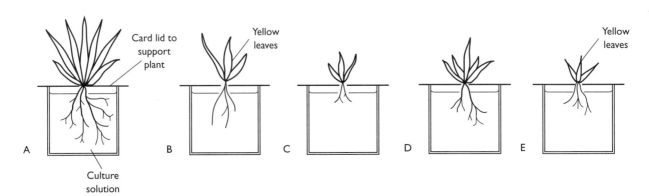

Fig. 5.13 Water culture experiments

(a)   Why is distilled water used instead of tap water?
(b)   Why is air bubbled through the mineral solution?
(c)   Why is a light-proof cover placed around each vessel?
(d)   Which minerals are needed to make chlorophyll?
(e)   Which mineral is needed for healthy root growth?

▷ Uptake of water and minerals

Plants obtain the water and minerals they need from the soil.

Key points

▷   plants absorb water and minerals through their **roots**;

▷   some root cells have root **hairs** which increase their **surface area** and therefore increase the **rate** of uptake;

▷   water moves into roots by **osmosis**;

▷   minerals move into roots by **diffusion** and **active transport**;

How is water absorbed?

Most water is absorbed by the region just behind the root tip where there are root hairs to increase the surface area. There is a film of water around soil particles and the root hairs are in close contact with this.

The cytoplasm of the root hair cells contains a mixture of sugars and salts, so water molecules will move into the cell by **osmosis**. The solution inside these cells then becomes more dilute than that of cells closer to the centre of the root: the result is a **concentration gradient** across the root, causing water to move towards the centre. Eventually it passes into the **xylem vessels** and is transported upwards. (See Fig. 5.14.)

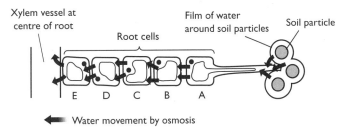

Fig. 5.14 Uptake of water by osmosis

Water moves into cell A by osmosis, because there is a higher concentration of water molecules in the soil than in the cytoplasm of cell A. This dilutes the cytoplasm of cell A, so water molecules move to cell B by osmosis. The cytoplasm of cell B is now more dilute, so water molecules move on to cell C. This continues until the water molecules reach the xylem vessels. These are long, narrow tubes, rather like drain-pipes. They are made of columns of dead cells which no longer have cytoplasm or end-walls.

How are minerals absorbed?

Plants need a variety of minerals in order to stay healthy, e.g. nitrate ions, phosphate ions, potassium ions, magnesium ions. These minerals are dissolved in the film of water surrounding the soil particles. Most minerals are absorbed by the region just behind the root tip where there are root hairs to increase the surface area. Minerals are absorbed in two ways:

1.   **By Diffusion**
     If there is a higher concentration of a particular mineral ion in the soil than in the cytoplasm of the root cell, then ions will diffuse into the cell. This depends on a concentration gradient being present, and will allow cells to accumulate **small** amounts of minerals.

2.   **By Active Transport**
     Ions are moved across the root cell membrane, into the cell, using carrier proteins. This process uses energy, so root hair cells have lots of mitochondria to generate

energy. This allows root cells to accumulate **large** amounts of mineral ions, i.e. does not depend on a concentration gradient.

Once the mineral ions are inside the root cell, they move towards the centre of the root and into the **xylem vessels.**

▷ **Transport of water and minerals**

Key points
▷ tubes called **xylem vessels** carry water to all parts of the plant;
▷ water movement in plants depends on **transpiration** – this is the evaporation of water through the leaf stomata;
▷ transpiration rate depends on temperature, air movement, humidity and time of day;
▷ transpiration rate can be measured using a **potometer**;
▷ minerals are transported in xylem vessels and phloem tubes.

Water and minerals move upwards from the roots through xylem vessels to reach all parts of the plant. Xylem vessels are long, narrow tubes which run through the root system and shoot system.

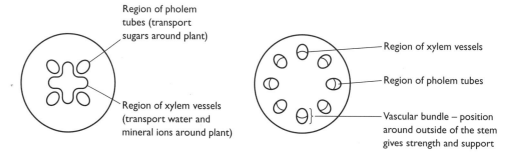

Fig. 5.15 Position of xylem vessels in a flowering plant (a) in root (b) in stem

Transport of water

Water moves up through the xylem vessels due to **transpiration**. Transpiration is the evaporation of water from the leaves of the plant, through stomata (Fig. 5.16).

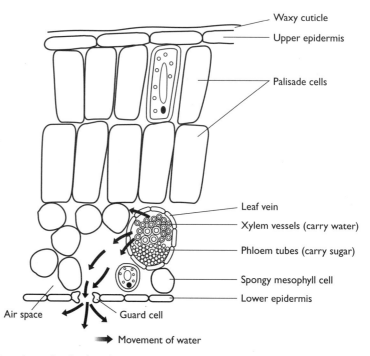

Fig. 5.16 Section through a leaf to show transpiration

In a healthy plant there is an unbroken column of water from the roots, through the stem, up to the leaves; all of this water is in the xylem vessels. As water evaporates from the leaves by transpiration, more water is pulled into the plant, and up through the xylem vessels to take its place. This process is called **transpiration pull** (Fig. 5.17).

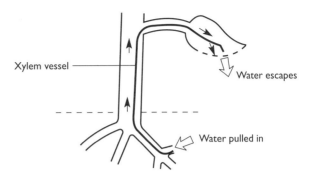

Fig. 5.17 Mechanism of transpiration pull

Evidence: transpiration pull depends on leaves. If leaves are removed from a plant, water movement is much slower. When deciduous trees lose their leaves in winter, there is very little water movement.

Factors affecting the transpiration rate
1. **Temperature** – transpiration occurs faster at warm temperatures than cool temperatures.
2. **Air movement** – transpiration occurs faster on windy days than on still days.
3. **Humidity** – transpiration occurs faster on dry days than on humid days (when there is already lots of water vapour in the air).
4. **Time of day** – transpiration occurs faster during the day than at night. This is because many plants open their stomata during the day and close them at night (by changing the shape of the guard cells).

'Try to learn these factors. They are very important.'

Measuring the transpiration rate
1. **Using a mass potometer**
    A plant is carefully uprooted and placed in a conical flask of water. A layer of oil is added to prevent evaporation of the water. The mass is measured at regular intervals (Fig. 5.18).

    As water is lost from the leaves by transpiration, the mass of the apparatus will decrease. Transpiration rate can be calculated, i.e. mass loss per hour. This experiment can be carried out with a potted plant if the pot is covered in a polythene bag to prevent evaporation of water from the soil.

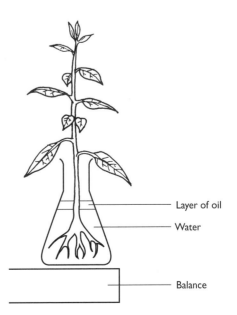

Fig. 5.18 Mass potometer

2.   **Using a bubble potometer**

The roots of a plant are cut off underwater so that no air bubbles get into the xylem vessels. The shoot is then inserted through the bung of the potometer, and the joints sealed with vaseline so that it is air-tight (Fig. 5.19).

'Exam questions are often set on this topic.'

At the start of the experiment, the whole potometer is filled with water. An air bubble is then introduced to the capillary tubing. As the shoot transpires, the air bubble will move through the capillary tubing towards the shoot.

The **rate** of transpiration is calculated by measuring the distance moved by the bubble in a particular time, e.g. 10 minutes.

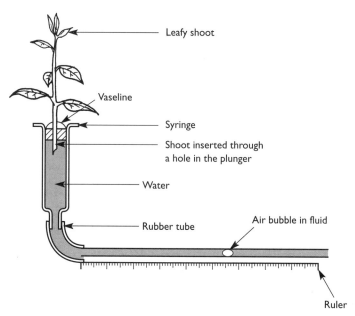

- Leafy shoot
- Vaseline
- Syringe
- Shoot inserted through a hole in the plunger
- Water
- Rubber tube
- Air bubble in fluid
- Ruler

Fig. 5.19 Bubble potometer

Transport of minerals

Mineral salts move with water because they are dissolved in it. However, they are also transported inside phloem tubes. Minerals are used by cells all over the plant, but especially at the growing points (tips of shoots and roots).

▷ Transport of sugars

Glucose is made in the leaves during photosynthesis. Some will remain in the leaves, but the rest will be moved to other parts of the plant.

Key points
▷   tubes called **phloem tubes** carry sugar around the plant;
▷   it is moved from the leaves (where it is made by photosynthesis) to other parts of the plant;
▷   movement of sugar is called **translocation**.

How sugar is moved around

Sugar is made in leaves by the process of photosynthesis. It is moved to other parts of the plant through phloem tubes, e.g. to the roots to be stored, to the tips of the roots and shoots to provide energy for growth. The movement of sugar solution through the phloem tube is called **translocation**. Phloem tubes are found in the roots and shoots (see Fig. 5.15) and are made up of living cells. Translocation is a complex process which seems to require energy.

Evidence for translocation

1. **Ringing experiments**

   If a ring of tissue around the outside of the stem, including the phloem tubes, is removed, translocation cannot occur. Sugar solution, which would normally move downwards in the phloem tubes, accumulates above the ring (Fig. 5.20).

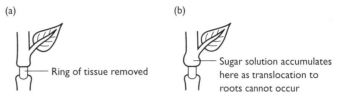

Fig. 5.20 Ringing experiment (a) immediately after removal of ring; (b) several days after removal of ring

2. **Radioactive isotopes**

   If part of a plant is provided with a radioactive form of carbon dioxide ($^{14}CO_2$), it will make radioactive sugar during photosynthesis. The route followed by this sugar in translocation can be observed by placing the plant on photographic film (the radioactivity causes 'fogging') (Fig. 5.21).

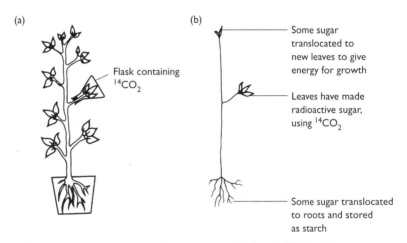

Fig. 5.21 Radioactive isotopes (a) some leaves are provided with $^{14}CO_2$, (b) appearance of photographic film

▷ Reproduction in flowering plants

> This topic is not part of the National Curriculum for England and Wales at Key Stage 4.

Asexual reproduction

There are two important features of asexual reproduction:

1. only one parent is involved;
2. offspring are genetically identical to the parent and to each other.

Many plants can reproduce asexually, e.g. with bulbs, runners or tubers. This is useful when the parent plant is well suited to its surroundings.

Sexual reproduction

There are two important features of sexual reproduction:

1. male and female gametes join at fertilization (usually from two different parent plants);
2. offspring are similar, but not identical to the parents and to each other.

Sexual reproduction always involves flowers (which contain the plant's sex organs), and seeds are produced.

This is useful when conditions are changing and it is beneficial for offspring to be different to their parents. Seeds can be dispersed a long way from the parent plant, and this helps to avoid overcrowding, and to colonise new areas.

There are five main processes involved:

1.   production of gametes;
2.   pollination;
3.   fertilization;
4.   seed development;
5.   seed dispersal.

1. Production of gametes

Male gametes are pollen grains. These are made inside the anther.
Female gametes are the egg cell nuclei. These are made inside the ovary.
The flower contains the sex organs of the plant.

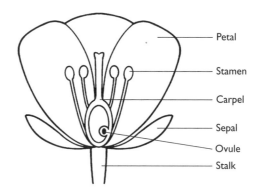

Labels: Petal, Stamen, Carpel, Sepal, Ovule, Stalk

Fig. 5.22 Parts of a flower

2. Pollination

This is the transfer of pollen from an anther to the stigma. Pollen cannot move on its own, and is usually transferred in one of two ways:
Insect pollination: insects are attracted to the flower by the brightly coloured petals and nectar, and when they are gathering nectar, pollen will stick onto their body. This will be brushed off when they visit another flower.
Wind pollination: the anthers hang outside the flower where wind can easily blow pollen away. Wind-pollinated flowers have feathery, net-like stigmas to catch pollen as it is blowing in the wind.

If pollen is transferred from an anther to the stigma of a different plant, it is known as **cross-pollination.**

If pollen is transferred from an anther to a stigma on the same plant, it is known as **self-pollination.**

3. Fertilization

Once a pollen grain has been transferred to the stigma, a pollen tube will start to grow. It grows down through the carpel until it reaches the ovule.

The pollen grain nucleus travels through the pollen tube to reach the egg nucleus, and joins to it – this is fertilization. See Fig. 5.23.

4. Seed development

Once fertilization has occurred, the petals, sepals and stamens shrivel and drop off. The ovary increases in size and develops into a fruit. The ovules will develop into seeds. Each seed contains an embryo plant and a foodstore to give it energy when it starts to grow. Seeds have a tough coat (the testa) to protect them from harm, and they are dormant so they will not start to grow until conditions are right.

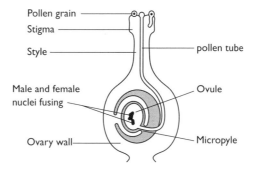

Fig. 5.23 Growth of the pollen tube and fertilization

5. Seed dispersal
It is important that seeds are spread away from the parent plant so that they are not over-crowded (this avoids competition for resources), and so that they can colonise new areas. Seeds are dispersed in a variety of ways:

Wind dispersal: seeds are light and may have wings or a parachute of hairs to help them float through the air.

Animal dispersal: fruits containing seeds may have hooks (so they will get caught in animal fur and be carried on the outside of the body), or may be brightly coloured and sweet tasting (so they will be eaten and carried inside the gut).

Water dispersal: seeds are buoyant and have a waterproof coat so they can float away from the parent.

Self-dispersal: the fruits dry out and split open, releasing the seeds.

REVISION ACTIVITY 7   How are each of the following seeds dispersed?

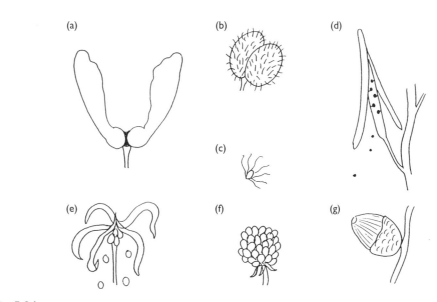

Fig. 5.24

▷ **Germination and growth**

When seeds are released from the parent plant they are dormant, but they have the potential to develop into a new plant in the right conditions.

Key points

▷   when a dormant seed starts to grow, we call it **germination**;

▷   germination requires water, oxygen and a suitable temperature;

▷   the seedling uses food stores from inside the seed until it can make its own food by photosynthesis;

▷   plant growth occurs mainly at the meristems, although secondary growth can occur.

Seed structure

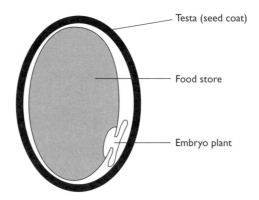

Fig. 5.25 Inside a seed

The seed has a tough coat, the testa, to protect it from damage. Inside the testa is an embryo plant which will start to grow (germinate) when conditions are right. The food store (cotyledons or endosperm) provides the energy for growth.

Germination

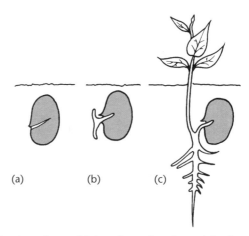

Fig. 5.26 Stages in germination of a seed (a) seed coat breaks and food stores are broken down to provide energy (b) embryo plant starts to grow (c) root and shoot develop

Conditions needed for germination

Seeds will only break dormancy and start to germinate when conditions are right. They need three things:

1. water;
2. oxygen;
3. a suitable temperature (this varies from species to species).

This helps to ensure that the seedling will be able to survive once it has started to germinate.

Growth

Plants differ from animals because growth continues throughout life, but it is confined to particular regions. The main growth points are the root and shoot tips (called meristems) where mitosis occurs rapidly. If these are pinched out, lateral buds will develop, forming side branches. See Fig. 5.27.

In woody plants, e.g. trees, secondary growth also occurs. This adds new xylem and phloem tissue to the stem, making it thicker. Secondary growth occurs during the summer, but stops in the winter: this is responsible for the annual rings you can see when a tree is cut down.

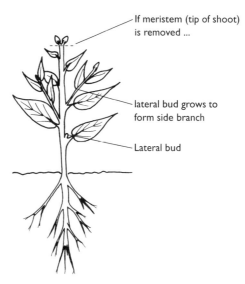

Fig. 5.27 Growth of lateral buds

> **Plant hormones**   Scientists have identified chemicals produced by plants which help to co-ordinate growth and development – some people call these plant hormones.

Key points

▷   chemicals in plants (plant hormones) control growth and developments;

▷   they are needed for the plant to function efficiently;

▷   farmers and gardeners can use plant hormones to control parts of the plant life cycle.

What do plant hormones do?

There are at least five types of plant hormones and they each have different effects. Together they regulate growth and development.

Table 5.3

Hormone	Effects
Auxins	▷ Make plant shoots bend towards the light (phototropism) ▷ Make plant roots grow downwards in response to gravity (geotropism) ▷ Prevents leaves and fruits falling off plants ▷ Make roots develop ▷ Encourage fruit development
Gibberellins	▷ Make plants grow taller ▷ Encourage germination of seeds ▷ Encourage fruit development ▷ Affect flowering time
Cytokinins	▷ Increase growth rate ▷ Keep leaves healthy once plant is dug up ▷ Encourage germination of seeds
Abscissic acid	▷ Slows down growth ▷ Makes leaves and fruits fall off ▷ Closes stomata
Ethene	▷ Ripens fruit ▷ Causes flowering ▷ Encourages bud growth

Commercial applications of plant hormones

Farmers and gardeners can use plant hormones to control parts of the plant life cycle and increase crop production. Examples of this include:

▶ **Synthetic weedkillers**: auxins are sprayed onto weeds and will disrupt their growth pattern so that they grow very quickly, and then die.

▶ **Hormone rooting powders**: a stem cutting can be dipped into auxin, and this will help new roots to form.

▶ **Fruit development**: plants can be treated with ethene to cause fruit ripening, then abscissic acid so that the fruit falls and can be harvested at a time suitable to the farmer.

REVISION ACTIVITY 8 | Which hormone(s) would you use if you wanted to:

(a) slow down growth?
(b) encourage seed germination?
(c) prevent fruits falling off?
(d) make fruits fall off?
(e) cause flowering?
(f) prevent harvested spinach leaves going yellow?

▷ ## SOLUTIONS TO REVISION ACTIVITIES

S1 Wear goggles.
Switch the Bunsen burner off **before** heating the ethanol – ethanol is very flammable, so it is dangerous to have it near a naked flame.

S2 (a) Light

(b) Carbon dioxide or temperature

(c) CO_2: add some sodium hydrogen carbonate to the water when photosynthesis is at its maximum rate. If the rate increases, carbon dioxide was a limiting factor.
Temperature: raise the temperature of the water by 5–10°C when photosynthesis is at its maximum rate. If the rate increases, temperature was a limiting factor.

S3 The bell jar is covered so that the plant has no light for photosynthesis. If it photosynthesised, it would use carbon dioxide, so the results would not be accurate.

S4 (a) In flask A (live peas), because live peas are respiring, and respiration produces heat.

(b) Because vacuum flasks are well-insulated to reduce heat loss.

(c) They are soaked in TCP to prevent growth of bacteria and fungi. The microbes would make heat when they respire, so it would not be a fair test.

S5 In bright light, the rate of photosynthesis is **more** than the rate of respiration.
In dim light, the rate of photosynthesis is **equal to** the rate of respiration
In the dark, the rate of photosynthesis is **less** than the rate of respiration.

S6 (a) Tap water contains dissolved minerals, so it would not be a fair test. Distilled water is pure water.

(b) Air is bubbled through because the roots need oxygen for respiration.

(c) The vessel is covered to exclude light. This prevents the growth of algae in the water. The algae would compete with the plants for minerals so it would not be a fair test.

(d) Nitrate and magnesium are needed to make chlorophyll.

(e) Phosphate is needed for healthy root growth.

S7 (a) wind

(b) animals (caught on fur)

(c) wind

(d) self-dispersal (pod bursts open)

(e) self-dispersal

(f) animals (carried in the gut)

(g) animals (buried as a food store).

S8 (a) Abscissic acid

(b) Cytokinins, Gibberellins

(c) Auxins

(d) Abscissic acid

(e) Ethene

(f) Cytokinins

 EXAMINATION QUESTIONS

▷ **Question 1** The diagram shows part of a simple plant living in water. The cells are joined end to end.

(a) The diagram shows the structure of a cell.

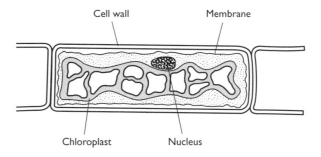

Fig. 5.28

Which labelled part of the cell carries out photosynthesis?   *(1)*

(b) Microscopic animals were placed in the water around the plant.
The plant carries out photosynthesis when light shines on it. This gives off oxygen which is used by the animals.
The microscopic animals do **not** eat the plant cells and they are **not** sensitive to light.

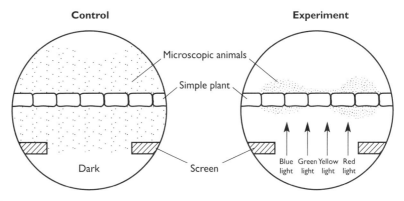

Fig. 5.29

    (i) Describe what happens when the lights are switched on.   *(3)*
    (ii) Which colours of light make the plant produce most oxygen?   *(1)*
                                                    (MEG)

▷ **Question 2**   (a) (i) What is the name of the type of apparatus shown below?   *(1)*

(ii) What process is being investigated?   *(1)*

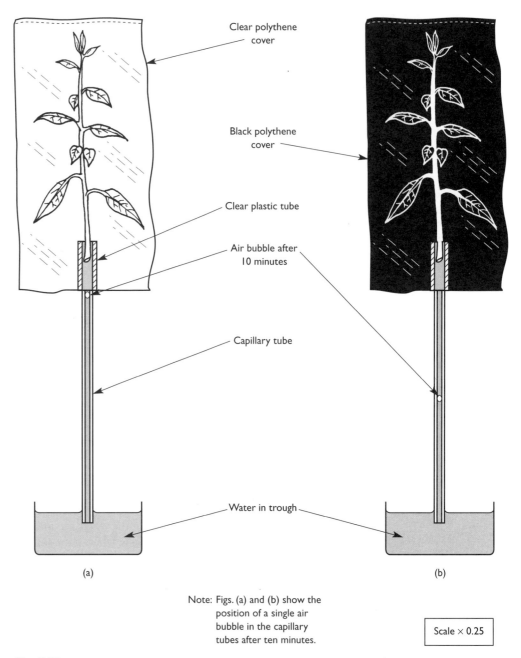

Note: Figs. (a) and (b) show the position of a single air bubble in the capillary tubes after ten minutes.

Scale × 0.25

Fig. 5.30

(b) A pupil recorded the rise of the bubble shown in diagram **A**, every minute for ten minutes, by measuring the distance between the base of the bubble and the bottom of the capillary tube in the trough. The same procedure was repeated with the plant enclosed by the black polythene as shown in diagram **B**. Again, the results were recorded for ten minutes.

(i) Why was the same plant used each time?   *(1)*

(ii) Complete the table below using the information provided by the diagrams **A** and **B**   *(2)*

REMEMBER THE DIAGRAMS ARE DRAWN TO X 0.25 SCALE

Table 5.4

Time in minutes		0	2	3	4	5	6	7	8	9	10
actual distance of bubble base from bottom of capillary tube in trough(mm)	Plant with clear polythene	0	48	72	100	124	148	176	200	224	
	Plant with black polythene	0	24	36	52	60	72	88	100	112	

(c) (i) Which experiment has the **slowest** rate of water uptake?   *(1)*

   (ii) Calculate the rate of water uptake in mm per minute for the plant covered in clear polythene.   *(2)*

(d) Which factor, besides light, was affecting the rate of water loss from the plant in the investigation?   *(1)*

(e) A liquid gathered on the inside of the polythene bag. What chemical would you use to prove that this liquid is water?   *(1)*

(f) Name a gas which would increase inside the black polythene bag.   *(1)*

(WJEC)

▷ **Question 3**   The diagrams show the results of an investigation into the mineral requirements of wheat seedlings.

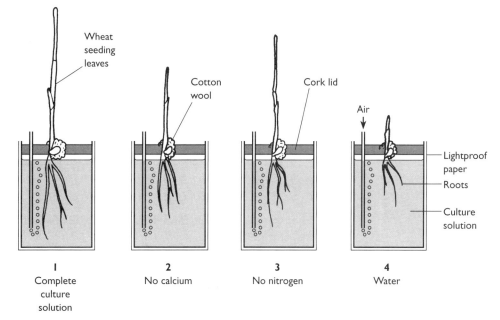

Fig. 5.31

Table 5.5

Tube	Mineral content	Total length of leaves/mm
1	Complete	24.0
2	No calcium	13.5
3	No nitrogen	21.0
4	None	5.5

(a) On graph paper, show the results as a bar chart.   *(4)*

(b) Why were tubes 1 and 4 included in the investigation?   *(1)*

(c) Explain the results for tube 2.   *(2)*

(d) Why must air be bubbled through the tubes?   *(3)*

(NICCEA)

▷ **Question 4**   Use the information the following paragraph and your own knowledge to answer (a) to (e).

> The diagram shows ten large, sealed vessels containing hydrogen carbonate indicator solution (HCIS). HCIS is both sensitive, detecting small changes, and specific to carbon dioxide. HCIS containing atmospheric concentration of carbon dioxide, approximately 0.03%, is orange-red in colour. At higher carbon dioxide concentrations the indicator goes yellow. Lowering the dissolved carbon dioxide concentration results in a change in colour from orange-red to purple-red.
>
> In the following experiment the HCIS was orange-red in colour at the start.

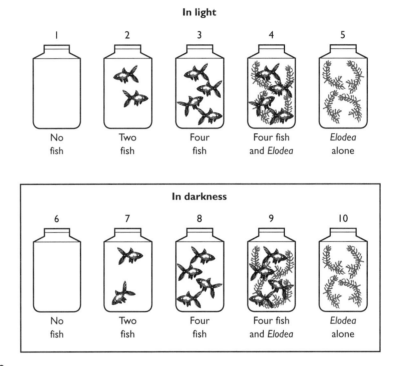

Fig. 5.32

(a) What was the concentration of carbon dioxide in each of the vessels at the start of the experiment?

_____%   *(1)*

(b) (i) What happened in HCIS for a colour change to occur?   *(1)*
     (ii) What has to happen in HCIS for the colour to change from orange-red to yellow? *(1)*
     (iii) What has to happen in HCIS for the colour to change from orange-red to purple-red?   *(1)*

(c) Which **two** basic chemical processes in cells are likely to have an effect on the colour of the HCIS during the course of the experiment?
Explain your answer.   *(4)*

(d) Predict a difference in the result for vessel 3 compared to vessel 2. Suggest an explanation for your prediction.   *(3)*

(e) At the end of the experiment the colours in vessels 5 and 10 were different. The HCIS in vessel 5 went purple-red.
    (i) Which chemical process in the plant cells, which would affect the colour change, took place in vessel 5 but not in vessel 10?   *(1)*
    (ii) Why did the chemical process not take place in the plant cells in vessel 10?   *(1)*
    (iii) What colour would you predict the HCIS to be in vessel 10 at the end of the experiment?
Explain your answer.   *(2)*

(f) At the end of the experiment there had been a colour change in vessel 9 but **not** in
vessel 4.
(i) What colour would you predict the HCIS to be in vessel 9?
Explain your answer.   *(2)*
(ii) Give an explanation for the lack of colour change in vessel 4.   *(3)*

(MEG)

▷ **Question 5**   Leaves are organs of photosynthesis. They come in all shapes and sizes but all of them are
adapted to absorb as much light as possible.
(a) Give **two** ways in which leaves are adapted to absorb light.

1.   _____

2.   _____   *(2)*

(b) The diagram shows a cross-section through a leaf.

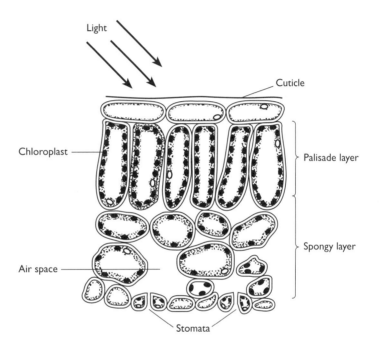

Fig. 5.33

Explain the following observations.
(i) The cuticle is transparent.   *(1)*
(ii) Most chloroplasts are found in the palisade layer.   *(1)*
(iii) Air spaces are found mostly in the spongy layer.   *(1)*

(c) What is the substance in chloroplasts which absorbs light?   *(1)*

(d) Explain how each of the following affects the rate of photosynthesis in a potted plant.
(i) Moving it nearer to the window.   *(1)*
(ii) Moving it to a colder room.   *(1)*

(e) Complete the following word equation for photosynthesis.

$$\text{_____ + water} \xrightarrow[\text{chlorophyll}]{\text{sunlight}} \text{carbohydrates + _____}$$ *(1)*

(f) The diagram (Fig 5.34) shows the carbon cycle.

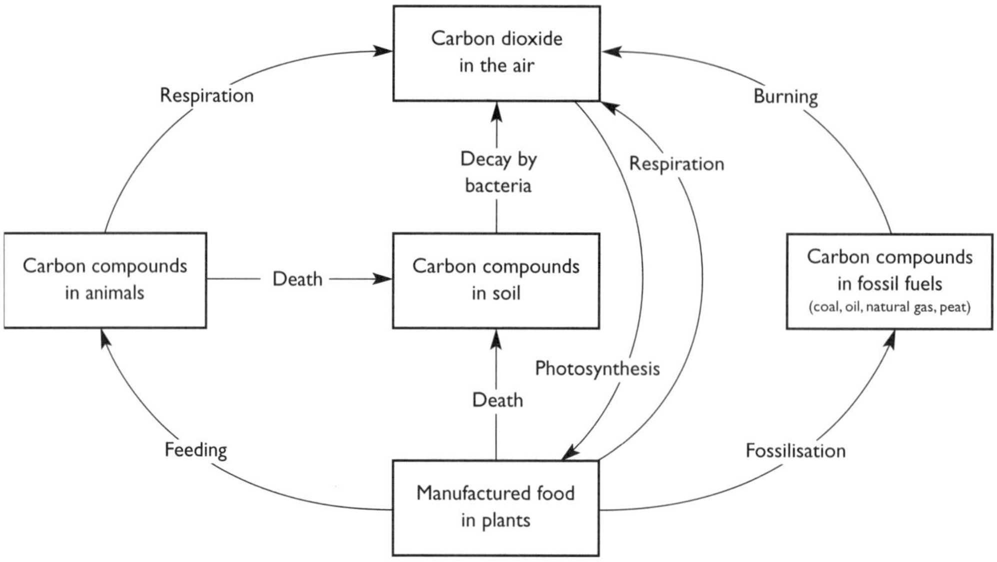

Carbon dioxide
in the air

Respiration

Burning

Decay by
bacteria

Respiration

Carbon compounds
in animals

Death

Carbon compounds
in soil

Carbon compounds
in fossil fuels
(coal, oil, natural gas, peat)

Photosynthesis

Death

Feeding

Fossilisation

Manufactured food
in plants

Fig. 5.34 The carbon cycle

Use the information in the diagram to help you explain why photosynthesis is important to all living things on planet Earth.

_____

_____

_____

_____

_____

_____

_____

_____

_____

(5)

(MEG)

▷ **Question 6**   (a)   An experiment was carried out to investigate the effects of strawberry pips on the growth of strawberries. The pips were removed from young strawberries and their appearance after one week is shown in the drawings below.

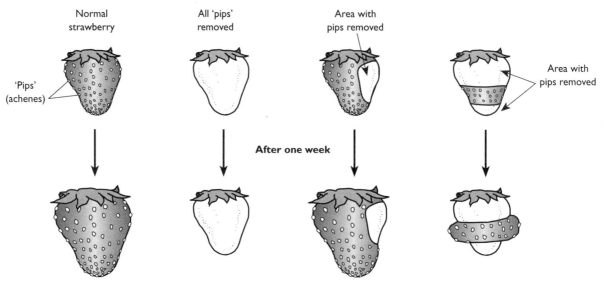

Normal
strawberry

All 'pips'
removed

Area with
pips removed

Area with
pips removed

'Pips'
(achenes)

After one week

Fig. 5.35

State the conclusion based on the results.   *(1)*

(b)   The graphs below show the growth of **three** strawberries over a period of time.

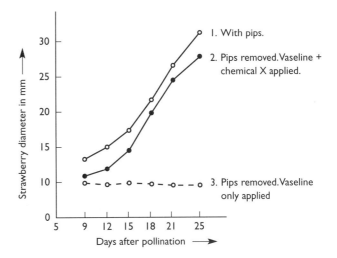

Fig. 5.36

(i)   What was the diameter of the complete strawberry after 12 days?   *(1)*
(ii)   Explain how you can tell that chemical **X** caused the growth and not the vaseline.   *(1)*
(iii) Use the drawings and the graphs to explain why the pips seem to produce a chemical similar to **X**.   *(1)*
(iv)   Biotechnologists can make chemical **X** in large amounts. Suggest a use for it.   *(1)*
(WJEC)

    ANSWERS TO EXAMINATION QUESTIONS

▷ **Question 1**   (a)   Chloroplast.

(b)   (i)   The plant cells photosynthesise. (1)
              They produce oxygen. (1)
              The animals move to the areas where there is a lot of oxygen. (1)
              They use oxygen for respiration. (1)
      (ii)   Red and blue light.

▷ **Question 2**   (a)   (i)   potometer
                          (ii)   transpiration rate

(b)   (i)   so that it was a fair test (so the results could be compared)
      (ii)   A = 240mm   B = 128mm

(c)   (i)   plant with black polythene (B)
      (ii)   240mm in 10 minutes = 24mm per minute

(d)   humidity (amount of water vapour)

(e)   cobalt chloride

(f)   carbon dioxide (from respiration).

▷ **Question 3** (a)

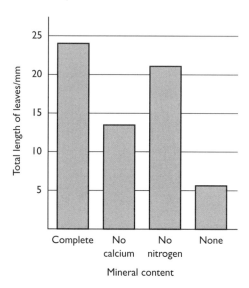

Fig. 5.37

(b) As a comparison, or control.

(c) Calcium is needed for growth (1): both roots and shoot grow slowly when it is absent. (1)

(d) Root cells need oxygen (1) for respiration / to make energy (1) for growth and active transport. (1)

▷ **Question 4** (a) 0.03%

(b) (i) the carbon dioxide concentration must change
(ii) higher carbon dioxide levels cause this
(iii) lower carbon dioxide levels cause this

(c) Respiration (1) makes carbon dioxide, i.e. increases the level. (1)
Photosynthesis (1) uses carbon dioxide, i.e. decreases the level. (1)

(d) Vessel 3 will go yellow sooner / go more yellow than vessel 2. (1)
This is because there are more fish, so more carbon dioxide is produced (1) by respiration. (1)

(e) (i) photosynthesis
(ii) it was dark
(iii) yellow (1) because the plant was respiring (1)

(f) yellow (1) both fish and *Elodea* are respiring (1)
(ii) the fish are making carbon dioxide when they respire. (1) *Elodea* is using carbon dioxide for photosynthesis. (1) The processes are balanced out, i.e. there is an equal amount made and used, therefore there is no change in colour.

▷ **Question 5** (a) thin / flat / contain chlorophyll / have a large surface area

(b) (i) so light can pass through the cuticle to reach the palisade cells
(ii) because they are near to the surface of the leaf, and get a lot of light for photosynthesis
(iii) close to the stomata where air enters the leaf / because the cells are irregular in shape so they don't fit together closely.

(c) chlorophyll

(d) (i) increases the rate because it has more light
(ii) decreases the rate, because enzymes work more slowly.

(e)
$$\textbf{carbon dioxide} + \text{water} \xrightarrow[\text{chlorophyll}]{\text{light}} \text{carbohydrates} + \textbf{oxygen}$$

(f)   **Plants** use carbon dioxide to make carbohydrates. (1)
      Carbohydrates can be converted to proteins and fats. (1)
      Animals eat plants to obtain food (to make energy during respiration). (1)
      Bacteria and fungi break down dead plants and animals and feed on them. (1)
      All of these depend on plants being able to make their own food. (1) Without plants, animals would have nothing to eat, so they would die out. (1)

▷ **Question 6**   (a)   The pips contain a substance which causes growth.

(b)   (i)   15mm
      (ii) When **X** and vaseline are added it grows, but if only vaseline is added, it does not grow.
      (iii) When pips are removed, growth does not occur, but when pips are present growth occurs. When **X** is present, growth occurs. Therefore, **X** may be similar to a chemical found in pips.
      (iv) It would increase fruit size.

▷ **STUDENT'S ANSWER WITH EXAMINER'S COMMENTS**

Table 5.4 shows the results of an investigation into the effect of width of stomatal pore on the rate of stomatal transpiration. Results were obtained for a plant growing in still air and on a separate occasion, in moving air.

Table 5.4

Width of stomatal pore/micrometers	Rate of stomatal transpiration/abritary units	
	Still air	Moving air
0	0	0
2	25	25
5	45	45
8	55	130
16	65	215
20	65	250
25	65	275

(a)   Draw a graph of the results on the axes below.
      Plot the points using different symbols for the two conditions.
      Join the points using straight lines.
      Label the curves drawn.

'Good. Points are plotted neatly and joined with a ruler. Different symbols have been used for the 2 lines, but this student would lose a mark because the lines are not labelled.

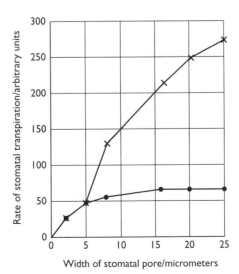

Fig. 5.38   (continued)

'Yes, but it levels off after 16 micrometers.'

(b) What is the effect of increasing stomatal pore width, on transpiration, over the range 0 to 20 micrometers, in still air and moving air?

still air: *as the stomata get wider the rate of transpiration increases* ✓

'It would be better to say that the rate is fairly constant.'

moving air: *as the stomata get wider the rate of transpiration increases* ✓

It keeps on increasing right to the end. ✓   (3)

'Yes. To get the last mark, the student should have explained that the lettuces would wilt, because the roots are not yet capable of taking up more water. Also, a bright day makes transpiration faster, because stomata are more fully open.'

(c) Explain how your graph shows that it would be unwise for a gardener to transplant lettuce seedlings on a bright breezy spring day.

Transpiration would be very fast. ✓

The lettuces would lose a lot of water ✓

(3)

(MEG)

SUMMARY

▷   leaves are thin and flat, and have specialised cells to enable them to carry out photosynthesis and transpiration;

▷   photosynthesis is the way in which plants make sugar in the light:

water + carbon dioxide $\xrightarrow{\text{light}}$ sugar + oxygen;

▷   if any raw materials are in short supply, or if conditions are wrong, the rate of photosynthesis will be slowed down – the factor determining the rate is called the limiting factor;

▷   sugar made in photosynthesis can be used in respiration, stored as starch or be converted to other materials, e.g. protein, chlorophyll;

▷   plants carry out respiration at all times to make energy;

▷   when the rate of photosynthesis equals the rate of respiration, we call this the compensation point. It occurs in dim light;

▷   plants need a variety of minerals, including nitrate and magnesium to develop properly. They get these minerals from the soil;

▷   plants absorb water by osmosis through their root hairs. Water travels upwards through xylem vessels due to transpiration;

▷   transpiration is the loss of water through stomata on the underside of leaves by evaporation. Transpiration rate depends on external factors, e.g. temperature, humidity, amount of light, amount of wind;

▷   transpiration rate can be measured using a potometer;

▷   plants absorb minerals by diffusion and active transport through their root hairs. Minerals travel upwards through xylem vessels;

▷   sugars travel from the leaves (where they are made by photosynthesis) to all parts of the plant through phloem tubes;

▷   many plants can reproduce asexually and sexually;

▷   during sexual reproduction pollen (the male gamete) is transferred to the stigma by winds or insects;

▷   a pollen tube grows, and the pollen grain nucleus travels through this to join to the egg cell nucleus;

▷   a seed develops inside a fruit, and is dispersed away from the parent plant;

▷   in the right conditions (water, oxygen, the correct temperature) seeds will germinate to develop into new plants;

▷   plant growth and development is controlled by plant hormones;

▷   farmers and gardeners can use plant hormones to control stages of the plant life cycle and increase crop production.

Variation, inheritance and evolution

> ## GETTING STARTED

MEG	SEG	LONDON	NEAB	WJEC	NICCEA	SEB

There is a huge variety of living organisms on Earth. Scientists have sorted organisms into groups, based on their similarities and differences – this is classification.

However, organisms of the same type (species) are not identical to each other: this variation is due to genetic factors and environmental factors.

In this chapter you will focus mainly on genetic variation, i.e. how offspring inherit features from their parents. We can draw genetic diagrams to show this – these diagrams are called monohybrid crosses. Some diseases are caused by faulty genes, and genetic diagrams can be used to follow the inheritance pattern of these diseases.

Humans use two very different techniques to increase the probability of organisms producing a particular type of offspring: these are selective breeding and genetic engineering.

Many biologists agree with the theory that was first put forward by Darwin and Wallace explaining evolution by natural selection.

TOPIC		STUDY	REVISION 1	REVISION 2
Variation				
Principles of classification				
Classification of plants				
Classification of animals				
Using keys				
Types of variation				
Causes of variation				
Genes and variation				
Asexual reproduction				
Sexual reproduction				
Mutation				
Inheritance				
Sex determination in humans				
Genetics problems (monohybrid crosses)				
Genetic diseases				
Selective breeding				
Cloning				
DNA				
Genetic engineering				
Natural selection and evolution				
Natural selection				
Evolution				
Evidence for evolution				

WHAT YOU NEED TO KNOW

▷ **Variation**   Variation is the way that living things differ from each other. We can classify organisms into groups depending on their features, but even within groups, organisms are not identical to each other.

This section of the book deals with two main themes:

1.   How do we classify organisms?
2.   Why are individuals from the same species different from each other?

Principles of classification

> ### Key points
>
> ▷   classification means sorting organisms into groups depending on their features;
>
> ▷   organisms have been classified into five main groups, called kingdoms;
>
> ▷   all organisms have been given a Latin binomial name, e.g. daisy is *Bellis perennis*.

In the past, organisms were classified into two main groups: plants and animals. We now know that this is not correct; there are many living things which do not fit into either of these groups. Scientists have developed a new classification system with five main groups or kingdoms. These are:

Fungi
Plants
Animals
Prokaryotes (bacteria and other similar microbes)
Protoctists (simple, single-celled organisms).

Within each kingdom, organisms are sorted out into smaller and smaller groups, based on their similarities and differences. Figure 6.1 shows how some animals are classified (many steps are left out).

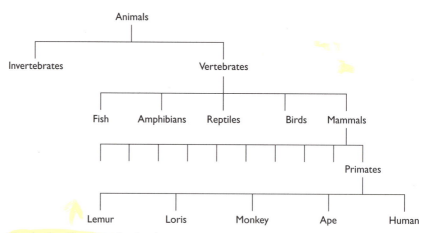

Fig. 6.1 Simple classification of animals

Within a kingdom, organisms are divided into different **phyla** (in Fig. 6.1, these are invertebrates and vertebrates). In each phylum, organisms are divided into **classes**, (e.g. fish, amphibians, reptiles, birds and mammals). In a class, organisms are divided into **orders**, e.g. primates, then into families and finally into the **genus** and **species**, e.g. *Homo sapiens* (humans).

Organisms belonging to the same **genus** are closely related and have many similarities, e.g. lion, tiger and leopard all belong to the same genus.

Organisms belonging to the same **species** will not look identical to each other, but key features within a species are always the same for all organisms in that species,

e.g. all dogs belong to one species,
all humans belong to one species.

Members of a particular species can breed together to produce offspring which will survive, and which will be fertile (capable of breeding themselves).

Latin binomial names

When scientists have classified organisms, they give them a binomial name. This is in two parts (a genus name and a species name), and is always in Latin,

e.g. oak tree – *Quercus petraea*
daisy – *Bellis perennis*
human – *Homo sapiens*

This is useful because:

▷ it tells other scientists which organisms belong to the same group, e.g *Panthera leo* (lion), *Panthera tigris* (tiger) and *Panthera paradus* (leopard) are all part of the same genus.

▷ all scientists use these names, no matter which country they come from, so they are able to understand each other.

This system was devised by a Swedish scientist, Linnaeus, in the eighteenth century. Whenever new organisms are discovered, a binomial name is invented for them.

Classification of plants

Key points

▷ all plants have cell walls made of cellulose;

▷ all plants can photosynthesise;

▷ the plant kingdom is divided into four main groups:

mosses
ferns
conifers
flowering plants.

Mosses (Bryophytes) e.g. Sphagnum

▷ small land plants which live in damp places
▷ no proper roots
▷ simple stem and leaves
▷ no xylem or phloem tubes
▷ no flowers or seeds
▷ reproduce by making **spores**
▷ spores are released from a capsule

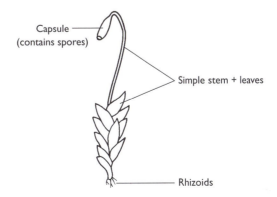

Capsule (contains spores)
Simple stem + leaves
Rhizoids

Fig. 6.2 Moss

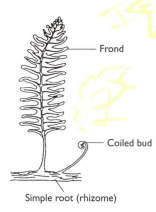

Frond

Coiled bud

Simple root (rhizome)

Fig. 6.3 Fern

Ferns e.g. bracken, maidenhair fern

▷ larger land plants which live in damp, shady places
▷ simple roots, stems and leaves (called **fronds**)
▷ xylem and phloem tubes present to carry water and sugars
▷ fronds are coiled inside the bud
▷ no flowers or seeds
▷ reproduces by making **spores**
▷ spores are usually grouped in clusters on the underside of fronds.

Conifers e.g. pine, larch

▷ trees or shrubs which often live in dry areas
▷ proper roots, stems and leaves
▷ simple xylem and phloem tubes to carry water and sugars
▷ leaves are usually needle shaped
▷ no flowers
▷ produces seeds inside **cones**

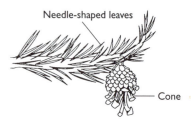

Needle-shaped leaves

Cone

Fig. 6.4 Conifer

Flowering plants

▷ live on land or in water, very variable in size
▷ proper roots, stems and leaves
▷ xylem and phloem tubes present
▷ have **flowers** which contain reproductive organs
▷ produce seeds which are enclosed in a **fruit**
▷ can be divided into two main types: monocots and dicots

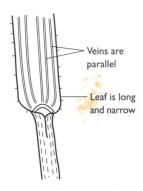

Veins are parallel

Leaf is long and narrow

Fig. 6.5 Flowering plant: monocot

Monocots, e.g. grass, daffodil, iris, barley, maize

▷ have narrow leaves with **parallel veins**
▷ have one seed leaf (cotyledon) inside seeds

Dicots, e.g. daisy, ivy, rose, oak, sycamore

▷ have broad leaves with a **network of veins**
▷ have two seed leaves (cotyledons) inside seeds.

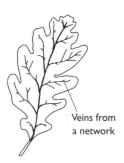

Veins from a network

Fig. 6.6 Flowering plant: dicot

Classification of animals

Key points

▷ animal cells never have a cell wall;

▷ animals feed on organic material, e.g. proteins, carbohydrates;

▷ animals are divided into two main groups,
   invertebrates
   vertebrates

▷ Invertebrates have no bones or skeleton inside their bodies, e.g. insects, spiders, earthworms;

▷ vertebrates have a skeleton inside the body, including a backbone, e.g. fish, birds, mammals.

Invertebrates

Invertebrates have no bones or skeleton inside their body. There are many groups of invertebrates, and we will consider six in detail:

annelids	crustaceans
molluscs	arachnids
insects	myriapods

Annelids (ringed worms) e.g. earthworms

▶ body is divided into **segments**
▶ no legs
▶ most have bristles (chaetae) to anchor them in the soil
▶ damp body surface (covered in mucus)

Fig. 6.7 Annelid

Molluscs, e.g. snails, slugs, limpets, mussels

▶ soft body
▶ no legs
▶ body may be protected by one or two **shells**

Fig. 6.8 Mollusc

Insects, e.g. housefly, locust, dragonfly

▶ body has a hard covering (**exoskeleton**)
▶ body has three distinct regions (head, thorax and abdomen)
▶ three pairs of legs
▶ usually two pairs of **wings**
▶ one pair of **antennae**

Fig. 6.9 Insect

Crustaceans, e.g. woodlice, crabs, shrimps

▶ body has a hard covering (**exoskeleton**)
▶ many legs or 'leg-like structures'
▶ two pairs of **antennae**

Fig. 6.10 Crustacean

Arachnids, e.g. garden spider, harvestman, mites

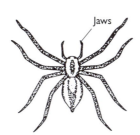

Jaws

Fig. 6.11 Arachnid

▶ body has a hard covering (**exoskeleton**)
▶ four pairs of legs
▶ no antennae

Myriapods, e.g. centipedes, millipedes

▶ body has a hard covering (**exoskeleton**)
▶ body is divided into many **segments**
▶ one or two pairs of legs on each segment
▶ one pair of **antennae**

Fig. 6.12 Myriapod

Vertebrates

Vertebrates have a skeleton inside the body, including a backbone. There are five groups of vertebrates;

fish
amphibians
reptiles
birds
mammals

Fish, e.g. trout, carp, cod, pike

▷ body covered in **damp scales**
▷ no legs
▷ **fins** to move through water
▷ breathe using **gills**
▷ cold blooded
▷ always live in water
▷ lay eggs with no shells in water

Fig. 6.13 Fish

Amphibians, e.g. frogs, toads, newts

▷ moist body covering (**no scales**)
▷ four legs
▷ breathe using **lungs** (when adult)
▷ cold blooded
▷ adults live on land, but lay eggs in water
▷ lay eggs with no shells

Fig. 6.14 Amphibian

Reptiles, e.g. crocodile, lizard, tortoise, snake

▷ body covered with **dry scales**
▷ most have four legs
▷ breathe using **lungs**
▷ cold blooded
▷ mostly live on land, some feed in water
▷ lay eggs with soft, leathery shells on land

Fig. 6.15 Reptile

Birds, e.g. starling, crow, owl, gull

▷ body covered with **feathers**
▷ two legs
▷ one pair of **wings**
▷ breathe using **lungs**
▷ warm blooded
▷ most live on land
▷ lay hard shelled eggs on land

Fig. 6.16 Bird

Mammals, e.g. humans, dogs, squirrels

▷ skin covered in **hair or fur**
▷ most have four legs
▷ breathe using **lungs**
▷ warm blooded
▷ most live on land
▷ eggs develop **inside** the mother's body so babies are born live
▷ babies fed on **milk** from the mother's mammary glands

Fig. 6.17 Mammal

Using keys

Scientists have found over two million different types of organisms living on Earth. It is not possible for anyone to remember the names of all these organisms, or to be able to identify them immediately. Instead we use a key – this is a list of questions about the organism which enables us to identify it.

Key points

▷   you must observe the organism you are trying to identify very carefully;

▷   always start at the beginning of a key;

▷   there are two types of keys: branching keys,
                                    number keys.

Branching key

This is set out as a flowchart (Fig. 6.18). For each question there is a simple choice and only one of the answers can be correct.

This type of key is easy to use, but is only suitable for a small number of organisms because it takes up a lot of space.

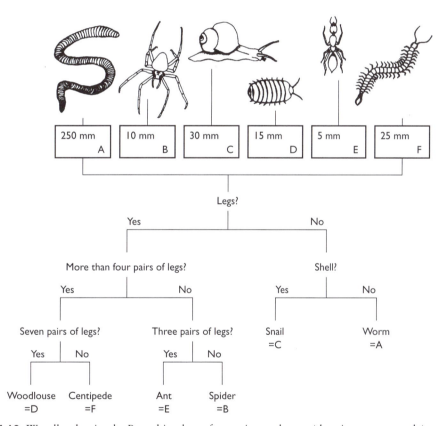

Fig. 6.18 Woodland animals: Branching key of some invertebrates (drawings not to scale).

Number key

This is set out as a list of questions. For each question there is a simple choice and an instruction about what to do next, e.g. go to 2.

1.	Legs present?	Yes:	go to 2	(B,D,E,F)
	....	No:	go to 5	(A,C)
2.	More than four pairs of legs	Yes:	go to 3	(D,F)
	....	No:	go to 4	(B,E)
3.	Seven pairs of legs present?	Yes:	woodlouse	(D)
	....	No:	centipede	(F)
4.	Three pairs of legs present?	Yes:	ant	(E)
	....	No:	spider	(B)
5.	Shell present?	Yes:	snail	(C)
	....	No:	earthworm	(A)

This type of key can hold much more information in a small space.

Sometimes you are required to show which numbers you have used to reach the name of the organism.

REVISION ACTIVITY I   Use the key to name each of the leaves shown in Fig. 6.19. As you work through the key for each leaf, tick the boxes in Table 6.1 to show how you got your answer.
Leaf A has been done for you.

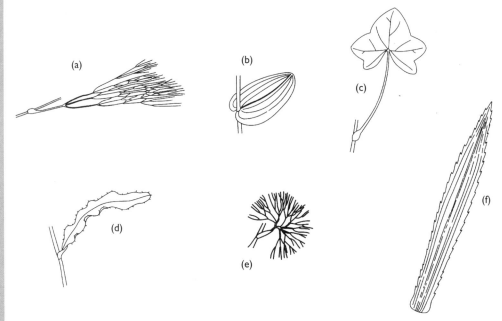

Fig. 6.19 Water plants

Key			*Name of plant*
1.	(a)	Leaf of many fine strands – go to number 2	
	(b)	Leaf formed of a flat blade – go to number 3	
2.	(a)	Strands branch into threes	**River crowfoot**
	(b)	Strands branch irregularly	**Round-leaved crowfoot**
3.	(a)	Leaf has a toothed edge – go to number 4	
	(b)	Edge of leaf smooth – go to number 5	
4.	(a)	Flat leaf sharply toothed	**Water soldier**
	(b)	Wavy leaf with many small teeth	**Curled pondweed**
5.	(a)	Oval leaf without lobes	**Perforated pondweed**
	(b)	Leaf has five main lobes	**Ivy-leaved crowfoot**

Table 6.1 Key questions used

Leaf	I(a)	I(b)	2(a)	2(b)	3(a)	3(b)	4(a)	4(b)	5(a)	5(b)	Name of plant
A	✔		✔								**River crowfoot**
B											
C											
D											
E											
F											

Types of variation

Key points
▶ variation is usually defined as differences between individuals of the same species;
▶ there are two main types of variation, continuous and discontinuous.

Continuous variation

- ▶ Individuals do not fit into clearly defined groups.
- ▶ Measurement is usually involved, e.g. of height, length.
- ▶ There is a range of values from the greatest to the least.
- ▶ This type of variation occurs when the feature is controlled by several genes, e.g. human height, or when the feature is influenced by the environment of lifestyle, e.g. human mass.
- ▶ Examples include human height, length of insect pupae, human mass, IQ.
- ▶ We display the data as a histogram (bars touching).

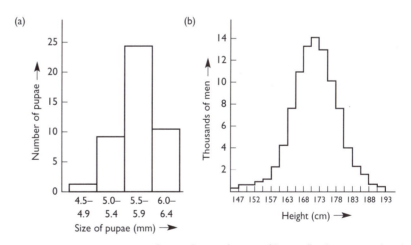

Fig. 6.20 Continuous variation: (a) Number and size of pupa of house fly (b) Human height

Discontinuous variation

- ▶ Individuals fit into clearly defined groups.
- ▶ Measurement or observation may be involved.
- ▶ This type of variation occurs when the feature is controlled by a single gene, e.g. human blood group, or when the environment does not directly affect that characteristic, e.g. human eye colour.
- ▶ Examples include height in pea plants, human blood groups, human eye colour.
- ▶ We can display the data as a histogram (bars completely separate) or as a pie chart.

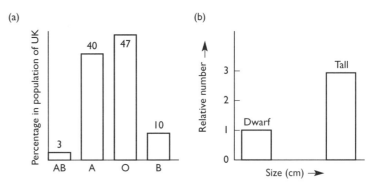

Fig. 6.21 Discontinuous variation: (a) Human blood groups (b) Height in pea plants

Causes of variation

Key points

▷ most variation is inherited, i.e. it has genetic causes;

▷ the environment organisms live in can cause variation, even when the organisms are genetically identical;

▷ mutation increases variation.

Genetic variation

This is the biggest cause of variation. Genes are passed on from parents to offspring during reproduction.

If one parent passes on **all** their genes to their offspring, the new individual will be genetically identical to that parent: we call this **asexual reproduction** (see p. 179).

In **sexual reproduction** gametes contain **some** genes from a parent, and when the offspring develops after fertilization they will have a mixture of genes from their two parents, so they will not be identical to either (see p. 180).

Genetic variation happens in three main ways.

1. **Offspring inherit a mixture of genes from both their parents.**
   In this way, they have features from both, but are not identical to either parent

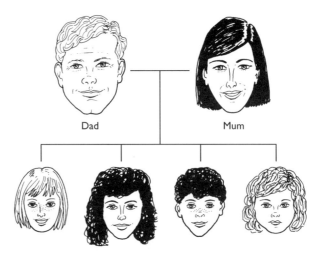

Fig. 6.22 Family tree to show genetic variation

This happens because gametes are **haploid**, i.e. they contain half the normal number of chromosomes (so they have half the normal number of genes). When gametes are formed by meiosis, they are not all identical to each other: different gametes from the same individual will contain different combinations of genes.

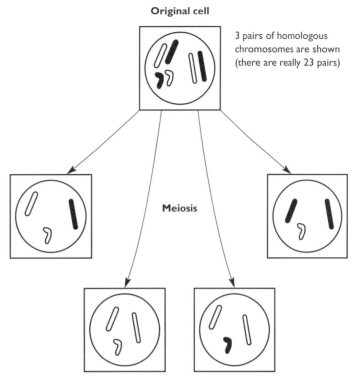

Fig. 6.23 Independent assortment

This is sometimes called independent assortment of genes.

2. **Genes are swapped between chromosomes during meiosis.**
   Sometimes during **meiosis** (the type of cell division which produces gametes), chromosomes become tangled together and break. When they repair themselves, they may join up wrongly and genes are swapped from one chromosome to another. This increases variation: the process is called **crossing over.**

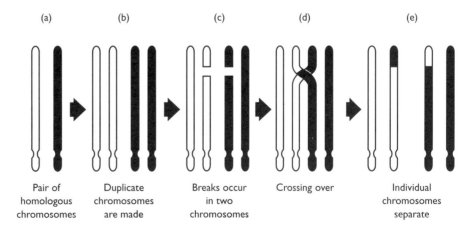

Fig. 6.24 Crossing over during meiosis

3. **Mutation can occur.**
   When a cell is about to divide (by mitosis or meiosis), an extra set of chromosomes must be made: this process is called **replication.**
   Sometimes a copying mistake is made during replication, and this results in a faulty gene. Copying mistakes like this are called mutations (see pp. 180–2).

Environmental variation
Even genetically identical organisms can show variation if they are exposed to different environmental factors,

▶ Two genetically identical animals fed different diets may show variation (one many suffer from a deficiency disease).

▶ Two genetically identical seedlings given different quantities of minerals may show variation: plants deficient in magnesium have yellow leaves.

▶ Identical twin humans who have different lifestyles may show variation. Exercise will increase the size of muscles, and exposure to UV light will darken the skin.

Genes and variation

Key points

▷ chromosomes are lengths of DNA carrying large numbers of genes;

▷ a gene is a small section of DNA which contains instructions for a single feature of the organism;

▷ genes exist in alternative forms called alleles; this increases variation;

▷ genes are passed on from parents to offspring during reproduction;

▷ genes are present in pairs in body cells (these cells are diploid), and singly in gametes (these cells are haploid);

▷ organisms which have the same genes are said to be genetically identical – they are clones.

What are chromosomes?
Inside the nucleus of all cells are long threads of DNA called chromosomes. Most of the time it is impossible to see them, even with a powerful microscope, because they are so thin. Just before the cell divides, they coil up so they are shorter and thicker, and they can be seen with a microscope.
Each chromosome carries thousands of genes.

In body cells, chromosomes occur in pairs (called homologous pairs), and each chromosome of the pair carries the same set of genes. These cells are diploid.

In gametes, chromosomes occur singly (only one chromosome from each pair is present), and these cells are haploid.

What are genes?
A gene is a small section of DNA which contains instructions for a single feature of the organism. It is not possible to see genes on a chromosome, but scientists know that most chromosomes contain thousands of genes.

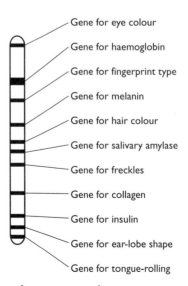

Fig. 6.25 Possible arrangement for genes on a chromosome

In fact, each gene is an instruction to make a particular protein inside the body, and these proteins determine how the body works. A particular gene will always occupy the same position on a chromosome.

The **genotype** is the genetic make-up that a particular individual has. Genes are usually given letter symbols, e.g. Bb.

The **phenotype** is the appearance or characteristics of an individual, e.g. blue eyes, black hair.

What are alleles?

Genes can exist in alternative forms called alleles. For example, the gene controlling fur colour in mice has two alleles, one for brown fur and one for black fur; the gene controlling blood group in humans has three alleles – the allele for group A, the allele for group B, and the allele for group 0.

When biologists are studying inheritance, alleles are usually given symbols,

e.g. B = allele for black fur
  b = allele for brown fur

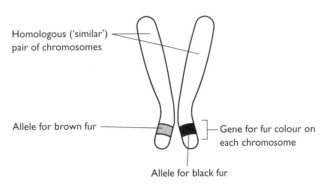

Fig. 6.26 Alleles for fur colour in mice

Usually one of the alleles is 'stronger' than the other, and this is called the **dominant allele**. If a mouse has the alleles Bb, the allele for black fur (B) is dominant so the mouse will have black fur. The dominant allele is given a capital letter symbol.

The 'weaker' allele is called the **recessive allele**. If a mouse has the alleles Bb, the allele for brown fur (b) is recessive, and it will be masked by the dominant allele, so the mouse has black fur. Brown-furred mice must have two alleles for brown fur (bb).

Diploid and haploid cells

In body cells, chromosomes occur in pairs, and each chromosome of the pair contains the same set of genes. However, they may contain different alleles for those genes. For example, a mouse body cell will contain two genes for fur colour (one of each chromosome of a particular homologous pair).

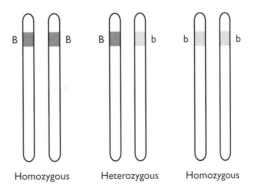

Fig. 6.27 Homozygous and heterozygous individuals

If the two alleles are the same, we say the individual is **homozygous** for that gene, e.g. BB, or bb.

If the two alleles are different, we say the individual is **heterozygous** for that gene, e.g. Bb.

Whenever chromosomes occur in pairs (homologous pairs) and there are two alleles present for a particular gene, we say the cell is **diploid**. All body cells are diploid.

In gametes, only one chromosome from each pair is present, so there is only one allele for a particular gene. We say these cells are **haploid**: haploid cells always contain half as many chromosomes as diploid cells (for the same species).

REVISION ACTIVITY 2 This section contains lots of very important new words. Match the words in the box to the definitions underneath.

homozygous	genotype	dominant	haploid
heterozygous	phenotype	recessive	diploid
chromosome	gene	homologous	allele

(a) a long thread of DNA _____

(b) a body cell with pairs of chromosomes _____

(c) a 'strong' allele _____

(d) an individual who has two identical alleles _____

(e) a 'weaker' allele _____

(f) a gamete with single chromosomes (not paired) _____

(g) the appearance of an individual _____

(h) the genes an individual has _____

(i) an individual who has two different alleles for a particular gene _____

(j) an instruction about a single feature _____

(k) a matching pair of chromosomes _____

(l) alternative forms of a gene _____

Chromosome number

Under normal circumstances, the diploid number of chromosomes remains constant for a particular species, and this is called its chromosome number. The number will vary from species to species. e.g.

Table 6.2

Species	Chromosome number (diploid)
Human	46
Onion	16
Tomato	24
Goldfish	100
Potato	48
Mouse	40

The haploid number, i.e. the number of chromosomes present in the gametes, is always half of the diploid number.

Occasionally the number of chromosomes in an organism or species will vary, usually due to an error in **meiosis** (cell division which produces gametes). People with Down's syndrome have 47 chromosomes, rather than 46. If a whole set of chromosomes do not separate properly during meiosis, a diploid gamete can be formed leading to a triploid zygote. This is called **polyploidy**, and it is fatal in animals, but can actually benefit plants. (See section on selective breeding, pp. 193–5).

Asexual reproduction

Key points
▶ only one parent is involved;
▶ the offspring are genetically identical to the parent and to each other;
▶ the offspring are called clones;
▶ gametes and fertilization are not involved.

Variation and asexual reproduction

Under normal circumstances, asexual reproduction does not cause variation because

▶ only one parent is involved;
▶ that parent passes on a full set of genes to each offspring;
▶ the offspring are therefore genetically identical to the parent and to each other. They are called clones.

This type of reproduction is very useful if environmental conditions are stable, and if the organism is well adapted to those conditions.

However, variation can occur as a result of mutation (see pp. 180–2). This is the only cause of variation during asexual reproduction.

Examples of asexual reproduction

Asexual reproduction occurs in:

▶ many microbes, e.g. bacteria (binary fission)
    yeasts (budding)
▶ many plants, e.g. daffodils, onions (bulbs)
    strawberries
    grass
    potatoes
▶ simple animals, e.g. hydra (budding)

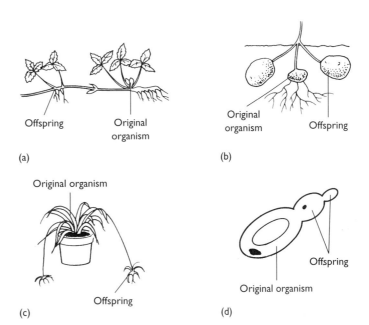

Fig. 6.28 Asexual reproduction (a) in strawberry plants (runners) (b) in potato plants (tubers) (c) in spider plants (d) in yeast (budding)

Sexual reproduction

Key points

▷ usually two parents are involved;

▷ gametes from each parent join at fertilization;

▷ the offspring inherits genes from each parent;

▷ the offspring are similar, but not identical, to the parents and to each other.

Variation and sexual reproduction

Sexual reproduction increases the amount of variation in a population, because:

▷ Gametes are **haploid** (they contain only one of each pair of alleles for a particular feature). When gametes are formed by meiosis, different combinations of alleles come together in different gametes, i.e. the gametes from one individual are not identical to each other. **This is independent assortment.**

▷ When meiosis occurs, pieces of chromosomes may break off and be transferred to other chromosomes, i.e. genes may be swapped between chromosomes. This is called **crossing-over**, and it increases variation.

▷ When fertilization occurs, gametes fuse together, i.e. genes from two parents join to form the **zygote**. The zygote will inherit some features from each parent, but will not be identical to either of them.

▷ There is a large amount of **variation** already present in the population, i.e. adults will choose which individuals to mate with depending on the characteristics they have. This variety leads to **choice**, which increases variety even more.

This type of reproduction is very useful if environmental conditions are changing, because offspring will be different to their parents and they may be better adapted to the new conditions, i.e. more likely to survive.

Mutation can occur in sexual reproduction, increasing variation even more (see pp. 180–1).

Examples of sexual reproduction

Sexual reproduction occurs in:

▷ Some microbes, e.g. yeast
▷ many plants,   e.g. daffodils
                        strawberries
                        grass
                        potatoes
▷ most animals,   e.g. hydra
                        earthworms
                        humans

Mutation

Key points

▷ a mutation is a change in genetic material (genes);

▷ mutations normally occur when the DNA is being copied before cell division;

▷ mutations may be harmful, neutral or beneficial;

▷ the mutation rate can be increased by exposure to mutagens, e.g. UV light, chemicals in tobacco;

▷ mutations increase variation in a population, and are important in natural selection.

How do mutations happen?

Mutations are changes in genetic material (genes). They can happen in two ways.

1. **DNA is not copied properly before cell division**

   When a cell is about to divide (by mitosis or meiosis), a new set of chromosomes must be made so that the new cells have their own set of chromosomes. This process is called **replication**; the DNA copies itself to make the new chromosomes.

   Sometimes mistakes are made in this copying process so that the new chromosomes are faulty. Usually they are small mistakes, involving only one gene, so they are called **gene mutations** or point mutations. However, they can be a serious problem for the individual if a very important gene is affected.

2. **Chromosomes are damaged and break**

   If chromosomes break, they will normally repair themselves (the DNA will rejoin), but they may not repair themselves correctly. This can lead to large changes in the structure of the DNA, and may affect large numbers of genes. The damage may even be visible under the microscope – these are called **chromosome mutations**.

   There are several types of chromosome mutations, e.g.

   deletion – some DNA is missing
   duplication – some DNA has been copied twice
   inversion – some DNA is the wrong way around
   translocation – some DNA is in the wrong place, i.e. it has joined onto another chromosome

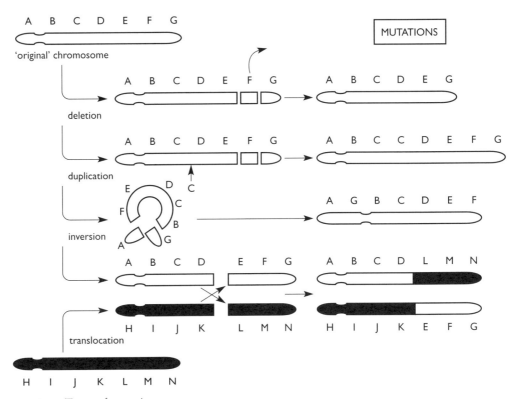

Fig. 6.29 Types of mutations

Chromosome mutations often cause a serious problem for the individual because many genes are affected. They may even be lethal (cause death).

Mutagens and the mutation rate.

Mutations happen naturally, for no obvious reason. However, scientists have found that the mutation rate is increased if organisms are exposed to **mutagens**. These are factors in the environment which increase the mutation rate, and include:

▶ X-rays, gamma radiation and UV light;
▶ chemicals in tobacco smoke.

It is wrong to say that mutagens cause mutation, because not every individual who is exposed to mutagens suffers from mutations. However, we know that increased exposure to mutagens increases the risk of mutations occurring.

Why are mutations important?

Mutations are important because they increase variation in a population.

Most mutations are harmful to the individual concerned. A mistake in replication or chromosome damage leads to faulty genes which do not work properly. If the mutation is in a body cell, it may cause cancer, e.g.

▷ increased exposure to UV light (sunbathing or on sunbeds) is linked to skin cancer;
▷ increased exposure to chemicals in cigarette smoke (particularly hydrocarbons in tar) is linked to lung cancer.

If the mutation is in a gamete, it will not affect the individual producing the gamete, but will affect the zygote that develops from it, i.e. the offspring. The genetic disease sickle cell anaemia and haemophilia can be caused in this way. Once a mutation like this has occurred, it can be passed on through many generations of the same family.

Some mutations are neutral to the individual concerned, i.e. they do not cause harm or benefit. This can happen if:

▷ the change in DNA is so small that it does not affect the way that the gene works, e.g. if only a single base on the DNA is affected;
▷ the affected gene is not vital for survival, e.g. a mutation could cause an individual to have a different ear-shape, but this is neither harmful nor beneficial to them.

A small number of mutations are beneficial to the individual concerned, i.e. they would make the individual more likely to survive. Examples of this type of mutations include:

▷ change in wing colour of peppered moths (see p. 207): the original moths were pale, but the mutant dark moths were better camouflaged in industrial areas, so they were more likely to survive;
▷ antibiotic resistance in bacteria: most bacteria are killed by antibiotics, but mutant resistant bacteria are not killed.

When mutations occur this increases variation in a population, and provides the raw material for natural selection (see p. 206).

---

see p. 207
see p. 206

REVISION ACTIVITY 3

(a) Write a definition for:
   (i) mutation
   (ii) replication
   (iii) mutagen
(b) Explain why
   (i) it is wrong to say that mutagens cause mutations
   (ii) only a small percentage of mutations are beneficial, most are harmful or neutral.

▷ Inheritance

Inheritance means the way that parents pass on characteristics to their offspring through genes. A famous scientist called Mendel first worked out how this happened in the nineteenth-century, and we still use the rules he developed when studying patterns of inheritance. These rules are the same for all plants and animals, and allow us to draw genetic diagrams (called monohybrid crosses) to explain how characteristics are inherited.

This section of the book deals with two main themes:

1. How do parents pass on characteristics to their offspring?
2. How can humans manipulate this process, to get the types of offspring most useful to them?

Sex determination in humans

Key points

▷ the sex of an individual (its gender), is determined at fertilization;

▷ gender is controlled by a pair of sex chromosomes;

▷ females are always XX, males are always XY;

▷ all eggs (ova) carry one X chromosome;

▷ sperm carry either one X or one Y chromosome; there are equal numbers of the two types of sperm.

In humans, gender is controlled by a pair of sex chromosomes. There are two types of sex chromosomes, called X and Y. They look different from each other: the X chromosome is bigger, and it is a different shape.

Females always have two X chromosomes, so they are described as XX. When female gametes (ova) are formed by meiosis, the gametes are haploid, so all ova carry one X chromosome (plus 22 other chromosomes).

Males always have one X chromosome and one Y chromosome, so they are described as XY. When male gametes (sperm) are formed by meiosis, the gametes are haploid. Equal numbers of two different types of sperm cells formed – half the sperm cells will carry an X chromosome (plus 22 other chromosomes) and half will carry a Y chromosome (plus 22 other chromosomes).

The sex (gender) of a baby depends on which type of sperm cell fertilizes the egg.

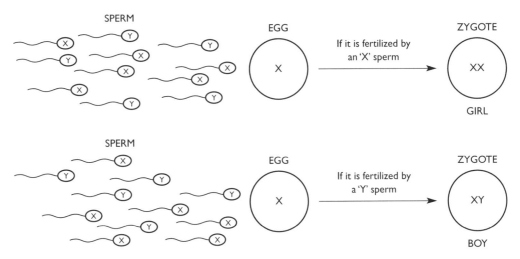

Fig. 6.30 Fertilization

Events can be summarised using the following diagram (Fig. 6.31).

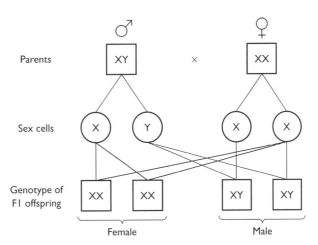

Fig. 6.31 Sex determination

REVISION ACTIVITY 4 Explain why roughly equal numbers of boys and girls are born.

Genetics problems (monohybrid crosses)

You may need to read the section 'Genes and variation' on pp. 176–8 before reading this part.

Key points

▶   a monohybrid cross shows how a single feature is inherited;

▶   you should use the genotypes of the parents to predict the possible genotypes of the off-spring;

▶   in most cases, one allele will be dominant to the other (the weaker one is called the recessive allele);

▶   in a few cases, neither allele is dominant or recessive – they are said to be co-dominant;

▶   some alleles are sex-linked, because they are carried on the X chromosome.

Glossary of important terms used in genetics problems

gene	a section of DNA which carries instructions about a single feature
allele	an alternative form of a gene, e.g. gene for eye colour has an allele for blue eyes and an allele for brown eyes
homozygous	an individual with two identical alleles for a particular gene. Symbols are AA or aa
heterozygous	an individual with two different alleles for a particular gene. Symbol is Aa
true-breeding	homozygous
dominant	the 'stronger' of the two alleles, this is always shown in the phenotype if it is present
recessive	the 'weaker' of the two alleles. This is only shown in the phenotype if there are two recessive alleles present
genotype	the genes an individual has
phenotype	the appearance or characteristics of an individual
Punnett square	an easy way of showing possible offspring in a genetic diagram
F1	the first set of offspring, i.e. the 'children' of the original parents
F2	the second set of offspring, i.e. the 'grandchildren' of the original parents
co-dominance	neither allele is dominant or recessive, and they both show equally in the phenotype
sex-linkage	alleles for these features are carried on the X chromosome

Setting out genetics problem

Suppose we are told that a black mouse and a brown mouse are mated together: how can we predict what colour fur the baby mice will have?

Before we can set out the problem, we need two key pieces of information:

1.   Which allele is dominant, and which allele is recessive?
2.   What are the genotypes of the parents?

A typical genetics problem would be worded like this:

'In mice, the allele for black fur is dominant to the allele for brown fur. A homozygous black furred mouse is mated with a homozygous brown furred mouse. What colour fur would the offspring have?'

There are five steps to answering this question:

1.   Choose symbols to represent the alleles.
2.   Write down the genotypes of the parents.
3.   Write down the gametes each parent can produce.
       Remember: a homozygous individual produces **one** type of gamete,
                          a heterozygous individual produces **two** types of gamete.
4.   Draw a Punnett square or cross to show the offspring which are produced.
5.   Write a short statement about the numbers or ratio of the offspring produced.

Step 1   B is the allele for black fur
          b is the allele for brown fur

Step 2   Parents

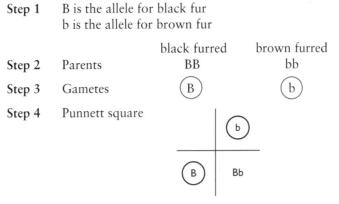

Fig. 6.32

Step 5   All the offspring are Bb, so they all have black fur.

We can look at a second example still involving fur colour in mice.

'A heterozygous black mouse is mated with a brown mouse. What phenotypes would the offspring have?'

Step 1   B is the allele for black fur
          b is the allele for brown fur

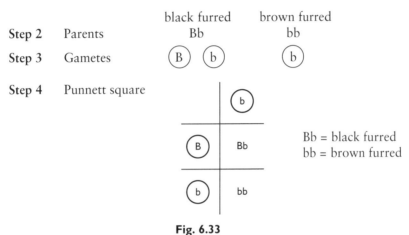

Bb = black furred
bb = brown furred

Fig. 6.33

Step 5   Half of the offspring will be brown, and half will be black. It is a 1 : 1 ratio.

There is an alternative way to set this out, not involving a Punnett square:

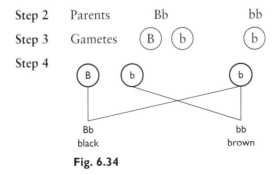

Fig. 6.34

Step 5   Half the offspring will be brown, and half will be black. It is a 1:1 ratio

If you use this method, you must be sure that you always join a male gamete to a female gamete.

Example 3: 'Two heterozygous black mice are mated together. What will be the ratio of phenotypes of their offspring?'

Step 1   B is the allele for black fur
b is the allele for brown fur

Step 2   Parents   black furred   black furred
Bb   Bb

Step 3   Gametes   Ⓑ ⓑ   Ⓑ ⓑ

Step 4   Punnett square

	Ⓑ	ⓑ
Ⓑ	BB	Bb
ⓑ	Bb	bb

BB = black fur
Bb = black fur
Bb = black fur
bb = brown fur

Fig. 6.35

Step 5   Three-quarters of the offspring will be black, and one-quarter will be brown. The ratio is 3 : 1.

The rules for genetics problems are the same, no matter which organisms are involved. You must:

1. Choose suitable symbols for the alleles (the dominant allele has a capital letter and the recessive allele has a lower-case letter).
2. Look carefully at the information you are given in the question, e.g. about phenotypes of the parents, whether they are homozygous or heterozygous.
3. Set out the problem carefully, using the steps outlined in the examples. Never miss steps out, or guess at the answer.
4. Make sure you have actually answered the question. You could be asked 'What are the phenotypes of the offspring?', or 'They have eight babies, how many of them have black fur?', or 'What is the ratio of black to brown mice?'

REVISION ACTIVITY 5   In pea plants, the allele for tall (T) is dominant to allele for dwarf (t). Complete the diagram to show what happens when a heterozygous tall plant is crossed with a dwarf plant. What percentage of the offspring are tall?

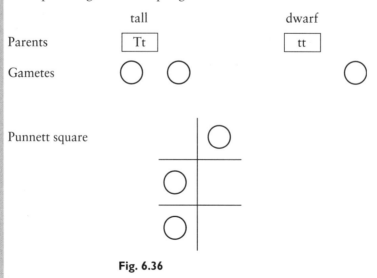

Fig. 6.36

Answer _____

REVISION ACTIVITY 6
'Remember to use the five step outlined on page 184'

In pea plants the allele for round seed is dominant to the allele for wrinkled seed. Show what would happen if two heterozygous round seed plants are crossed together. What will be the ratio of phenotypes of the offspring?

REVISION ACTIVITY 7

(a) In fruit flies, the allele for long wing (L) is dominant to the allele for short wing (ℓ). A scientist carried out the breeding experiments shown below. Tick the boxes to show the phenotypes of the offspring in each breeding experiment

Table 6.3

Cross	Genotypes of parents	Phenotypes of offspring	
		Long wing	Short wing
1.	LL × LL		
2.	Lℓ × $\ell\ell$		
3.	Lℓ × Lℓ		
4.	LL × $\ell\ell$		

(b) What would the genotypes of the parents be if all of the offspring were short winged?

Problems with pedigrees
Sometimes, the question will give you information in the form of a pedigree, or family tree. You will probably have to draw your own genetic diagrams to work out the answer.

Example 1: Tongue rolling in humans is controlled by a single gene. The allele for rolling (R) is dominant to the allele for non-rolling (r).

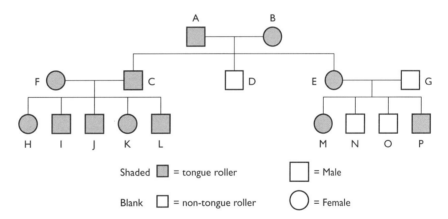

Fig. 6.37 Family pedigree: tongue-rolling

What is the genotype of B?
                         C?
                         D?
                         E?
                         P?

In order to answer this question, we must look very carefully at the information we are given.

A and B: can both roll their tongues, they have children who can (C and E) and a child who can't
∴ they are both heterozygous (Rr)

C and F: can both roll their tongues
all their children can roll their tongues
∴ they are probably both homozygous (RR)

E: can roll her tongue, so may be Rr or RR. Her husband G cannot, so he must be rr.
Some of their children can roll (M and P) and some cannot (N and O)
∴ E must be heterozygous (Rr)

From this, we can give the answers
B = Rr, C = RR, D = rr, E = Rr, P = Rr

Co-dominance (incomplete dominance)
In a few cases, neither allele is dominant or recessive.
They are both equally dominant, and both show equally in the phenotype.

Example 1
A red flowered plant is crossed with a white flowered plant. The alleles for flower colour are co-dominant. Show the cross; and show what would happen if two of the offspring are crossed together.

In these problems, you should use two different capital letter symbols for the two alleles.
e.g. R is the allele for red flowers
      W is the allele for white flowers

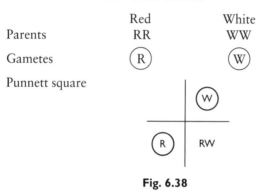

Fig. 6.38

All the offspring are pink-flowered (RW). If two of these pink-flowered plants are crossed together:

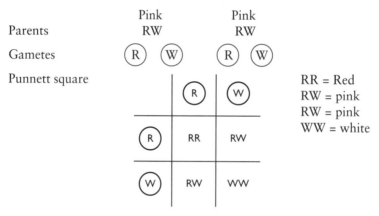

RR = Red
RW = pink
RW = pink
WW = white

Fig. 6.39

One-quarter of the offspring will be red flowered, half will be pink flowered, and one-quarter will be white flowered.
The ratio is 1:2:1.

REVISION ACTIVITY 8   What would happen if:

(a) a pink flowered plant (RW) was crossed with a red flowered plant (RR)?
(b) a pink flowered plant (RW) was crossed with a white flowered plant (WW)?

Human blood groups
The ABO blood group system in humans is another example of co-dominance.
   There are three possible alleles : A, B and O. All humans have two of these alleles, e.g. AA, AO, BB, BO, AB, or OO.

The rules of dominance are:

Allele A is dominant to allele O.
Allele B is dominant to allele O.
Alleles A and B and co-dominant (equally dominant).

The alleles a person has determines his or her blood group.

Table 6.4

Genotype	Blood group (phenotype)	Reason
AA	A	two alleles for blood group A
AO	A	allele A is dominant to allele O
BB	B	two alleles for blood group B
BO	B	allele B is dominant to allele O
AB	AB	alleles A and B are co-dominant
OO	O	two alleles for blood group O.

Example 1

A woman (genotype BO) and her husband (genotype AA) have four children. What would you expect their blood groups to be?

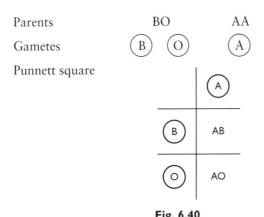

Fig. 6.40

You would expect half the children to be blood group A, and half to be blood group AB.

Example 2

Problems are sometimes set out using the following symbols:

A woman with the genotype $I^A I^B$ is married to a man with the genotype $I^O I^O$ and they have one child whose blood group is AB. Could the husband be the father of this child?

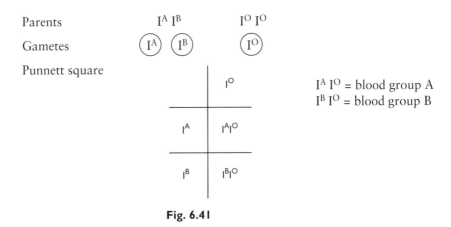

$I^A I^O$ = blood group A
$I^B I^O$ = blood group B

Fig. 6.41

No, this man could not be the father of a child with blood group AB.

REVISION ACTIVITY 9 I^A, I^B and I^O are the alleles of the gene which controls human blood groups.

(a)   Using these symbols, what are the possible genotypes of people with the following blood group?

(i)   Group AB _____

(ii)   Group O _____

(iii)   Group B _____

(b)   Which blood group is the result of co-dominance? _____

Sex linkage

Some alleles are carried on the X chromosome, so they are described as sex-linked. This means that women have two of these alleles (because they have two X chromosomes), but men only have one.

Red-green colour-blindness is an example of a sex-linked condition. The allele for normal vision (N), is dominant to the allele for colour-blindness (n). There are five possible genotypes.

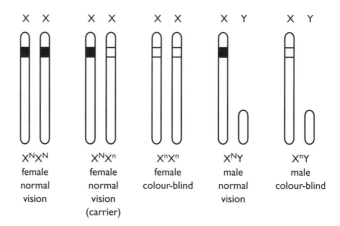

Fig. 6.42 Genotypes for colour vision

Remember: A woman can be heterozygous for colour-blindness (a carrier); a man can never be hetrozygous.

Example 1

A woman hetrozygous for red-green colour-blindness is married to a normal man and they have one child. If it is a girl, what is the probability she is colour-blind?

N is the allele for normal vision.
n is the allele for colour-blindness.

Parents   Mother $X^N X^n$ Father $X^N Y$

Gametes X^N X^n X^N Y

Punnett square

	X^N	Y
X^N	$X^N X^N$	$X^N Y$
X^n	$X^N X^n$	$X^n Y$

$X^N X^N$ = normal girl
$X^N Y$ = normal boy
$X^N X^n$ = carrier girl
$X^n Y$ = colour-blind boy

Fig. 6.43

The probability of their daughter being colour-blind is 0.

REVISION ACTIVITY 10   A colour-blind man is married to a woman with normal vision ($X^N X^N$). What are the possible genotypes of their children?

Haemophilia is another sex-linked condition (see p. 193 for more on this).

Genetic diseases

Key points
▷   genetic diseases are caused by faulty genes, and can be passed on from parents to offspring;
▷   cystic fibrosis, Huntington's disease, sickle cell anaemia and haemophilia are all genetic diseases;
▷   genetic diseases cannot be cured, but in many cases the symptoms can be treated;
▷   heterozygous individuals are often called carriers, because they can pass the disease on.

Autosomal dominant diseases, e.g. Huntington's disease
Diseases like this are caused by a **dominant allele,**

e.g. H is the allele for Huntington's disease
        h is the allele for normal health

an individual with the genotype   **HH** has the disease
                                                  Hh has the disease
                                                  hh does not have the disease

People who have this disease often do not show any symptoms until they are over 40 years of age. By this time they may have married and had children, and passed the disease on to the children without realising that they were affected. The symptoms are loss of control over movement and thought processes.

REVISION ACTIVITY 11   (a)   Look at the family tree. If Sam has the genotype Hh, give the genotypes of Alice, Jo, Liz and Ben.

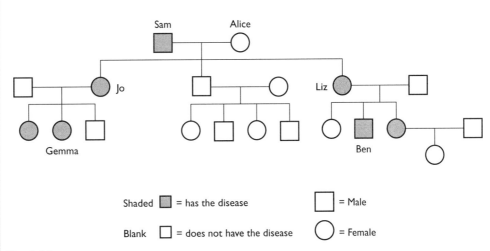

Shaded ■ = has the disease   □ = Male

Blank □ = does not have the disease   ◯ = Female

Fig. 6.44

(b)   Gemma and Ben are cousins. If they married and had one child, what is the probability that it would have this disease?

Autosomal recessive diseases, e.g. cystic fibrosis
Diseases like this are caused by a recessive allele,

e.g. C is the allele for normal health
        c is the allele for cystic fibrosis

an individual with the genotype CC does not have the disease
                                 Cc does not have the disease (but is a carrier)
                                 cc has cystic fibrosis.

People who have this disease produce very thick, sticky mucus which blocks the air passages in the respiratory system, and causes problems with digestion and absorption in the gut.

REVISION ACTIVITY 12 Look at this family tree (Fig. 6.45). Julie and John are both carriers for cystic fibrosis, so we would expect a quarter of their children to have the disease.

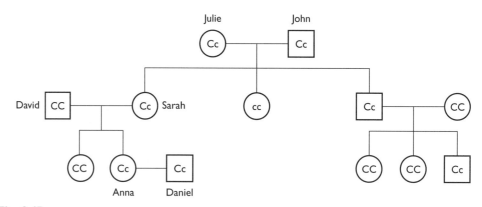

Fig. 6.45

(a) How many children do they have?
(b) How many are carriers?
(c) How many have the disease?
(d) Could Sarah and David ever have a child with cystic fibrosis? Explain why.
(e) Could Anna and Daniel ever have a child with cystic fibrosis? Explain why.

Diseases showing co-dominance, e.g. sickle cell anaemia
Diseases like this are caused by a **recessive allele**, and heterozyous individuals are affected.

e.g. B is the allele for normal blood
       b is the allele for sickle cell anaemia

an individual with the genotype BB is normal
                                 Bb has sickle cell trait
                                 bb has sickle cell anaemia

In this disease haemoglobin is faulty, so it cannot carry oxygen properly, and red blood cells are the wrong shape (they are 'sickled', not biconcave disc-shaped).

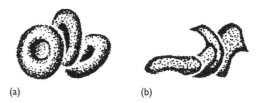

(a)   (b)

Fig. 6.46 Red blood cells: (a) normal (b) sickled

People with sickle cell anaemia have all their red cells affected like this, and are likely to die. People with sickle cell trait have 30–40% of their red cells affected like this. In parts of Africa, one-third of the population has sickle cell trait: this is beneficial to them, because they are protected from malaria.

REVISION ACTIVITY 13 Look at this family tree for sickle cell anaemia

(a) How would you describe Lee and Mary?
(b) Which of their children is likely to die from this disease?
(c) Which is most at risk from malaria?

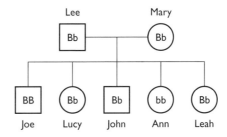

Fig. 6.47

Sex-linked diseases, e.g. haemophilia
Diseases like this are caused by a faulty allele carried on the X chromosome.
e.g. H is the allele for normal blood clotting
       h is the allele for haemophilia

an individual could have the genotype $X^H X^H$ female, normal
                                          $X^H X^h$ female, carrier
                                          $X^h X^h$ female, haemophiliac
                                          $X^H Y$ male, normal
                                          $X^h Y$ male, haemophiliac

In this disease, the blood does not clot properly, so a person could bleed to death after a cut. This is unlikely to happen now as doctors can give injections of 'clotting factors' to haemophiliacs – these are blood proteins which are needed for blood to clot properly.

Selective breeding

Key points

▶ this is sometimes called artificial selection;

▶ it is carried out by humans to obtain plants or animals with the characteristics humans require, i.e. to benefit humans;

▶ it may take many years to develop organisms with the required characteristics;

▶ the organisms obtained will still belong to the same species, but they are often described as different breeds or varieties.

General principles of selective breeding
Selective breeding has been carried out by humans for thousands of years to develop the crop plants and domestic animals we have today. There are five main steps in any breeding programme:

1. Look for individuals with the characteristics you require, e.g. short stem plants.
2. Breed together two of these individuals (or self-pollinate if it is a plant).
3. Collect the offspring, and select those which have the characteristics you require.
4. Breed from these offspring.
5. Repeat these steps over many generations.

Selective breeding in plants
Breeding programmes like this have been carried out to produce the varieties of crop plant we have today,
       e.g. Apples: Cox's pippins, Granny Smiths, Bramleys, Red delicious, Golden delicious
             Potatoes: King Edwards, Cara, Desirée, Jersey royals

As well as differences in taste and appearance, crop plants can be bred to:

▶ be resistant to diseases;
▶ be resistant to frost;
▶ give a high yield;
▶ have a short stem (so they are less likely to be damaged by bad weather).

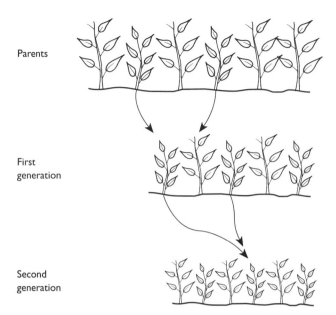

Fig. 6.48 Selective breeding to obtain shorter stems

An example of selective breeding is **wheat**. Wheat which is used to make bread today has been developed over thousands of years from wild wheat and wild grass (see Fig. 6.49).

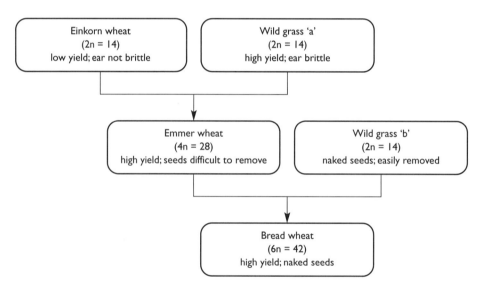

Fig. 6.49 Selective breeding of wheat

Selective breeding of wheat for bread has been going on for about 10 000 years. Much of the early selective breeding of wheat took place in the Middle East. The original wild wheat was not suitable for cultivation because the 'ear' (i.e. the collection of seeds in the fruit) was brittle, and broke off during harvesting. This was replaced by another variety, called **Einkorn** wheat, which was non-brittle. However, Einkorn wheat gave a low yield, and was replaced by another variety, **Emmer** wheat. This was selectively bred from Einkorn wheat and from a wild grass relative of wheat. During this selective breeding, the chromosome number was increased, by a process known as **polyploidy**. Emmer wheat is still grown in parts of India and Russia. However, the grain (i.e. seeds) of Emmer wheat are difficult to remove from the surrounding chaff during threshing. Modern bread wheat has 'naked' seeds which are easily removed during mechanised threshing. This has resulted from selective breeding of Emmer wheat with a wild grass. The selective breeding processes involved in the production of modern wheat are summarised in Fig. 6.49. Notice the increase of chromosome number which accompanied this process. (2n = diploid number.)

Selective breeding in animals

The domestic animals we have today have been developed from breeding programmes lasting hundreds of years,

> e.g. Cattle: Fresian, Jersey, Hereford, Aberdeen Angus
> Dogs: Labradors, Alsatians, Poodles, Chihuahua

Animals are useful to humans as:

▷ a source of food:
▷ a source of raw material for clothing:
▷ transport;
▷ hunting and livestock control;
▷ guard dogs;
▷ guide dogs.

One common technique in selective breeding of farm animals is **artificial insemination**. Semen is collected from the male, and 'injected' into the female. This method is an advantage for farmers who do not have suitable male animals for breeding, and also avoids the need for animals to be moved over large distances for selective breeding.

Selective breeding in domestic animals can be a slow process compared with that of crops, because generation times are long, and relatively few offspring are produced from which to choose for further selective breeding.

An example of selective breeding is **milk yield in cattle**. To develop cows with an increased milk yield you would carry out the following steps:

▷ test the milk yield of the cows you have to breed from;
▷ select the cow with the highest milk yield (A);
▷ select a bull descended from a cow with a high milk yield (B);
▷ cross A and B, and select female calves;
▷ wait for these calves to mature, then test their milk yield;
▷ select the cow with the highest milk yield (C), then repeat these steps again.

Cloning

Key points

> ▷ cloning means producing large numbers of genetically identical individuals;
>
> ▷ cloning can occur naturally, e.g. when bacteria or yeasts reproduce asexually;
>
> ▷ artificial clones can be formed in animals by separating embryos at an early stage;
>
> ▷ artificial clones can be formed in plants by taking cuttings and micropropagation.

Cloning in bacteria and yeasts

Bacteria and yeasts form natural clones due to asexual reproduction.

Bacteria form clones by binary fission. In ideal conditions this will occur roughly every 20 minutes, so large numbers can be produced quickly.

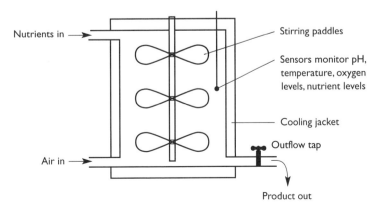

Fig. 6.50 Fermenter

'See Fig. 6.28'

Yeasts form clones by budding. In ideal conditions, new individuals are formed every 30 minutes, so large numbers are produced quickly.

Scientists who want to obtain large numbers of identical microbes normally grow them in a fermenter. This is a large container where conditions are very carefully controlled, e.g. correct pH, correct temperature, enough oxygen, suitable nutrients. (See Fig. 6.50.)

Cloning in animals, e.g. sheep, cattle.

This occasionally happens naturally when identical twins are born. Humans can form artificial clones by taking an embryo at an early stage of development, e.g. after a test-tube fertilization procedure, and splitting the embryo into separate cells. each of these cells will then develop into a new embryo, genetically identical to the original. The new embryos can be implanted into the uteruses of 'surrogate mothers', i.e. females who were not related to the original embryo, and these surrogate mothers will give birth at the end of their pregnancy. The offspring produced are a clone, i.e. they are genetically identical to each other

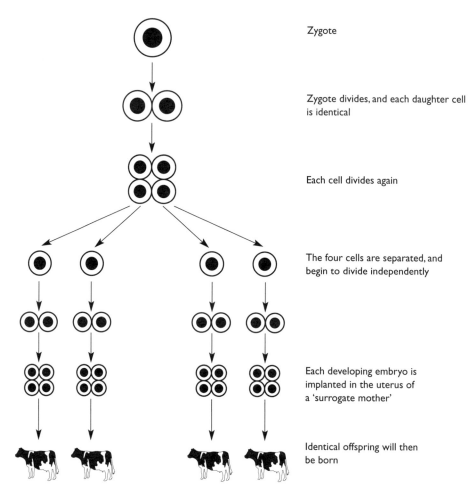

Zygote

Zygote divides, and each daughter cell is identical

Each cell divides again

The four cells are separated, and begin to divide independently

Each developing embryo is implanted in the uterus of a 'surrogate mother'

Identical offspring will then be born

Fig. 6.51

Cloning in plants

Cloning in plants occurs naturally when plants reproduce asexually, e.g. by bulbs, corms, tubers, runners, etc. However, humans can produce artificial clones in plants in two main ways:

1. Taking cuttings

Plant growers often take stem cuttings of plant like geraniums to increase the number of plants they have. There are five main steps in this process (see Fig. 6.52):

1. use a sharp knife to make a slanting cut just below a node;
2. remove the leaves close to the bottom of the cutting;
3. dip the cut end into hormone rooting powder;
4. leave the cutting with the cut end suspended in water. After a few days new roots will form;
5. plant carefully in soil, and it will continue to grow.

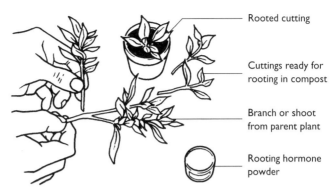

Fig. 6.52 Taking cuttings

2. Micropropagation

This is usually carried out on a large scale by plant breeders to produce very large numbers of identical plants very quickly.

At the tip of the roots and shoots of plants are areas called **meristems**. Here the cells divide rapidly by mitosis, so the meristems are known as growing points.

If cells are removed from the meristem and placed in suitable conditions, new plants will develop (Fig. 6.53). The new plants will be genetically identical to each other.

There are four main steps in this process

(a)   use a sharp knife to remove the meristem from the shoot;
(b)   cut the meristem into small pieces;
(c)   place the pieces onto sterile nutrient medium, e.g. agar jelly, and new plants will start to grow;
(d)   when the plantlets are big enough to handle, plant them carefully in soil, and they will continue to grow.

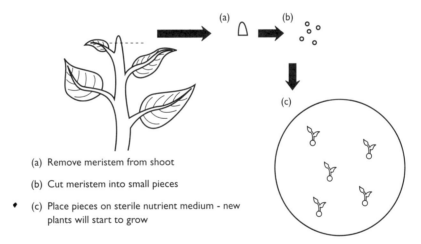

(a) Remove meristem from shoot

(b) Cut meristem into small pieces

(c) Place pieces on sterile nutrient medium - new plants will start to grow

Fig. 6.53

DNA

Inside the nucleus of all plant and animal cells there are long threads of DNA called chromosomes. Each chromosome carries hundreds of genes, and each gene codes for a single protein.

The DNA inside the cell will replicate (make a copy of itself) before the cell divides, so that each daughter cell will carry the genetic information coded on the chromosomes.

The genetic information is in the form of the genetic code; this depends on the order of bases in the DNA. Three adjacent bases will code for each amino acid.

When proteins are being made, a copy of one gene, called the RNA template, is made inside the nucleus, then this moves out into the cytoplasm. Amino acids are joined together according to the genetic code on the RNA.

Key points

▶ chromosomes are made of DNA;

▶ each chromosome carries hundreds of **genes**;

▶ each gene codes for one **protein**;

▶ DNA is made up of repeating units called **nucleotides**;

▶ DNA is a **double helix**, i.e. two strands of nucleotides are twisted together in a spiral shape;

▶ **base-pairing** holds the two strands together;

▶ when DNA replicates, **identical** strands of DNA are formed;

▶ an RNA copy of part of the DNA moves from the nucleus to the cytoplasm during protein synthesis;

▶ amino acids line-up on the RNA according to the order of the bases (**genetic code**) and are joined together to make a protein.

Structure of DNA

DNA is short for **deoxyribonucleic acid**. The structure of DNA was worked out by a British scientist, Francis Crick, and an American scientist, James Watson, in 1953. It is made up of a large number of repeating units called **nucleotides**. One nucleotide looks like this (Fig. 6.54).

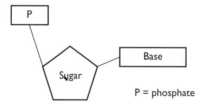

Fig. 6.54 A nucleotide

The nucleotides are joined together to make a long chain, (Fig. 6.55).

There are four types of bases which can be included. They are called: adenine (A)
thymine (T)
cytosine (C)
guanine (G)

A molecule of DNA is made up of two strands of nuleotides joined by their bases (see Fig. 6.56). Look carefully at how they are joined together.

▶ **Adenine always bonds to thymine.**
▶ **Cytosine always bonds to guanine.**

This is called **base pairing**.

The shape of the strands causes the molecule to twist into a **helix** (spiral) shape. It looks like a twisted ladder, where the rungs are the pairs of bases (see Fig. 6.57).

Replication of DNA

A typical human body cell, e.g. skin cell, bone cell, has 46 chromosomes. When that cell divides by mitosis, two daughter cells are formed, each with 46 chromosomes. This means that new chromosomes must have been formed. In fact, the DNA makes a copy of itself – the scientific term for this is **replication**.

There are four main stages in replication (Fig. 6.58)

(a) The DNA molecule is double-stranded and helix shaped.
It untwists and begins to separate into two strands.
The bonds between the bases are broken.

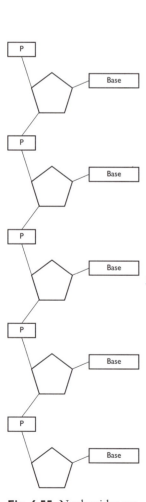

Fig. 6.55 Nucleotides are joined to form a long chain

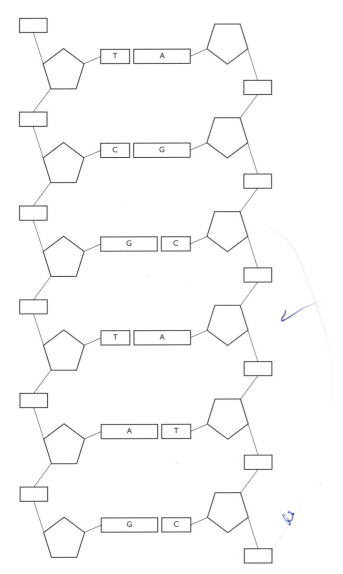

Fig. 6.56 Structure of DNA (showing base pairing)

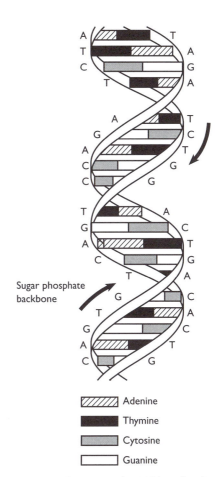

Sugar phosphate backbone

	Adenine
	Thymine
	Cytosine
	Guanine

Fig. 6.57 Structure of a DNA molecule

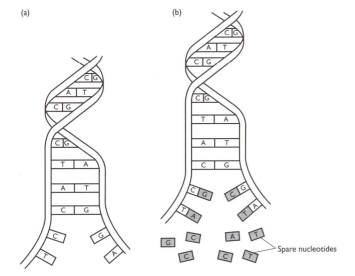

Spare nucleotides

Fig. 6.58 Stages in the replication of DNA

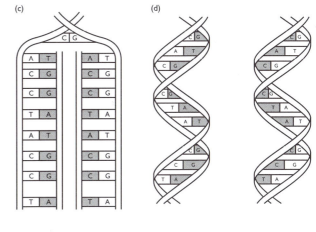

(b) Spare nucleotides inside the nucleus pair up with the bases on the separated strands.

(c) As the helix unwinds, more nucleotides pair up with the bases on the separated strands. Eventually the whole DNA molecule will separate in this way.

(d) There are now two molecules of DNA, each double-stranded. Each one twists up to form a helix shape. The two DNA molecules are **identical** to each other.

Genes and proteins

The DNA in chromosomes carries hundreds of genes. Each gene **codes** for one protein; that means that it carries the instructions to make one protein.

Remember, each protein is made up of a chain of **amino acids.** Altogether, there are 20 different amino acids, and proteins are different from each other due to the **type** of amino acids they contain, and the **order** of the amino acids (Fig. 6.59).

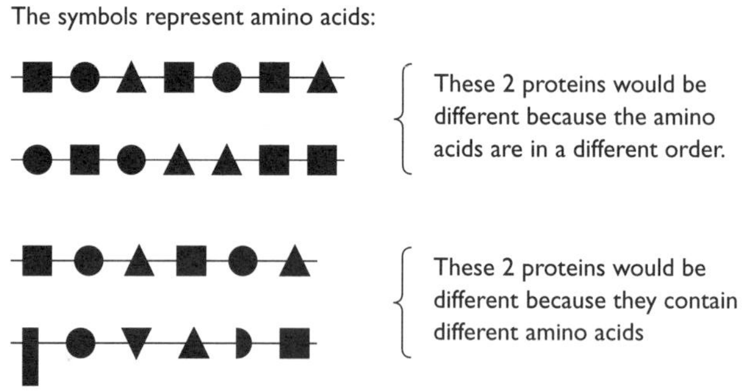

The symbols represent amino acids:

These 2 proteins would be different because the amino acids are in a different order.

These 2 proteins would be different because they contain different amino acids

Fig. 6.59 Amino acids are joined to make proteins

'Proteins control thousands of important reactions within the body.'

To be healthy, a human must have thousands of different proteins, all working properly,
e.g. amylase to digest starch
insulin to control blood sugar level
growth hormone to regulate growth.

So, a gene must carry instructions for the type of amino acids, and the order of amino acids, to make a protein. It does this through the **genetic code**, i.e. the order of the bases on the DNA molecule. Each set of three bases is called a **triplet**, or **codon**, and it will code for a single amino acid.

Protein synthesis

DNA (in chromosomes) carries the instructions for making a particular protein, and the chromosomes are inside the nucleus.

Protein synthesis (putting together the right amino acids in the right order) occurs in the cytoplasm of the cell. The chromosomes are too big to move out of the nucleus, so a copy is made of part of the DNA (one gene), and this moves out into the cytoplasm. This copy acts as a pattern, or **template**, to make the protein, and is made of a substance called **RNA** (ribonucleic acid).

The RNA is much shorter than the DNA it is copied from; it is exactly the length of a single gene. It is single stranded, i.e. made up of one chain of nucleotides, and contains organic bases. However, it never contains **thymine** – this is replaced with **uracil** (U).

RNA is made by base-printing with the DNA on a process called **transcription**. The RNA is complementary to one of the DNA strands – this means that the bases match it.

'There is no thymine (T) in RNA – it is replaced with uracil (u).'

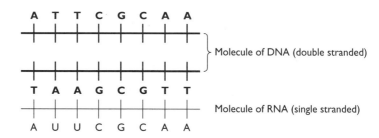

Fig. 6.60

There are four main stages in protein synthesis (see Fig. 6.61).

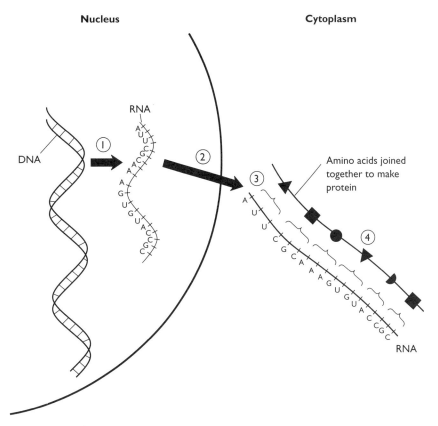

Fig. 6.61 Protein synthesis

1. DNA inside the nucleus unwinds, and a RNA copy is made of one gene.
2. The RNA (RNA template) moves out of the nucleus into the cytoplasm.
3. The bases (A, U, C and G) on the RNA are 'read' in groups of three. Each group of three bases (a triplet or codon) codes for one amino acid.
4. Amino acids line up against the RNA in the right order, and these are joined together to make a protein.

Protein synthesis is a difficult topic: it might help you to think of a model to explain it.

DNA is equivalent to a recipe book. It has thousands of different recipes (genes) in it.

RNA is like a single recipe from that book. It contains instructions to make one dish (one protein).

Amino acids are like the ingredients you use. The recipe book does not contain the ingredients, it tells you how to put them together to make the dish.

Protein synthesis is like following a recipe to put the right ingredients together in the right order.

REVISION ACTIVITY 14

(a) Use the words in the box to complete these sentences.

helix	cytosine	sugar	base-pairing
guanine	thymine	guanine	nucleotides
double	adenine	genetic	thymine

DNA is a large _____ stranded molecule made up of thousands of _____.
Each nucleotide consists of a _____ , a phosphate and a base. There are four
types of base: _____ , _____ , _____ , and _____. The two
strands in DNA are joined by _____ ; this means that adenine is joined to
_____ , and cytosine is joined to _____ . The shape of the molecule makes
it twist into a _____ (spiral). It carries the _____ code.

(b) Why is DNA described as a **double helix**?
(c) Adenine and thymine are sometimes described as complementary – what does this mean?
(d) What does 'genetic code' mean?

Genetic engineering

These are techniques which have been developed quite recently to transfer DNA from one type of organism to another.

A gene is taken from one organism (called the **donor**) and joined to a vector which will transfer it to a different organism (called the **recipient**). The recipient will then be able to make the protein which was coded for on that gene, i.e. it will have acquired a new characteristic. So far, there have been three main uses of genetic engineering

1. to transfer genes into bacteria, so that they can make useful products, e.g. insulin, human growth hormone;
2. to transfer genes into plants and animals, so that they acquire new characteristics, e.g. they are resistant to disease;
3. to transfer genes into humans, so that they no longer suffer from genetic diseases, e.g. cystic fibrosis.

Although there are undoubtedly benefits to be gained from these applications of genetic engineering, it is important to consider the potential dangers.

There are strict legal guidelines which control the **types** of experiment which can be carried out, and which safeguard the **health** of the scientists and the general public.

Key points

▷ genetic engineering transfers DNA from one organism to another;

▷ DNA from a donor is cut into fragments using enzymes;

▷ DNA fragments are transferred to vectors;

▷ vectors carry the donor DNA into recipient cells;

▷ the recipient cell has a new gene and therefore has a new characteristic;

▷ the recipient cell can be cloned to make thousands of identical copies of the gene.

Techniques of genetic engineering

We will consider the example of the gene for human growth hormone being transferred to a bacterium (*E. coli*). The bacterium makes the protein (human growth hormone), then it can be collected and used to treat people who do not make enough of this hormone themselves.

Donor organism	:	human
Vector	:	plasmid (small piece of bacterial DNA)
Recipient organism	:	*E. coli* (bacterium)
Product	:	human growth hormone (HGH)

Transferring the gene: There are four main stages in this process (see Fig. 6.62).

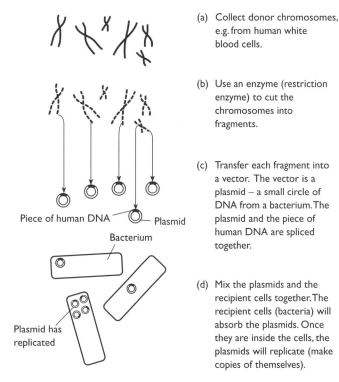

(a) Collect donor chromosomes, e.g. from human white blood cells.

(b) Use an enzyme (restriction enzyme) to cut the chromosomes into fragments.

(c) Transfer each fragment into a vector. The vector is a plasmid – a small circle of DNA from a bacterium. The plasmid and the piece of human DNA are spliced together.

Piece of human DNA — Plasmid

Bacterium

Plasmid has replicated

(d) Mix the plasmids and the recipient cells together. The recipient cells (bacteria) will absorb the plasmids. Once they are inside the cells, the plasmids will replicate (make copies of themselves).

Fig. 6.62 Stages in gene transfer (diagrams not to scale)

One of the recipient cells now has several copies of the gene for human growth hormone, and will be able to make this protein.

Cloning the gene: In order to make large quantities of human growth hormone, we must have large quantities of bacteria carrying the HGH gene. The easiest way to do this is by **cloning** – allowing the bacteria to reproduce asexually, to produce millions of offspring, each containing the gene for HGH.

The cloning procedure is carried out in a large container, called a **fermenter**. The conditions inside the fermenter must be very carefully controlled, i.e. correct pH, correct temperature, enough oxygen, suitable nutrients. This gives the bacteria the ideal (optimum) conditions to grow, and to make the protein.

'See Fig. 6.50'

The product is collected by opening the outflow tap on the fermenter. However, it must be carefully purified and have any contaminants removed before it can be used.

Uses of genetic engineering
Genetic engineering is a relatively recent invention, and new techniques and uses are being developed all the time. Currently there are three main uses:

1. To transfer genes into bacteria so they can make useful products
The techniques are outlined in Fig. 6.62. The genetically engineered bacteria are grown in large fermenters, then the products are collected and carefully purified. Products made in this way include:

▷ **Human growth hormone** – this is given to people whose pituitary glands do not make enough, so they would not grow properly.
▷ **Insulin** – this is given to people whose pancreas does not make enough insulin, so they cannot control their blood sugar level effectively (see p. 87). These people are diabetic; previously they were given animal insulin, but this often caused side effects.
▷ **Rennet** – this is an enzyme used in the cheese-making process to make milk clot. Vegetarian cheeses contain rennet made by bacteria, whereas other cheeses contain rennet from animals.
▷ **Proteases/lipases** – these enzymes are added to biological washing powders to digest 'biological stains', e.g. food containing proteins and fats.

2. To transfer genes into plants and animals so that they acquire new characteristics

The techniques used to transfer genes into plants and animals are more complex than the procedure outlined earlier in this section, but the principles are the same. This time there is no product to collect, but the recipient organism has a new characteristic which makes it more useful to humans.

> e.g. gene for **frost resistance** has been transferred from fish to tomato plants. This means that the plants will be able to grow in colder weather, so farmers will make more profit.

Other organisms which have been modified in this way include:

▷ **cereal plants** which have been given the gene for disease resistance, so they are more healthy and produce a higher yield of grain;

▷ **cattle** which have been given the gene for increased growth rate, so they reach their adult size more quickly, and can be sold or used for food sooner;

▷ **crop plants** which have been given a gene which makes them glow when they are diseased. This means that diseased plants can easily be identified and removed before the disease spreads;

▷ **trout** which have been given a gene to make them paler, so they can be more easily seen by fishermen;

▷ **fruits and vegetables** have been given a gene to make a vaccine to protect people from diseases;

▷ **crop plants** which have been given a gene making them resistant to herbicide (weed-killer). This means that fields can be sprayed with herbicides and the crop plants will not die.

One recent, and very controversial, application of this technology is the development of **transgenic pigs**. These pigs have been given a human gene so that all cells in their bodies contain human 'marker proteins' (antigens). Organs from these pigs, e.g. kidneys, hearts, could be transplanted into humans, because the 'marker proteins' would stop them being rejected.

Once the required gene has been transferred into the recipient organism, it must be cloned to make many copies, so that many organisms carrying this gene will be formed. Cloning of animals and plants is a more complex process than of bacteria (see p. 195 for details of cloning).

3. To transfer genes into humans so that they no longer suffer from genetic diseases

This process is known as **gene therapy**, and is currently being developed. It is suitable for people who have genetic diseases caused by a single faulty gene, e.g. cystic fibrosis.

This disease occurs when a person has two copies of the 'faulty gene', i.e. is homozygous, so they make a 'faulty' version of a cell protein. This results in very thick, sticky mucus being produced in the lungs and gut, instead of clear, runny mucus. The airways of the lungs become clogged, and the lungs can be permanently damaged. The mucus in the gut prevents food being digested and absorbed effectively.

For gene therapy to be **successful**, three things must occur

'This is a very complex process. Gene therapy has been tried for very few genetic diseases so far.'

1. the exact **position** of the gene must be known so that it can be 'cut out' from the chromosome;

2. it must be attached to a **vector** to get it inside human cells. Plasmids will not work inside human cells, so the vector must be a virus or an artificial chromosome. The gene must be inserted into the right **type** of cell, e.g. cells lining the air passages;

3. once it is inside the cells, the gene must be **active**, i.e. it must cause protein synthesis so that the 'correct' version of the protein is made.

Implications of genetic engineering

When scientists carry out genetic engineering, they are permanently altering an organism's DNA, and therefore altering its features. They do this because the modified organism will be useful to humans in some way, or to prevent disease.

However, there are potential dangers associated with altering DNA, and these must be considered together with the advantages.

Example 1. *Using bacteria to make human growth hormone*

Advantages
- large amounts of growth hormone are available to treat humans who need it
- it does not cause side-effects in the people who use it
- manufacturers make a large profit

Disadvantages
- none apparent so far

Example 2. *Making crop plants disease resistant*

Advantages
- less plants are damaged or killed by disease
- higher yields of crops are produced, so more food is available for human consumption
- farmers make a large profit

Disadvantages
- the genetically-engineered plants might grow much better than other plants, i.e. be more successful, so some plants may die out
- animals which depend on those plants, i.e. for food, or as a habitat to live on, will be affected
- food webs may become disturbed as numbers of plants and animals change, i.e. the balance of nature is affected
- if some breeds die out there is less variety in the population, so natural selection cannot occur properly

Example 3. *Gene therapy to treat genetic diseases*

Advantages
- the person no longer has a dangerous disease
- they do not have to use medicines or drugs to treat the symptoms
- they will be healthier and live longer

Disadvantages
- only the body cell genes can be changed, not the genes in eggs or sperm, so the person's children might still have the disease
- if the transfer process goes wrong, then other genes might be affected, causing severe health problems for that person.

A Moral dilemma?

These are some of the questions currently being asked about genetic engineering:

'Think carefully about the issues raised here. How would you answer?'

- What would happen if genetically engineered organisms 'escaped' into the environment? How would this affect the balance of nature?
- Is it right to change animals and plants so that farmers can make a bigger profit? Does it cause harm to the organisms involved?
- Is it right to alter human genes? Should this only be done to prevent disease, or should 'better humans' be developed?
- Who should decide how plants, animals and humans should be changed?

REVISION ACTIVITY 15

(a) Put these steps in genetic engineering into the correct order.

  A. Collect product, e.g. human growth hormone
  B. Transfer the gene into a vector, e.g. plasmid
  C. Identify the gene for human growth hormone
  D. Grow the bacteria in a fermenter
  E. Cut out the gene using enzymes
  F. Transfer the vector containing the gene into bacteria, e.g. *E. coli.*

  □□□□□□

(b) Scientists have just used genetic engineering to develop fruits and vegetables containing a vaccine. People who eat them would be protected from some diseases.
  (i) Think of two reasons why this is a better way to vaccinate people than the injection method.
  (ii) Why would it be better to transfer the gene to bananas instead of potatoes?

(c) Give three advantages and three disadvantages of using transgenic pigs in human organ transplants. Would you be prepared to have a transplant like this? Do you think you would want your child to have a transplant like this?

▷ Natural selection and evolution

Charles Darwin and Alfred Wallace first put forward the idea of evolution by natural selection in 1856. They suggested that some individuals have characteristics which increase their chances of survival, so they will survive to breed and produce offspring like themselves. Gradually, over thousands of years, changes will build up in a population and new species will be formed.

Natural selection

> ## Key points
>
> ▷ individuals have to compete for resources to stay alive;
>
> ▷ the individuals who have characteristics which increase their chances of survival will be most likely to breed;
>
> ▷ they will produce offspring like themselves;
>
> ▷ peppered moths are a good example of natural selection;
>
> ▷ mutation is the raw material for natural selection.

Principles of natural selection

Natural selection means that some individuals are more likely to survive than others because they have certain characteristics – this is sometimes called 'survival of the fittest'. Darwin suggested that there were six key points in this theory.

1. In any population there is variation, i.e. the members of a species are not identical to each other.
2. Individuals have to compete with each other to survive. They might compete for food, water, space or a mate.
3. Some individuals are more likely to survive than others, because of their features, e.g. they are bigger, stronger, more aggressive, grow faster, etc. We call this a selective advantage.
4. The individuals who have a selection advantage, i.e. are well suited to their environment, will survive and breed. Individuals who do not have a selection advantage are more likely to die.
5. When the survivors breed, they will produce offspring like themselves, i.e. they will pass on their successful features to the next generation.
6. If the environment or conditions change, then the features needed to survive in it will change, so natural selection is a continuous process.

You can see from these points that variation is very important for natural selection to occur properly; if individuals were identical to each other, none of them would have a selection advantage. Individuals are not identical to each other due to sexual reproduction (see p. 180 for more details of this). Mutation is very important because this increases variation in populations: mutation is sometimes described as the raw material for natural selection. You will probably find it easier to understand this if you consider the following examples.

Example 1. Penicillin-resistant bacteria

Normal bacteria, e.g. *Neisseria gonorrhoea* which causes sexually transmitted disease gonorrhoea, are killed by penicillin (an antibiotic).

If a mutation occurs and a bacterium is formed which is resistant to penicillin, it will have a selective advantage, i.e. it will be more likely to survive, and when it reproduces, it will produce offspring like itself. Bacteria can only reproduce asexually, so all the offspring of this mutant individual will be resistant to penicillin. See Fig. 6.63.

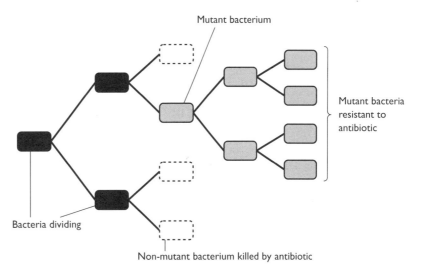

Fig. 6.63 Mutant bacteria are resistant to antibiotics

Example 2. Peppered moths

Normal peppered moths are a pale, speckled colour. They spend most of the day resting on lichen-covered tree trunks, where they are well camouflaged.

If a **mutation** occurs and a dark moth is formed, it will not be so well camouflaged, so it is more likely to be eaten by birds, i.e. it will not survive.

However, in industrial areas mutant dark moths have a **selection advantage**. Here pollutant gases, e.g. sulphur dioxide, have killed the lichens, and the tree trunks are covered by soot. Dark moths are well camouflaged, so they are less likely to be eaten by birds. They will survive and breed, and produce offspring like themselves.

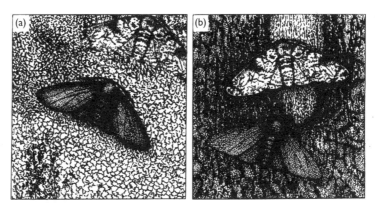

Fig. 6.54 Pale and dark forms of the peppered moth: (a) Lichen covered tree in unpolluted area. (b) blackened tree in polluted area

Biologists have collected a lot of data about the numbers of pale and dark moths in Britain. The first set of data compares the numbers of the two types of moths in Manchester in 1848 and 1894 (Table 6.5)

Table 6.5 Increase in relative numbers of dark form of peppered moth in industrial area

Year	Percentage of each form	
	Dark	Pale
1848	1	99
1894	99	1

This suggests that as the amount of pollution due to industry increased, dark moths had a selective advantage, so the proportion of dark moths in the population increased.

The second set of data shows the proportions of pale and dark moths in different parts of Britain in 1958.

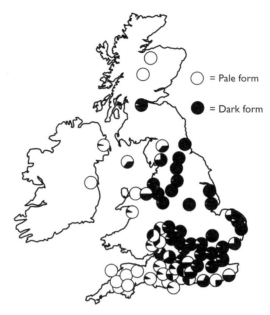

Fig. 6.65 Distribution of pale and dark forms of the peppered moth in Britain in 1958. (Republished from the journal *Heredity*, with permission)

This data suggests that

▷ dark moths have a selective advantage in industrial areas, e.g. Leeds, Sheffield, Manchester, London;

▷ dark moths have a selective advantage in rural areas if the prevailing wing blows pollutant gases in that direction, e.g. coast of East Anglia;

▷ pale moths have a selective advantage in rural areas where there is no air pollution, e.g. North of Scotland, Cornwall and Devon, East coast of Ireland.

> **Remember** Pale moths cannot 'turn into' dark moths. For the proportions of moths in the population to change, pale moths must be dying sooner, and dark moths living longer. If the dark moths breed more successfully, more dark moths will be born, so gradually the numbers of dark moths increases.

REVISION ACTIVITY 16

Most rats are killed by Warfarin (rat poison), but in parts of South Wales there are rats which are resistant to it.

(a) Where have these resistant rats come from?
(b) Which rats have a selection advantage? Explain why.
(c) If you did a survey in 20 years' time, what would you expect to find about the number of rats resistant to Warfarin?
(d) What could people in South Wales do to kill rats?

Evolution

This theory explains why there are so many different types of living organism on Earth, and where they all came from. It suggests that all living things have descended (or evolved) from a **common ancestor** – a simple organism living millions of years ago.

When Charles Darwin and Alfred Wallace first suggested the idea of evolution by natural selection in 1856, it was very controversial. Today many scientists believe this theory to be correct; but remember, it is a theory, not a proven fact. Because evolution is thought to have occurred over the millions of years, it is not possible to see absolute proof of the process today.

Key points

▷   some individuals in a population are better suited to their environment than others – we say they have a selection advantage;

▷   these individuals are more likely to survive and breed, and produce offspring like themselves – this is natural selection;

▷   over long periods of time, the characteristics of the population will change, as small changes accumulate;

▷   eventually a new species will be formed;

▷   scientists think that all existing species are related to each other, i.e. they evolved from a **common ancestor**;

▷   the time-scale for evolution is very long – this process has taken millions of years;

▷   evidence for evolution includes the fossil record, comparative anatomy and data from natural selection.

How do new species form?

In order to understand this idea, you need to be confident with the principles of **natural selection** (see p. 206).

When natural selection occurs, the characteristics of a population gradually change. Scientists think that if some members of the population are **isolated** from the rest, they will change so much that eventually they become a new species.

This could happen if:

▷   a barrier separates part of a population from the rest, e.g. a river becomes wider, so animals cannot cross it;

▷   conditions on one side of the barrier are different to conditions on the other side, e.g. land may be swampier on one side;

▷   the two populations are completely separate from each other, and they cannot interbreed;

▷   natural selection will occur on both sides of the barrier. On one side animals which can cope with swampy conditions have a selection advantage, while on the other side animals adapted to drier conditions have a selection advantage;

▷   gradually the characteristics of the two populations will change due to natural selection;

▷   if the river dries up and the two populations can mix again, they may no longer interbreed because they have become too different to each other. We could then say a new species had evolved.

A **species** is a group of individuals of the same type who can breed together to produce fertile offspring. They need not look identical to each other.

REVISION ACTIVITY 17   The Galapagos Islands are situated in the Pacific Ocean about 1000 km west of Ecuador in South America.

When Charles Darwin visited the Galapagos islands in 1835, he noticed **six** different varieties of beak amongst the finches on the islands. The diagram (Fig. 6.56) shows these beak shapes and the main food eaten by the finches. Darwin suggested that, originally, the large ground finches came to these islands from South America and that all the other types evolved from these.

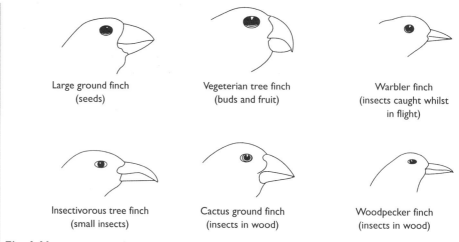

Large ground finch
(seeds)

Vegeterian tree finch
(buds and fruit)

Warbler finch
(insects caught whilst
in flight)

Insectivorous tree finch
(small insects)

Cactus ground finch
(insects in wood)

Woodpecker finch
(insects in wood)

Fig. 6.66

Explain, in detail, how the varieties of beak shape could have come about and enabled the finches to survive.

How are organisms related to each other?

The theory of evolution suggests that organisms are all descended from a **common ancestor** – a simple organism which lived millions years ago. If this is true, we should be able to draw a 'family tree' to show how the organisms which are alive today evolved.

Scientists have drawn a family tree like this based on fossil evidence and by comparing the types of organisms alive today (looking for similarities and differences between them).

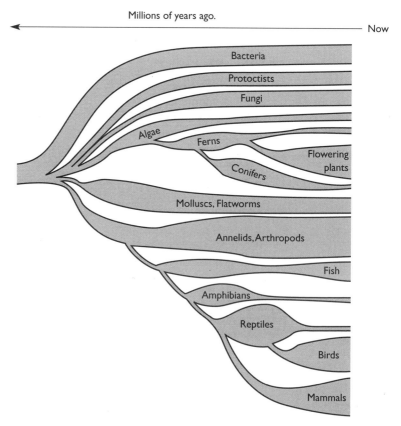

Millions of years ago.

Now

Bacteria

Protoctists

Fungi

Algae

Ferns

Conifers

Flowering plants

Molluscs, Flatworms

Annelids, Arthropods

Fish

Amphibians

Reptiles

Birds

Mammals

Fig. 6.67 Family tree based on evolutionary evidence

Evidence for evolution

Key points

▷ there are four main pieces of evidence for evolution:
1. The fossil record.
2. Comparison of body structure (anatomy).
3. Comparison of chemicals in the body.
4. Evidence from natural selection.

The fossil record

If organisms die in the right circumstances, fossils may be formed. This happens if:

(a) the organism is covered in a layer of mud or earth soon after it dies (most likely if it dies in a river or shallow sea);

(b) the sediment covering it becomes deeper, and is gradually changed into sedimentary rock.

Fig. 6.68 Fossil formation

There are different types of fossils, formed in different ways, e.g.

▷ shells or teeth (hard parts of the organism) may be preserved unchanged in rock;
▷ bones may be replaced gradually by other minerals so the fossil is eventually completely made of rock;
▷ the organic remains may decay, but leave an impression in the rock.

The fossil record provides evidence of organisms which were alive millions of years ago. It tells us three main things:

1. The simplest organisms developed first, and over time, organisms have gradually become more complex.
2. If you look at fossils in date order (the oldest fossils are found in the deepest, oldest rocks), it is possible to create 'family trees' as related organisms evolve. This evolution is probably in response to changes in the environment.
3. Many organisms have died out (become extinct) because when environmental conditions changed, they could not cope with this change. Scientists have estimated that the organisms alive today represent only 1% of the types of organisms which have lived on Earth, i.e. for every species alive today, another 99 species have become extinct!

However, scientists are sometimes criticised when they use the fossil record as evidence for evolution because it is incomplete. This means that it is not possible to follow every step in an evolutionary pathway, so scientists have had to make guesses at some points.

There are several reason why the fossil record is incomplete:

▷ Soft-bodied organisms e.g. invertebrates do not form fossils as well as vertebrates. Since invertebrates account for millions of years of early evolution, this part of the fossil record is patchy.
▷ Organisms are much more likely to be fossilised if they are covered in sediment soon after they die. This means that there are lots of fossils of organisms living near lakes, rivers and in shallow seas, but far fewer fossils of organisms living on land.
▷ Fossils are found deep in sedimentary rock, so there are probably millions of fossils which have not yet been found by humans.

Evolution of the horse

The fossil record showing how the horse is thought to have evolved is often studied because:

▷   lots of fossils have been formed;
▷   it is possible to see lots of intermediate steps (gradual changes) in the evolutionary pathway;
▷   it is possible to link these changes to changing environmental conditions;
▷   it is possible to compare the fossils with animals which exist today (modern horses).

These fossils have been found in sedimentary rock in North America. The earliest horse fossils suggest that they were alive about 54 million years ago. Since then, new types of horses have evolved to suit the changing environmental conditions. The main changes are:

▷   height of the animal;
▷   foot structure (number of 'toes' in contact with the ground);
▷   tooth structure.

Table 6.5 shows the main changes which have occurred over 54 million years (lots of steps have been left out).

Table 6.6

Name and when it lived	Height (to shoulder)	Foot structure	Tooth structure	Lifestyle
Hyracotherium 54 million years ago	0.4m	Four 'toes' in contact with ground – larger surface area spreads weight.	Small molar teeth.	Lived on soft, marshy ground. Ate soft vegetation.
Mesohippus 38 million years ago	0.6m	Three 'toes' in contact with ground. Middle 'toe' enlarged.	Small molar teeth.	Lived in drier places (forests and prairies).
Merychippus 26 million years ago	1.0m	One 'toe' in contact with ground.	Longer molar teeth. Crown covered by cement	Lived in very dry conditions – it could run faster on hard ground. Ate tougher vegetation.
Pliohippus 7 million years ago	1.0m	One 'toe' in contact with ground. – other 'toes' much smaller. Foot bones are thicker, hoof appears.	Very long teeth covered by cement.	Could run very fast on dry ground. Teeth are adapted for eating grass.
Equus (modern horse) 1 million years ago	1.6m	Leg and foot bones longer, proper hoof formed.	Large teeth with enamel and cement on crown to grind food. More molars develop.	Can run very fast on dry ground. Has strong teeth to chew and grind grass.

REVISION ACTIVITY 18   (a)   Look at these diagrams of horses and their feet, and put them into the correct order to show an evolutionary pathway.

Table 6.7   First

Horse					Modern horse
Foot					

(b)   Why do you think it would be an advantage to the horse to be taller?

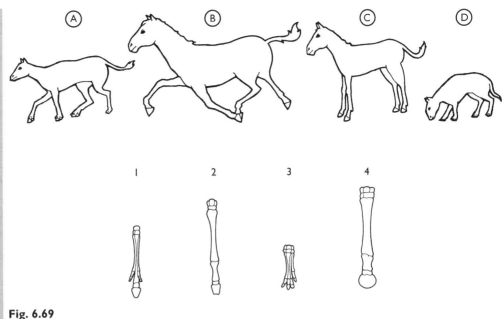

Fig. 6.69

Comparison of body structure (comparative anatomy)
Organisms which are descended from a common ancestor are likely to have similar structures inside their bodies: these are called **homologous structures**. A good example of this is the **pentadactyl limb in vertebrates**. If we look at the bone structure in the fore limb of different vertebrates, e.g. frog, bird, lizard, whale, rabbit, human, we see the same basic **pattern**.

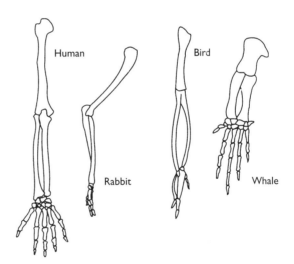

Fig. 6.70 Pentadactyl limb

There are differences in detail because the animals are adapted for different types of loco-motion, e.g. hopping, flying, walking on two legs, but the basic pattern is the same.

Comparison of chemicals inside the body (comparative biochemistry)
Organisms which are descended from a common ancestor are likely to have similar chemicals, e.g. proteins, inside their bodies.

A good example of this is the protein **cytochrome c** which is important in the process of respiration, and is present in all known organisms. It is a long chain of amino acids (between 104 and 112, depending on species).

▷ If we compare human cytochrome c and monkey cytochrome c, only one amino acid is different. This suggests that they are closely related on an evolutionary pathway.

▷ If we compare human cytochrome c and kangaroo cytochrome c, ten amino acids are different. This suggests that they belong to the same group (mammals) but are less closely related.

▷ If we compare human cytochrome c and yeast cytochrome c, 45 amino acids are different. This suggests that they are not closely related on an evolutionary pathway. However, the fact that more than half of the aminos acids are the same suggests that millions of years ago humans and yeast shared a **common ancestor**.

Evidence from natural selection

Even over a very short timespan (less than 200 years) we can see how populations change as a consequence of changing their environment,

e.g. peppered moths, due to air pollution
bacteria, due to use of antibiotics.

If changes like this were allowed to accumulate over thousands of years, it is possible to see how new species could evolve.

When humans carry out **selective breeding** they are deliberately changing the characteristics of a population by breeding together selected individuals. This process shows how much characteristics can change – think about the differences between chihuahuas and rottweilers!

▶ SOLUTIONS TO REVISION ACTIVITIES

S1

Table 6.8

Leaf	\multicolumn{10}{c	}{Key questions used}	Name of plant
	1(a)	1(b)	2(a)	2(b)	3(a)	3(b)	4(a)	4(b)	5(a)	5(b)	
A	✔		✔								**River crowfoot**
B		✔				✔			✔		Perforated pondweed
C		✔				✔				✔	Ivy leaved crowfoot
D		✔		✔			✔				Curled pondweed
E	✔			✔							Round-leaved crowfoot
F		✔		✔		✔					Water soldier

S2 (a) a long thread of DNA   chromosome

(b) a body cell with pairs of chromosomes   diploid

(c) a 'strong' allele   dominant

(d) an individual who has two identical alleles   homozygous

(e) a 'weaker' allele   recessive

(f) a gamete with single chromosomes (not paired)   haploid

(g) the appearance of an individual   phenotype

(h) the genes an individual has   genotype

(i) an individual who has two different alleles for a particular gene   heterozygous

(j) an instruction about a single feature   gene

(k) a matching of chromosomes   homologous

(l) alternative forms of a gene   alleles

S3 (a) (i) **mutation**   – a change in genetic material (DNA)
(ii) **replication** – when DNA makes a copy of itself before cell division
(iii) **mutagen**   – a factor which increases the mutation rate

(b) (i) Sometimes a mutagen may be present, but mutation does not occur. Also a mutation may occur without a mutagen being present. However, mutagens do increase the rate of mutation.

(ii) A random change in a gene which is working well is unlikely to improve it (think about what would happen if you hit a clock that was working well with a hammer!). A very small change may have no effect at all, i.e. it may be a neutral mutation.

S4 Roughly equal numbers of boys and girls are born because:

(a) there are roughly equal **numbers** of the two types of sperm (X-sperm and Y-sperm);

(b) both types of sperm are **equally likely** to fertilize the ovum.

S5

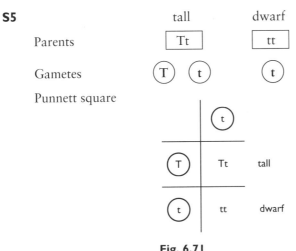

Fig. 6.71

Answer **50% are tall, 50% are dwarf**

S6 R is the allele for round seed
r is the allele for wrinkled seed

	Round seed	Round seed
Parents	Rr	Rr
Gametes	(R) (r)	(R) (r)

	(R)	(r)
(R)	RR	Rr
(r)	Rr	rr

RR = round seed
Rr = round seed
Rr = round seed
rr = wrinkled seed

Fig. 6.72

Ratio is 3 round seed : 1 wrinkled seed plant

S7 (a)

Table 6.9

Cross	Genotypes of parents	Phenotypes of offspring	
		Long wing	Short wing
1.	LL x LL	✔	
2.	Lℓ x $\ell\ell$	✔	✔
3.	Lℓ x Lℓ	✔	✔
4.	LL x $\ell\ell$	✔	

(b) $\ell\ell \times \ell\ell$ (both homozygous recessive)

S8 (a) Half the offspring would be pink, half would be red.

(b) Half the offspring would be pink, half would be white.

S9 (a) (i) $I^A I^B$
(ii) $I^O I^O$
(iii) $I^B I^B$ and $I^B I^O$

(b) AB

S10 Colour-blind man must be $X^n Y$

Woman   Man
Parents $X^N X^N$ $X^n Y$

Gametes (X^N) (X^N) (X^n) (Y)

	(X^n)	(Y)
(X^N)	$X^N X^n$	$X^N Y$
(X^N)	$X^N X^n$	$X^N Y$

$X^N X^n$ = carrier girl
$X^N Y$ = normal boy

Fig. 6.73

S11 (a) Alice = hh, Jo = Hh, Liz = Hh, Ben = Hh

(b) Gemma = Hh   Ben = Hh

Parents   Hh   Hh
Gametes (H) (h) (H) (h)

	(H)	(h)
(H)	HH	Hh
(h)	Hh	hh

HH – has the disease
Hh – has the disease
Hh – has the disease
hh – does not have the disease

Fig. 6.74

The probability that their child has the disease is 75% (0.75).

S12 (a) three children

(b) two are carriers (Cc)

(c) one has the disease (cc)

(d) No, because a child with cystic fibrosis must get a gene for it from both parents to be cc. David cannot pass the gene to his children, because he is CC.

(e) Yes, because they are both carriers (Cc). A child could inherit the cystic fibrosis gene from both of them to be cc.

S13 (a) Lee and Mary are both **carriers** for this disease.

(b) Ann.

(c) Joe, because heterozygous people (Bb) are protected from malaria.

S14 (a) DNA is a large **double** stranded molecule made up of thousands of **nucleotides**. Each nucleotide consists of a **sugar**, a phosphate and a base. There are four types of base: **adenine, guanine, cytosine** and **thymine**. The two strands in DNA are joined by **base-pairing**; this means that adenine is joined to **thymine**, and cytosine is joined to **guanine**. The shape of the molecule makes it twist into a **helix** (spiral). It carries the **genetic** code.

(b) Double = consists of two strands of nucleotides.
Helix = twisted into a spiral shape.

(c) This means that they are bonded together during base-pairing.

(d) The genetic code is the order of bases on the DNA. It is set of instructions for making proteins. Each group of three bases codes for one amino acid (amino acids are the building blocks proteins).

S15 (a) ⬚C⬚E⬚B⬚F⬚D⬚A

(b) (i) Vaccines have to be stored in cold conditions, e.g. fridges. They have to be given with sterile needles. In some parts of the world, it is difficult to get fridges and enough needles to all the people to all the people who need to be vaccinated.
The genetically engineered vaccine plants could be grown where they are needed. They would also be cheaper to produce.
(ii) Bananas are eaten raw; cooking would damage the vaccine.

(c) **Advantages**
No waiting lists for organ transplants.
People would be less likely to die from kidney failure, heart and lung disease, etc.
The organs are unlikely to be rejected.
The person can live a normal life.
It costs less than treating them long term, e.g. with dialysis.

Disadvantages
The pig is being killed to save human life.
Scientists do not know if there will be future problems, e.g. side affects after many years.
Some people may not want to receive animal organs.
The pig organs may be vulnerable to animal viruses.
If pigs have a shorter life-span than humans, their organs may not remain healthy for long enough.

S16 (a) They are mutants.

(b) The Warfarin-resistant rats have a selective advantage, because they are more likely to survive.

(c) It would have increased.

(d) Use other poisons, or use rat-traps.

S17   The shape and length of a bird's beak is determined by genes. Variation occur in the genetic information that determines beak characteristics, i.e. by mutations. Birds are in competition with each other (and other species) for limited amounts of food. New beak characteristics which provide improved adaptions for feeding give the bird a selective advantage. These birds have an increased chance of survival and will be more likely to breed. The characteristics are therefore many likely to be inherited by future generation.

S18   (a)

Table 6.9

Horse	D	A	C	B
Foot	3	1	2	4

(b)   Taller horses have a selection advantage because:
  ▷ they have longer legs, so they can run faster;
  ▷ they can see further, so they can avoid predators.

EXAMINATION QUESTIONS

▷ **Question 1**   The following list includes some of the major groups of living organisms.

Amphibians, Annelids, Birds, Bony fish, Flowering plants, Insects, Reptiles.

Complete the table by using groups chosen from the list. Each group may be used either once or not at all.

Table 6.11

	Features	Name of group
(a)	Body has scales. Shelled eggs are laid on land.	
(b)	Body is segmented. Skin soft and moist. Body has no limbs.	
(c)	Roots, stem and leaves. Flowers which produce seeds.	
(d)	Body has hard exoskeleton. Two pairs of wings and three pairs of legs.	

(4)
(NICCEA)

▷ **Question 2**   (a)   How does the chromosome content of a sex cell (sperm or ovum) differ from the chromosome content of a body cell?

(1)
_____

(b)   Put the following parts of a cell in order of increasing size.   *(3)*

| amino acid   chromosome   gene   nucleus |

smallest ▮ _____

_____

_____

largest _____

(c)   The sex chromosomes of a body cell are paired either as **XX** or **XY** according to the sex of the person.
    The rearrangement of these chromosomes before and after fertilisation should produce equal numbers of male and female children. Explain how this would happen.
    You may draw a diagram if it helps your answer.   *(4)*
(SEG)

▷ **Question 3**   The diagram (Fig. 6.75) below shows the inheritance of eye colour in a family. The gene for brown eyes is dominant (**B**) and the gene for blue eyes is recessive (**b**).

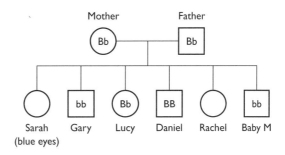

Fig. 6.75

Key: ☐ Male   ◯ Female

(a) Which of the following statements is true?
   A   Lucy and Daniel both have blue eyes
   B   Lucy and Daniel have different colour eyes
   C   Lucy and Daniel have the same coloured eyes
   D   All the males in the family have brown eyes
   Answer: Statement _____ is true   *(1)*

(b) What is the sex and eye colour of baby M?

_____   *(2)*

(c) In the family shown, Rachel has an identical twin. Rachel has brown eyes.

   (i)   Who is Rachel's identical twin? _____   *(1)*

   (ii) Explain how you decided on your answer.

_____

_____

_____   *(2)*

(LONDON)

▷ **Question 4**   (a) In the fruit fly, wing type is controlled by one pair of alleles. The diagram (Fig. 6.76) shows two types of wings, normal and vestigal.

Fruit flies

Fig. 6.76

The normal winged fly is heterozygous and the vestigial winged fly is homozygous. Explain the meaning of

(i)   homozygous _____

(ii) heterozygous _____   *(2)*

(b) A normal winged fly of unknown genotype was crossed with a vestigial winged fly. The allele for normal wing, A, is dominant to the allele for vestigial wing, a. The offspring are shown below (Fig. 6.77).

Fig. 6.77

(i) From the diagram determine the ratio of normal winged flies to vestigal winged flies.

_____ *(1)*

(ii) Give the genotype of this normal winged parent fly.

_____ *(1)*

(NICCEA)

▷ **Question 5** (a) A student growing pea plants was surprised to see four plants in one batch which were white (albino) instead of the normal green colour.
He became interested in the plants and treated them as shown in the diagram below.

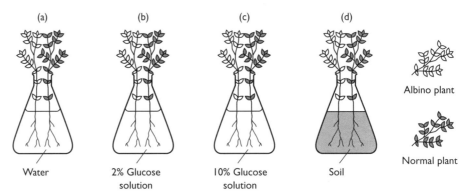

Fig. 6.78

All the plants were approximately 15 cm tall at the beginning of the experiment.
He kept them in sunlight and recorded the following results after two weeks.

Table 6.12

Flask	Plant type	Condition of plant after two weeks
A	Normal	Healthy, 18 cm tall
	Albino	Dead
B	Normal	Healthy, 22 cm tall
	Albino	Healthy, 19 cm tall
C	Normal	Wilted, 16 cm long
	Albino	Wilted, 15 cm long
D	Normal	Healthy, 27 cm tall
	Albino	Dead

(i) Suggest why the normal plant growing in soil grew taller than the normal plant growing in water. *(1)*

(ii) Explain why **both** plants in the 10% glucose solution had wilted after two weeks. *(3)*

(iii) What is the evidence in the experiment which suggests that albino plants cannot make glucose? *(2)*

(b) The albino condition is caused by a recessive allele (**a**). The green colour of normal plants is caused by the dominant allele (**A**). Explain, with the aid of a genetic diagram, how albino plant could be produced from apparently normal green plants.   *(3)*

(c) The albino pea plants would never flower and produce seeds and the allele which causes the albino condition is very rare.

   Describe one way by which scientists could produce more albino pea plants from the albino plant growing in 2% glucose solution.   *(3)*

(LONDON)

▷ **Question 6**   The Creamy Milk Farm Company wanted to breed cows that would give high yields of milk rich in butterfat. Butterfat gives milk a creamy taste.

   The best cows convert food to milk efficiently producing little waste. This quality is shown by a high food conversion factor.

   A cow's temperament affects its milk yield. Calm cows give a higher milk yield; nervous cows give a reduced milk yield.

   The table below (Fig. 6.79) shows the qualities of three cows (Tornado, Turbo and Tango) and the average qualities of the daughters of a bull, Black Star.

Breeding stock	Qualities			
	Food conversion factor	Temperament	Average annual milk yield (litres)	Percentage of butterfat in milk
Tornado 	Low	Nervous	3500	4.0
Turbo 	Medium	Calm	5000	3.0
Tango 	High	Nervous	4500	3.5
Daughters of Black Star 	Low	Calm	2500	5.5

Fig. 6.79

Use the information in the table to answer the following questions.

(a) Which cow converted food to milk most efficiently? *(1)*

(b) Which cow produced the most butterfat per year?

Name of cow _____

Explain how you found your answer. *(3)*

(c) State **one** feature carried by the daughters of Black Star which the company would wish to be absent in future offspring.

Give a reason for your answer. *(2)*

(d) The company intend to mate Black Star with **one** of three cows, Tornado, Turbo or Tango.

Suggest which cow should be chosen to give the best chance of an improved yield of creamy milk.

Give reasons for your answer. *(3)*

(e) If the calf from these parents is a bull, how can the company find out if he possesses the desired characteristics to achieve their aim? *(2)*

(LONDON)

▷ **Question 7** The drawings below show two tomato plants. Plant P is normal. Plant Q is from a strain which has been genetically engineered to resist attack by caterpillars.

Each plant had ten caterpillars of the same type placed on it two days before the drawings were made.

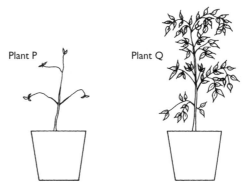

Plant P   Plant Q

Fig. 6.80

(a) Describe how such genetically engineering tomato plants can be produced. *(4)*

(b) Suggest **two** ways in which the genetically engineered plant Q could be resistant to attack by caterpillars.

1 _____

2 _____ *(2)*

(c) The caterpillar-resistant strain of tomato plant could have been produced in a different way by selective breeding.

State **one** advantage that genetic engineering has over selective breeding. *(1)*

(LONDON)

▷ **Question 8** Farmers growing soya beans have a problem because weeds compete with their crop. A genetically engineered variety of soya bean may solve their problem. A bacterial gene which can boost photosynthesis has been inserted into the plant. The new soya bean plants can withstand glyphosate, a herbicide, which disrupts photosynthesis and kills plants.

Use the information above to help you answer the following questions.

(a) A field of the genetically engineered soya beans is sprayed with glyphosate.

Explain the effects this would have on the yield. *(6)*

(b) Sometimes crop plants can interbreed with weeds. Explain **one** problem which could be caused if the genetically engineered soya beans did this.   *(2)*

(LONDON)

▷ **Question 9**   The diagram (Fig 6.81) shows two forms of a moth which rests on trees.
These moths are eaten by birds.
     When large quantities of coal were burned the air was heavily polluted with soot.

(a) What could happen to the colour of the tree trunks in a heavily polluted area?   *(1)*

(b) A survey of dark coloured and light coloured moths was carried out in a polluted area and an unpolluted area.
Moths were collected in the morning, marked on the underside and released.
They were collected again later the same day.
The results are shown in the tables below.
Table 6.14 shows the number of moths marked, released and recaptured.

Table 6.14

area		number of moths	
		light coloured	dark coloured
unpolluted	released	496	473
	recaptured	62	30
polluted	released	64	154
	recaptured	16	82

Fig. 6.81

Table 6.15 shows the percentage of moths recaptured in these areas.

Table 6.15

area	% recaptured	
	light coloured	dark coloured
unpolluted	12.5	6
polluted		53

(i) Calculate the percentage of light coloured moths recaptured in the polluted area. Show your working.   *(2)*

(ii) Why were the moths marked on the underside rather than on the upperside?   *(1)*

(iii) Suggest an explanation for the difference in the percentage of light coloured and dark coloured moths recaptured in the unpolluted area.   *(3)*

(c) This is an example of natural selection. Describe the principles of natural selection.   *(3)*

(d) Nowadays the level of soot pollution is much lower than when the survey was done.
     Suggest what effect reduced soot pollution might have on the populations of dark coloured and light coloured moths.   *(1)*

(MEG)

▷ **ANSWERS TO EXAMINATION QUESTIONS**

▷ **Question 1**   (a) Reptiles   (b) Annelids   (c) Flowering plants   (d) Insects

▷ **Question 2**   (a) Sex cells (gametes) have half the normal number of chromosomes: we say they are haploid. A body cell is diploid.

(b) amino acid; gene; chromosome; nucleus.

(c) All ova carry one X chromosome. (1)
     Half the sperm carry an X chromosome, and half carry a Y chromosome. (1)
     When fertilization occurs, the zygote may be XX (a girl) or XY (a boy). (1)

Both are equally likely, because there are equal numbers of the two types of sperm, (1) and both are equally likely to fertilize the ovum. (1)

▷ **Question 3** (a) Statement C is true. (1)

(b) Blue eyes, (1) boy. (1)

(c) (i) Rachel's twin is Lucy. (1)
  (ii) Rachel is a girl with brown eyes, so her identical twin, must be a girl, (1) with brown eyes; (1) it must be Lucy.

▷ **Question 4** (a) (i) **homozygous** means an individual has two identical alleles for a particular feature, e.g. AA or aa.
  (ii) **heterozygous** means an individual has two different alleles for a particular feature, e.g. Aa.

(b) (i) 1:1 ratio
  (ii) Aa (1)

▷ **Question 5** (a) (i) Soil contains minerals the plant needs, water does not. (1)
  (ii) The root cells are immersed in a strong glucose solution, so water moves out of the cells (1) by osmosis. (1) The cells become plasmolysed (1) so the plants wilt.
  (iii) In Flask B, albino plants grow well when they are given glucose, (1) but they cannot grow in water (Flask A) or soil (Flask D). (1)

(b) If both parent plants are heterozygous (**Aa**), you would expect a quarter of the off-spring to be albino. (1)

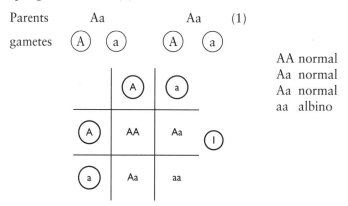

AA normal
Aa normal
Aa normal
aa albino

Fig. 6.82

(c) Take a cutting (see p. 196 for details) from the albino plant, (1) grow it in 2% glucose solution, (1) describe main steps of taking a cutting (see p. 197). (1)

▷ **Question 6** (a) Tango (high food conversion factor) (1)

(b) Tango (1)
Butterfat yield depends on annual milk yield and percentage of butterfat in milk.
Tango has the highest total (4500 × 3.5).

(c) Daughters of Black Star have a low food conversion factor (1) and a low milk yield. (1)

(d) There are two possible answers to this; make sure you explain your reasons to get full marks.
  Tornado is not a good choice. She is nervous, with a low food conversion factor and medium milk yield and percentage butterfat.
  Turbo is a good choice. She is calm, with a medium food conversion factor and a high milk yield. She has a low percentage butter fat, but Black Star has high butterfat, so that it is not a problem.
  Tango is a good choice. She has a high milk yield and high conversion factor. She is nervous with a low butter fat percentage, but Black Star is calm and has high butter-fat, so that is not a problem.

Tango or Turbo. (1)
Give two reason for your choice, as outlined. (2)

(e) Breed the bull with a cow with good characteristics, (1) measure milk yield, butterfat, etc. in any female calves produced by this mating. (1)

▷ **Question 7** (a) Identify a gene for resistance to insects in another organism, (1) cut it out using enzymes, (1) join it to DNA in a vector, e.g. bacteria, (1) clone the vectors, e.g. in a fermenter, (1) then infect the plants with the vectors. (1)

(b) The plant could:
taste unpleasant, smell unpleasant, be poisonous, be prickly, have tough leaves, have slippery leaves.

(c) Genetic engineering is quicker than selective breeding, (1) and it is more likely to produce organisms with the required characteristics. (1)

▷ **Question 8** (a) If the field was sprayed with glyphosate:
the crop yield would increase (1)
because weeds would be killed (1)
so they would no longer compete with crop plants (1) e.g. for light, water, minerals (1)
so crop plants have more resources and will grow better (1)
crop plants are not harmed by glyphosate (1)

(b) If they interbreed, they could produce hybrid offspring, (1) i.e. weeds which have the gene for glyphosate resistance, (1) so the weedkiller would be ineffective. (1)

▷ **Question 9** (a) The tree trunks become darker

(b) (i) percentage light moths recaptured in polluted
$$\text{area} = \frac{16}{64} \times 100 \ (1)$$
$$= 25\% \ (1)$$
(ii) Moths are marked on the underside so that the mark does not make them more visible to predators, i.e. does not increase their risk of being eaten. (1)
(iii) In the unpolluted area, tree trunks are covered in lichen, so they are pale. (1)
Light coloured moths are well camouflaged, so they are more likely to survive. (1)
Dark coloured moths are easily seen, so they are more likely to be eaten by predators. (1)

(c) There is variation, i.e. individuals are different. (1)
Some individuals have a selection advantage, i.e. they are well suited to their environment. (1)
They are more likely to survive and breed. (1)
They will have offspring like themselves. (1)

(d) Less soot will lead to a **decrease** in the number of dark moths, and an **increase** in the number of light moths.

STUDENT'S ANSWER WITH EXAMINER'S COMMENTS

(a) The diagram below shows portion of a DNA molecule during replication. The letters A, C, G and T represent the four bases; A = Adenine; C = Cytosine; G = Guanine; T = Thymine.

Complete the diagram by writing in the correct letters (A, C, G or T) in the empty boxes.   *(2)*

'Correct. This student knows that A bonds to T, and C bonds to G.'

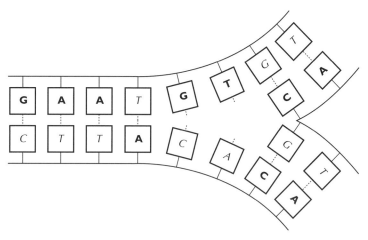

Fig. 6.83

'A mistake in copying DNA is a mutation, and it can lead to a faulty protein.'

(b) In mitosis, why is it necessary for exact copies of the DNA to be passed to each new cell?

DNA carries the genetic code. A mistake in copying means the new cells are not the same. ✓   *(2)*

(c) The order of the bases in a DNA molecule acts as a code that enables a cell to make proteins.

Table 6.16 shows the codes for some of the amino acids found in human cells.

Table 6.16

Amino Acid	DNA code	Amino Acid	DNA code
Phenylalanine	AAA	Leucine	AAT
Tyrosine	ATA	Cysteine	ACA
Histidine	GTA	Glutamine	GTT
Isoleucine	TAA	Methionine	TAC
Asparagine	TTA	Lysine	TTT
Valine	GAA	Alanine	CGA
Glutamic acid	CTT	Glycine	CCA

'Correct. The information has been transferred from the table properly.'

(i) Complete the boxes to show the amino acids which would be linked if the code of bases was:

DNA Sequence   TAACCAACA

Amino Acid Sequence   *isoleucine, glycine, cysteine* ✓   *(1)*

(continued)

(ii) In the box below, write down the sequence of bases which would act as a code for the following chain of amino acids:

Amino Acids Alanine, Valine, Histidine

'Correct.'

DNA Sequence *CGA, GAA, GTA* ✓ *(1)*

(d) Changes in base sequence can occur when a DNA molecule replicates. These changes may lead to altered genes.

(i) What name is given to the changes in DNA which can cause altered genes?

*'No, Down's syndrome is not caused by a faulty **gene**, it is due to an extra **chromosome**. Cystic fibrosis is a suitable answer.'*

mutation ✓ *(1)*

(ii) Name one human disease which is caused by a faulty gene.

Downs syndrome ✗ *(1)*

(iii) Explain why changes made during the replication of DNA can sometimes benefit a species of animal or plant.

'Good. This student has given an example to make the answer clear. She could have said . . . 'to increase it's chance of survival.'

It might cause a selective advantage, like the mutation in peppered moths, so there are better camouflaged. ✓ *(2)*

(e) Nature conservationists who have studied populations of hedgehogs for many years now think that there are two types of hedgehog living in Britain.

One type is the 'town' hedgehog which runs away when approached by road vehicles. The other type is the 'country' or 'normal' hedgehog which curls up when approached by road vehicles and is frequently run over and killed. The difference between the two types is thought to be caused by a gene.

Explain the process which has resulted in 'town' hedgehogs becoming much more common than the 'normal' ones in places where there is heavy traffic.

*'This question is all about natural selection. This student has got the right idea, but should have also included the following points: The town hedgehogs' behaviour is due to a **mutant gene**, and the town hedgehogs have a **selective advantage**.'*

In towns, hedgehogs are likely to be run over and killed by cars. Town hedgehogs run away, so they are not so likely to be killed. ✓ *They live longer, so they will have more babies, and their babies will also run away from cars.* ✓ *This explains why the number of town hedgehogs will increase.* ✓ *(5)*

(LONDON)

SUMMARY

Classification

▷ all living things are classified into five kingdoms: prokaryotes (bacteria and other similar microbes), protoctists, fungi, plants and animals;

▷ plants are classified into four main groups: mosses, ferns, conifers and flowering plants – you should know the main external features of each group;

▷ animals are often classified as invertebrates or vertebrates:

  invertebrates include insects, spiders, crustaceans, molluscs and segmented worms

  vertebrates include fish, amphibians, reptiles, birds and mammals

  you should know the main external features of each group;

▷ biologists use simple keys to identify unknown organisms. These may be branching keys or number keys.

Genes and variation

▷ variation means that individuals within a species are different from each other – it can be caused by genes (inherited from parents) or by the environment;

▷ a gene is a length of DNA carrying instructions about a particular feature of an individual – genes are part of chromosomes, which are found in the nucleus of all cells;

▷ genes exist in alternative forms called alleles, e.g. there is a gene for eye colour, with alleles for blue eyes, brown eyes, etc;

▷ body cells contain pairs of chromosomes, so they have two copies of each gene – this number of chromosomes is called the diploid number, and in humans it is 46;

▷ gametes contain single chromosomes, so they have one copy of each gene – this number of chromosomes is called the haploid number, and in humans it is 23 (the haploid number is always half of the diploid number);

▷ meiosis (cell division) produces haploid gametes;

▷ when male and female gametes (both haploid) fuse at fertilization, the zygote that is formed is diploid; it receives genes from both parents, so it inherits features from both parents;

▷ two of the chromosomes are called sex chromosomes: females are always XX and males are always XY;

▷ An individual's phenotype is his or her appearance or characteristics, e.g. blue eyes. The genotype is the alleles he or she has, e.g. bb;

▷ if an individual has two identical alleles, we say he or she are homozygous, e.g. , or BB – he or she has two different alleles, we say he or she is heterozygous, e.g. Bb;

▷ some alleles are dominant to others (we normally show these with a capital letter symbol), and will always show in the phenotype;

▷ other alleles are recessive (we use a lower case letter symbol for these), and will only shown in the phenotype if there are two of them,

  e.g.   BB – brown eyes   Bb – brown eyes   bb – blue eyes
    allele B is dominant, allele b is recessive;

▷ you must be able to draw simple genetic diagrams to show how features are inherited;

▷ some diseases are caused by faulty genes, and can be passed on from parents to children, e.g. cystic fibrosis, sickle cell anaemia, Huntington's disease. In some cases, parents are carriers (heterozygous), e.g. Aa, and can pass on the allele for the disease, even through they have no symptoms themselves;

▷ some conditions are sex-linked, because the allele is carried on the X chromosome, e.g. red-green colour-blindness, haemophilia. Men suffer from these conditions much more often than women;

▷ some alleles show incomplete dominance (co-dominance), where neither is dominant or recessive. In this case, both alleles will show equally in the phenotype, e.g. blood group AB individuals.

SUMMARY CONT.

DNA and protein synthesis

▷ DNA is found in the nucleus of all cells, and it carries genetic information in the form of a genetic code. It is a large molecule made of two strands of nucleotides twisted together – it is sometimes called a double helix. The strands are linked by bases which are matched together: adenine links to thymine, cytosine links to guanine;

▷ DNA carries information to make all the proteins in the body; one gene carries information to make one protein. Protein synthesis occurs in the cytoplasm, and the DNA must remain in the nucleus, so a copy of the gene is made from RNA. RNA passes out of the nucleus into the cytoplasm and acts as a template (pattern) for protein synthesis;

▷ the genetic code is the order of bases on the DNA (and its copy made from RNA). The bases are read in groups of three (a codon, or triplet), and each group codes for a single amino acid. The correct amino acids are joined together in the correct order to make a protein;

▷ genetic engineering means transferring DNA (a gene) from one organism to another, so that the recipient can make new proteins. The gene for insulin has been transferred from humans to bacteria, so the bacteria can make insulin, and this can be used by diabetics;

▷ cloning means producing genetically identical offspring from a single parent. It may be natural, e.g. when yeasts or bacteria reproduce asexually, or when plants reproduce asexually with bulbs or runners;

▷ it may be artificial, e.g. when gardeners take plant cuttings, or carry out micropropagation, or when embryos are spilt in animal breeding;

▷ selective breeding (sometimes called artificial selection) is a way of choosing parents to obtain a particular type of offspring . It is important in the development of crop plants, e.g. for disease resistance, or to get high yields, and in the development of domestic animals, e.g. breeds of dog, breeds of cattle;

▷ when a cell divides, the DNA must be copied so that the new cell gets a set of chromosomes. Sometimes the DNA is copied inaccurately and we say a mutation has occurred. This can happen naturally, but it is increased by exposure to radiation and to some chemicals.

Natural selection and evolution

▷ mutations increase variation – they may be helpful or neutral, but are usually harmful to the organisms;

▷ due to variation, some individuals are better suited to their environment than others, so they are more likely to survive – they will breed and produce offspring like themselves: this process is called natural selection;

▷ natural selection is most obvious when conditions are hostile, i.e. there is competition for resources, and the individuals who are not suited to the environment die out;

▷ gradually, the features of the population change, and the accumulation of changes over a long period of time is called evolution. The fossil record is incomplete, but it suggests that many species have evolved in this way.

Chapter 7

Living organisms in their environment

GETTING STARTED

| MEG | SEG | NEAB | LONDON | WJEC | NICCEA | SEB |

If we study living organisms in isolation from each other, we only see a part of the total picture. Biologists need to study organisms in their natural environment and to consider how they interact with their environment and with each other.

In this chapter, you will look at the different techniques for studying organisms in field-work, and you will consider the ways in which they interact, e.g. competition, predator–prey relationships. You will look at the impact of humans on the natural environment, and on the organisms which live in it. You will find out how materials and energy pass through ecosystems, and how humans can manage ecosystems to get maximum crop yield.

TOPIC	STUDY	REVISION 1	REVISION 2
Ecology			
Ecological fieldwork			
Adaptation and competition			
Predator–prey relationships			
Factors affecting population size			
Humans and the environment			
Human effects on the environment			
Human population size			
Changes in the biosphere			
Conservation			
Energy and nutrient transfer			
Food chains and food webs			
Ecological pyramids			
Energy transfers in ecology			
Decay			
Importance of decay			
Carbon cycle			
Nitrogen cycle			
Managed ecosystems			
Pest control			

WHAT YOU NEED TO KNOW

▷ **Ecology**

Ecology is the study of organisms in their natural habitats. This includes finding out exactly **which** organisms are present, **where** they are, and **how many** there are.

For an organism to be successful, i.e. to survive and breed, it must be **well adapted** to its habitat, i.e. it must have features which help it to survive. You must be aware of the conditions in a particular habitat before you can identify features which will increase survival.

There are several very important terms you should be familiar with in this topic:

'You must know the meaning of these terms.'

ecology	study of living things in their natural surroundings.
habitat	the place where an organism lives, e.g. rock pool habitat, pond habitat, woodland habitat.
population	all the members of a particular species within a habitat, e.g. a rock pool may have a population of limpets.
community	all the types of living things within a habitat, e.g. a rock pool may have a community which includes seaweeds, limpets, topshells, periwinkles, shrimps and small fish.
ecosystem	all of the living and non-living things in a habitat, e.g. plants, animals, rocks and water in a rock pool would make up the rock pool ecosystem.
environment	an organism's surroundings.

Ecological fieldwork

Fieldwork is an important part of Biology, so you need to plan your work carefully before you go out. Make sure you take a **key** to help you to identify the organisms you find, and take suitable equipment to trap or record the organisms.

Always replace animals where you found them, and take care not to damage living things or their habitat in any way.

For each habitat there are **key pieces of information** which should be collected:

- temperature;
- pH of soil or water;
- variety of plants present, i.e. number of species;
- type of plants present, i.e. names of species;
- distribution of plants, i.e. where they are growing;
- variety of animals present;
- type of animals present;
- distribution of animals.

Key points

- you will need keys to identify plants and animals;
- record plants or non-moving animals by using transects or quadrats;
- record moving animals using nets, beating trays, or traps;
- estimate the number of plants by quadrat sampling;
- estimate the number of animals by the mark – recapture method;
- always replace animals where you found them, and make sure you do not harm living things or damage their environment in any way.

Techniques for recording plants

1. Line transect

Place a tape or string between two poles and record any plant which **touches** the tape (Fig. 7.1). If the transect is too long, record plants touching the tape at **regular intervals** e.g. every 10 cm.

Suitable for:	▷ plants which grow close to the ground;
	▷ areas which involve a change from one habitat type to another, e.g. edge of a pond, field border adjoining hedgerow.

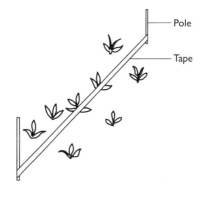

Fig. 7.1 Line transect

2. Point transect

Place a tape or string between two poles. The tape should be 0.5 m above the ground. Place a piece of doweling or a metal strip vertically against the tape at **intervals**, e.g. every 10 cm and record every plant it **touches** (Fig. 7.2).

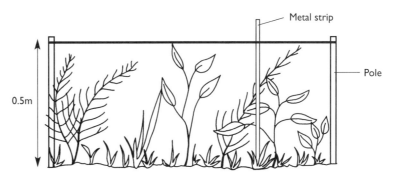

Fig. 7.2 Point transect

Suitable for: areas where there are several **'layers'** of plants.

3. Belt transect

Place a tape or string between two poles and place a quadrat on it. Record all plants **within** the quadrat. (Fig. 7.3). Either move the quadrat so that all plants on the belt are recorded, or so that plants at regular intervals, e.g. 1 m are recorded.

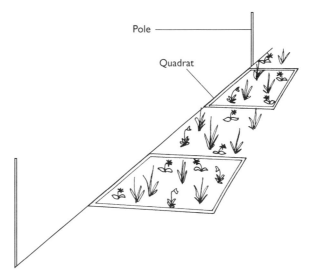

Fig. 7.3 Belt transect

Suitable for: ▷ long transects;
                 ▷ collecting large amounts of data.

4. Quadrat

This is a frame (usually 0.5 m × 0.5 m) which is placed on the ground, and plants inside it are identified. It can either be placed **randomly**, e.g. by throwing it or using random number tables, or in a **fixed pattern**, e.g. a belt transect.

(a) It can be used to assess the **variety** of plants present, e.g. in a rocky shore habitat there may be three species present in one quadrat, in grassland there may be 25 species present.

(b) It can be used to assess which plant is the **dominant species** in a particular habitat. We can estimate the area inside a quadrat taken up by each species, this is **percentage cover**. In Fig. 7.4, species **A** occupies about 80% of the quadrat, while species **B** occupies the remaining 20%.

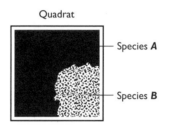

Fig. 7.4 Estimation of percentage cover

(c) It can be used to estimate **number of plants** present. In a field 100 m × 100 m there are too many daisy plants to count. We can **sample** the field using a quadrat (Fig. 7.5).

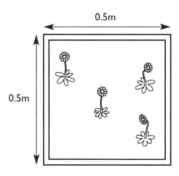

Fig. 7.5 Estimation of number of plants

Area of quadrat   =   0.5 × 0.5 m
                   =   0.25 m^2

Number of daisy plants present
                   =   4

If we place nine other quadrats in this field, we record these results:

Quadrat number	1	2	3	4	5	6	7	8	9
Number of daisy plants	0	6	11	3	2	10	0	0	1

'This method is most accurate when the plants are evenly distributed.'

Total number of daisy plants = 37

Mean number per quadrat   = $\dfrac{37}{10}$ = 3.7

One quadrat has an area of 0.25 m^2

The whole field has an area of $100 \times 100 = 10,000m^2$ so the field is 40,000 times bigger than one quadrat.

We can use this information to **estimate** the number of daisy plants in the field.

There are 3.7 daisy plants in one quadrat, so in the whole field there will be

   $3.7 \times 40,000$ daisy plants
   = 148,000 plants.

This gives us a **rough estimate** of the daisy plants in the field.

Techniques for recording animals

1. Nets
Use a fine mesh net on a wire frame to collect small animals from water (a sieve could also be used for this.) Empty the net into a white enamel dish containing a small amount of water so that you can see the animals clearly.

   Some nets have a glass tube at the base to collect trapped animals (Fig. 7.6). These are called **plankton nets.**

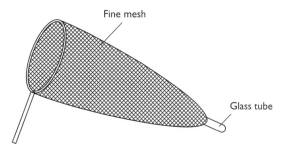

Fig. 7.6 Net

Suitable for: collecting small animals from ponds, streams or rock pools.

---

2. Beating tray
Place a large piece of white card or material (e.g. old sheet) under the branches of a bush or tree. Gently hit the branches to shake off any animals attached to the bark or leaves – take care **not** to damage the branches (Fig. 7.7). The animals will fall onto the card and can be identified.

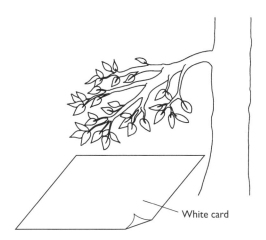

Fig. 7.7 Beating tray

Suitable for: small animals living in hedgerows or trees e.g. caterpillars, beetles.

---

3. Pitfall trap

Bury a container e.g. yogurt pot or jam jar, so that the top is level with the ground. Balance a stone over the top so that it will not fill with water if it rains. Leave it for 24 hours, then collect and identify the animals which have crawled into it, (Fig. 7.8).

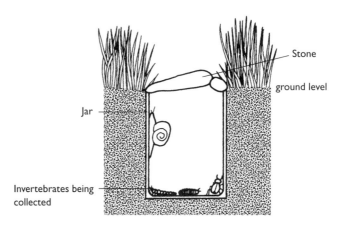

Fig. 7.8 Pitfall trap

Suitable for: small animals in grassland or woods, e.g. beetles, spiders.

4. Tullgren funnel

Collect a sample of leaf litter and put it on the gauze platform inside the funnel. Small animals will move away from the heat and light, and will fall into the alcohol, which kills them (Fig. 7.9).

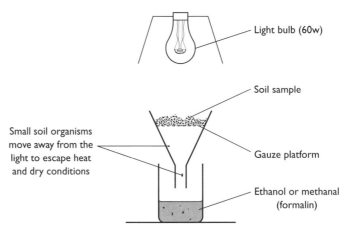

Fig. 7.9 Tullgren funnel

Suitable for: small animals in leaf litter, e.g. beetles, millipedes, worms.

5. Quadrats

Some animals do not move at all, or move only slowly, e.g. barnacles, limpets, mussels on rocky shores. These can be recorded using a quadrat.

Estimating number of animals in a habitat

The easiest way to do this is **mark–recapture technique**. This method works for animals which can move around easily, e.g. beetles as long as:

(a)   you have a way of trapping them, e.g. pitfall trap,
(b)   you have a way of marking them, e.g. spot of paint on body.

It involves five stages:

1.   Set up the trap to catch the animals you are investigating, e.g. beetles.
2.   Record how many are caught, and mark each one.
3.   Release the marked beetles in the area you are investigating.
4.   Some time later, e.g. 24 hours, set up the trap again.
5.   Record how many marked and unmarked beetles are caught.

You can use this formula to work out the total number of beetles in the area you are investigating:

$$\text{Total number of beetles} \quad = \quad \frac{\text{number caught 1st day} \times \text{number caught 2nd day}}{\text{number of marked beetles caught 2nd day}}$$

e.g. if I caught and marked 27 beetles on the first day, then caught 30 beetles on the 2nd day, but only 6 of them were marked

$$\text{Total number of beetles} \quad = \quad \frac{27 \times 30}{6}$$

$$= \text{135 beetles}$$

When using this method, you must make sure that:

▶ marked beetles are **equally likely to survive**, i.e. brightly coloured paint would make them more noticeable to predators, so they would be less likely to survive;
▶ you leave a **suitable time** between stages 3 and 4 for the beetles to spread out.

REVISION ACTIVITY I   (a)   Which method would you use to investigate the number of:
   (i)   limpets on the shore?
   (ii) tadpoles in a pond?
   (iii) slugs in a garden?
   (iv) buttercups in a field?

(b)   (i)   I set a pitfall trap in my garden and caught 47 beetles. I marked them and released them. Two days later I set the trap again, and caught 56 beetles, and 7 of these were marked. Estimate the number of beetles in my garden.
   (ii) Why shouldn't you mark them with fluorescent paint?

Adaptation and competition

Key points

▶ to be successful in a particular habitat, organisms must adapted to live there. This means that they have features which will help them to survive;

▶ to understand adaptation, you must be aware of the conditions in a habitat;

▶ organisms compete with each other for the resources they need to stay alive;

▶ not all organisms are successful in competition. The least successful organisms may die.

Adaptation: general points

Organisms are successful because they are **adapted** (suitable) for the habitat where they normally live. This means that they have certain features which help them to survive.

1. Desert Habitat

Conditions: very little water,
               very hot during the day and very cold at night,
               sand may be blown by wind.

'Think about why they are successful.'

Successful plant: cactus

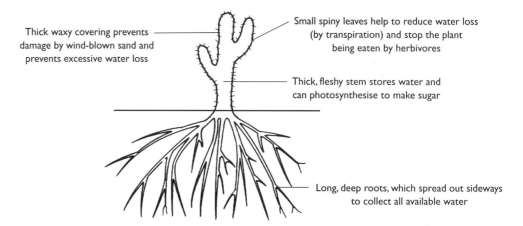

Thick waxy covering prevents damage by wind-blown sand and prevents excessive water loss

Small spiny leaves help to reduce water loss (by transpiration) and stop the plant being eaten by herbivores

Thick, fleshy stem stores water and can photosynthesise to make sugar

Long, deep roots, which spread out sideways to collect all available water

Fig. 7.10 Cactus

Successful animal: camel

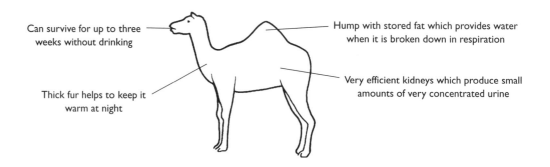

Can survive for up to three weeks without drinking

Hump with stored fat which provides water when it is broken down in respiration

Thick fur helps to keep it warm at night

Very efficient kidneys which produce small amounts of very concentrated urine

Fig. 7.11 Camel

2. Stream Habitat (Britain)

Conditions: freshwater, i.e. water with some minerals in it, temperature varies throughout the year, flow rate may be rapid or slow.

Successful plant: water crowfoot

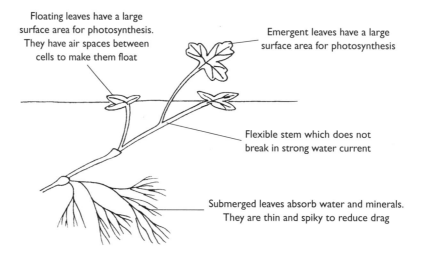

Floating leaves have a large surface area for photosynthesis. They have air spaces between cells to make them float

Emergent leaves have a large surface area for photosynthesis

Flexible stem which does not break in strong water current

Submerged leaves absorb water and minerals. They are thin and spiky to reduce drag

Fig. 7.12 Water crowfoot

Successful animals: mayfly nymph

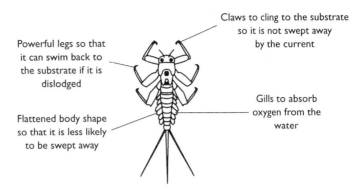

Powerful legs so that it can swim back to the substrate if it is dislodged

Claws to cling to the substrate so it is not swept away by the current

Flattened body shape so that it is less likely to be swept away

Gills to absorb oxygen from the water

Fig. 7.13 Mayfly nymph

Adaptations to the rocky shore ecosystem
The rocky shore can be divided into three regions, based on the tides (Fig. 7.14)

upper shore: is usually uncovered, except when there are very high tides,
middle shore: is covered and uncovered by water twice each day,
lower shore: is usually covered by water, except when there are very low tides.

Within these three regions there are many different types of habitat, e.g. rock pools, cracks and crevices in rocks, areas under boulders, etc.

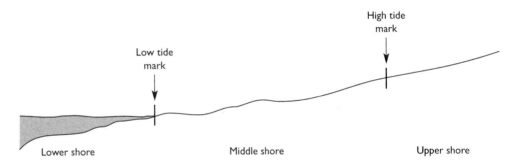

High tide mark

Low tide mark

Lower shore   Middle shore   Upper shore

Fig. 7.14 Profile of a rocky shore

As a result of the tides, conditions vary significantly

daily:
▷ amount of **water** covering an organism changes as the tide goes in and out (twice each day);
▷ **temperature** varies due to the tides. Organisms that are covered in water will have a reasonably constant temperature compared with those that are uncovered;
▷ amount of **light** that reaches an organism varies. When the tide is in, less light can penetrate the water.

Seasonally:
▷ the heights of the **tides** vary so that different regions of the shore are covered and exposed. The highest tides are in spring and autumn.

Organisms which live on a rocky shore must be able to cope with the following problems:

▷ drying out when they are left uncovered;
▷ large changes in temperature;
▷ being moved around and swept off the rocks by the power of the waves;
▷ animals must get enough oxygen from the water to survive;
▷ plants must trap enough light for photosynthesis.

'Zonation is a key concept on rocky shores – make sure you understand why it occurs.'

The differing conditions on different parts of the shore leads to **zonation**, i.e. animals and plants have a particular region of the shore where they can survive best, and where they are abundant.

1. Rocky shore plants

The only plants found on rocky shores are seaweeds. These are algae which attach themselves to rocks with a holdfast. They have no proper roots, stems or leaves; but they have a region called the thallus which can photosynthesise (Fig. 7.15).

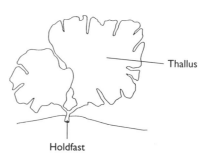

— Thallus

Holdfast

Fig. 7.15 Seaweed (Ulva)

Seaweeds can be divided into three groups:

(a) **green seaweeds**, e.g. *Ulva* (sea lettuce) are found mainly on the upper shore. They are usually small and can withstand drying out when uncovered.

(b) **brown seaweeds**, e.g. *Fucus vesiculosus* (bladder wrack) are found on the middle and lower shore. Some have air bladders so that they will float closer to the surface of the water. Some are very large and can withstand being pounded by the waves.

(c) **red seaweeds**, e.g. *Corallina* are found in rock pools and on the lower shore. These vary a lot in size and can live permanently underwater.

2. Rocky Shore Animals

There is a large variety of animals found on unpolluted rocky shores. Many of them are fixed to the rock, or move very slowly, so they are easy to record. Animals you might see include:

sponges
sea anemones
molluscs, e.g. periwinkles, limpets
crustaceans, e.g. barnacles, crabs, shrimps
starfish
fish, e.g. blenny, wrasse

Their position on the shore will depend on several factors:

e.g. how they feed,
how they prevent themselves drying out,
how they prevent themselves being damaged by waves.

An example of a rocky shore animal from the upper shore, is the Periwinkle (*Littorina neritoides*):

▷ lives in rock crevices;
▷ clamps itself to rock when tide is out to reduce water loss;
▷ shell protects it from predators;
▷ feeds on algae on rock surfaces of upper shore.

Fig. 7.16 Periwinkle

3. Collecting data on rocky shores

Plants: use line or belt transects, quadrats.
Animals: use belt transects or quadrats for fixed animals and nets for swimming animals, e.g. fish, shrimps.

4. Ideas for fieldwork

'Remember to check the tides when you are planning fieldwork.'

(a) Investigate zonation of plants or animals.
(b) Investigate how plants or animals prevent themselves being swept off rocks.
(c) Investigate the size and shape of limpets from different regions of the shore.
(d) Investigate the rate at which different types of seaweed dry out when exposed to air.

Always avoid disturbing or damaging the habitat.

Adaptations to the pond ecosystem

A pond is a small area of quite shallow, stagnant water (Fig. 7.17). It can be divided into four regions:

1. Surface film: small animals and plants live on the surface film of water or hang underneath it.
2. Vegetation zone: this consists of floating and submerged plants and the animals that live on them.
3. Open water: floating plants and swimming or drifting animals are found in this region.
4. Muddy bottom: light and oxygen are scarce here, but several types of animal thrive in these conditions.

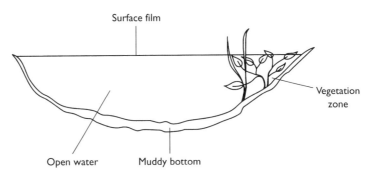

Fig. 7.17 Profile of a pond

Conditions will vary much more in small ponds than larger ones.

daily:

▶ amount of **oxygen** varies. At night, plants have no light for photosynthesis so they stop producing oxygen. All pond organisms continue to use oxygen for respiration, so oxygen levels will fall very low. During the day more oxygen is made by photosynthesis.

▶ **temperature** is higher during the day than at night.

seasonally:

▶ amount of **light** varies. In the summer there is more light, so plants grow faster.

▶ **temperature** varies. In summer it is warmer so many animals will be more active.

▶ amount of **water** varies. In summer some ponds will become much shallower, or even dry up, as water evaporates in the heat.

1. Pond plants

Most of the plants found in ponds are algae or flowering plants; mosses and ferns are very rare. Algae are mainly microscopic, and live in open water or on the surface of stones or leaves, e.g. *Spirogyra, Chlorella*. Flowering plants can be divided into three main groups:

(a) Rooted plants with floating leaves, e.g. water-lily (*Nymphaea***)**

Roots anchor the plant at the bottom of the pond, but are not very important for absorbing water or minerals. The leaves have air spaces so they will float to obtain maximum light for photosynthesis. The stomata are on the upper surface of the leaf and this surface is usually waxy so water does not collect there.

(b) Floating plants, e.g. duckweed (*Lemna***)**

Small, circular fronds (leaves) float on the surface of the water and short roots hang down. These help to balance the plant and collect minerals from the water. Gas exchange occurs through stomata on the upper leaf surface and through the roots.

(c) Submerged plants, e.g. Bladderwort (*Utricularia***)**

There are no roots, but horizontal stems with many small leaves absorb water and minerals. Some of the leaves have small sac-like bladders to trap tiny water organisms which provide the plant with minerals. Bladderwort grows best in ponds where the water contains few minerals because it has an advantage over the other plants there.

Plants are important in ponds in the following ways:

▶ they produce oxygen when they photosynthesise
▶ they are an important food source for animals
▶ they provide an important place for animals to shelter and lay their eggs.

2. Pond animals

The variety of animals will depend on the size and permanence of the pond. Some of the animals will spend their whole life there, while others have a complicated life-cycle and spend only part of it in the pond, e.g. dragonflies, frogs. Animals you might see include:

flatworms
annelid worms
molluscs, e.g. pond snails
crustaceans, e.g. water fleas, waterlice
insects, e.g. pondskater, water boatman, midge larva
fish
frogs (or tadpoles)

An example of a pond animal that lives on the **surface film** is the **pondskater** (*Gerris*):

▶ small animal which walks on surface film of water;
▶ four long legs angled away from the body to spread its weight;
▶ very light for its size;
▶ carnivore which feeds on other animals on or near the watersurface.

Fig. 7.18 Pondskater

3. Collecting data in ponds

Plants: ▶ use nets or jars;

Animals: ▶ use nets for surface film or open water;
            ▶ search vegetation by hand;
            ▶ dig up a small amount; e.g. a teaspoonful, of bottom mud and place in a white enamel dish with some water.

4. Ideas for fieldwork

(a) Investigate the distribution of plants or animals in a pond.
(b) Investigate the growth rate of duckweed with different amounts of light.
(c) Investigate the growth rate of duckweed with different amounts of minerals.
(d) Investigate which type of substrate pond snails prefer, e.g. sandy, muddy, gravel, etc.

> If you remove animals from a pond, make sure you return them to the same pond, and to the correct region of the pond. Avoid disturbing or damaging the habitat in any way.

Adaptations to the woodland ecosystem

Woods can be divided into two types: broad-leaved (deciduous) woods and coniferous woods. In this section we will consider **broad-leaved** woods.

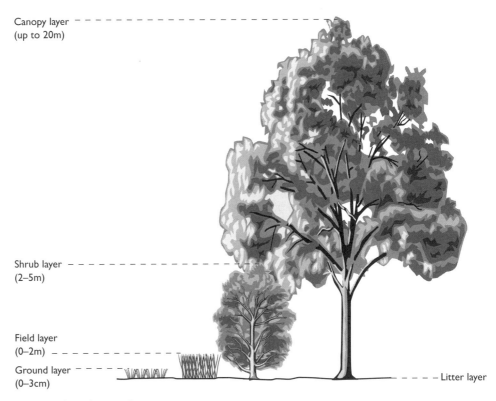

Canopy layer (up to 20m)

Shrub layer (2–5m)

Field layer (0–2m)

Ground layer (0–3cm)

Litter layer

Fig. 7.19 Profile of a wood

A typical wood can be divided into five regions:

In **coniferous** woods, the trees form a much denser canopy layer, so less light penetrates through to the woodland floor. There are far fewer plants in the shrub, field and ground layers and consequently the number of animals is smaller.

Conditions will depend on the size of the wood, the type of soil present and how closely the trees are growing.

daily: ▷ amount of **light** and **temperature** will vary between day and night.

seasonally: ▷ amount of **light** varies as leaves in the canopy layer grow in spring and fall in autumn;

▷ **daylength** varies throughout the year. This is important because it triggers flowering in many plants and behaviour patterns, e.g. mating or hibernation in some animals.

1. Woodland plants

A typical wood contains a large variety of plants, including lichens, mosses, ferns and flowering plants. Many of these plants can cope well with shady conditions.

Tree layer: there is usually one dominant species, e.g. oak (*Quercus*) or two species may be equally dominant, e.g. oak and ash.

Shrub layer: this includes hawthorn, hazel, elder and young trees.

Field layer: this region includes ferns, bramble, bluebell, dogs mercury, wild garlic.

Ground layer: mosses, lichens and grasses are found in this layer.

Litter layer: only dead and decaying plants are found here.

Many plants found in the field layer have adaptations for living in the shade, e.g.

'These are important adaptations.'

▷ early growth and flowering before the leaf canopy forms;

▷ plants grow taller to make the best use of available light;

▷ plants have larger leaves than those of the same species growing in sunny places. This gives a larger surface area for the absorption of light;

▷ leaves contain more chloroplasts to trap sunlight.

An example of a woodland plant is the **bluebell**. See Fig. 7.20 overleaf.

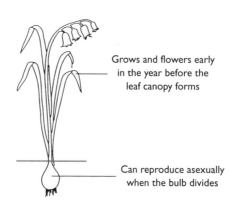

Grows and flowers early
in the year before the
leaf canopy forms

Can reproduce asexually
when the bulb divides

Fig. 7.20 Bluebell

2. Woodland animals
There is a huge variety of animals in a typical wood, including:

annelid worms, e.g. earthworm
molluscs, e.g. snail, slug
crustaceans, e.g. woodlice
arachnids, e.g. spiders, harvestmen
insects, e.g. butterflies, moths, beetles, ants
myriapods, e.g. centipedes, millipedes
birds, e.g. crows, rooks, woodpeckers, owls
mammals, e.g. dormice, woodmice, squirrels.

Many of these animals will be very secretive or nocturnal, and therefore difficult to observe.

An example of a woodland animal from the Field layer is the **speckled wood butterfly**

▶ eggs are laid on underside of grass leaves;
▶ caterpillars are green, so are well camouflaged on grass;
▶ caterpillars have strong jaws to feed on grass;
▶ adult is mottled brown colour (well camouflaged);
▶ adult is active even at low temperatures, e.g. in shady woods.

Fig. 7.21 Woodland
butterfly

3. Collecting Data in Woods
Plants: use line, point or belt transects, or quadrats

Animals: use beating trays for animals in shrubs or trees
                 pitfall traps for animals in ground layer
                 Tullgren funnel for animals in litter layer.

4. Ideas for fieldwork
(a) Investigate distribution of plants or animals in a wood.
(b) Compare heights of a single species of plant growing in the sun and shade.
(c) Compare leaf area of a single species of plant growing in the sun and the shade.
(d) Investigate the numbers of a particular animal species using mark–recapture techniques.
(e) Compare the animals found in a deciduous and a coniferous wood.

> **If you remove any animals from the wood, make sure they are returned to the correct region. Avoid damaging or disturbing the habitat in any way.**

REVISION ACTIVITY 2   Bill noticed some tiny white insects called springtails in the soil below an oak tree. Springtails feed on fungi which decay the leaves.

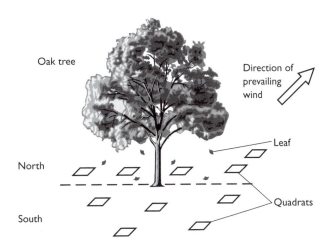

Fig. 7.22

He investigated the distribution of the insects around the tree using five quadrats to the north and five to the south of the tree.

Bill took an equal sample of soil from each quadrat. He counted the number of spring-tails in each sample using a Tullgren funnel (see p. 236).

(a)   (i)   Why did Bill take an equal sample of soil from each quadrat?
      (ii) Why did he use a lamp?
      (iii) Why was the wire mesh used?

(b)   The results of the investigation are shown in the table below.

Table 7.1

	North of tree					South of tree				
Number of springtails per soil sample	20	30	45	10	25	10	15	20	5	5

(i)   The average number of springtails per sample in the south was 11.
      Calculate the average number of springtails per sample in the north. Show your working.
(ii) Explain the difference in the number of springtails on different sides of the tree.

Competition

Organisms must **compete** with others for the things they need to stay alive (we call these **resources**). Often these resources are in short supply, so only the most successful competitors will survive; less successful organisms will die.

Plants compete for:

▶   light, to photosynthesise;
▶   water;
▶   mineral salts, e.g. nitrates, phosphates;
▶   space.

'Try to learn these examples.'

Animals compete for:

▶   food;
▶   space (sometimes called territory);
▶   a mate;
▶   also, they must avoid being eaten by predators.

Competition may be between organisms of different species: we call this **interspecific competition**, e.g.

▶   in a wood; trees, ferns, bluebells and mosses may be competing for light;
▶   in a field; grasses, dandelions and groundsel may be competing for minerals from the soil.

Competition may be between organisms of the same species: we call this **intraspecific competition**, e.g.

▶ in a field of maize the individual plants are competing with each other for light and minerals;

▶ in a rockpool, periwinkles are competing with each other for food (algae).

If resources are scarce, some organisms will not get the things they need to stay alive, so they will die. This is an important step in **natural selection** (see p. 209).

Predator–prey relationships

Key points

▶ carnivores which hunt and eat other animals are called **predators**;

▶ the animals they eat are called their **prey**;

▶ there is a close relationship between numbers of predators and numbers of prey.

If a predator relies mainly on a particular prey for its food, the populations are likely to be strongly affected by each other. For instance, if the prey population increases, the population of the predator will also increase, at least initially. This is because the predators will tend to survive for longer, and reproduce more successfully, if there is abundant food available. However, an increase in predator numbers will cause a reduction in the prey population. This, in turn, will result in reduction in predator numbers.

There are two important features of predator–prey relationships:

▶ the number of predators is always less than the number of prey;

▶ after an increase in the prey population, there is a time-lag before the predator population increases.

This is the time need for the predator to respond to the increased food availability, and to reproduce.

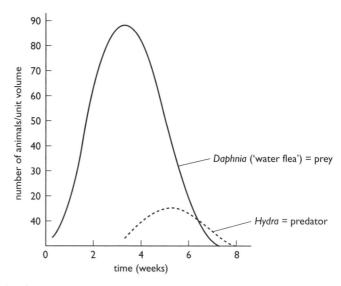

Fig. 7.23 Example of a simple predator–prey relationship

When predator numbers increase, more prey will be eaten so the number of prey animals decreases. This will lead to a food shortage for predators, so the predator numbers will fall.

This cycle of dependency will be repeated many times.

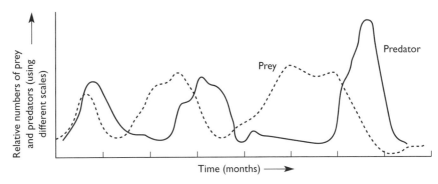

Fig. 7.24 Fluctuations of predator–prey populations over time

Factors affecting population size

> ### Key points
>
> ▷ a population is a group of organisms of the same species in a habitat;
>
> ▷ the number of organisms in a population is determined by several factors;
>
> ▷ increased reproductive rate and immigration will increase the population size;
>
> ▷ increased death rate and emigration will decrease the population size.

Increase in population size

This occurs for three main reasons:

1. **Increased reproductive rate**
    i.e. more offspring are being born and are surviving. This may happen if more food or space becomes available, or the number of sexually mature adults increases.
2. **Decreased death rate**
    i.e. organisms are living longer. This may happen if more food becomes available, or the number of predators falls.
3. **Immigration**
    i.e. individuals move into the population from outside. This occurs in animals, e.g. birds which have a regular migration pattern, and it occurs in plants, e.g. seeds may be moved by wind or animals, and may colonise a new area.

Decrease in population size

This occurs for three main reasons:

1. **Increased death rate** (mortality)
    More organisms than usual may die due to disease or lack of food.
2. **Decreased reproductive rate**
    Fewer organisms than usual are being born. This may be due to lack of food or space, or lack of available breeding partners.
3. **Emigration**
    i.e. individuals move out of the population to live elsewhere.

Patterns of population growth

When a small number of individuals is placed in a habitat, the population growth will follow a predictable pattern

There are four main stages:

1. Lag phase: when organisms are adjusting to their new environment.
2. Log phase: when numbers are increasing very rapidly.
    This continues until resources, e.g. food or space, limit further increases.
3. Stationary phase: when the number of organisms remains constant.
4. Post-stationary phase: several things can happen at this stage, depending on the conditions:

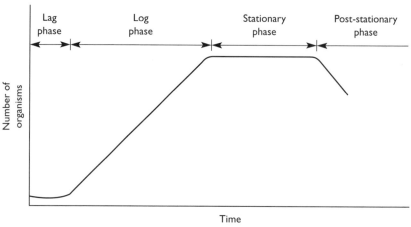

Fig. 7.25 Population growth

(a) numbers may remain constant for a long period;
(b) numbers may fall slightly, then remain constant.
     Both (a) and (b) represent the **carrying capacity**: the number of organisms which can be supported long-term in a particular habitat.
(c) numbers may drop dramatically (population crash) due to disease or bad weather conditions;
(d) numbers may decrease, then increase, then decrease again (population fluctuation) due to predator–prey relationships.

Measuring population size
To get accurate data about patterns of population growth, you must know the numbers of organisms present. Read the section on fieldwork techniques to find out how this is done.

Humans and the environment

The human population continues to expand, unlike populations of most other species which are stable or declining. This places increasing demands on the environment as humans need more living space, more food and more resources, and produce more waste products and pollution. Many other species and habitats are now at risk due to human activities.

Conservation is a way of limiting the damage that humans do to their environment.

Human effects on the environment

> **Key points**
>
> ▷ humans usually have a harmful effect on other species and their natural habitats;
>
> ▷ human activities pollute air, water and land;
>
> ▷ humans use land for farming, mining and building, which damage natural habitats;
>
> ▷ overfishing and deforestation are examples of humans exploiting living resources.

Pollution
Pollution is the presence in the environment of substances in the wrong amounts, in the wrong place and at the wrong time. Most pollution occurs as a direct result of human activities. It tends to cause most concern when it affects humans, but most organisms in most habitats are likely to be affected by pollution. Each of the main types of habitat – air, land and water – are affected by pollution.

Despite our improved understanding of the causes and effects of pollution, the problem is likely to become more serious as the human population continues to expand. One type of pollution, which has global rather than simply local effects, is carbon dioxide. This is described in more detail on p. 256.

1. Air pollution

Most air pollution is due to **fossil fuels** being burned by industry, in homes or in vehicles.

Primary pollutants are produced directly and released into the air.

Secondary pollutants are formed in the air from chemical reactions between primary pollutants.

Table 7.2

Air pollutant	Source	Damaging effects
Primary pollutants		
sulphur dioxide	combustion of fossil fuels (mainly industry)	'dieback' in trees, reduced crop plant growth
nitrogen oxides	combustion of fossil fuels (mainly vehicles)	'dieback' in trees, reduced crop plant growth
carbon monoxide	combustion of fossil fuels (mainly vehicles)	human respiratory disease
carbon dioxide	combustion of fossil fuels	global warming?
chlorofluorocarbons (CFCs)	aerosol cans, refrigerators	destruction of ozone layer
particulate matter	smoke (mainly from industry)	human respiratory disease, cancer
radioactive substances	nuclear tests, nuclear power stations	increased mutation rates
lead	lead vehicle exhaust, from leaded petrol	mental development in children impaired
Secondary pollutants:		
ozone	formed from chemical reaction with nitrogen oxides and UV light	'dieback' in trees, reduced crop plant growth
acid rain	mixture of sulphuric and nitric acids, derived from sulphur dioxide and nitrogen oxides in rainwater	death of freshwater fish, corrosion of stone buildings

A clear relationship has been shown between human respiratory disease and air pollution. For example, the incidence of deaths due to respiratory disease (bronchitis, pneumonia) and heart failure dramatically increases during episodes of very high pollution (Fig. 7.26). In the UK, the Clean Air Act (1956) has done much to reduce high levels of air pollution, though emissions of certain pollutants (e.g. from vehicles) continue to increase. In some cities in the world (e.g. Mexico City, Los Angeles), this is a major problem.

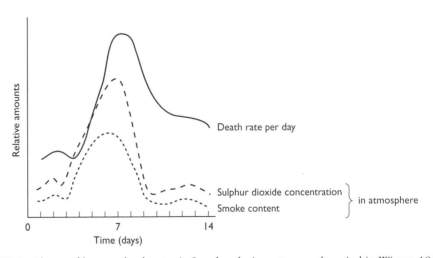

Fig. 7.26 Incidence of human death rates in London during a two week period in Winter, 1952.

The effects of air pollutants on natural ecosystems are numerous and complex. For example, the effects of acid rain on lakes and forests depends on how sensitive these habitats are in a given area. The sensitivity of water and soil depends on several factors, including the normal pH (acidity or alkalinity) of the surrounding soil. Acid rain has been widely attributed to be the cause of forest 'dieback' (large-scale death or poor growth of trees) in North America and in Europe. Although acid rain may be the principal cause, the presence of other factors such as disease and drought may increase the vulnerability of the forest.

One striking example of the likely effects of acid rain is on the occurrence of lichen species. Lichens are symbiotic associations of fungi and algae, often found growing on trees and buildings. Some lichen species are very sensitive to acid rain, and it has been shown that the number of species declines at distances closer to sources of air pollution, such as city centres (Fig. 7.27).

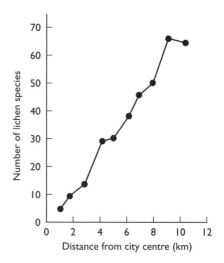

Fig. 7.27 Changes in the number of lichen species with distance from city

2. Water pollution

Water pollution consists mainly of chemicals from industry and agriculture and sewage from human habitation. **Toxic pollutants** accumulate in aquatic ecosystems, and become incorporated into food chains. **High levels of nutrients** and hot water from pollution result in excessive growth of bacteria, which reduces the amount of dissolved oxygen in water. This, in turn, can cause death in aquatic animals.

There are two main types of water pollution: **toxic substances** and **excess nutrients**.

(a) **Toxic substances**

These include:

  ▶ wastes discharged from industrial and mining sites into rivers, lakes and oceans, e.g. cyanide, lead, mercury, zinc;
  ▶ oil spills at sea;
  ▶ dumping of radioactive waste at sea;
  ▶ agricultural chemicals, e.g. pesticides, herbicides, which have been washed into rivers, lakes and oceans.

Aquatic animals may be affected directly, if they absorb the pollutant, or indirectly if it contaminates food chains. Humans can be affected either by consuming contaminated fish and other aquatic organisms, or by drinking water which contains dissolved toxins. Although many toxic substances occur at fairly low concentrations, many accumulate in the body over time.

(b) **Excess nutrients**

Many waste substances are in fact also nutrients. Organic waste such as **sewage** (effluent) is a food source for bacteria, which break it down. However, such bacteria are often oxygen-demanding, and their activity reduces the amount of dissolved oxygen available to other organisms. The activity of bacteria is further increased by the presence of hot water, which often accompanies the discharge of effluents. The amount of oxygen consumed by aquatic organisms is called the **biochemical oxygen demand (BOD)**. Polluted water typically has a high BOD value.

Nutrients such as **nitrates** and **phosphates** are contained in fertilisers, which are widely used in agriculture to promote crop growth. However, not all these nutrients are absorbed by the crops. Surplus amounts contained in the soil may eventually soak into streams, rivers and lakes. High levels of nitrate from urine also released from the sewage of human populations and farm animals. These nutrients are then used particularly by aquatic algae, which grow very rapidly (= 'algal bloom'). When the algae die, they are broken down by bacteria, which consume much of the dissolved oxygen in water. This process of excess growth with a lowering of dissolved oxygen is called **eutrophication.**

REVISION ACTIVITY 3   Put these steps in the process of eutrophication into the right order.

    A.   Bacteria change sewage into nitrates.
    B.   Plants in the water die due to lack of light.
    C.   Algae absorb nitrates and grow very quickly.
    D.   Sewage flows into the river.
    E.   A mat of algae on the surface prevents light from reaching plants in the water.
    F.   Animals in the water die due to lack of oxygen.
    G.   Decomposers break down dead plants, and use oxygen in the water to do this.

Correct order | D | | | | | | |

REVISION ACTIVITY 4   Fig. 7.28 shows the concentration of oxygen, the numbers of bacteria and the numbers of fish in a river over a distance of 50 km, measured from point **P** which is upstream from a source of pollution.

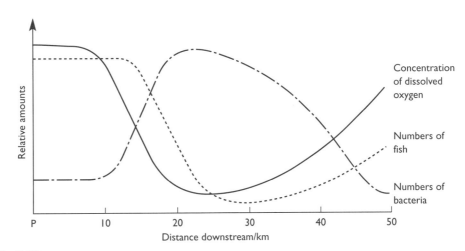

Fig. 7.28

(a) At what distance from point P did the river become polluted?

(b) (i) With reference to the three curves on the graph, describe the effect of the pollution.
      (ii) Suggest a possible cause of the pollution.

(c) The oxygen concentration 50 km downstream from point P is returning to its original level, yet the numbers of fish are still much reduced. Suggest two reasons for this.

3. Land Pollution

This is mainly due to disposal of human refuse, and contamination by agricultural chemicals.

    Disposal of refuse: humans produce millions of tonnes of waste each year, and this is usually buried in landfill sites or burned. Dumping refuse in landfill sites is a problem because:

▷   it destroys natural habitats;
▷   it is a breeding ground for disease and animals which may carry it;
▷   as the refuse decomposes, methane is released. If buildings are eventually constructed on the landfill site there may be subsidence as pockets of methane gas escape; there is also a risk of explosion.

Recycling can reduce the amount of refuse.

    Agricultural chemicals, e.g. fertilisers, pesticides, herbicides, are deliberately sprayed onto crops and the soil. When it rains, they will be washed into rivers and eventually into the sea. Pesticides and herbicides are persistent – they remain active in the environment for long periods of time.

Urbanisation and industrialisation

As the human population increases, more land is used for towns and cities and for transport networks, i.e. roads, railways, airports, etc. This damages natural environments and may cause organisms to become extinct.

We now live in an increasingly industrialised society; we use machines to carry out everyday tasks,

e.g. transport
heating our homes
communicating with others
manufacturing processes
housework, gardening, leisure activities.

This increases the amount of natural resources which we use (particularly fuels) and increases pollution levels.

Agriculture

A major purpose of agriculture is to produce food for human consumption. Both the efficiency and the intensity of food production are being continually increased to meet the demands of the human population. There are several environmental implications of this:

▶ **Land clearance**
Land is cleared for cultivation and for grazing; this reduces the number of potential habitats available. Tropical forests are cleared for timber and land use on a massive scale; this destroys important habitats and makes the soil unstable. Destruction of a habitat reduces variation and hence the so-called gene pool. This decreases the diversity of species and makes land more exposed and vulnerable to wind, which can blow away topsoil; this is called **erosion**.

▶ **Monoculture**
Monoculture is the cultivation of a single species of crop on a particular area of land, for instance wheat and barley. Monoculture is an 'artificial' situation because there will normally be a **succession** leading to a greater diversity of species. This is resisted in monoculture by the use of selective **herbicides** to prevent the growth of weeds, and **pesticides** to remove insect and other pests. Herbicides are used to control or eliminate weeds. Several herbicides contain an impurity called **dioxin**, which is highly poisonous to wildlife and to humans. Insecticides are used to kill insect pests. Organochlorine insecticides, including DDT, do not break down very rapidly in the environment (i.e. they are not biodegradable), which can result in pollution problems. DDT and similar pesticides accumulate in the tissues of animals, and become concentrated, particularly in those occupying higher trophic levels. The pollutant therefore becomes concentrated along the food chain. One result of DDT has been to reduce the thickness of egg shells in birds of prey, causing a decrease in successful reproduction. A further problem with DDT is that many insect pests have now become resistant to it.

▶ **Over-production**
Maximum use is made of available agricultural land by intensive cultivation, including the use of nitrate fertilisers. One possible effect of this over-exploitation of soil is that it becomes more susceptible to erosion by wind and water. This may lead to desertification. Over-use of fertilisers may cause minerals such as nitrates to be leached away; nitrates can accumulate in aquatic ecosystems, resulting in **eutrophication**. Eutrophication involves rapid, excessive growth of aquatic plants which then die and decay; their decomposition lowers oxygen levels in the aquatic environment (see p. 271).

Fishing

Fishing is important in many human communities as a source of protein and oil, and also to provide feed for domestic animals and ingredients for fertilisers used in agriculture. In many coastal and island countries, fish can provide up to 90% of the proteins required by humans. Most (about 90%) of fish and shellfish that are consumed are caught by fishing boats.

There have been dramatic increases in the intensity and efficiency of commercial fishing methods. This has resulted in **overfishing** in many areas of the world. Overfishing results in a depletion of younger fish, so that the 'breeding stock' is unable to maintain previous population levels. A **commercial extinction** level is reached, beyond which it is unprofitable

'Exam questions on the effects of humans on the environment are almost guaranteed!'

to continue fishing for a particular species. Some countries have introduced laws to control net mesh sizes to reduce this problem; larger-mesh nets allow juvenile fish to escape, and so go on to reproduce. Other control methods include restrictions on where or when fishing is permitted, to allow fish populations to recover. **Aquaculture** and **fish farming**, in which captive fish and shellfish are bred specifically for food, is being used increasingly to supply human needs. (see p. 272).

Mining

Mining is used to obtain a wide range of minerals, as well as coal. Minerals are both metallic (e.g. iron, copper, aluminium) and non-metallic (e.g. phosphates). Various techniques are used, mainly with heavy machinery, to obtain mineral from the surface and underground. Mining is essential to meet human needs for energy and many raw materials. If mining is done carefully, the mined area can be allowed to recover to a large extent after mining operations have been completed.

However, mining can result in serious environmental degradation, for example by land disturbance, erosion, air pollution and water pollution. Underground mining produces proportionally much less land disturbance than surface mining, but is more expensive and dangerous.

For any given mineral which is being mined, there are finite amounts available for extraction. The exact amounts are uncertain in many cases, because reserves have not all been identified. At each site, the amount of mineral that can be extracted is also limited by economic depletion levels, beyond which it is not economic to continue mining. The rate at which minerals are used up also depends on how efficiently they are mined and used (Fig. 7.29).

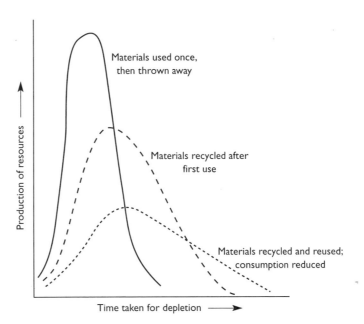

Fig. 7.29 The rate at which non-renewable resources are used up depends on the way which they are used

Deforestation

Forests cover about 34% of the world's land surface. However, about half the world's forests have been removed (**deforestation**) during the last 30 years, often to provide additional land for cultivation and occupation. Forests are an important source of timber for construction, as a fuel and for paper. Forests also provide rubber, foods and natural medicines. Forests have a much wider ecological role in stabilising the Earth's climate, especially in the circulation of carbon dioxide, oxygen and water and are important in preventing soil erosion. In tropical rain forests in particular, forests are centres of genetic diversity, since many of the world's species exist in these ecosystems. It is estimated that at least 50% of the world's species live in tropical rain forests, even they only occupy about 7% of the world's land area.

Forests are a potentially renewable resource, providing timber extraction does not exceed the rate of natural forest regeneration. In tropical areas, local people cause some deforestation by shifting cultivation and the collection of fuelwood. However, timber extraction to meet the demand of developing countries often occurs at much higher rates, which are not sustainable. It also opens up the forest for further exploitation. Intensive deforestation has many direct and indirect effects, including increased soil erosion and flooding, and displacement of indigenous people. It is also predicted that, with fewer trees to absorb carbon dioxide, deforestation will contribute to global warming.

Human population size

Key points

▷ human population is increasing rapidly due to better nutrition and health care;

▷ as the population size increases humans use more land, more resources, and produce more pollutants and waste;

▷ the world's resources are finite so some slowing of the population increase will be necessary to avoid a global catastrophe.

Why is the human population increasing?

The world human population has approximately doubled in the last 30 years; from 2.5 billion in 1950 to 5.6 billion in 1993. A further doubling (to about 10.8 billion) is expected by the year 2045. The increase in the world's total human population is currently exponential (i.e. the 'log' phase – see p. 299), increasing at about 1.8% each year. The human population increase produces a 'J'-shaped curve when plotted as a graph.

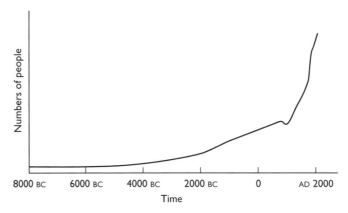

Fig. 7.30 Human population growth curve

There are four main factors influencing human population size:

1. Birth rate and death rate

There has been a slight decline in birth rate throughout the world. However, it is the relative difference between birth rate and death rate which determines actual population increase. Birth rate exceeds death rate in many countries, particularly in the developing world.

Factors which tend to increase birth rate (natality) and decrease death rate (mortality) include an increased availability of food, improved sanitation and better medicine and health care. Antibiotics such as penicillin and streptomycin and insecticides such as DDT, have made a major impact on disease control. Selective breeding of crops and domestic animals, and increased mechanisation in agriculture have had a dramatic effect on food production. However, two-thirds of the world's population is still without sufficient food.

2. Age structure of the population

The relative number of individuals in each age group in the population is very important in determining both current and future increases in population. Population increase is strongly influenced by the relative number of people of 'reproductive age' (i.e. who can have children). However, even if the number of children born to parents is reduced, the total population will still increase in many countries, because a high proportion of individual belong to younger age groups, and many will be future parents (Fig. 7.31). In developing countries, the proportion of individuals under 15 years old is approximately 40%, compared with 28% in developed countries. This, along with the increasing proportion of old people in the population who need to be supported, has been called a 'demographic time-bomb'.

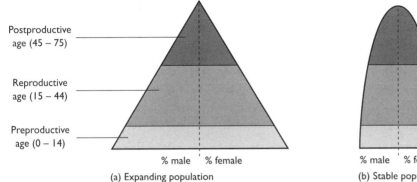

Postproductive
age (45 – 75)

Reproductive
age (15 – 44)

Preproductive
age (0 – 14)

% male   % female

(a) Expanding population

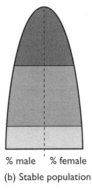

% male   % female

(b) Stable population

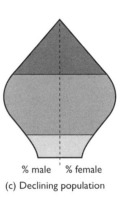

% male   % female

(c) Declining population

Fig. 7.31 Age structure in human populations

3. Generation time

The age when women begin to have children is an important factor for human population growth for two reasons. First, having children later in life means there is 'less time' to have children. Second, an older woman may be more aware of the consequences of having more children than she can cope with, and may also have taken on other responsibilities. In some countries, the minimum age allowing marriage is relatively high, which 'delays' the onset of the next generation.

4. Fertility and birth control

'Fertility' is an expression of the number of children born to each family, in each generation. Currently, the number of children in each family throughout the world is on average 4.7. In developing countries, the average is higher (5.7) than in developed countries (2.6). If the human population is to stop growing, the number of children born to each family would need to be reduced to about 2.5; the replacement number. This number is more than two (i.e. the number needed to 'replace' the parents in each new generation) because not all females survive to reproduce (especially in developing countries), or have less than two children. Even if this replacement number was immediately implemented, the world's population would continue growing until the year 2100.

Birth control by **contraception** is currently used by many adults to limit the size of their family. Contraception in some communities is either not available, or not understood, or not acceptable. This is a complex issue because it involves personal choices, but the effects of continued population growth affect society in general, for instance because of the world's limited resources. Rates of food production and distribution are being increased, but this is not a long-term solution to the problem of an ever-increasing human population.

Effects of continued increases in the human population

The **number** of humans is directly related to the **impact** they have on the environment, e.g.

- amount of land used for towns, cities, transport;
- amount of land used for growing crops;
- amount of pollution (of air, water, land);
- amount of refuse to be destroyed;
- amount of resources used, e.g. stone, fuels, timber, metal ores, etc;
- amount of fishing, logging, etc, i.e. exploitation of living resources.

Industrialised societies, e.g. Britain, USA, place particularly heavy demands on the environment because:

(a) we use large amounts of fuel for transport, manufacturing processes, heating, etc;

(b) we expect a high level of 'consumer goods', and we want to replace these whenever we choose, e.g. clothes, furniture, electrical appliances, etc. Often we do not recycle our waste;

(c) we expect a large choice of food, and to eat foods which are 'out of season'; this increases the transport costs and the land needed to grow the food.

Changes in the biosphere

> ## Key points
>
> ▷ the biosphere is the layer of air surrounding the earth's surface;
>
> ▷ some types of pollution cause long-term changes in the biosphere, and have large effects on systems on earth;
>
> ▷ damage to the ozone layer and the greenhouse effect are both changes in the biosphere;
>
> ▷ they both lead to global warming.

Depletion of the ozone layer

Ozone (O_3) collects naturally in the upper atmosphere, and this layer forms a barrier to cosmic rays, e.g. ultra-violet rays.

Some pollutants, e.g. chlorofluorocarbons (CFCs) found in aerosols, in expanded polystyrene packaging and in refrigerators, damage the ozone layer when they are released. The ozone layer becomes thinner, and 'holes' have appeared over the North and South poles.

This results in less UV radiation being absorbed, so more reaches the earth's surface, and this has two main effects:

1. increased temperature, i.e. global warming;
2. increased UV radiation is linked to an increase in skin cancer.

The greenhouse effect

Some pollutant gases are called 'greenhouse gases' because they form a layer in the atmosphere which acts like glass in a greenhouse. They allow high-energy solar radiation to pass through to the earth's surface. Much of this energy is 'bounced back' towards space as heat, which greenhouse gases 'trap'. This causes global warming.

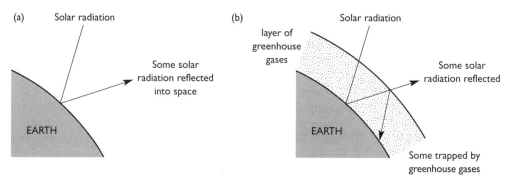

Fig. 7.32 The greenhouse effect (a) greenhouse gases at a low level, (b) greenhouse gases at a high level

Greenhouse gases include:

▷ carbon dioxide
▷ methane
▷ CFCs
▷ nitrous oxide

Although methane, CFCs and nitrous oxides are not present in high quantities, they have much more absorbing power than CO_2. Water vapour and particulate matter in the atmosphere also act as greenhouse gases. There is still some uncertainty about whether recent increases in the world's temperature are due to global warming, or part of a regular series of long-term temperature fluctuations which have occurred in the past. However, the amount of greenhouse gases in the atmosphere is known to be rising.

Carbon dioxide is particularly important in the greenhouse effect because it represents about 49% of all greenhouse gases. Carbon dioxide concentrations in the atmosphere have increased from 0.027% to over 0.033% during the last 100 years. Further, more rapid increases are expected in the future. There are two major reasons for the increase in CO_2 in the atmosphere: **fossil fuel burning** and **deforestation.**

'Look at the section on the carbon cycle if necessary.'

The burning of fossil fuels accounts for about 80% of the increases of CO_2 in the atmosphere. Most (76%) comes from industrialised countries. The burning of fossil fuels (oil and coal) is likely to increase well into the future.

Deforestation accounts for about 20% of the increased CO_2 levels in the atmosphere. There are three reasons for this. First, timber removal means there are fewer trees to absorb CO_2 by photosynthesis. Second, deforestation is often accompanied by burning of remaining vegetation, to prepare the land for cultivation. Third, any unburnt vegetation may quickly die and decompose, releasing CO_2. The regrowth of vegetation after deforestation is often insufficient to offset these effects.

Possible effects of global warming

Various predictions have been made concerning global warming. Possible temperature increases during the next 50 years have been suggested in the range 1.5–5.5°C, if concentrations of greenhouses rise at current rates. One problem is that, by the time there is a indisputable evidence for a link between greenhouse gas concentrations and global warming, the ecological problem will be too big to solve.

Possible effects of global warming might include increased crop yields (which will also be able to utilise higher CO_2 concentrations), but insect pest populations might also increase and there might be less soil water available.

In tropical areas of the world, decreased availability of water might lead to the formation of deserts. In coastal areas throughout the world, some melting of polar icecaps would result in flooding. Other predicted effects include the spread of tropical disease over a wider area, increased frequency of droughts, hurricanes and cyclones, and also forest fires.

Conservation

> ### Key points
>
> ▷ conservation involves **action** by individuals as well as governments and industry;
>
> ▷ habitats are being destroyed by human activities;
>
> ▷ organisms living in those habitats will decline and may be at risk of extinction;
>
> ▷ conservation works towards maintaining **a natural ecological balance** in our surroundings.

Whenever humans interfere with a natural environment, they will change the ecological balance, e.g.

▷ when land is cleared to build houses and roads, large areas of habitat are destroyed;

▷ when water flow is changed, e.g. marshy land is drained, or estuaries are dammed up to make marina areas, natural habitats are destroyed;

▷ when crop plants are grown, rather than native wild plants, food webs in that area will be affected;

▷ when animals are hunted for sport, or for products which can be used by humans, e.g. furs, ivory, whale oils, their numbers will fall and they may become extinct;

▷ when natural resources are taken from the land, e.g. in mining, quarrying, logging, habitats are destroyed. Deforestation causes particular damage as it can speed up the process of erosion;

▷ when chemicals, e.g. pesticides, herbicides, are released into the environment, plants and animals may be killed;

▷ some pollutants cause major changes which affect all living things, e.g. excess carbon dioxide gas is linked to the greenhouse effect and global warming; CFCs damage the ozone layer allowing harmful radiation to reach the earth.

Conservation involves doing things to **limit the impact** of humans on the environment, and to maintain a **natural ecological balance**, e.g.

▷ controlling building in green-belt areas, so that local habitats are saved;

▷ preventing the destruction of important habitats by giving them legal protection, e.g. as national parks, nature reserves or SSSIs (sites of special scientific interest);

▷ allowing wild plants to live alongside crop plants by retaining hedgerows and avoiding the use of herbicides;

▷ protecting endangered species by law, e.g. in Britain it is illegal to disturb bats, or to pick or damage fen orchids;

▷ maintaining the diversity of habitats by responsible management, e.g. coppicing, dredging ditches;

▷ recycling natural resources wherever possible to limit environmental damage. Glass, metal, paper and plastics can all be recycled, saving energy and valuable natural resources, and preventing damage to habitats;

▷ encouraging organic farming so that living things are not harmed by agricultural chemicals, e.g. pesticides, herbicides, artificial fertilisers;

▷ limiting the release of pollutants by enforcing or improving existing laws, and by reducing energy use by individuals, e.g. walking or cycling instead of using a car.

Although some of these conservation measures depend on laws and decisions made by governments, there are lots of things that all of us can do in our everyday lives to help to conserve our environment.

▷ Energy and nutrient transfer

This topic is fundamental in the study of ecology. Food chains (and food webs) consist of feeding relationships between different types of organism. When one organism is consumed by another, the nutrients it contains are 'passed on'. This allows nutrient to be recycled within living communities.

When organisms die they decay, and the nutrients in them pass to decomposers. Minerals like carbon and nitrogen are released, and can be re-used by other organisms. This cycling of materials is a very important part of the study of ecosystems.

Glossary of important terms used in this topic:

food chain	a flow chart to show feeding relationships between organisms
food web	a set of linked food chains
trophic levels	the stages in a food chain or web
producer	a plant which makes its own food by photosynthesis. Producers are always found at the start of food chains
consumer	an animal which feeds on plants or other animals. These can be put in order in a food chain as primary consumers, secondary consumer, tertiary consumer, etc.
herbivore	an animal which eats plants, i.e. a primary consumer
carnivore	an animal which eats other animals
top carnivore	an animal at the end of a food chain, i.e. it is not eaten by anything
omnivore	an animal which eats plants and animals, therefore it belongs to more than one trophic level in a food web
scavenger	a large animal which feeds an animal remains, e.g. ravens and foxes
detritus feeders	smaller animals which feed on fragments of organic material, e.g. earthworms and beetles
decomposers	bacteria and fungi which make organic material decay
parasites	small organisms which live on or in a host and cause it harm, e.g. ticks and fleas
saprophytes	decomposers (bacteria and fungi)
biomass	the amount of biological material. This value is obtained by weighing the organism.

pyramid of numbers	a diagram showing the number of organisms at each trophic level of a food chain; the length of the bars is proportional to the number of organisms
pyramid of biomass	a diagram showing the mass of organisms at each trophic level of a food chain; the length of the bars is proportional to the mass of the organisms

Food chains and food webs

> ## Key points
>
> ▷ a food chain is a sequence of feeding relationships between organisms;
>
> ▷ food chains involve the transfer of energy and nutrients;
>
> ▷ food chains always begin with a producer (a plant);
>
> ▷ the other organisms in the food chain are consumers (animals);
>
> ▷ each stage of a food chain is called a trophic level;
>
> ▷ food chains are normally linked to form food webs;
>
> ▷ the other organisms in the food chain are consumers (animals);
>
> ▷ each stage of a food chain is called a trophic level;
>
> ▷ food chains are normally linked to form food webs;
>
> ▷ the energy passed along food chains comes from the Sun;
>
> ▷ herbivores are animals which eat plants;
>
> ▷ carnivores are animals which eat other animals.

Food chains

A food chain is a sequence of **feeding relationships** between organisms living within the same community. Feeding relationships involve the transfer of **energy** and **nutrients** (as food) from one organism to another, down the food chain. In natural communities, normally several food chains are interconnected to form **food webs**.

Different organisms obtain their food in different ways. In other words, they occupy a different 'feeding level', or **trophic level**, within the food chain. An example of a simple food chain is shown here, with four of the main trophic levels.

'The arrow represent **energy** *passing along the food chain – they* **must** *point the right way!'*

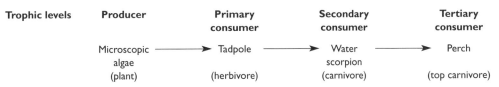

Trophic levels	Producer	Primary consumer	Secondary consumer	Tertiary consumer
	Microscopic algae (plant)	Tadpole (herbivore)	Water scorpion (carnivore)	Perch (top carnivore)

Fig. 7.33 Example of a food chain

Food webs

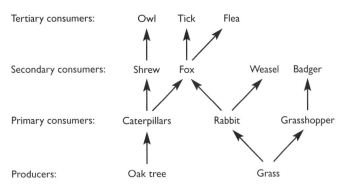

Fig. 7.34 Example of a food web

Food webs arise when organisms consume, or are consumed by, two or more other organisms. In other words, food webs consist of two or more interacting food chains. In fact, it is unusual for a consumer to restrict its **diet** (i.e. food intake) to a single species. One reason for this is changes in the availability of food, for instance during different seasons. Another reason is that the full range of nutrients needed by an organism will not necessarily be available from a single source. Some animals (the **omnivores**) even obtain their food from more than one trophic (feeding) level. In a food web, all the organisms are linked together so if one factor changes, it will affect lots of other organisms.

e.g. **if a disease killed the rabbits**

▶   numbers of weasels and foxes would decrease;
▶   amount of grass would increase;
▶   number of grasshoppers would increase;
▶   number of badgers would increase.

e.g. **if another owl was introduced to the area**

▶   number of shrews would decrease;
▶   numbers of caterpillars would increase.

Ecological pyramids

Key points

> ▶   there are two types of ecological pyramids, pyramids of number and pyramids of biomass;
> ▶   pyramids of number show the number of organisms at each trophic level;
> ▶   they are sometimes the 'wrong shape';
> ▶   pyramids of biomass show the mass of organisms at each trophic level;
> ▶   they are always the 'right shape'.

Pyramids of number
These are diagrams that show the number of organisms at each trophic level. The length of the bars is proportional to the number of organisms.

e.g.   algae ⟶ tadpoles ⟶ water scorpion ⟶ perch

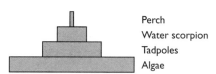

Perch
Water scorpion
Tadpoles
Algae

Fig. 7.35 Pyramid of numbers

The bar for producers is **always** at the bottom of the diagram.

Pyramids of number are **usually** a typical pyramid shape with a broad base, but in certain circumstances they are the 'wrong shape'.

Example 1: narrow producer bar

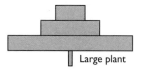

Large plant

Fig. 7.36

This happens when the producer is a large plant with lots of smaller herbivores feeding on it.

Example 2: wide consumer bar

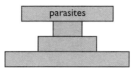

Fig. 7.37

This happens when one of the consumer levels is a parasite, e.g. ticks or fleas. Lots of these tiny animals can live on a host.

Example 3: complex shape

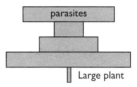

Fig. 7.38

This happens when you have a combination of the two examples above.

Pyramids of biomass
These are diagrams which show the mass of organisms at each trophic level. The length of the bars is proportional to the mass of organisms.

e.g. algae ⟶ tadpoles ⟶ water scorpion ⟶ perch

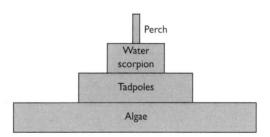

Fig. 7.39 Pyramid of biomass

The bar for the producers is **always** at the bottom of the diagram.
    Pyramids of biomass are **always** a typical pyramid shape with a broad base. This is because they take account of the relative size of organisms.
    If you look at the pyramids of numbers on pp. 260–1 (examples 1, 2 and 3) and draw pyramids of biomass for those food chains you find that they are a typical pyramid shape.

Remember

▶ pyramids of numbers can be the 'wrong shape';
▶ pyramids of biomass are always the 'right shape' because they take account of the size of the organisms involved;
▶ pyramids of biomass are always widest at the base and narrowest at the top because energy is lost at each trophic level. Read the next section to find out more about this.

(a) Match the pyramids of numbers shown in Fig. 7.40 to the food chains

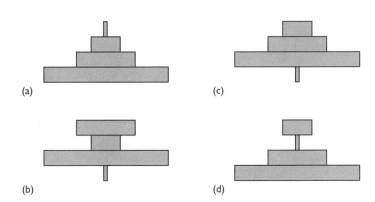

Fig. 7.40

(i) grass ⟶ rabbit ⟶ fox ⟶ fleas
(ii) rose bush ⟶ greenfly ⟶ ladybird ⟶ blue tit
(iii) algae ⟶ tadpoles ⟶ water beetles ⟶ perch
(iv) oak tree ⟶ caterpillars ⟶ shrews ⟶ ticks

(b) Sketch a pyramid of biomass for each food chain.

(c) Give two reasons why your pyramids of biomass are that shape.

Energy transfers in ecology

Key points

▷ all the energy for food chains and webs comes from the sun;

▷ plants change light energy into chemical energy (in sugar) when they photosynthesise;

▷ chemical energy (in food) is passed along food chains;

▷ a lot of energy is 'lost' at each trophic level;

▷ a small amount of energy (about 10%) is passed on to the next trophic level;

▷ this 'lost energy' limits the length of food chains.

How is energy passed along a food chain?

Plants use light energy from the sun for photosynthesis. Chlorophyll (inside chloroplasts) traps light energy and this energy is used in the process of making sugar.

$$\text{carbon dioxide} + \text{water} \xrightarrow{\text{light}} \text{sugar} + \text{oxygen}$$

However, plants do not make use of **all** the available light energy (see Fig. 7.41):

▷ some is the wrong wavelength for photosynthesis;
▷ some is reflected from the leaf surface;
▷ some passes straight through the leaf.

About 10% of the available energy is used to make sugar. The plant will use some of this in respiration to meet its own energy needs, e.g. active transport to get minerals into the roots.

Only 5% is used for growth or stored as starch, so only 5% can be passed on to the next organism in the food chain.

When a herbivore eats a plant, it does not make use of all the available energy:

▷ it may not eat all parts of the plant, e.g. roots may be left;
▷ the food may not be digested properly, so some energy is lost in faeces and in urine.

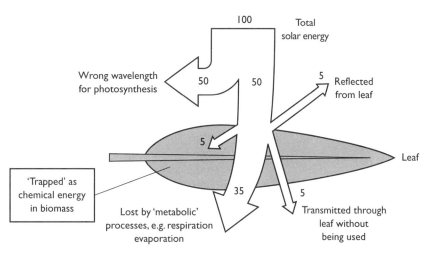

Fig. 7.41 How is light energy used by plants?

About 35% of the food energy it takes in is actually available to the animal. Most of this will be used for respiration to meet its own energy needs, e.g. moving around, staying warm, vital body processes, e.g. heart beat, etc.

Only about 5% is used for growth, or stored as glycogen or fat, so only 5% can be passed on to the next organism in the food chain.

This explains why pyramids of biomass are 'pyramid' shaped, i.e. broader at the base. As energy is lost at each trophic level, less energy is available to support the animals higher up the pyramid, so their total mass decreases.

We can summarise energy flow through food chains in a diagram like Fig 7.42:

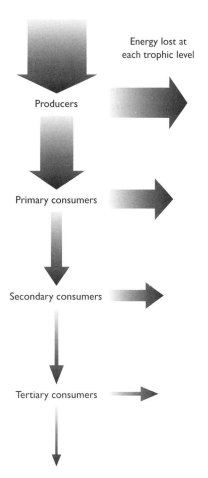

Fig. 7.42 Summary of energy flow

When an organism dies the energy in it passes to decomposers (bacteria and fungi) when they make it decay. Decomposers also obtain energy from urine and faeces when they are broken down.

How is energy lost?

Energy is lost in five main ways:

1. moving around;
2. keeping a constant body temperature;
3. vital body processes, e.g. heart beat, etc;
4. as heat lost to the surroundings;
5. in undigested food, i.e. lost in faeces.

Are all organisms equally efficient?

Some organisms are much more efficient at energy transfers than others. If you look at the list of ways that energy is lost, the most efficient organisms:

▶ do not move around much;
▶ are cold blooded (ectothermic), i.e. do not keep their body temperature constant;
▶ have a small surface area: volume ratio, so they lose less heat over their body surface;
▶ eat foods which are easily digested.

In general, carnivores are more efficient in energy transfer than herbivores, because they can digest their food more easily.

On average animals pass on about 10% of the energy they take in to the next stage of the food chain. In reality this varies from about 2% (for the least efficient animals) to 30% (for the most efficient animals).

REVISION ACTIVITY 6 For each pair, which animals would you expect to be most efficient in energy transfer? Explain why.

(a) cow or rabbit

(b) cow or trout (carnivore).

Energy transfer and humans

This information has implications for human food production. Humans are omnivores, i.e. can eat plants and other animals. It has been estimated that the same area of land can provide about ten times more plant protein than animal protein; this is because many herbivores, including beef cattle and sheep, are relatively inefficient at energy transfer.

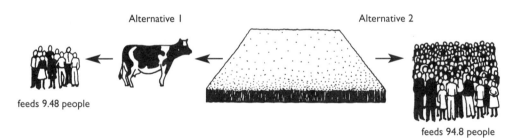

Alternative 1   Alternative 2

feeds 9.48 people

feeds 94.8 people

Fig. 7.43 Diagram showing two alternative ways in which the corn produced by one hectare of land could be used

As the human population continues to rise, more food will need to be made available by increased production. One way of achieving this is for humans to eat less meat, i.e. to shorten the food chain.

Ecosystems and productivity

The efficiency of the process by which plants convert solar energy into 'trapped' forms (chemical energy and biomass) is known as **net primary productivity**. Ecosystems with the highest productivity are tropical forests, swamps, marshes and estuaries. The lowest productivity occurs in desert, Arctic tundra and open oceans. Agricultural land is intermediate in productivity, although output is usually increased by management techniques, such as by the use of fertilisers, herbicides and pesticides. The energy contained in the high-productivity ecosystems is important for the animals which live there. However, it is mostly not energy which can easily be used by humans.

In tropical forests, most of the nutrients are 'locked up' in the trees, and the soils are fairly nutrient-poor. Some tropical forests are being cut down to create land for grazing. However, the soils are unable to support high crop production over several years. Combined with the loss of energy in food chains described below, grazing cattle on land created by removal of tropical rain forests is not efficient. This is why an area of tropical rain forest in Central America about the size of a small kitchen (about 5 m²) is lost to provide grazing to make one quarter-pounder hamburger!

Decay

Key points
▷ all organic matter will eventually decay (break down);   ▷ decay involves enzymes within the organic matter, and living organisms: scavengers, detritus feeders and saprophytes (decomposers);   ▷ rate of decay depends on several factors, e.g. temperature, amount of air, etc.;   ▷ decay is very important in the cycling of nutrients.

Importance of decay

The materials which make up organisms are being constantly transferred between organisms, and also between organisms and their non-living environment. The processes which are involved in these transfers include **nutrition, excretion, egestion,** and **death and decay**.

All living things will eventually die, and useful chemicals will be released when they decay. In addition to this, living organisms produce organic waste products which can decay, e.g. leaves fallen from plants, animal faeces, insect exoskeletons which are shed during growth.

The process of decay is important for two reasons

1. it causes the breakdown of waste products and the remains of dead organisms, so these do not 'pile up';
2. it releases valuable substances into the environment to be re-used by other organisms.

Process of decay

There are four main stages in the process of decay:

1. **Autolysis:** enzymes inside the organism start to break down body tissues, e.g. protease enzymes break down proteins to make amino acids.
2. **Scavengers and detritus feeders:** these are animals which feed on the remains of dead organisms or their waste products. **Scavengers** are fairly large animals which feed on animal remains. Each habitat will contain animals which feed in this way:

'These are important animals in every ecosystem.'

> e.g. woodland   – raven, fox
> rocky shore – crab
> pond   – water louse

Detritus feeders are usually smaller animals which will feed on small fragments from the dead organism (detritus). Detritus tends to collect at the lower levels of a habitat, so that is where detritus feeders are found:

> e.g. woodland   – beetles, earthworms (in the litter layer)
> rocky shore – barnacles, mussels (filter detritus from water)
> pond   – gnat larvae (filter detritus from water).

3. **Fungi:** they will grow on the dead organism and produce enzymes to digest the cells and their contents. They absorb the nutrients from the cells into their hyphae – this is

called **external digestion.** Fungi are particularly important in the decay of plant material (including wood), because they produce cellulase enzymes.

4. **Bacteria:** these microscopic, single-celled organisms complete the process of decay. They secrete enzymes which digest organic material, releasing nutrients and minerals – this is **external digestion.** They absorb the nutrients and use them to grow and reproduce. Eventually the whole organism will decompose.

Fungi and bacteria which feed in this way are called **saprophytes,** or decomposers. Saprophytes are an important part of any food chain, because they release the nutrients 'locked up in' dead organisms so they can be re-used. Large numbers of saprophytes are found in soil.

Key factors in the process of decay

Remains of organisms do not always decay at the same rate; in some conditions they can be quite well preserved for long periods of time.

The rate of decay is affected by:

1. **Temperature:** saprophytes work faster at warm temperatures than at cool temperatures.
2. **Moisture:** saprophytes work faster when there is a suitable amount of water.
3. **Air:** most saprophytes use the oxygen in air to cause decay.

This information is useful if we want to prevent saprophytes from working, e.g. to keep food fresh. Think about some of the ways that humans treat food to prevent it 'going off'.

e.g. freezing it   – used for meat, fish, vegetables
      drying it   – used for milk, soup, fruits (raisins, currants)
      vacuum packing it   – used for cold meats, cheese.

The role of living things in decay and the cycling of nutrients

There are four types of organism involved in the process of decay:

1. **Scavengers** – these are usually quite large animals which feed on animal remains. They will tear off pieces which they digest internally. Examples of scavengers include ravens and foxes (woodland habitat), crab (rocky shore habitat), water lice (pond habitat).
2. **Detritus feeders** – these are usually smaller animals which feed on fragments of organic material (detritus). They may filter this from water, or extract it from soil, and digest it internally. Examples of detritus feeders include beetles and earthworms (woodland habitat), barnacles and mussels (rocky shore habitat) and gnat larvae (pond habitat).
3. **Fungi** – these grow over the surface of the organic material and secrete enzymes which begin to digest it (this is external digestion). Once digested, the nutrients can be absorbed into the hyphae. Examples of fungi which feed in this way include *Mucor* (pin mould).
4. **Bacteria** – these grow on the remaining organic material and secrete enzymes to digest it externally. This will continue until the organism is fully decomposed. *Pseudomonas* is a bacterium which feeds in this way.

Scavengers and detritus feeders are important because they speed up the rate of decay by breaking the organic material into small pieces, i.e. increasing the surface area. If they are not present, decay will still occur, but it will take much longer.

Bacteria and fungi (saprophytes) are important because they release nutrients from dead organisms or their waste.

Susan wanted to find out more about the decay process in soil. She placed 30 leaf discs in two mesh bags and buried them 8 cm below the soil surface.

The bags were examined at intervals. The amount of leaf disc lost was recorded. Susan's results are shown below (see Fig. 7.44).

(a) In which bag did the leaves break down at the faster rate?

(b) Name **two** groups of organisms which may have caused the disappearance of some of the material from bag **A**, but not from bag **B**.

(c) Name **one** other type of organism which could have caused the decay process in bag **B**.

(d) If Susan buries the bags at a depth of 1 m, the decay is slower. State **two** reasons why.

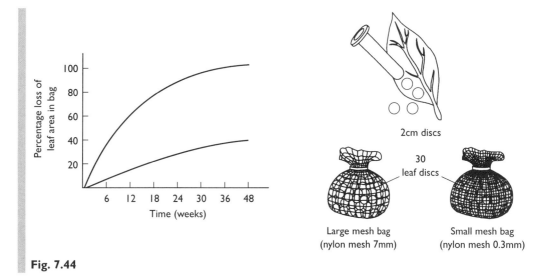

Fig. 7.44

Carbon cycle

Key points

▶ this is an example of cycling of nutrients;

▶ all living things need carbon to make proteins, carbohydrates and fats;

▶ carbon can be transferred between organisms and the environment by a series of processes, e.g. respiration, photosynthesis, decay and combustion;

▶ decomposers are important in the carbon cycle.

There are five key processes in the carbon cycle:

1. **photosynthesis:** plants convert carbon dioxide into sugar (carbohydrate). This is sometimes described as 'fixing carbon'.

2. **respiration:** all living things convert carbohydrate to carbon dioxide when they respire, i.e. they release carbon dioxide.

3. **decay:** when decomposers (bacteria and fungi) feed on organic material and make it decay, they release carbon dioxide.

4. **feeding:** when animals feed on plants or other animals, organic substances containing carbon, e.g. proteins, carbohydrates and fats are passed along the food chain.

5. **combustion:** when organic matter is burned, carbon dioxide is released. This may be fresh organic matter, e.g. wood, or fossil fuels (oil, coal, gas) which were formed from organisms living millions of years ago.

'There a lots of different ways to draw this diagram. Make sure you understand it – don't just learn it parrot fashion.'

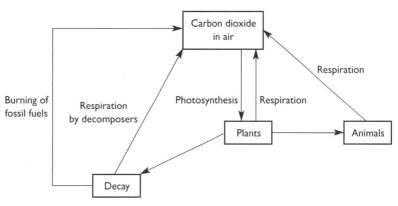

Fig. 7.45 The carbon cycle

The diagram below shows the carbon cycle.

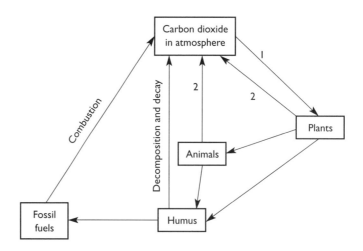

Fig. 7.46

(a) (i) Name the process which is shown by arrow 1.
    (ii) Name the raw material, other than carbon dioxide, which is needed for process 1.

(b) Name the process shown by the arrows labelled 2.

(c) Name **two** groups of organisms which bring about decomposition and decay.

(d) Name **two** fossil fuels in common use.

Nitrogen cycle

Key points

▶ this is an example of cycling of nutrients;

▶ all living things need nitrogen to make proteins and nucleic acids;

▶ nitrogen can be transferred between organisms and the environment by a series of processes, e.g. nitrogen fixation, nitrification, denitrification, decay;

▶ bacteria are very important in the nitrogen cycle;

▶ although about 78% of the air is nitrogen gas, only nitrogen fixing bacteria can use this;

▶ nitrogen can be added to soil in the form of nitrate fertilisers, manure or compost.

There are six key processes in the nitrogen cycle:

1. **Nitrogen fixation:**   nitrogen fixing bacteria change nitrogen gas into nitrates. Some of these bacteria live free in the soil, and some live in root nodules of plants like peas, beans and clover (legumes).

2. **Absorption by plants:**   plant roots absorb nitrate and it is used inside the plant to make proteins and nucleic acids.

3. **Feeding:**   when animals feed on plants or other animals, nitrogen (in protein) is passed along the food chain.

4. **Decay:**   when decomposers feed on organic matter containing protein, they release ammonia (contains nitrogen).

5. **Nitrification:**   nitrifying bacteria (in the soil) change ammonia into nitrate. This is a two-step process
    ammonia $\longrightarrow$ nitrite $\longrightarrow$ nitrate

6. **Denitrification:**   denitrifying bacteria (in the soil) change nitrate into nitrogen gas.

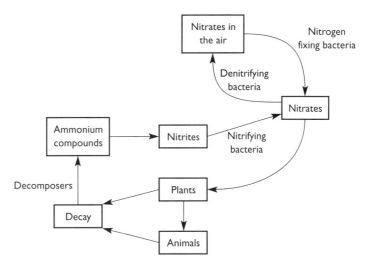

Fig. 7.47 Nitrogen cycle

In addition to the processes involving living things, nitrate can be added to the nitrogen cycle by:

(a) **lightning**: converts nitrogen gas to nitrates;

(b) **fertilizers**: add nitrate to the soil. This is necessary because most crops are not left to decay where they grew so when a farmer harvests a crop he is taking nitrogen out of the natural cycle. To keep the land fertile, he must put extra nitrogen back into the cycle.

Nitrate can be lost from the nitrogen cycle by:

(a) **leaching**: nitrate is very soluble in water, so it may be carried into rivers and lakes. This causes **eutrophication** (see p. 271);

(b) **harvesting of crops**.

To summarise

1   There is a lot of nitrogen gas in the air, but only nitrogen fixing bacteria can use it.
2.   Plants can only use nitrogen in the form of nitrate.
3.   There are four important types of microbe involved in the nitrogen cycle:

(a)   nitrogen fixing bacteria   –   change nitrogen into nitrate
(b)   nitrifying bacteria   –   change ammonia into nitrate
(c)   saprophytes   –   break down dead organic material to ammonia
(d)   denitrifying bacteria   –   change nitrate into nitrogen gas

---

REVISION ACTIVITY 9   (a)   Put these steps in the cycling of nitrogen into the correct order.
A   The roots of plants take up nitrates.
B   Dead leaves decay and ammonium compounds are formed.
C   Nitrates are formed in the soil.
D   Living plants make protein.
E   Nitrites are formed in the soil.

Correct order | B | | | | | | |

(b)   With which step in part (a), i.e. A, B, C, D, or E, do you associate the following bacteria:
(i) decomposers?
(ii) nitrifying bacteria?

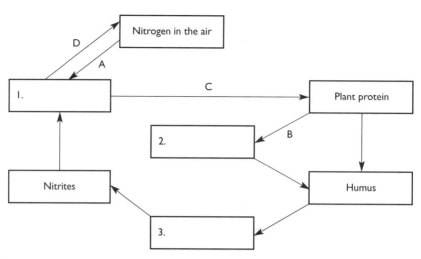

Fig. 7.48

(a) Complete the empty boxes using these words

ammonia   animal proteins   nitrates

(b) What process is occurring at A?
What process is occurring at B?
What process is occurring at D?

(c) Inside some plants, atmospheric nitrogen can be converted to nitrate which is used to make plant protein. Explain how this could happen.

Managed ecosystems

Key points

▷ Production of food, either from crops or animals, is more efficient if conditions are carefully controlled.

▷ There are four main principles:
  1. to provide optimum conditions for growth e.g. temperature, nutrients
  2. to improve efficiency of energy transfer so that more energy is used for growth and less is 'wasted'
  3. to start with 'high yield' organisms which may have been obtained by selective breeding or genetic engineering
  4. to eliminate diseases and predators which will reduce yield.

▷ As well as maximising the profit to be made, the farmer must consider the costs of the process and the responsibilities to the environment and to the organisms involved.

Animal husbandry

Farm animals are kept for the **products** they make, e.g. milk, eggs, or to be killed and used as meat. In both of these cases the animal is fed on a crop, and uses the energy in this food to make the product or to grow. This results in the following type of food chain

grass $\longrightarrow$ cow $\longrightarrow$ human
corn $\longrightarrow$ hen $\longrightarrow$ human

We have already seen that energy transfer through food chains is not very efficient, with only 10% of the animal's food intake being used to grow. Around 90% is 'wasted' on movement, keeping warm and vital body processes.

1. Principles of animal husbandry

Farmers reduce this energy loss by keeping animals in carefully controlled conditions. In particular they:

'These are the principles of factory farming.'

▷ **restrict movement** – animals may be kept in confined spaces so that they do not use energy unnecessarily.
▷ **control food intake** – animals are fed the optimum (ideal) amount of food for rapid growth, and have this food delivered to them i.e. they do not have to move around to find it.
▷ **control temperature** – birds and mammals are endothermic: this means that they maintain a constant body temperature. Many farm animals are kept in heated buildings so that they do not use energy to keep warm.

Farmers must also ensure that animals are not at risk from **predators** or **disease**.

If large numbers of animals are confined in warm buildings, disease can spread rapidly. Many farmers routinely give animals **antibiotics** with their food, to control diseases. However, this can cause problems for two reasons:

1. bacteria can develop **resistance** to the antibiotics, so the drugs can no longer be used to treat sick animals;
2. it is important that there are no traces of the drug present in meat or other animal products, as some people are **allergic** to antibiotics.

Farmers try to maximise the amount of product they obtain by using **high-yield animals.** Some of these have been developed over many years through **selective breeding,**

> e.g. cows with high milk yield,
> pigs with low back-fat ratio.

Some have been developed more recently through **genetic engineering,**

> e.g. animals with genes for disease resistance,
> pigs with genes for increased growth rate.

Some animals are given injections of **hormones** which will increase their growth rate or milk yield.

The farmer must balance the demands of maximum food production (and therefore high profits) against the cost and responsibilities of the production process. The costs include energy to heat buildings, drugs to prevent or treat disease, and food. Farmers must also pay high prices for good breeding animals.

2. Responsibilities to animals

It is important that the welfare of animals is considered at all stages of food production. There is some evidence that animals which are used to make large amounts of food products e.g. milk, eggs, are more likely to suffer from some **health problems** than other animals. For example:

▷ dairy cows have a greater risk of **mastitis** (infection of the udder) than other cows, due to the large volumes of milk produced;
▷ dairy cows have an increased risk of **lameness**, due to walking difficulties caused by an enlarged udder;
▷ hens kept for egg production have an increased risk of **broken bones**, due to repeated use of body calcium (from their bones) to develop egg shells.
Many people feel that this harm to animals is unacceptable.

3. Responsibilities to the environment

When large numbers of animals are kept in confined spaces for food production, there is often a problem with disposal of **waste products.**

For example in dairy farms, cows will produce large amounts of urine and faeces. In the past, when farmers were involved in mixed farming, i.e. they kept animals and grew crops, these waste products would have been used as **fertilisers**. Now, most dairy farmers keep large numbers of cows (so they have large amounts of waste) and do not grow crops, so they do not need fertiliser.

'Eurotrophication is a major problem when waste gets into fresh water.'

If this waste is allowed to drain into streams or ponds, it will cause **eutrophication,** i.e. minerals, especially nitrate, in the waste will make algae in the water grow faster. They will form a mat on the water surface, blocking out the light for other plants. When the algae die, saprophytes will make them decompose and oxygen is removed from the water. This results in deoxygenated streams and ponds which cannot support animal life.

Fish farming (aquaculture)

> ## Key points
>
> ▷   some fish are not suitable for fish farming because they grow slowly, or have a complex life-cycle or expensive diet;
>
> ▷   fish are reared in tanks then kept in outdoor cages until they are big enough to be killed;
>
> ▷   movement and food intake are carefully controlled;
>
> ▷   fish farming still accounts for less than 10% of the fish we eat.

This involves rearing fish in an enclosed area until they can be used for food.

Currently, less than 10% of the fish we eat are obtained in this way, whilst 90 % are caught using nets or hooks and lines.

Some fish are unsuitable for fish farming, for the following reasons:

▷   they have a very **slow** growth rate, and may take around five years to reach their adult size, e.g. cod, plaice;

▷   many popular fish, e.g. cod, haddock, sole, are carnivores, found at the top of food chains. It is therefore **expensive** to provide them with suitable food.

'The fish farmer must consider public demand for the product.'

The best profit returns come from fast-growing, fresh water herbivores, e.g. carp, but these are not popular with the public.

1. Principles of fish farming

Eggs and sperm are collected from captive adult fish, and fertilisation occurs in tanks. The eggs are kept in controlled conditions until they hatch, then the larvae are provided with suitable high-energy food for rapid growth.

When the larvae have grown enough, they are transferred to outdoor **cages**. For freshwater fish, e.g. trout, these cages are usually in lakes. For marine fish, e.g. salmon, the cages may be in sea lochs, or in the open sea.

The cages keep the fish in one place, and allow them to be fed easily, while preventing losses from predators. Fish can be kept in the cages for 1–2 years, before being killed for food.

Within a food chain, energy is lost at each trophic level, e.g. in moving around and carrying out vital body processes. Fish farmers try to maximise energy transfer by:

▷   **restricting movement** – larvae are kept in small tanks and adults are kept in cages, so that they do not use energy unnecessarily.

▷   **controlling food intake** – for maximum growth rate, fish must be given large quantities of nutrient-rich food. This is normally processed into pellets made from molluscs and small fish (of varieties humans do not choose to eat, e.g. sand eels), with added vitamins and minerals. Such a diet is very expensive.

▷   **controlling temperature** – fish are ectothermic i.e. they do not control their body temperature, so they do not use energy keeping warm. However, they will grow faster if they are kept in warm conditions. It is easy to control the temperature of the indoor stages i.e. eggs and larvae, but once the fish have been transferred to outdoor cages, it is virtually impossible.

Large numbers of fish kept in tanks or cages are at risk of **disease**, e.g. from parasites such as lice, and from fungi and bacteria. This is avoided in two ways:

1.   spraying the water in the cage area with **pesticides** to kill parasites. This is only effective if the cage is in a relatively enclosed area, e.g. small lake.

2.   adding antibiotic and anti-fungal **drugs** to the fish diet.

Farmers try to maximise the amount of product they obtain by using **high-yield fish**. Some of these have been developed by selective breeding, and others by genetic engineering.

Farmers must balance the demands of maximum food production (and therefore high profits), against the costs and responsibilities of the production process. The cost include energy to heat indoor stages, drugs and pesticides to prevent disease, and very high food costs.

2. Responsibilities to animals
Fish farming represents a major change in the lifestyle of many fish, e.g.

▷   they can no longer migrate;
▷   they can no longer range over large areas of water to feed;
▷   they are kept at very high density i.e. large numbers of fish per cage.

Although little work has been done on the effects of these changes, it is likely that they are detrimental to the fish involved.

3. Responsibilities to the environment
Problems arise as a result of two of the management procedures

'These problems are greater if the cages are in an enclosed area, e.g. small lake.'

▷   when caged fish are fed on processed, pelleted food, some of it will fall through the bottom of the cage and settle on the lake or sea bed. Here the pellets will disintegrate, releasing their nutrients. This has a damaging effect on the natural food web in this region.
▷   when the cage area is sprayed with pesticides to kill fish parasites, e.g. sea lice, the pesticide will spread through the water and affect other invertebrates, disrupting food webs.

Pest control

Key points
▷   pest control is important because pests account for large crop losses and increased disease amongst plants and animals;
▷   chemical control relies on use of chemical pesticides to kill pests;
▷   biological control relies on use of natural predators to kill pests.

Importance of pest control
Every year pests attack crop plants and animals, causing reduced crop yield. The main problems are:

▷   pests feed on crop organisms, so yield is reduced;
▷   pests compete with crop organisms for resources, so yield is reduced;
▷   pests can directly cause disease in crop organisms;
▷   pests can make infection by pathogens more likely;
▷   pests can spoil food when it is being stored or transported.

These factors lead to a reduced amount of food (very important in some parts of the world, where food is in very short supply), and to massive economic losses for farmers.

Chemical control of pests
This involves using herbicides, fungicides or insecticides (together these are called **pesticides**) to kill the pests.

The chemicals can be:

▷   sprayed onto the crop;
▷   applied as powders or smokes in enclosed areas;
▷   watered into the soil so that plants absorb them though their roots;
▷   sprayed onto animals;
▷   added to animal feed, or sprayed onto the food source of wild pests.

The advantages and disadvantages of chemical control are:

Advantages

1.   The chemicals kill pests.
2.   They are quite easy to use.

Disadvantages

1. The chemicals are expensive.
2. They are **non-specific**, i.e. they may kill other organisms as well as the pest.
3. Many pesticides are **persistent**, i.e. they remain in the environment, or in the bodies of organisms, for a very long time.
4. Many pesticides **accumulate** in the bodies of organisms over time, as they are passed along food chains.
5. They may harm **humans** if they are taken into the body directly, e.g. inhaled, or if they are ingested as part of the diet.
6. Pests may become **resistant** to them as a result of mutation, so they are no longer effective.
7. Farmers may have to use increasingly **large amounts** of pesticides to get the same effect, as pests become tolerant.

Case Study: use of DDT

DDT is an insecticide which can be used to kill lice, fleas, greenfly, etc. It was first used in Britain in 1939, and was important in controlling disease-carrying insects, e.g. fleas, mosquitoes, and as a garden insecticide.

DDT is persistent, and it accumulates along food chains, so animals can pick up large amounts of DDT in their diet,

$$\text{DDT added}$$
$$\downarrow$$
$$\text{e.g. plants} \longrightarrow \text{greenfly} \longrightarrow \text{blue-tits} \longrightarrow \text{birds of prey}$$

DDT may accumulate in amounts large enough to kill birds of prey, or to stop them breeding successfully. By the 1950s and 1960s, populations of birds of prey (sparrow hawks, peregrine falcons, eagles) were decreasing, and DDT was banned in Britain.

Biological control of pests

This involves using natural predators to kill the pests. Examples of biological control include:

▶ using the caterpillar moth (*Cactoblastis*) to kill cacti (*Opuntia*);
▶ using a parastic wasp (*Encarsia*) to kill whitefly;
▶ using a virus (*Myxomatosis*) to kill rabbits;
▶ using ladybirds to kill scale insects;
▶ using bacteria (*Bacillus thuringiensis*) to kill caterpillars.

The predator may kill the pest by:

(a) feeding on it directly;

(b) acting as a parasite, e.g. laying its eggs inside the pest – when the young develop they will kill the pest;

(c) causing a disease so pest dies;

(d) making the pest infertile.

The advantages and disadvantages of biological control are:

Advantages

1. The predators kill the pests.
2. The predators are **specific**.
3. The predators will breed in the environment, so they do not need to be constantly re-applied.
4. They do not cause harm to other organisms or accumulate in food chains.
5. They are unlikely to harm humans.
6. Pests cannot become resistant to them.

Disadvantages

1. They do not kill all the pests; they work by controlling pest numbers, and keeping them at a manageable level.
2. The predator itself may become a problem in the environment, e.g. cane toads were introduced to Australia to kill beetles (the pest), but there are now such large numbers of cane toads that they are regarded as a pest.

Case Study: use of bacteria to kill caterpillars

The bacterium *Bacillus thuringiensis* is a natural predator of blackfly caterpillars. The bacteria can be mixed with water and sprayed onto the caterpillar's food plants. Within a few days of taking in the bacteria, the caterpillars start to die. This method has been used to clear the caterpillars from huge areas of West Africa where the adult blackflies carry the disease river blindness which affects humans. This has decreased the level of river blindness in West Africa.

Remember:

There is no single ideal method for killing pests. Chemical control is effective, but it is likely to harm other organisms. Biological control is specific, but will not get rid of all pests.

▷ **SOLUTIONS TO REVISION ACTIVITIES**

S1 (a) (i) quadrats (sample and multiply up)
             (ii) nets (mark and recapture)
             (iii) pitfall trap (mark and recapture)
             (iv) quadrats (sample and multiply up)

(b) (i) Total number $=$ $\dfrac{\text{number caught 1st day} \times \text{number caught 2nd day}}{\text{number of marked beetles caught 2nd day}}$

$$= \frac{47 \times 56}{7}$$

$$= 376$$

(ii) This makes them more visible to predators, so they are less likely to survive.

S2 (a) (i) So he could compare the quadrants (it would be a fair test).
             (ii) Animals move away from the heat and light to the base of the funnel.
             (iii) To stop the soil falling into the beaker.

(b) (i) Average number $= \dfrac{130}{5} = 26$

(ii) More leaf litter collects on the north side of the tree, so more fungi are found there. Springtails feed on fungi, so there will be most on this side of the tree.

S3 | D | A | C | E | B | G | F |

S4 (a) 8 km (this is when dissolved oxygen levels start to fall).

(b) (i) The pollution caused an increase in numbers of bacteria, resulting in a decrease in the concentration of dissolved oxygen, hence numbers of fish. This effect was reduced at increasing distances downstream from the source of pollution.
     (ii) Wastes discharged from sewage works.

(c) The numbers of other organisms, needed by the fish for food, are still reduced. Toxic substances may be still be present in the water, or in the food chain.

Comments

(b) (i) needs answering carefully, so that you give yourself a chance to show your understanding of the processes involved.
     (ii) Several answers are possible here, e.g. dairy, farm waste, paper mill, etc.

(c) Another possibility is that the fish have not had time to reproduce, following a 'pulse' of pollution.

S5 (a) (i) d (ii) c (iii) a (iv) b

(b) They are **all** like this:

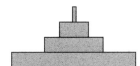

Fig. 7.49

(c) It is this shape because
  (i) energy is lost at each trophic level so it gets narrower towards the top;
  (ii) it takes account of the size of organisms, so it is the correct pyramid shape.

S6 (a) cow because (i) it is less active;
  (ii) it loses less heat though its skin because it is bigger (so uses less energy keeping warm).

  (b) trout because (i) it does not keep a constant body temperature, so it does not use energy keeping warm;
  (ii) it is a carnivore, so its food is more easily digested.

S7 (a) A

  (b) large soil organisms – insects/millipedes/ worms/woodlice

  (c) micro-organisms – bacteria, fungi (saprophytes/decomposers)

  (d) (i) less air for action of aerobic microbes
  (ii) fewer soil organisms at this depth
  (iii) may be colder (soil not warmed by Sun)

S8 (a) (i) photosynthesis
  (ii) water (not light, because light is a source of energy, not a raw material)

  (b) respiration

  (c) bacteria and fungi

  (d) coal, oil, gas

S9 (a) | B | E | C | A | D |

  (b) (i) B
  (ii) E and C

S10 (a) 1 = Nitrates
  2 = Animal protein
  3 = Ammonia

  (b) A = Nitrogen fixation
  B = Feeding
  D = Denitrification

  (c) Some plants (legumes e.g. peas, beans, clover) have root nodules which contain nitrogen fixing bacteria. The bacteria change nitrogen gas into nitrate, and the plant uses nitrate to make protein.

EXAMINATION QUESTIONS

▷ **Question 1**   In order to estimate the abundance of buttercups in a small lawn, a square frame was placed at three random places and the number of buttercups in each frame was counted. The results are represented (see Fig. 7.50 on p. 277):

(a) What is the name given to the frame?   *(1)*

(b) What is the average number of buttercups per frame?   *(1)*

(c) What is the area of each square?   *(1)*

(d) How many buttercups would you expect to find in an area of 1m²?   *(1)*

(e) How would you use your answer in (d) to estimate the number of buttercups in the lawn? Mention any other measurements you would need to take.   *(3)*

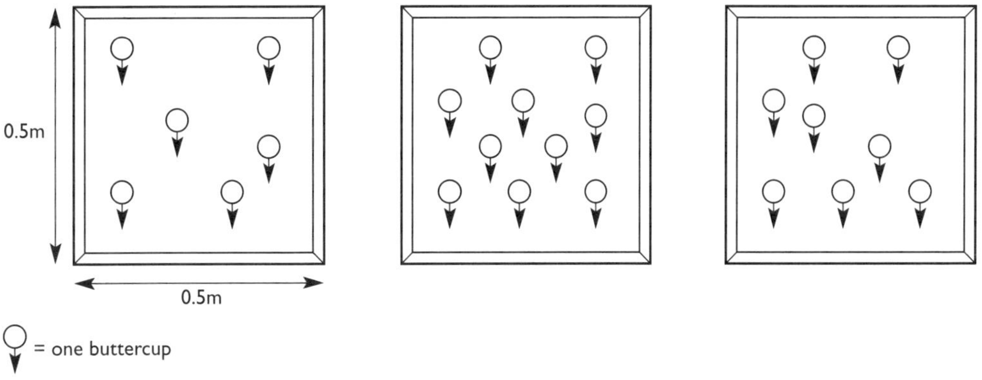
0.5m
0.5m
= one buttercup

Fig. 7.50

(f) How could you make your estimate more reliable? *(2)*

(g) What technique would you use to study the distribution of buttercups along the edge of a straight path through a field? *(1)*

(WJEC)

Question 2

The table below shows what some of the living things in a wood do at different times of the year.

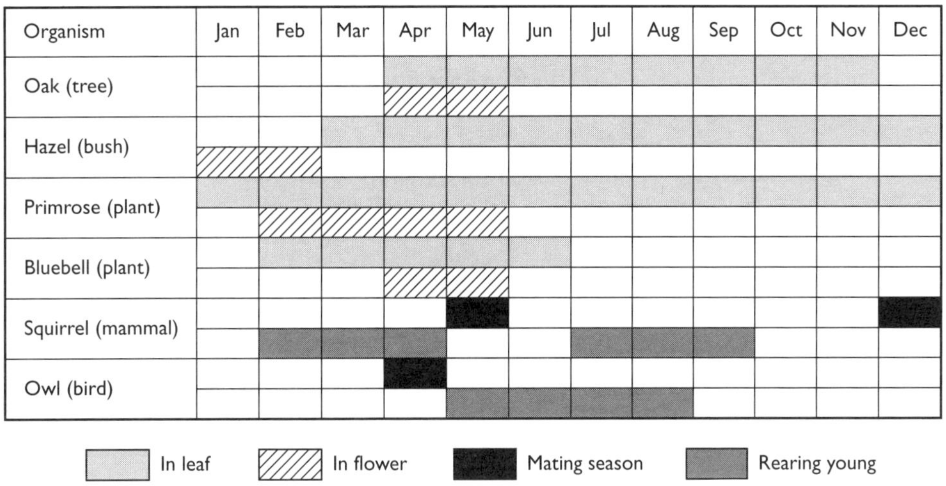
Organism
Jan
Feb
Mar
Apr
May
Jun
Jul
Aug
Sep
Oct
Nov
Dec
Oak (tree)
Hazel (bush)
Primrose (plant)
Bluebell (plant)
Squirrel (mammal)
Owl (bird)
In leaf
In flower
Mating season
Rearing young

Fig. 7.51

(a) Use information from the table to help you to answer the following questions.

(i) For how many months are there leaves on the oak trees? *(1)*

(ii) There are no leaves on the oak tree for the whole of one season. Which season is this? *(1)*

(iii) Suggest **one** change in the environment which might cause oak trees to lose their leaves. *(1)*

(iv) Bluebells live on the floor of the wood. Explain why it is an advantage to the bluebells to produce leaves in February rather than later in the year. *(1)*

(v) When do the owls mate? *(1)*

(vi) Explain **one** advantage to the owls of rearing their young in summer rather than in winter. *(1)*

(b) One food chain in the wood is:

Hazel tree nuts ⟶ squirrels ⟶ owls

(i) What does this food chain tell us? *(2)*

(ii) Which one of the organisms in the food chain is a producer? *(1)*

(iii) This year the hazel bushes have produced very few nuts.
Explain, as fully as you can, how this might affect the populations of:
1. squirrels;
2. owls. *(4)*

(c) An area of the floor of the wood 1m² was fenced off so that animals could not reach it. The graph below shows the depth of leaf litter (dead leaves) inside the fence over the next few months.

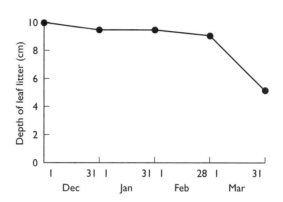

Fig. 7.52

Explain, as fully as you can,

(i) why the depth of the leaf litter decreased; *(1)*
(ii) how this decrease happened. *(1)*
(iii) In which month does leaf litter disappear fastest? Explain why? *(2)*

(NEAB)

▷ **Question 3**   A pupil placed some damp grass clippings on a compost heap. Every two days for twelve days the temperature inside the clippings was measured. The results were as follows:

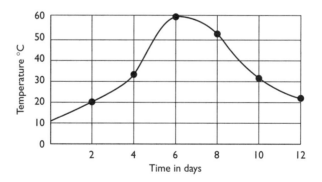

Fig. 7.53

(a) (i)   What was the temperature on day 10? *(1)*
(ii) In which two-day period did the greatest change occur? *(1)*
(iii) Suggest what caused the temperature to rise during days 1–6. *(1)*

(b) The number of living animals in a sample of the clippings was also recorded and shown in the table:

Day	2	4	6	8	10	12
Number of animals	8	28	4	12	36	170

(i) What was the average number of animals in the six samples collected? *(1)*

(ii) Suggest why there are so few animals in the sample on days 6–8. *(1)*

(c) An experiment was set up as shown in the diagram using methylene blue which turns colourless when oxygen is not present.

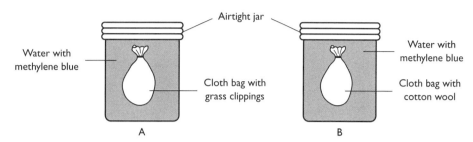

Fig. 7.54

The results were as follows:

	Colour of methylene blue	
	Jar at start	*Jar after two days*
A	Blue	Colourless
B	Blue	Blue

(i) What gas is present at the start of the experiment? *(1)*

(ii) Explain why this gas disappears. *(2)*

(WJEC)

▷ **Question 4** Black aphids are tiny insects. They can do a lot of damage to crops.

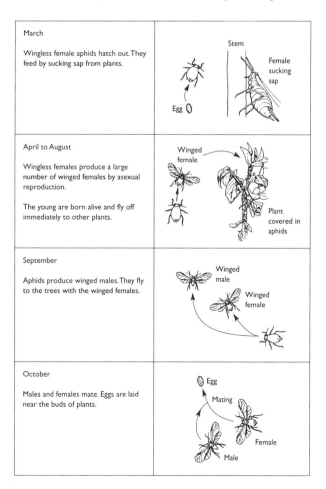

Fig. 7.55

(a)   Explain **two** ways in which aphids are adapted to survive.   *(4)*

(b)   The black aphid population is controlled by predators as ladybirds.
      (i)   Write out a food chain for the aphids, ladybirds and plants.   *(2)*
      (ii) from the organisms in this food chain choose

      one producer   _____

      one consumer   _____

      one carnivore   _____

      one herbivore   _____   *(4)*

(c)   Aphids can be killed by spraying them with a pesticide.
      Explain what could happen to the population of ladybirds if a lot of aphids were killed.*(2)*
                                                                              (MEG)

▷ **Question 5**   (a)   The diagram below shows a marine food web.

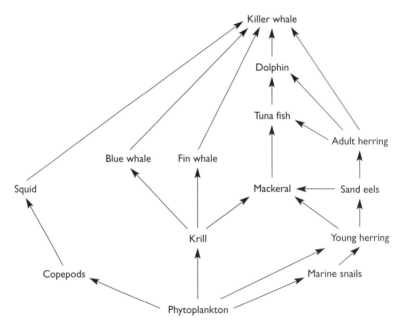

Fig. 7.56

Using the information in the food web:

(i)   Write a food chain consisting of **four** organisms.   *(2)*
(ii) Name **three** secondary consumers.

      1   _____

      2   _____

      3   _____   *(1)*

(iii) Give **three** reasons why reducing the number of adult herring by fishing is likely
      to change the number of sand eels.

      1   _____

      2   _____

      3   _____   *(3)*

(iv) Explain why there is more energy available to a whale feeding on krill than a
      whale feeding on fish.   *(4)*

(b) An additional threat to marine animals involves organic pollution of the seas. The diagram below shows how a large proportion of this organic waste can be recycled and thereby reduce possible marine pollution.

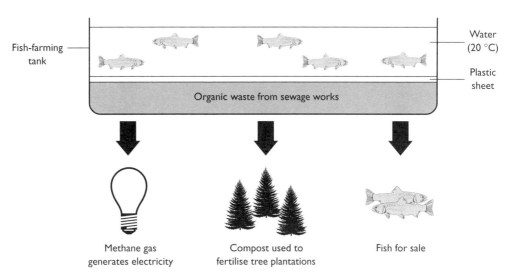

Fig. 7.57

(i)   Explain how the release of organic waste into the sea could
  1   increase plant growth
  2   kill fish   (2)
(ii) Explain how the organic waste helps to keep the water in the fish tank at 20°C. (2)
(iii) Suggest why the compost produced is used to fertilise tree plantations rather than crops for human consumption.   (1)

(NICCEA)

▷ **Question 6**   The diagram shows the energy flow through a food chain.

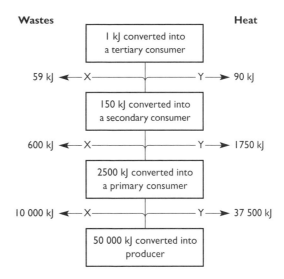

Fig. 7.58

Use the information in the diagram to help answer the following questions.

(a) What processes, in the consumers, account for the energy flow represented by the letters X and Y?

X _____

Y _____   (2)

(b) What percentage of the energy available in the primary consumer is available for the secondary consumer? (Show your working.) *(2)*

(c) Why are there rarely more than five trophic levels in a food chain? *(2)*

(NICCEA)

▷ **Question 7** The diagram below shows tomatoes being grown in a glasshouse.

Group A were grown in a 'grow bag' containing compost. Group B were grown in a tube through which organic 'slurry' flowed constantly.

The tomato plants in Group B were much taller and more productive than those in Group A.

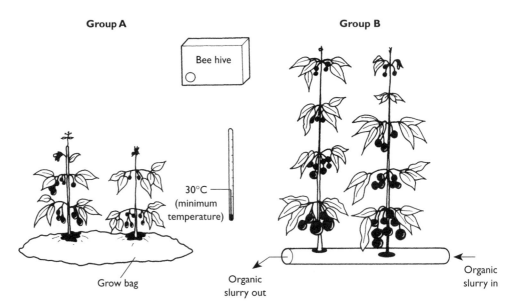

Fig. 7.59

(a) Explain how the factors shown in the diagram affect the growth and productivity of both groups of tomato plants. *(4)*

(b) Even though tomato plant can flower and fruit at any time of the year, it has proved uneconomic to grow tomatoes in glasshouses in Britain between November and February. Suggest **two** reasons why this is so. *(2)*

(LONDON)

▷ **Question 8** (a) The table below shows the energy content and amount of insecticide in the organisms of a food chain.

Organisms in food chain	Energy content as percentage of original energy	Amount of insecticide in body mass (mg/kg)
Human	1	1.00
Fish	4	0.1
Microscopic animals	20	0.01
Microscopic water plants	100	0.001

(i) Calculate the percentage loss of energy between the microscopic water plants and microscopic animals.

Energy loss = _____ % *(1)*

(ii) Food chains involving humans should be kept as short as possible.
Use information from the table to explain this. *(3)*

(iii) How are insecticides useful to farmers?   *(1)*
(iv) Explain why fish contain insecticides.   *(2)*

(b) Fish farming is an important way of increasing the amount of food available. The diagram below shows a simple fish farming system.

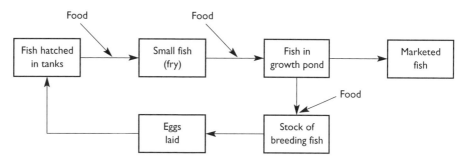

Fig. 7.60

Describe the advantages and disadvantages of a fish farming system like the one shown. *(3)*
(LONDON)

▷ **Question 9**   The prickly pear cactus did not grow in Australia until 1840 when Doctor Carlyle introduced the plant into his garden. The cactus quickly spread outside the garden. Within a few years it covered large areas and prevented other plants, including crops, from growing properly. Methods of control available at that time did not work. In 1925, eggs of a species of moth from Argentina were brought to Australia and placed on some prickly pear cactus plants. The caterpillars of this moth quickly ate the cactus plants and large areas were cleared. The cactus population increases from time to time but when this happens the population of the moth also increases.

(a) Give **two** methods which might have been used to control the cactus before 1925.   *(2)*

(b) The use of the moths is a an example of biological control.
   (i)   Apart from being more successful, give **two** advantages of this method over the earlier methods.   *(2)*
   (ii) Give **two** factors that must be considered when choosing an organism to control another organism.   *(2)*
   (iii) Why is it important that the control agent does not destroy the pest completely?   *(2)*

(c) In Britain, aphids can be a serious pest to crops, and biological methods have been used to control them.
   (i) Why are aphids a serious pest to crops?   *(2)*
   (ii) Describe a biological control method that has been used on aphids.
(LONDON)

▷ **Question 10**   Professor John Lawton researches into the problem of controlling the spread of bracken. Bracken is a fern which threatens upland farms partly because it poses a health risk to people and animals. Professor Lawton is waiting for government permission to release the Conservular caterpillar which feeds on the bracken.
   The Secretary of State has to decide whether the Conservular caterpillar can be released.
   The article printed on p. 284 describes some of the problems faced by the Secretary of State.

Upland farms are artificial ecosystems, created and maintained mainly for the rearing of sheep and cattle. These farms are being threatened by the spread of bracken. Up to now the only treatment for bracken has been to use herbicides.
   Use the article to explain as fully as you can what advice you would give to the Secretary of State. Explain the arguments for and against that lead to your decision.
   You will not receive marks for simply copying extracts from the article.   *(8)*
(NEAB)

David the caterpillar to bracken's Goliath

Yorkshire farmer Maurice Cotrill has just forked out £500 to have a helicopter hover over his land and spew out loads of chemicals aimed at destroying one of the most pervasive and dangerous weeds know to man – bracken. In a little box in a laboratory near Ascot, Berkshire, lies a tiny caterpillar which could have done the job for nothing.

Whether or not that caterpillar and thousands of its chums will ever be let loose on the massive carpet of bracken that is sweeping over Britain at the rate of 53 square kilometers a year has to be decided by the Secretary of State for the Environment.

Weed control through the release of imported insects has never been tried in Britain before. If the Secretary of State permits the experiment, the caterpillar is in for the feast of its life, because five years of painstaking research have proved that bracken is its only food. However, is that the full story? Will the beast stop there or will it go on, wreaking unforeseen devastation? Can scientists predict what will happen when imported insects are released into the wild?

Bracken is poisonous – more than 20 000 sheep and 1 000 cattle suffer poisoning each year. Its spores are carcinogenic, posing a threat to hill walkers. Bracken costs a depressing £4m a year to control while rendering useless grazing land valued at £5m annually. 'Bracken is one factor which is leading to hill farming becoming uneconomic', says the director of the Ramblers Association. 'We are worried about that because the more uneconomic hill farms become, the more prospect there is of the forestry industry taking over.'

The National Farmers Union are concerned about the consequences of the caterpillar getting out of control. What if it stared consuming garden ferns? What if it loved potatoes? On the other hand, the caterpillar might help to preserve important uplands where wildlife flourishes when bracken is kept at bay. However the experiment takes the scientists into unknown territory.

World-wide, 94 species of weeds have been controlled by biological releases involving 215 types of animal in 50 countries. Professor Lawton says that approximately one-third have achieved effective control and the remainder have failed.

Fig. 7.61

▷ **Question 11** Consider the following data concerning human population for 1970 and 1988. Doubling time is the time taken for the population to double in size. Birth rate is the number of births per one thousand population

Region	Year	Birth rate	Death rate	Doubling time of population (years)	% below 15 years of age
Africa	1970	47	20	27	44
	1988	44	15	24	42
Europe	1970	18	10	88	25
	1988	13	10	266	21
United States	1970	18	10	70	30
	1988	16	9	99	22
Russia	1970	18	8	70	28
	1988	20	10	68	26
Mexico	1970	44	10	21	46
	1988	30	6	29	42

(a) Which region's birth rate is **not** following the general trend? *(1)*

(b) Which regions had the highest population below puberty in 1988? *(1)*

(c) Which region's population was **most** affected by birth control in 1988? *(1)*

(d) (i) Which region would have the largest population in the year 2000? *(1)*

   (ii) Suggest two factors which this region would need to develop to cope with a large population increase. *(1)*

(WJEC)

▷ **Question 12**   The arrows on the diagram below show the energy flow to and from the Earth.

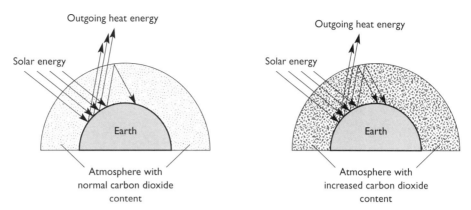

Fig. 7.62

(a) Use the diagram to explain the greenhouse effect.   *(3)*

(b) Give two consequences of the greenhouse effect.   *(2)*

(c) Name two gases, other than carbon dioxide, which also contribute to the greenhouse effect.   *(2)*

(d) The drawings below show some changes which Man could make to reduce the amount of carbon dioxide in the atmosphere.

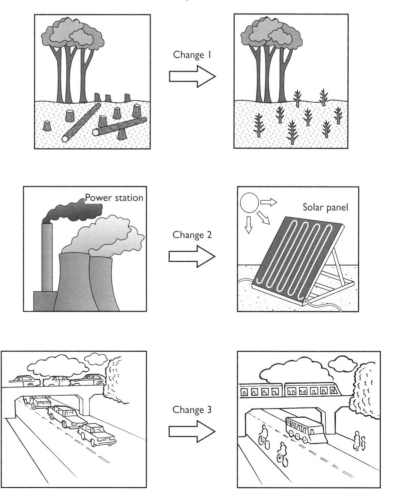

Fig. 7.63

Explain how each change would help reduce the carbon dioxide level in the atmosphere.   *(6)*

(NICCEA)

ANWERS TO EXAMINATION QUESTIONS

▷ **Question 1** (a) quadrat

(b) average $= \dfrac{6 + 10 + 8}{3} = \dfrac{24}{3} = 8$

(c) area $= 0.5 \times 0.5 = 0.25$ m^2

(d) total in 1m^2 $= 8 \times 4 = 32$

(e) Calculate the area of the lawn,
(by measuring length and width and multiplying) (1)
multiply up, e.g. area in m$^2 \times 32$, (1)
to find the total number in the lawn.

(f) Take more samples, i.e. more than three quadrats, (1) in several areas of the lawn. (1)

(g) A line transect or point transect. (1)

▷ **Question 2** (a) (i) 8 months
(ii) Winter
(iii) Fall in temperature/shorter day length.
(iv) In February there is more light for photosynthesis, because leaves have not grown on trees yet. (1)
(v) April
(vi) There is more food/it is warmer.

(b) (i) Owls eat squirrels, squirrels eat nuts from hazel trees. (1)
(ii) Hazel tree.
(iii) 1. There will be fewer squirrels. (1)
There is not enough food to support a large population. (1)
2. There will be fewer owls. (1)
There are fewer squirrels for the owls to eat. (1)

(c) (i) The leaf litter was decomposing (rotting). (1)
(ii) Decomposers (bacteria and fungi) were breaking it down. (1)
(iii) March, (1) because the temperature is warmer. (1)

▷ **Question 3** (a) (i) 30 °C
(ii) From day 4 to day 6.
(iii) Decomposers breaking down organic material/respiration by decomposers.

(b) (i) Average $= \dfrac{8 + 28 + 4 + 12 + 36 + 170}{6} = \dfrac{258}{6}$
$= 43$
(ii) The temperature was too high.

(c) (i) Oxygen
(ii) Decomposers use it (1)
when they respire. (1)

▷ **Question 4** (a) They have piercing mouth parts (1) to suck sap from plants. (1)
They can reproduce asexually (1) to produce large numbers of identical offspring. (1)
Young are born alive (1) they can fly to plants immediately and feed. (1)
Males have wings (1) to fly to females and mate with them. (1)

(b) (i) plants $\longrightarrow$ aphids $\longrightarrow$ ladybirds
(1) for correct order,
(1) for arrows pointing the right way.
(ii) producer = plant (1)
consumer = aphid or ladybird (1)
carnivore = ladybird (1)
herbivore = aphid (1)

(c) ladybirds would die (1) because they would not have enough to eat. (1)

▷ **Question 5** (a) (i)   Phytoplankton ⟶ krill ⟶ fin whale ⟶ killer whale
                      Phytoplankton ⟶ krill ⟶ blue whale ⟶ killer whale
                      Phytoplankton ⟶ copepods ⟶ squid ⟶ killer whale
                      (1) for correct chain
                      (1) for arrows the right way.

        (ii)   Squid/blue whale/fin whale/ mackerel/young herring/sand eels.

        (iii) 1.   Fewer sand eels will be eaten by herring. (1)
                2.   If there are fewer adult herring, there will be fewer tuna fish. Tuna fish also eat mackeral, so the number of mackeral will rise, and more sand eels will be eaten. (1)
                3.   Mackeral eat young herring. If the number of mackeral falls, more young herring will survive. (1)

        (iv) Energy is lost at each trophic level of a food chain. e.g. by moving around, or lost as heat. (1)
            Whales feeding on krill are at the 3rd trophic level so not much energy has been lost. (1)
            Whales feeding on fish are at the 6th trophic level, so a lot more energy has been lost. (1)

      (b) (i)   Organic waste contains minerals which increase plant growth. (1)
            When organic waste decays, oxygen is used (by decomposers), and the low levels of oxygen kill fish. (1)
        (ii)   The organic waste is broken down to make methane gas, (1) and the gas is used to generate electricity for heating. (1)
        (iii) the compost may contain viruses or bacteria which could cause disease if they contaminated food. (1)

▷ **Question 6** (a) X = excretion (1)
             Y = respiration (1)

      (b) Energy in primary consumers = 2500 KJ
          Energy in secondary consumers = 150 KJ
          This is $\frac{150}{2500} \times 100$ (1) = 6% available (1)

      (c) Energy is lost at each trophic level, (1)
          so there is not enough energy left to support more animals, (1) only 0.002% of the original energy remains. (1)

▷ **Question 7** (a) **Beehive:** insects pollinate the flowers to increase yields of fruit. (1)
          Warm temperature: so photosynthesis is rapid, to make more food, so plants grow faster. (1)
          Grow bag: group A plants have minerals from the compost. These are needed for growth. (1)
          Slurry: group B plants have minerals from the slurry. More minerals are present, so they grow faster. (1)

      (b) It is too expensive to heat the greenhouses. (1)
          It is too expensive to provide artificial light (necessary because of short daylength). (1)
          Bees are less active in winter (too cold) so pollination is decreased. (1)

▷ **Question 8**   (i)   Energy loss = 100 − 20 = 80% (1)
        (ii)   Energy is lost at each trophic level, (1) e.g. by moving about, as heat, (1) so short food chains pass on most energy to humans / are most efficient. (1)
        (iii) Insecticides kill insects which damage crops / reduce crop yield. (1)
        (iv) Insecticides are sprayed onto crops, but rain washes it into rivers. (1)
            Fish pick up insecticide from the water, or from eating microscopic animals containing it. (1)

      (b) **Advantages**
         Less wild fish are killed; fish stocks are conserved, (1) fish are not eaten by predators, (1) fish grow quickly because they are kept warm and given high energy food, (1) high quality parents can be used for breeding. (1)

Disadvantages
It is expensive to heat the tanks and provide good quality food; (1) the fish's normal life cycle is disrupted – it cannot swim freely or migrate. (1)

To get full marks, you should give advantages **and** disadvantages.

▷ **Question 9**   (a)   Chemicals used to kill plants.
Cutting back the plant, or digging it up.
Burning the plant.

(b)   (i)   It does not damage the environment, (1) it is cheaper than using chemicals, or paying people to dig up plants. (1)
(ii)   The organism should be specific (it should harm only the pest). (1)
It should not grow out of control itself (it should have natural predators). (1)
It should not cause harm to the environment. (1)
(iii)   If it reduced the pest numbers dramatically, it would die out (1) because it would have nothing to feed on, (1) and the pest numbers could then increase.(1)

(c)   (i)   They feed on sap, so the plant grows more slowly; (1) they act as vectors to spread disease. (1)
(ii)   A natural predator of the aphids is added to the crops, (1) e.g. ladybirds, (1) and these feed on the aphids, reducing the numbers.(1)

▷ **Question 10**   You should organise your ideas into advantages and disadvantages of using the caterpillar to control bracken, then summarise your advice, i.e. should it be used or not.

Advantages
▶   Bracken is a health risk to animals and humans; it is poisonous to animals and causes cancer in humans.
▶   The conservular caterpillar only eats bracken, so it will not harm other organisms.
▶   Present methods of controlling bracken are very expensive (about £4m a year), but the caterpillars would be much cheaper.
▶   Bracken spreads very quickly, and damages grazing land, so **some** method of control must be used.
▶   The natural habitat is improved if bracken is controlled – other plants will flourish.
▶   The caterpillar is less harmful to the environment than herbicide chemicals.

Disadvantages
▶   The caterpillar will spread to other areas, it will be impossible to prevent its escape.
▶   It may feed on garden ferns, which are biologically similar to bracken.
▶   It may have no natural predators in Britain, so numbers may increase very rapidly.
▶   It may disrupt natural food chains and webs.
▶   Only one-third of biological control programmes like this have worked in other countries – this may not work, i.e. may not control bracken.
▶   Scientists cannot predict what will happen once the caterpillar is released. If there are major problems, it will be difficult to solve them.

▷ **Question 11**   (a)   Russia

(b)   Mexico and Africa

(c)   Mexico (birth rate fell most between 1970 and 1988)

(d)   (i)   Africa – it has a high percentage below 15 years of age, and a high birth rate.
(ii)   better food supplies,
better water-treatment/disease control,
more education facilities,
more housing.

▷ **Question 12**   (a)   In normal conditions some solar energy is reflected from the Earth's surface and escapes into space. (1) If carbon dioxide levels are high, the reflected solar energy cannot escape into space, it is trapped close to the earth. (1)
This causes global warming. (1)

(b) Global Warming can cause:
 ▶ melting of polar ice caps;
 ▶ spread of tropical diseases to new areas;
 ▶ increase in desert sizes;
 ▶ change in weather patterns.
 ▶ increase in flooding.

(c) methane, nitrogen oxides, ozone

(d) 1. **Planting new trees** will reduce the carbon dioxide levels by taking more carbon dioxide from the air for photosynthesis. (1) This is reversing deforestation. (1)
   2. **Changing from fossil fuels to solar energy.** Fossil fuels (coal, oil, gas) produce carbon dioxide when they are burned. (1) Electricity can be generated using solar power instead. (1)
   3. **Cars** produce large amounts of carbon dioxide when petrol is burned in the engine. (1) Reducing car use, e.g. by walking, using public transport (buses and trains) or using bicycles will reduce pollution. (1)

▶ **STUDENT'S ANSWER AND EXAMINER'S COMMENT**

The diagrams show pyramids of numbers for three ecosystems.

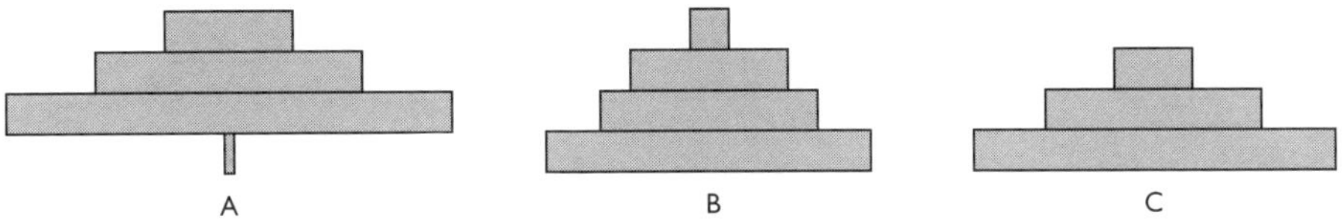

Fig. 7.64

(a) (i) Which ecosystem is likely to be area woodland? Explain your answer.

'Well explained.'

A because the bar for plants is narrow. This means that there are a small
number of large plants e.g. trees ✓   (2)

(ii) Construct a pyramid of biomass for an area of woodland (1)

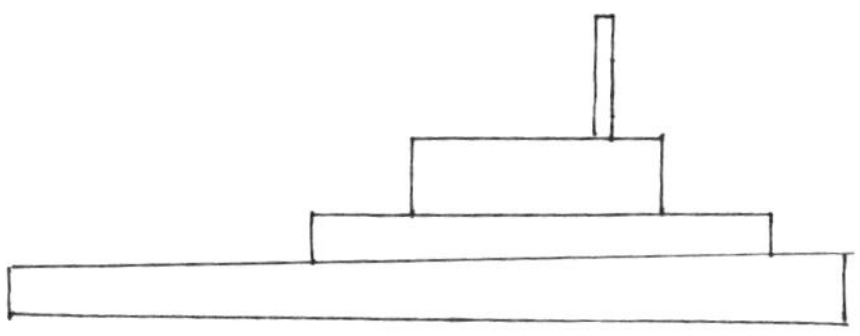

'This is basically correct, but the drawing is very careless. It should be symetrical'

Fig. 7.65

(iii) The pyramid of numbers below has four trophic levels. Identify the type of organism at each trophic level, using the words from the following list.

 carnivore   herbivore   parasite   producer

Write your answer on the lines beside the diagram.

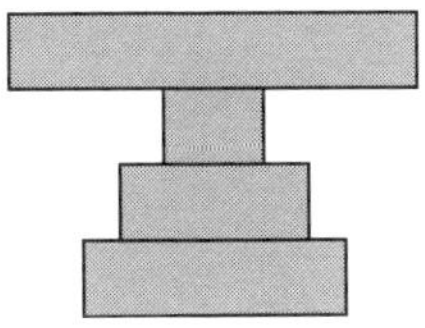

'Correct'

Trophic level 4	*parasite* ✓
Trophic level 3	*carnivore* ✓
Trophic level 2	*herbivore* ✓
Trophic level 1	*producer* ✓ (4)

Fig. 7.65

(continued)

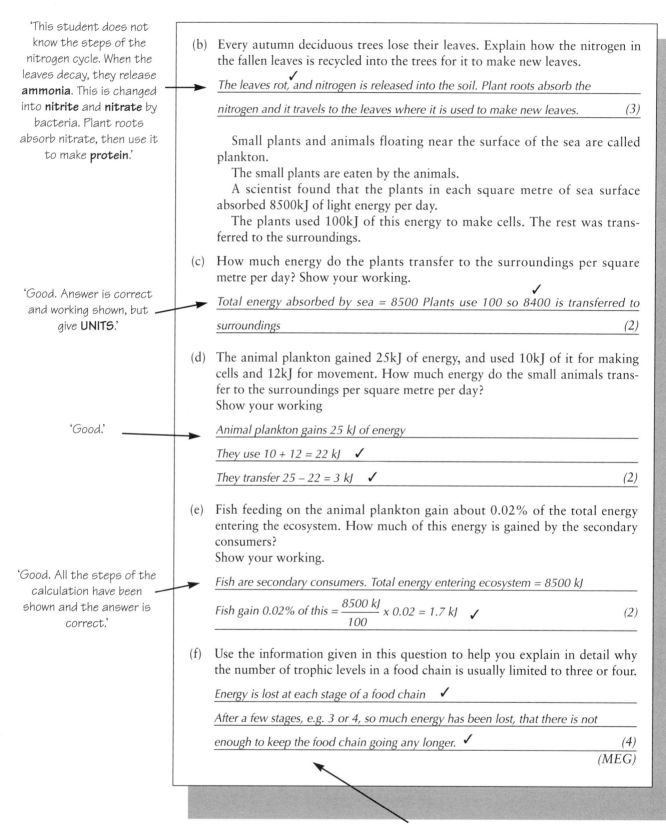

'This student does not know the steps of the nitrogen cycle. When the leaves decay, they release **ammonia**. This is changed into **nitrite** and **nitrate** by bacteria. Plant roots absorb nitrate, then use it to make **protein**.'

(b) Every autumn deciduous trees lose their leaves. Explain how the nitrogen in the fallen leaves is recycled into the trees for it to make new leaves.

The leaves rot, ✓ and nitrogen is released into the soil. Plant roots absorb the

nitrogen and it travels to the leaves where it is used to make new leaves.   (3)

Small plants and animals floating near the surface of the sea are called plankton.
The small plants are eaten by the animals.
A scientist found that the plants in each square metre of sea surface absorbed 8500kJ of light energy per day.
The plants used 100kJ of this energy to make cells. The rest was transferred to the surroundings.

(c) How much energy do the plants transfer to the surroundings per square metre per day? Show your working.

'Good. Answer is correct and working shown, but give **UNITS**.'

Total energy absorbed by sea = 8500 Plants use 100 so 8400 ✓ is transferred to

surroundings   (2)

(d) The animal plankton gained 25kJ of energy, and used 10kJ of it for making cells and 12kJ for movement. How much energy do the small animals transfer to the surroundings per square metre per day?
Show your working

'Good.'

Animal plankton gains 25 kJ of energy

They use 10 + 12 = 22 kJ ✓

They transfer 25 – 22 = 3 kJ ✓   (2)

(e) Fish feeding on the animal plankton gain about 0.02% of the total energy entering the ecosystem. How much of this energy is gained by the secondary consumers?
Show your working.

'Good. All the steps of the calculation have been shown and the answer is correct.'

Fish are secondary consumers. Total energy entering ecosystem = 8500 kJ

$$\text{Fish gain 0.02\% of this} = \frac{8500 \text{ kJ}}{100} \text{ x } 0.02 = 1.7 \text{ kJ} \quad ✓$$ (2)

(f) Use the information given in this question to help you explain in detail why the number of trophic levels in a food chain is usually limited to three or four.

Energy is lost at each stage of a food chain ✓

After a few stages, e.g. 3 or 4, so much energy has been lost, that there is not

enough to keep the food chain going any longer. ✓   (4)

(MEG)

'This is correct, but does not give enough details for 4 marks – the student has not used enough information from the question. He or she could have said that plants are quite efficient at energy transfer but animals are less efficient, because they use quite a lot of energy for moving around.'

SUMMARY

Ecology

▷ A population is all the individuals of one species in the same place, e.g. a population of limpets in a rock pool.

▷ A community is made up of individuals from different species in the same place, e.g. a rock pool community includes limpets, mussels, fish, seaweed, sea anemones.

▷ The habitat is the place where an organism lives, e.g. rock pool habitat, pond habitat, woodland habitat.

▷ The environment describes the type of habitat, and the conditions which exist there, e.g. temperature, rainfall, amount of light, type of soil, etc.

▷ The ecosystem is all of the living and non-living things in a habitat. It is the interaction between organisms and their environment.

▷ Organisms must be adapted (suitable) to live in a particular environment, otherwise they will not survive, e.g. fish have gills to absorb oxygen from water, polar bears have thick fur to keep them warn.

▷ Organisms compete for resources, e.g. food, space, light, water. Some organisms will not be successful and will die, others will survive and breed.

▷ The numbers of predators and prey are closely linked. If there are too many predators, the prey will be hunted too much and may die out, so then the predators would starve. If there are too few predators, prey numbers will increase (because they are not being eaten).

▷ Population size depends on conditions in the environment, competition and predation.

▷ Population size can be estimated during fieldwork by sampling in the environment.

In aquatic environment use nets and collecting jars.

In terrestrial environments use quadrats for plants; use nets, pitfall traps or mammal traps for animals.

Humans and the environment

▷ Human activities change the natural environment e.g. building, farming, fishing, mining, industry. They may destroy natural habitats, or may pollute the environment.

▷ Many fuels cause air pollution when they are burned. Acid rain is caused by sulphur dioxide, mainly from burned coal. Car exhaust gases include carbon monoxide and nitrogen oxides. Carbon dioxide is produced when any fuel is burned, and high levels of this gas are linked to the green house effect.

▷ Water is polluted by humans sewage, and farm waste, e.g. fertilisers containing nitrates and phosphates which are washed into rivers. This can have serious effects on aquatic organisms, e.g. eutrophication.

▷ As the human population increases in size, and it becomes more industrialised and dependent on machines, the impact on the environment increases. There are several reasons for this, e.g. more land is need for housing, roads and growing food; more fuel is needed for industry, houses and transport, so more air pollution occurs, more waste products are made, and these must be disposed of.

Transfer of nutrients and energy

▷ Food chains show the feeding patterns of organisms in a habitat. They always start with a producer (plant); this is eaten by a primary consumer (herbivore), which in turn is eaten by a secondary consumer (carnivore). The last organism in a food chain is called the top carnivore. The different steps in a food chain are called trophic levels.

▷ A pyramid of numbers is a scale diagram showing the number of organisms at each trophic level of a food chain.

▷ A pyramid of biomass is a scale diagram showing the mass of organisms at each trophic level of a food chain.

▷ Energy for food chains comes from the sun, and is transferred along the food chain as one organism eats another. The amount of energy available for transfer decreases as you progress along the food chain, because each organism uses some energy to stay alive.

▷ Each trophic level of a food chain contains less energy than the previous level, and contains less biomass than the previous level. This accounts for the triangular shape of a pyramid of biomass.

▷ Decay occurs when organisms called decomposers (bacteria and fungi) feed on dead organic material, e.g. dead organisms or their waste products. Decay occurs fastest when it is warm and damp, with plenty of air.

▷ The element carbon is found in carbon dioxide and in carbohydrates, protein and fats; the carbon cycle describes how it can be changed from one form to another in the environment.

Plants use carbon dioxide to make carbohydrate (during photosynthesis).

SUMMARY CONT.

Animals and plants change carbohydrate into carbon dioxide (during respiration).

Decomposers release carbon dioxide in the process of decay.

▷ The element nitrogen is found in the air, and in proteins and other compounds inside living things; the nitrogen cycle describes how it can be changed from one form to another in the environment. Bacteria are very important in the nitrogen cycle.

Nitrogen fixing bacteria change nitrogen gas into nitrate in the soil.

Plants can use nitrate to make proteins.

Decomposers change proteins and waste products into ammonium compounds.

Nitrifying bacteria change ammonium compounds into nitrate in the soil.

Denitrifying bacteria change nitrate into nitrogen gas.

▷ Efficient food production depends on efficient energy transfer, and control of pests and diseases. In agriculture or fish farming the aim is to control the ecosystem so that the crop organisms (animal or plant) gives the highest possible yield.

8

Extension topics

GETTING STARTED

MEG	SEG	NEAB	LONDON	WJEC	NICCEA	SEB

Each examination board chooses its own extension topics which must be studied in addition to the core topics to achieve Biology GCSE. In this chapter we will look at some of the most common extension topics.

Before you read through this, and start to revise, it is vital to know which syllabus you are following, and which extension topics you should be studying.

MEG A	D	C	SEG	LONDON	NEAB	WJEC	NICCEA	SEB	TOPIC	STUDY	REVISION 1	REVISION 2
									Micro-organisms			
✓	✓		✓	✓	✓	✓			Bacteria			
✓	✓		✓	✓	✓	✓			Viruses			
✓	✓		✓	✓	✓	✓	✓		Fungi			
				✓	✓	✓	✓		Protoctists			
✓		✓	✓	✓	✓	✓	✓	✓	Growing microbes in the lab			
	✓		✓	✓	✓	✓	✓	✓	Patterns of growth			
									Micro-organisms and disease			
✓	✓		✓	✓	✓		✓		Entry of pathogens			
✓	✓		✓	✓	✓		✓		Avoiding infection			
✓	✓	✓	✓	✓			✓		Food preservation + spoilage			
✓	✓			✓			✓		Bacterial infection			
✓	✓			✓			✓		Viral infections			
✓	✓			✓			✓		Fungal infections			
✓				✓					Protoctist infections			
✓	✓		✓	✓	✓	✓	✓		Immunity			
✓				✓			✓		Fighting infection with antibiotics			
									Biotechnology			
✓	✓	✓	✓	✓	✓	✓	✓	✓	Fermentation by yeasts			
	✓		✓	✓	✓	✓	✓		Antibiotic production			
✓	✓		✓	✓	✓				Foods from fungi			
✓	✓	✓	✓	✓	✓	✓	✓	✓	Yoghurt and cheese production			
✓									Vinegar production			
	✓				✓	✓		✓	Enzymes			
					✓	✓		✓	Gasohol			
			✓		✓	✓		✓	Biogas			
	✓		✓	✓		✓		✓	Sewage treatment			
✓	✓	✓			✓	✓		✓	Genetic engineering			
									Movement and support			
		✓	✓		✓			✓	Vertebrate skeletons			
			✓						Invertebrate skeletons			
		✓	✓					✓	Structure of bones			
		✓	✓			✓		✓	Joints			
			✓						Locomotion in animals			
			✓						Tropisms			

WHAT YOU NEED TO KNOW

▷ **Micro-organisms**

Key points
▷ There are four main types of micro-organisms:
1. bacteria,
2. viruses,
3. fungi,
4. protoctists
▷ all are microscopic;
▷ most are uni-cellular;
▷ some are beneficial to humans, some are harmful and others do not affect humans directly;
▷ most micro-organisms can easily be grown in the laboratory.

Bacteria

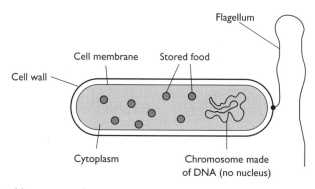

Fig. 8.1 A typical bacterium (shape can vary)

▷ bacteria are about one thousandth of a millimetre long;
▷ the shape varies between species. Some species are round (cocci), some are rod-shaped (bacilli) and some are helical (spiral-shaped);
▷ bacteria never have a proper nucleus;
▷ they have one chromosome, made of a long circular piece of DNA;
▷ they do not have any organelles in their cytoplasm;
▷ many bacteria have plasmids (small loops of DNA) in their cytoplasm;
▷ they have a cell wall made of carbohydrate not cellulose;
▷ some bacteria have a slime capsule outside the cell wall. This protects them;
▷ some have flagella so that they can move;
▷ some bacteria can photosynthesise, others are decomposers (feed on dead organic material);
▷ bacteria reproduce by binary fission (asexually);
▷ bacteria can be grown in nutrient broth or on nutrient agar in the laboratory;
▷ some bacteria are useful to humans e.g. in manufacturing cheese, yoghurt, vinegar some bacteria are harmful to humans e.g. pathogens which cause diseases (TB, whooping cough, salmonella);
▷ bacteria are killed by antibiotics;
▷ some bacteria can form vegetative spores: these are resistant to hostile conditions, e.g. heat, drought, and so increase survival.

Viruses

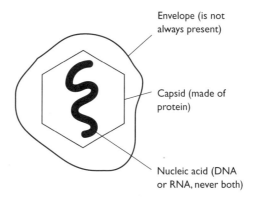

Fig. 8.2 A typical virus (polyhedral)

▶ viruses are about one millionth of a millimetre long (they are much too small to be seen with a light microscope);

▶ their shape varies between species; some are polyhedral, some are helical and some are complex;

▶ viruses are not like other living things: they do not have a proper cell structure and they do not carry out the seven processes of living things. Some scientists think that viruses are not really alive;

▶ they do not have a nucleus, cell membrane or cytoplasm;

▶ they have a short piece of nucleic acid (DNA or RNA, never both), surrounded by a protein coat called the capsid. Some viruses have an envelope around the capsid;

▶ viruses do not feed on anything;

▶ they replicate inside living cells. When they do this, the host cells are killed;

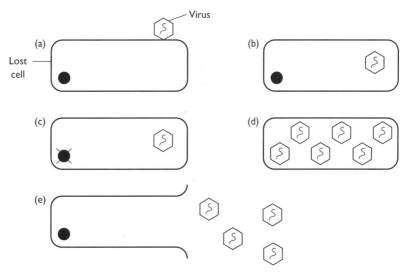

(a) Virus attaches to host cell
(b) Virus enters host cell
(c) Virus inactivates host cell nucleus
(d) Virus replicates (make copies of itself)
(e) Virus is released from host cells as it bursts open

Fig. 8.3 Replication of viruses

▶ viruses can only be grown inside living cells in the laboratory, e.g. in hens' eggs, or in infected plants;

▶ all viruses are pathogenic to their host (cause harm). Some viruses cause disease in humans, e.g. mumps, measles, flu, AIDS;

▶ viruses are not killed by antibiotics.

Fungi

There are two main types of fungi:

1. unicellular fungi;
2. multicellular fungi.

Unicellular fungi (yeasts)

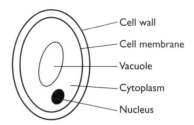

Fig. 8.4 Structure of yeast

▷ yeasts are about one hundredth of a millimetre long;
▷ they are oval or spherical shaped;
▷ they have a proper nucleus, cytoplasm and a cell membrane;
▷ they have lots of chromosomes, made of DNA;
▷ they have organelles in their cytoplasm, e.g. mitochondria;
▷ they have a cell wall made of chitin (not cellulose);
▷ they feed on sugars from their environment;
▷ they can reproduce in two ways:
  (a) by budding (asexual reproduction)
  (b) by making spores (sexual reproduction)
▷ yeasts can be grown in sugar solution in the laboratory;
▷ yeasts are useful to humans, e.g. in brewing and baking;
▷ some yeasts cause diseases in humans, e.g. thrush;
▷ yeasts are not killed by antibiotics.

Multicellular fungi (moulds)

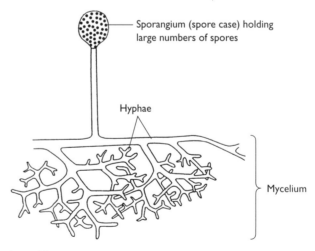

Fig. 8.5 Structure of mould

▷ each mould consists of a mycelium (mass of tangled threads called hyphae);
▷ the mycelium may be very large (many centimetres in diameter) but each of the hyphae is about one hundredth of a millimetre wide;
▷ the cells making up the mycelium have a proper nucleus, cytoplasm and cell membrane;

> they have organelles in their cytoplasm;
> they have a cell wall made of chitin;
> they are decomposers (feed on dead organisms and organic waste);
> they feed on external digestion. Enzymes are secreted from the tips of the hyphae, and these digest the food source. The digested nutrients are then absorbed back into the hyphae;
> moulds can reproduce in two ways, both of which involve making spores:
>   (a) asexually
>   (b) sexually
> moulds can be grown on nutrient agar or in nutrient broth in the laboratory;
> some moulds make antibiotics, e.g. penicillin;
> some moulds are useful in food production;
> some moulds cause disease in humans, e.g. athlete's foot;
> moulds are not killed by antibiotics.

Protoctists

Protoctists are simple, single-celled organisms.
Some are similar to animal cells, e.g. *Amoeba*, and some are similar to plant cells, e.g. *Chlorella*.

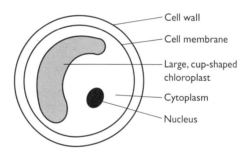

Fig. 8.6 Chlorella

> protoctists vary in size, but most are about a tenth of a millimetre long;
> the shape depends on the species; some are spherical, some are oval, some are ribbon-shaped;
> they have a proper nucleus, cytoplasm and cell membrane;
> they have organelles in their cytoplasm. Some have chloroplasts, so they can photosynthesise;
> some have a cell wall made of cellulose;
> most of them live in soil or water;
> some feed on food particles from their surroundings and others photosynthesise to make food;
> they reproduce in two ways:
>   (a) asexually by binary fission
>   (b) sexually (only a few species can reproduce sexually)
> protoctists can be grown in the laboratory:
>   (a) in a solution of sugars and minerals if they are 'animal like',
>   (b) in a mineral solution in the light if they are 'plant like';
> most protoctists do not affect humans directly, i.e. do not cause benefit or harm, but they are very important links in food chains;
> a few protoctists cause human diseases, e.g. malaria, sleeping sickness, dysentery;
> protoctists are not killed by antibiotics.

REVISION ACTIVITY I   (a) Complete this table about the features of different types of micro-organisms. Fill in the boxes with ✓, ✗, or 'S' for sometimes.

Features	Bacteria	Viruses	Fungi	Protoctists
are unicellular	✓	✓		
have a cell wall	✓	✗	✓	✓
have a proper nucleus	✗	✗	✓	✓
have cytoplasm	✓	✗	✓	✓
have organelles				
reproduce asexually	✓	✓	✓	✓
reproduce sexually	✗	✗	✓	✓
are useful to humans	✓	✗	✓	✗
are harmful to humans	✓	✓	✓	✓
are killed by antibiotics	✓	✗	✗	✗

(b) Put these microbes into size order, smallest first
    bacteria, viruses, algae, yeasts

Smallest ___v, b, y, a_____

REVISION ACTIVITY 2 Match up each of these terms with a type of micro-organism:

mould F	envelope ✓	chloroplasts P
capsid V	slime capsule b	mycelium F
sporangium F	hyphae F	bacillus b
polyhedral V	replicate V	chitin F
malaria P	decomposer b	AIDS V

Growing microbes in the lab

It is quite easy to grow bacteria, fungi and protoctists in the laboratory. They all need:

▶ a source of carbon, nitrogen and minerals;
▶ air;
▶ a suitable temperature.

Bacteria

Bacteria can be grown in a liquid, e.g. nutrient broth, or on the surface of a solid, e.g. nutrient agar. The nutrient broth or agar contains a carbon source (sugar), a nitrogen source (amino acids or ammonium salts) and minerals.

Bacteria grow best at a temperature of 25–35°C.

If they are grown on nutrient agar, **colonies** form. These are clones consisting of thousands of individual bacteria, all descended from one bacterium by asexual reproduction.

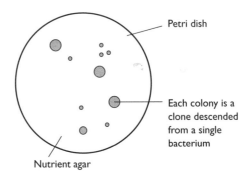

Fig. 8.7 Colonies of bacteria

Fungi

Fungi can be grown in a liquid, e.g. nutrient broth or on the surface of a solid, e.g. nutrient agar. The nutrient broth or agar contains a carbon source (sugar or starch), a nitrogen source (amino acids or ammonium salts) and minerals.

Fungi can grow well at lower temperatures than bacteria (20–25°C), but grow best at 25–35°C. Some fungi, e.g. yeasts, can grow without oxygen. In these circumstances they carry out **fermentation** (see p. 311).

If multicellular fungi are grown on nutrient agar, round patches of fungal growth are visible. This is the mycelium made up of thousands of minute hyphae.

Protoctists, e.g. algae

Algae, e.g. *Chlorella* can be grown in liquid when exposed to light (*Chlorella* uses light for photosynthesis). The liquid must contain a nitrogen source, e.g. ammonium salts and minerals.

Viruses

It is much more difficult to grow viruses than bacteria, fungi or protoctists, because viruses need living host cells in order to function properly. They get inside the host cells and replicate there, before killing the host cells as they emerge.

It is possible to keep viruses in the laboratory in one of three ways:

1. by infecting hens eggs with the virus, and allowing the virus to grow on the embryo and egg membranes (this is suitable for some animal viruses);
2. by infecting plants with the virus (this is suitable for plant viruses, e.g. tobacco mosaic virus);
3. by infecting bacteria with the virus (this is suitable for bacteriophages – viruses which use bacteria as their host).

Sterile technique

There are a series of steps you should follow to:

(a) avoid contaminating the microbes you want to grow with other organisms;
(b) avoid allowing the microbes you are growing to escape.

- wash your hands with soap and hot water before and after microbiology practicals;
- wipe the bench surface with disinfectant before and after microbiology practicals;
- keep windows and doors closed;
- report any spillages or breakages at once, and use disinfectant when they are cleared up;
- sterilise all growth media, e.g. nutrient agar, nutrient broth, and containers before use (by autoclaving them);
- never touch a growing medium, e.g. nutrient agar, or breathe directly over it;
- always work close to a lighted Bunsen burner;
- sterilise all instruments, e.g. wire loops, glass spreaders, etc. before and after use. Do this by dipping in alcohol and flaming (for glass instruments), or heating until they glow red (for metal instruments);
- tape petri dish lids securely, and label clearly;
- do not open petri dishes after incubation unless you are told to do so;
- dispose of unopened petri dishes by autoclaving or burning.

Patterns of growth

When bacteria, fungi or algae are grown in the laboratory, the following stages can be identified.

1. Lag phase:

   - growth is slow;
   - microbes are getting used to the new conditions;
   - microbes are making enzymes.

2. Log phase:

   - growth is rapid;
   - microbes are reproducing as quickly as possible (maximum rate = every 20 minutes);
   - nutrients are not scarce.

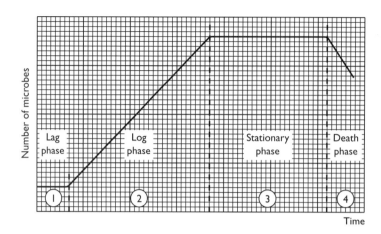

Fig. 8.8

3. Stationary phase:

> ▶ growth slows down;
> ▶ reproduction rate equals death rate, so numbers stay constant;
> ▶ this may be due to shortage of nutrients or oxygen, or a build up of waste products.

4. Death phase:

> ▶ numbers fall as an increasing number of microbes die;
> ▶ this is usually due to the build up of toxic waste products.

Factors affecting growth rate
There are seven main factors:

1. availability of food;
2. availability of oxygen;
3. temperature;
4. pH;
5. build up of waste products;
6. light (for algae only);
7. presence of chemicals, e.g. antibiotics, antiseptics, etc.

REVISION ACTIVITY 3

The table below shows the number of living yeast cells in a culture solution during a 24-hour period. The temperature of the solution was kept constant throughout the experiment.

Time (hours):	2	4	6	8	10	12	14	16	18	20	24
Number of living yeast cells (millions per ml):	10	60	90	200	400	600	650	700	700	50	0

(a) On a sheet of graph paper, plot a graph to show the changes in the population of yeast.

(b) Use the graph to estimate:
   (i) the number of yeast 7 hours after the beginning of the experiment
   (ii) the time taken for the population to reach 500 million cells per ml of culture solution
   (iii) how long the log phase lasted.

(c) Suggest two reasons for the changes in the yeast population during the last 8 hours of the experiment:

(d) What would be a suitable temperature for the culture solution?

> ### Key points
>
> ▷ microbes can enter the body in infected food or water, through wounds to the skin or by natural body openings;
>
> ▷ good hygiene can reduce infection levels;
>
> ▷ food preservation techniques and careful food handling can reduce food poisoning;
>
> ▷ bacteria, viruses, fungi and protoctists can all cause diseases in humans;
>
> ▷ the body responds to infection by destroying pathogens (this is immunity);
>
> ▷ bacteria can be killed by antibiotics.

Important terms

Make sure you understand the meaning of the following important terms:

pathogen:	an organism which causes disease.
antibody:	chemical made by white blood cells (lymphocytes) to kill pathogens.
antigen:	the part of the pathogen which lymphocytes recognise as 'foreign' or 'non-self'. It is usually a protein marker on the surface of the pathogen.
toxins:	poisons produced by pathogens.
antibiotics:	chemicals which kill bacteria. They do not kill viruses or fungi.
immunity:	the body's defences against disease.
immune response:	production of antibodies by white blood cells.
vector:	an animal which passes on a disease, but does not suffer from it itself, e.g. mosquitoes are vectors for malaria.

Entry of pathogens

Pathogens can enter the body through natural openings, or through wounds.

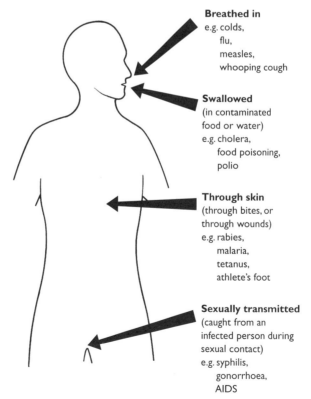

Breathed in
e.g. colds,
    flu,
    measles,
    whooping cough

Swallowed
(in contaminated
food or water)
e.g. cholera,
    food poisoning,
    polio

Through skin
(through bites, or
through wounds)
e.g. rabies,
    malaria,
    tetanus,
    athlete's foot

Sexually transmitted
(caught from an
infected person during
sexual contact)
e.g. syphilis,
    gonorrhoea,
    AIDS

Fig. 8.9 Transmission of diseases

Avoiding infection

Although it is impossible to avoid some pathogens, e.g. airborne pathogens which are inhaled, there are several simple steps that can be taken to avoid infection.

Personal hygiene
▶   Always wash hands after using the lavatory.
▶   Always wash hands before preparing food or eating.
▶   Wash hair, skin and clothes regularly.

Domestic hygiene
▶   Keep work surfaces and food preparation areas clean.
▶   Disinfect sinks, baths and toilets regularly.
▶   Vacuum carpets or sweep floors regularly.
▶   Do not allow household refuse to build up.

Water treatment and sewage treatment
▶   Drinking water should be fit for the purpose, i.e. it should not contain pathogens. In Britain drinking water is treated with chlorine before being pumped to holding tanks.
▶   Sewage should be treated to remove pathogens and organic matter before being released into rivers or the sea.

Food storage and preparation
▶   Food should be stored at low temperatures and prepared in clean conditions to avoid contamination.
▶   See p. 303 for further details of this.

Contact with infected individuals
▶   Contact should be avoided wherever possible.
▶   Towels, bedding, cups, etc. should not be shared, and should be washed in hot water.
▶   Infected people should avoid coughing or sneezing on others (many pathogens are airborne).
▶   Condoms will help to prevent the spread of sexually transmitted diseases.

Immunisation
▶   It is possible to be immunised (vaccinated) against many common diseases.
▶   See p. 308 for further details of this.

Food preservation and spoilage

Food preservation

Many of the foods we buy have been treated in some way to prevent them being broken down by microbes. This keeps the food fresh for longer, and helps to prevent disease. The micro-organisms which make food go off are called decomposers (bacteria and fungi).

There are nine main methods of food preservation (see Table 8.1):

1.   freezing
2.   drying
3.   canning
4.   vacuum packing
5.   salting
6.   sugaring
7.   pickling
8.   pasteurisation
9.   irradiation

Most of these methods rely on the fact that decomposers need **oxygen**, **water** and a suitable **temperature** to carry out the process of decay.

Food spoilage

If food is attacked by decomposers, chemicals in it are broken down, and this is called food spoilage. This is a problem for two reasons:

1.   the food looks and smells different, and becomes unfit to eat;
3.   if it is eaten, it could cause food poisoning.

Table 8.1 Methods of food preservation

Methods	Used for...	How it works	Why it works
Freezing	meat, bread, fruit, fish	Food is kept at a low temperature (–18°c)	Decomposers cannot break food down at this temperature (it is too cold for enzymes to work).
Drying	milk, potato, soup, custard, fruit	Water is removed from the food	Decomposers need water to break down food.
Canning	fruit, meat, fish, vegetables	Food is cooked and stored in airtight cans	Decomposers are killed when food is cooked. Cans are sealed so no more can enter.
Vacuum packing	bacon, cold meats, cheese	Food is sealed inside packages without air.	Decomposers need oxygen to break down food.
Salting	meat, fish	Food is packed in strong salt solution (brine).	Osmosis causes decomposers to lose water. They die.
Sugaring	fruit (jam)	Food is packed in strong sugar solution.	Osmosis causes decomposers to lose water. They die.
Pickling	vegetables, eggs	Food is packed in vinegar (acid).	Decomposers cannot survive in acid.
Pasteurisation	milk	Milk is heated to a high temperature, then bottles/cartons sealed.	Decomposers are killed when milk is heated. Containers are sealed so no more can enter.
Irradiation	fresh fruit and fish	Pre-packed food is treated with gamma-rays.	Decomposers are killed, and no more can enter the sealed packages.

Food poisoning
This occurs for one of two reasons:

1. there are large amounts of live bacteria on the food when it is eaten;
2. the food contains large amounts of toxins (produced by bacteria which may have later been killed by food processing).

Both the bacteria and the toxins can cause the symptoms of food poisoning

e.g. vomiting and diarrhoea,
       high temperature
       abdominal pain.

In babies, young children and elderly or ill adults food poisoning can cause serious illness. Severe vomiting and diarrhoea can cause dehydration which can be fatal.

Case Study: Salmonella food poisoning
Salmonella is a type of bacteria that lives in the gut of some animals, e.g. chickens, turkeys.
     If live bacteria are eaten by humans, they can cause serious food poisoning (symptoms: vomiting, diarrhoea).

How are the bacteria transferred to food?

▶ The bacteria are often present in the gut of poultry (they do not cause disease in these animals), i.e. the birds are **infected.**
▶ If the birds are kept in enclosed spaces, e.g. in a factory farm, faeces (containing large amount of bacteria) will accumulate in the bottom of cages or pens.
▶ The birds' feet will pick up these bacteria (from the faeces) and they will be transferred to the bird's skin so the chicken and turkeys you buy may have skin covered with *Salmonella* bacteria.

Also, when the dead poultry is being prepared for sale, the gut will be removed. If this contains *Salmonella* bacteria, they may spread into the body cavity or onto the skin. In addition, birds infected with *Salmonella* may produce infected **eggs.** If these eggs are eaten raw, e.g. in mousse, ice-cream, meringues, cake mixture, a person may be infected.

How are humans harmed?

If **large** numbers of bacteria are ingested, they enter the cells lining the small intestines. They kill these cells and prevent efficient absorption of digested food. The person is likely to be sick and to suffer from diarrhoea. Most people recover within seven days, but food poisoning can be very dangerous for babies, pregnant women, elderly people and those who are already ill.

How can food poisoning be avoided?

- Store food at low temperatures, i.e. in a fridge.
- Cook it thoroughly to kill bacteria.
- If it is not to be eaten immediately; cover it, cool it, and put it back into the fridge.
- Always defrost food thoroughly before cooking it.
- Avoid contaminating food, e.g. with knifes, chopping boards or hands which may have bacteria on them.
- Never use food which is past its 'use-by-date'.

REVISION ACTIVITY 4 | Explain why

(a) You should always defrost frozen food thoroughly before cooking it.

(b) You should store meat in a cold place, e.g. in a fridge.

(c) You should never re-freeze frozen food which has defrosted.

(d) Bread goes mouldy faster than biscuits stored in the same way.

(e) Irradiated foods may still cause food poisoning.

Bacterial infections

Bacterial infections include: cholera
tuberculosis (TB)
salmonella
tetanus
whooping cough
diphtheria.

Table 8.2

Disease	Caught by	Avoid infection by	Symptoms of infection
Cholera	drinking contaminated water	proper water treatment, or boil all water	vomiting and diarrhoea; can be fatal
TB	inhaling bacteria or direct contact with an infected person	immunisation	affects the lungs (coughing) and bones; can be fatal
Salmonella	eating infected food	good food hygiene cooking food properly	vomiting and diarrhoea
Tetanus	bacteria entering through wounds in the skin	immunisation	muscular spasms and convulsions; can be fatal
Whooping cough	inhaling bacteria	immunisation	affects the lungs and causes severe coughing; may be fatal in babies
Diphtheria	inhaling bacteria	immunisation	affects the respiratory system – causes difficulty in breathing; may damage the heart, kidneys and liver

Bacteria can multiply inside the body, and may produce toxins (poisons) which cause the symptoms of illness. Bacteria infections can be treated with **antibiotics.**

Viral infections

Viral infections include: influenza
                            hepatitis B
                            measles
                            polio
                            common cold
                            AIDS

Table 8.3

Disease	Caught by	Avoid infection by	Symptoms of infection
Influenza	inhaling virus	avoiding infected people, immunisation	fever, aching, sore throat, coughing
Hepatitis B	sexual contact, contact with infected blood	immunisation, use of condoms, avoid sharing needles in drug use	liver damage, nausea, vomiting
Measles	inhaling virus	immunisation, avoid infected people	red rash, sneezing, fever
Polio	drinking contaminated water, or eating contaminated food	immunisation	paralysis
Common cold	inhaling virus	avoid infected people	fever, sneezing, coughing
AIDS	sexual contact, contact with infected blood	use of condoms, avoid sharing needles in drug use	damage to immune system

Viruses invade living cells and replicate inside them. The cells are then killed when large numbers of virus particles are released. Each of these new virus particles can go on to infect another body cell, so tissues in the body are damaged as more and more cells die.

Virus infections cannot be treated with antibiotics. Anti-viral drugs do exist, but they often have bad side-effects for the person taking them, so they are only used for serious diseases.

Fungal infections

Fungal infections include: athlete's foot
                             thrush

Table 8.4

Disease	Caught by	Avoid infection by	Symptoms of infection
Athlete's foot	contact with fungi/ fungal spores from damp floors,etc. e.g. changing rooms	wear shoes (do not walk in bare feet), dry feet properly after exercise	skin becomes soft and breaks, especially between toes, itching
Thrush	The yeast lives in the gut of most people but can be transferred to (a) babies mouths (b) vagina of women		creamy patches inside the mouth thick, itchy vaginal discharge

Fungal infections usually affect the skin or body openings, e.g. mouth, vagina. The yeast which causes thrush lives in the gut of most people without causing illness, but if the number of yeast cells increases dramatically, or if it is transferred to the mouth or vagina, it can cause problems. Thrush is particularly common in pregnant women, women taking the contraceptive pill, women taking antibiotics and diabetics.

Fungal infection cannot be treated with antibiotics. Anti-fungal drugs (tablets or cream for the infected area) are effective.

Protoctist infections

Protoctist infections include: dysentery
malaria.

Table 8.5

Disease	Caught by	Avoid infection by	Symptoms of infection
Dysentery	eating contaminated food (flies spread the protoctist)	Cooking food properly, covering it to prevent contamination by flies	vomiting, diarrhoea, fever
Malaria	protoctist is passed on by mosquito bites	use insect repellent or mosquito nets, take anti-malaria tablets	Fever, damage to red blood cells and to liver

Malaria

Malaria is caused by the protoctist *Plasmodium*. This enters the body after a bite from an infected mosquito. The *Plasmodia* invade red blood cells and multiply inside them. When they burst out of the red blood cells, toxins are released and the person has a fever. The *Plasmodia* then infect more red blood cells and liver cells. causing serious damage. If the infected person is bitten by another mosquito which sucks their blood, *Plasmodia* are transferred to another mosquito ready to infect another human.

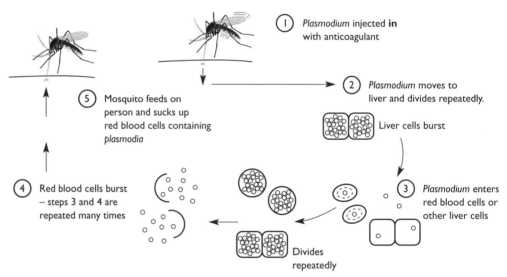

Fig. 8.9 Transmission of malaria (Plasmodium)

Mosquitoes act as **vectors** – they do not suffer from the disease, but they carry it from one person to another.

Malaria is a serious disease which kills about 2 million people each year.. It can be avoided by:

▶ avoiding being bitten, e.g. use insect repellent or mosquito nets;
▶ killing *Plasmodia* in the body, e.g. use anti-malaria drugs;
▶ killing mosquitoes, e.g. with insecticide;
▶ preventing mosquitoes breeding, e.g. by draining swamps.

Immunity

This is the way that the body fights infection. We can look at two main aspects:

1. natural immunity
2. artificial immunity.

Natural immunity (see also p. 121)
The body deals with infection in four main ways:

1. Barriers to infection

These are defences which protect the body from invasion by pathogens,
e.g. ▶ acid in the stomach to kill pathogens which enter in food or drink;
     ▶ cilia and mucus to trap pathogens which enter the respiratory tract;
     ▶ chemicals in tears and ear-wax to kill pathogens.

2. Phagocytosis

Some white blood cells (phagocytes) can locate, engulf and destroy pathogens.

3. Production of antibodies

Some white blood cells (lymphocytes) can produce chemicals called antibodies which
destroy pathogens. This is called the **immune response**.

4. Killing virus infected cells

Some white blood cells (T-lymphocytes) kill the person's own cells which have been
infected by viruses. This is **cell-mediated immunity**.

How does the immune response work?

▶ Lymphocytes are programmed to recognise 'foreign' or 'non-self' cells within the
   body. They can do this because all the cells of an individual have unique protein
   markers on the surface; foreign cells will have the wrong markers, so lymphocytes will
   recognise them as foreign.
▶ A lymphocyte which has recognised a foreign cell is said to be sensitised.
▶ It will divide repeatedly to form a clone of cells. Some of these will become **B-lymphocytes** which can make antibodies. Others will become **memory cells** which stay in the
   body for a long time, and can make the correct antibodies in the future.
▶ Antibodies travel around the body in the blood. They will stick to foreign cells or
   toxins and destroy them.
▶ If the same pathogen infects the body in the future, memory cells will start to make
   antibodies against it immediately.

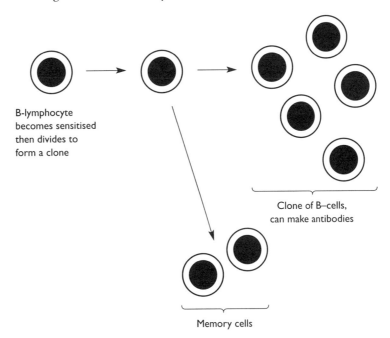

B-lymphocyte
becomes sensitised
then divides to
form a clone

Clone of B–cells,
can make antibodies

Memory cells

Fig. 8.10 B-lymphocytes and the production of antibodies

Antibodies can pass across the placenta from the mother to the foetus to protect it from
pathogens before it is born. If a women breastfeeds her baby, there are antibodies in breast
milk, so it is protected against pathogens.

Any material which causes lymphocytes to make antibodies is called an **antigen**.

Artificial immunity

Here the efficiency of the immune system is being improved by **vaccination** (immunisation). The purpose of a vaccine is to cause antibody production without causing the symptoms of the disease.

What are vaccines?

A vaccine contains antigens (material from a pathogen) which will protect humans from future infection. There are five main ways of making vaccines

▷   inject the dead pathogen into the body;
▷   inject live non-virulent pathogen into the body – this is a weakenened strain which will not cause disease (developed by selective breeding);
▷   inject modified toxin into the body – this has been chemically changed so it will not cause disease;
▷   inject fragments of pathogen into the body – these will not cause disease;
▷   inject safe antigens which have been made by genetic engineering.

How do vaccines work?

The vaccine contains **antigens**, but it is not capable of causing disease. When it is injected into the body, lymphocytes recognise the antigens as 'non-self', and make antibodies to destroy them. This is the **primary response**. Memory cells then remain in the blood for a long time: these cells are capable of recognising the same antigens if it ever enters the body again, and producing antibodies immediately.

If at some time in the future, the **pathogen** enters the body, memory cells recognise the antigens on its surface and antibodies are produced immediately. These destroy the pathogen before it makes the person ill; this is the **secondary response**.

There are three main differences between the primary response and the secondary response:

'Look at the graph showing primary and secondary response to infection on p. 124.'

1.   there is a delay before antibodies are produced in the primary response, but in the secondary response they are produced immediately;
2.   larger amounts of antibodies are produced in the secondary response;
3.   the antibodies remain in the blood for longer during the secondary response.

Memory cells remain in the body for several years, and they can 'remember' how to produce antibodies to destroy a particular pathogen. However, with some pathogens, e.g. tetanus bacteria, it is necessary to have regular **booster vaccinations** to improve the immune response.

Immunity is sometimes classified as:

Innate immunity – defences which are continually present to prevent attack by pathogens, e.g. phagocytes in blood, acid in stomach.

Acquired immunity – defences which develop during life, e.g. antibodies. If you make your own antibodies, as a result of infection or vaccination, it is **active acquired immunity**. If you get 'ready made' antibodies, e.g. through breast-feeding, or through an injection of antibodies, it is **passive acquired immunity**. Antibodies are sometimes injected directly into people who have been exposed to serious infections, and who would not have enough time to make their own antibodies.

Cell-mediated immunity

This is another type of **natural immunity**. It involves **T-lymphocytes** (T-cells). These are lymphocytes which destroy pathogens (viruses) without making antibodies. They can detect a virus-infected cell, and will kill the whole cell – this prevents it making new virus particles (see Fig. 8.12).

T-cells will not attack virus particles unless they are inside the person's own cells.

A T-cell can recognise a virus infected cell because some viral marker proteins are left on the cell membrane. The T-cell is then sensitised and divides to form a clone of cells – there are different cell types within the clone: killer T-cells,
helper T-cells,
suppressor T-cells,
memory T-cells.

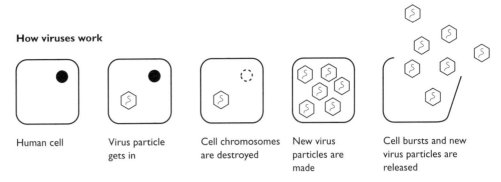

Fig. 8.11 How viruses work

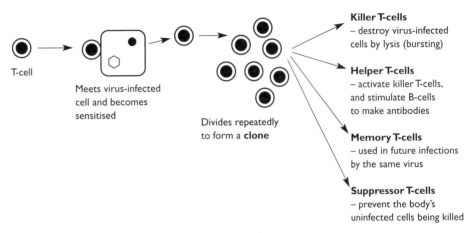

Fig. 8.12 T-cells and the distruction of infected cells

T-cells will also attack cancer cells and destroy them – this is because many cancer cells have 'faulty' (i.e. non-self) protein markers on them.

The disease **AIDS** (Acquired Immune Deficiency Syndrome) is caused by a virus (HIV) which attacks T-cells. It causes the breakdown of the whole immune system, and the person is likely to become ill with a variety of infections or types of cancer, and eventually will die from them.

Fighting infections with antibiotics

> **Key points**
>
> ▷ antibiotics are chemicals naturally made by fungi;
>
> ▷ antibiotics fight bacterial infections;
>
> ▷ some antibiotics kill bacteria; they are bacteriocidal;
>
> ▷ some antibiotics stop bacteria reproducing, they are bacteriostatic.

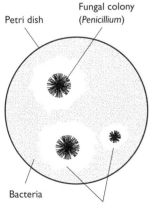

Fig. 8.13 Fungi make antibiotics

In 1928 Alexander Fleming (a Scottish scientist) made a very important discovery. He was growing bacteria in a petri dish on nutrient agar, and he found that the bacteria was unable to grow near to a fungus growing on the petri dish (see Fig. 8.13).

He deduced that the fungus, *Penicillium*, was making a chemical which was killing the bacteria; this was **penicillin**.

We now know that penicillin is a type of **antibiotic**; a chemical produced by fungi to kill bacteria. There are hundreds of different types of antibiotics, and some can be used as drugs to treat people with bacterial infections. It was not until more than ten years after Fleming discovered penicillin that it was first used to fight disease in humans. Two American scientists, Florey and Chain purified the antibiotic and calculated the dose needed to treat patients.

Antibiotics work in one of two ways:

1. some are bacteriocidal – they kill bacteria by damaging their cell walls;
2. some are bacteriostatic – they prevent bacteria reproducing by interfering with protein synthesis, or synthesis of cell membranes and cell walls, so the number of bacteria stays the same. These bacteria can then be killed by normal body defences, e.g. phagocytes, antibodies.

Problems with antibiotics
Bacteria can become resistant to them, so they no longer have any effect. This happens as a result of a **mutation** in the bacterial DNA, and it gives the bacterium a **selective advantage**, i.e. it is more likely to survive. The increase in the number of bacteria resistant to antibiotics has been linked to their over-use.

REVISION ACTIVITY 5

(a) Complete the sentences:
Malaria is a serious disease caused by a microbe called _____ which is a type of _____ . If a person is bitten by an infected female _____ , the pathogens enters the blood stream. It multiples in _____ cells and _____ cells. After a few days the infected cells burst open releasing more _____ and toxins. The toxins cause a fever, and the person feels very ill. More cells can be infected and this cycle is repeated over and over again. A person with malaria may suffer from anaemia because so many _____ cells have burst. The mosquito acts as a _____ because it carries the pathogen from one person to another.

(b) Suggest ways you could:
  (i)   prevent a person from being bitten;
  (ii) reduce the number of mosquitoes.

(c) Why are antibiotics not used to treat people with malaria?

REVISION ACTIVITY 6

(i)   Match up the diseases to the type of organism which cause them, e.g. bacteria, viruses, fungi, protoctists.

malaria	athlete's foot	cholera
flu	AIDS	thrush
measles	whooping cough	polio
TB	salmonella	hepatitis B

(ii) Which diseases could you treat with antibiotics?

(b) What is the difference between
  (i)   antibodies and antigens?
  (ii)   antibiotics and disinfectants?
  (iii) B-lymphocytes and T-lymphocytes?
  (iv)   active and passive immunity?
  (v)   innate and acquired immunity?

▷ **Biotechnology**   Biotechnology has been defined by the Department of Trade and Industry as 'the **exploitation of living organisms and biological processes**'. In simple terms this means using living organisms (usually micro-organisms) to make useful products for humans or to carry out important processes, e.g. sewage treatment. Some of the techniques now called biotechnology have been developed over thousands of years, e.g. brewing, whereas others are completely new inventions from the past 30 years, e.g. genetic engineering.

Key points

> biotechnology means using organisms (usually microbes) to make useful products, or to carry out important processes;

> moulds (fungi) are used to make antibiotics;

> yeasts (fungi) are used in brewing and baking;

> bacteria are used in yoghurt and cheese production, and to make vinegar;

> bacteria and fungi are used to manufacture enzymes;

> yeasts are used to make gasohol (fuel) from plant waste;

> bacteria are used to make biogas from domestic waste;

> bacteria and fungi are used in sewage treatment;

> bacteria and yeast have been modified by genetic engineering to produce useful products.

Fermentation by yeasts

See p. 296 for basic information on yeasts. Yeasts have been used for thousands of years in brewing and baking. When they are kept in anaerobic conditions (without oxygen), they ferment sugars like this:

$$\text{sugar} \longrightarrow \text{energy} + \text{carbon dioxide} + \text{ethanol}$$

Brewing

There are five main steps involved in alcohol production, e.g. wine production:

1. yeast and sugar are added to fruit juice;
2. it is kept in anaerobic conditions at a warm temperature;
3. yeast feeds on sugar, producing carbon dioxide and ethanol;
4. as ethanol builds up, it eventually kills the yeast, so fermentation stops;
5. dead yeasts are filtered off, and the wine is bottled.

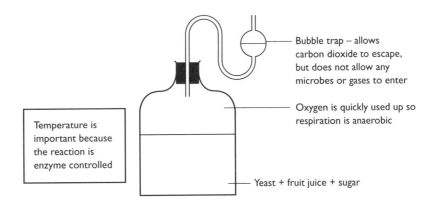

Bubble trap – allows carbon dioxide to escape, but does not allow any microbes or gases to enter

Oxygen is quickly used up so respiration is anaerobic

Temperature is important because the reaction is enzyme controlled

Yeast + fruit juice + sugar

Fig. 8.14 Making wine

REVISION ACTIVITY 7   Why is it important to

(a) add sugar?

(b) allow carbon dioxide to escape?

(c) keep the container at a warm temperature?

(d) have the container completely clean (sterile) when you start?

Baking

Bread is made from flour, water, salt and yeast. The yeast digests some of the starch (in flour) to make sugar, then uses the sugar for respiration. At first there may be oxygen present, but this is quickly used up, so fermentation (anaerobic respiration) occurs.

Due to mixing (kneading), the yeast is trapped inside the dough, and when it respires pockets of carbon dioxide are formed; this gives the bread a light texture.

There are six main steps involved in bread making

1. flour, water, salt and yeast are mixed to form a dough;
2. the dough is kneaded to distribute to yeast evenly;
3. it is put in a warm place for respiration to occur;
4. it is kneaded again – this helps to make the dough 'elastic', so the bread is light;
5. it is put in a warm place for respiration to occur. The dough will expand as carbon dioxide is produced;
6. it is baked. This sets the dough, trapping bubbles of carbon dioxide, and removes any trace of alcohol (it evaporates).

Antibiotic production

Antibiotics are chemicals made by moulds (fungi). They kill bacteria, and can be used as drugs to treat bacterial infections inside the body. The first antibiotic to be produced was made by the fungus *Penicillium*, so it was called **penicillin**. Today over a hundred different types of antibiotic have been discovered.

Growing fungi in a fermenter

To obtain large amounts of antibiotics, large amounts of fungi have to be grown. The most effective way to do this involves a large container called a fermenter.

Most fermenters have:

'Look at the diagram of a fermenter, Fig. 8.19 on p. 315.'

▷ a water-cooled jacket to remove the heat produced by microbes when they respire;
▷ stirring paddles;
▷ an air supply, because fungi need oxygen for respiration;
▷ probes to monitor temperature, pH, oxygen concentration and nutrient concentration so that conditions can be maintained at an optimum (ideal) level.

When are antibiotics produced?

Antibiotics are only produced when the growth of the fungus slows down (due to a lack of nutrients or a buildup of waste products).

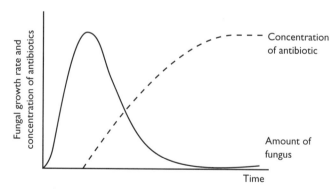

Fig. 8.15 Production of antibiotics

There are five main steps in antibiotic production:

1. add a starter culture of mould, e.g. *Penicillium*, to nutrients in a fermenter;
2. keep the fermenter at a suitable temperature, and monitor conditions carefully;
3. after 6–7 days, an antibiotic will have been produced;
4. empty the fermenter, and filter the contents to remove the mould;
5. purify the antibiotic, e.g. penicillin.

Foods from fungi
Fungi are involved in the production of several other types of food, e.g.

Mycoprotein

This is sometimes called single-cell protein. Fungi can be grown on a range of cheap or waste materials, e.g. sugar cane waste, dairy waste. The fungi can then be purified and processed for use as human or animal food. **Quorn** is an example of human food made of mycoprotein.

Advantages of using mycoprotein as a food source are:

▶ large amounts can be produced quickly in fermenters;
▶ it does not need large amounts of land as do growing crops or keeping animals;
▶ fungi feed on cheap or waste products, so it is economical to produce;
▶ mycoprotein has a high protein and fibre content, and it is low in fat.

Soy sauce

This is made from soya beans and wheat in a complex three-step fermentation process.

The final product is filtered to remove microbes, pasteurised then bottled for sale.

Yoghurt and cheese production

Both of these processes involve **lactic acid bacteria**. They feed on lactose (a sugar naturally found in milk) and convert it to lactic acid:

$$\text{lactose} \longrightarrow \text{lactic acid + energy}$$

Yoghurt production
There are three main steps in yoghurt production (see Fig. 8.16):

1. Pasteurisation

The milk is heated to about 90°c for 15–30 minutes to kill any microbes which may be present. The milk is then cooled.

2. Incubation with a starter culture

A starter culture of lactic acid bacteria, e.g. *Lactobacillus bulgaricus* and *Streptococcus thermophilus* is added, and the mixture is incubated at about 40°C for 4–6 hours, or at about 30°C for 12 hours. The lactic acid bacteria convert lactose in the milk to lactic acid, so the pH of the mixture falls to about 4.5. The acid conditions will denature milk proteins, so the mixture becomes thicker. It is now yoghurt.

3. Processing

The yoghurt is cooled and may have fruit, flavourings or colourings added to it, before being packed into containers. Some yoghurts are heat treated at this stage to kill microbes, and others are sold with 'live microbes' in them.

Cheese production
There are four main steps in cheese production:

1. Pasteurisation

The milk heated to about 70°C for 15 seconds to kill any microbes which may be present. The milk is then cooled.

2. Coagulation

A starter culture of **lactic acid bacteria**, e.g. *Streptococcus lactis* is added. This converts lactose in the milk into lactic acid, so the pH of the mixture falls. After about one hour **rennet** is added. This is an enzyme which coagulates milk protein (makes it solidify). Rennet can be obtained from calves' stomachs, or from genetically-engineered bacteria.

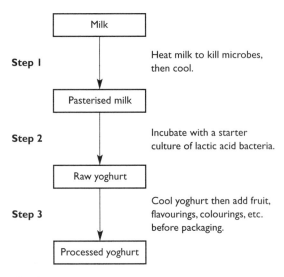

Fig. 8.16 Yoghurt production

The coagulated milk protein is called **curd**, and the watery liquid it separates from is **whey** (remember Miss Muffett!). Whey can be used in animal feed.

3. Curd extraction

The curds are collected and cut into small pieces, then heated to remove more whey. Salt is added before the cheese is pressed into moulds.

4. Ripening

The cheese is stored for up to one year to allow flavour to develop. This happens because enzymes in the milk or microbes in the cheese break down chemicals releasing waste products which have a strong flavour. For some varieties of cheese, microbes are deliberately added,

e.g. *Penicillium camemberti* to Camembert cheese, yeasts and moulds on the surface of brie, bacteria injected into Emmental cheese to make holes!

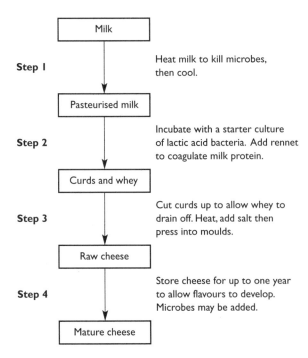

Fig. 8.17

Vinegar production

The chemical named for vinegar is acetic acid (ethanoic acid). It is made when **acetic acid bacteria** change ethanol (in wine or beer) into acetic acid. This is an aerobic process, so oxygen must be present.

ethanol + oxygen ⎯⎯⎯⎯⎯→ ethanoic acid + water + energy

Acetobacter is one type of bacteria which can do this.

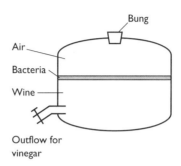

Fig. 8.18 Traditional method of vinegar production

Traditionally, barrels containing alcoholic drinks, e.g. beer, wine or cider were partly filled (so there was an air space), and a starter culture of *Acetobacter* was added. This grew on the surface of the liquid (in contact with the air) and converted the ethanol to vinegar. It was a very slow process, taking several weeks.

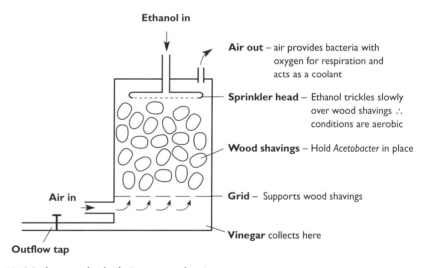

Fig. 8.19 Modern method of vinegar production

The modern method uses a **fermenter** loosely packed with wood shavings. The wood shavings are covered with a film of *Acetobacter*. Air is pumped upwards through the fermenter, and ethanol (in beer, wine, cider, etc.) is sprinkled through the fermenter from the top. The liquid which collects at the bottom of the fermenter may be recycled, i.e. may go through the fermenter more than once, to make sure that all ethanol has been converted to vinegar. This process takes 4–5 days.

Enzymes

Enzymes are protein produced by living cells. They act as **catalysts** – this means that they speed up the rate of chemical reactions. Enzymes work best at a particular temperature (called the optimum temperature), and at a particular pH. See also pp. 37–8.

Production of enzymes by micro-organisms

Biotechnology often involves production of large amounts of enzymes by microbes. Microbes are well suited for this because:

▷   they grow quickly, so can make large amounts of enzymes;
▷   they are easy to grow in fermenters;
▷   they can be fed on cheap or waste material;
▷   they can be modified by genetic engineering to produce different types of enzymes.

Examples of enzymes made in this way include:

▷   protease and lipase enzymes for use in biological washing powders;
▷   rennin for use in cheese making (for vegetarian cheese);
▷   enzymes for use in medical tests, e.g. to estimate blood cholesterol levels or blood glucose level.

Use of enzymes in manufacturing processes

Enzymes are an important part of many manufacturing processes, e.g.

▷   protease enzymes are used to pre-digest protein in some baby foods;
▷   protease enzymes are used in meat-tenderisers and marinades;
▷   sucrase enzyme is used to digest sucrose in the manufacture of soft-centred sweets;
▷   pectinase enzymes are used to extract juice from some fruits;
▷   enzymes are also important in   brewing,
                                      cheese making,
                                      textiles.

In industry, enzymes are used to make processes more economical, i.e. to bring about reactions more quickly, or at lower temperatures or pressures than normal.
    Industrial processes may:

▷   use whole micro-organisms containing enzymes, e.g. yeasts or bacteria;
▷   use enzymes extracted from living cells and trapped in beads (immobilised enzymes).

Both of these systems enable the enzymes to be re-used many times, and keep them separate from the product, i.e. prevent contamination of the product.

Gasohol

Gasohol is the name given to vehicle fuel produced by microbes. It is made when **yeasts** ferment plant waste, e.g. sugar cane waste in **anaerobic conditions**. The process takes place in large fermenters and dilute **ethanol** is produced; this can then be distilled.

       sugar ⟶ ethanol + carbon dioxide + energy

There are four main steps in gasohol production:

1.   **Collect plant waste,** e.g. cassava roots, sawdust, waste straw, molasses.
2.   **Treat it with enzymes** to break down complex carbohydrates and form glucose. This step is not necessary if the plant waste already contains sugars. Extract the sugars.
3.   **Add yeast to the sugars in the fermenter.** In anaerobic conditions ethanol will be produced.
4.   **Distill the dilute ethanol** to give pure ethanol which can be used as fuel.

This process was first carried out on a large scale in Brazil during the 1970s, and now all Brazilian cars are converted to use this fuel. It is particularly successful in Brazil because:

▷   the climate and agricultural system produce large amounts of sugar cane;
▷   there is a large quantity of plant waste available for fermentation;
▷   the plant waste left after removal of sugar can be burned to provide energy for the distillation stage

At the moment ethanol produced in this way is relatively expensive compared with oil, but there are some advantages to using it, e.g.

▷   it is a renewable energy source and will not run out;
▷   it is a profitable way of using plant waste;
▷   it produces less pollutants than oil or petrol.

It is possible that **genetically engineered yeasts** will be more efficient and increase the yield of ethanol in the future.

Biogas

Biogas is the name given to a mixture of methane and carbon dioxide produced by microbes. It is made when **bacteria** break down organic material in almost **anaerobic conditions**. This process does not require complex equipment, and has been used on a small scale for hundreds of years in some communities. Any organic material can be used, e.g. plant waste, animal dung, human faeces. The waste is put into a **digester** with a starter culture of bacteria, e.g. *Methanobacterium*, and left for several months.

Biogas digesters usually have the following features:

▶   They are underground; this strengthens the walls and keeps heat in.
▶   They are situated away from homes because
    (a)   methane is flammable and there is a risk of explosion,
    (b)   the decomposing organic waste smells unpleasant.
▶   They have very thick walls (so that they do not crack as gas is produced).
▶   There is an inlet pipe to add waste.
▶   There is an outlet pipe where gas can be trapped or removed for storage.
▶   It must be possible to open the digester periodically so that sludge can be removed.

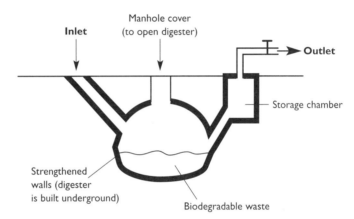

Fig. 8.20 Production of biogas

When organic waste is added to the digester bacteria break down proteins, carbohydrates and fats, producing methane (CH_4) and carbon dioxide. This can be used as domestic fuel, e.g. for heating and lighting, or it can be compressed for use in cars and tractors.

Some of the waste will not decompose fully and is known as **sludge**. It contains large amounts of minerals and can be used as fertiliser. A small amount of sludge is normally left in the digester when it is cleaned out; this contains bacteria which will act as a starter culture for the next batch of organic waste.

Using organic waste to make biogas is an advantage because:

▶   the raw material is a waste product, i.e. cheap and freely available;
▶   it reduces the amount of rubbish to be disposed of;
▶   the product can be used as domestic fuel, e.g. for heating or lighting, so it reduces the consumption of other fuels;
▶   the process is simple and requires no complex equipment;
▶   methane is a 'clean fuel' when it is burned.

Sewage treatment

The purpose of sewage treatment is to remove harmful materials from sewage, so that clean water can be returned to rivers or the sea.

What is sewage?

Sewage is defined as human faeces and urine, with waste domestic water, e.g. from washing, washing up, washing clothes, etc., and some rain water. (Detergents contain phosphates, faeces and urine contains nitrates.)

Industrial or factory waste may also be washed into the sewage system.

Why is sewage treatment important?

Although almost 99% of the material we call sewage is water, it is contaminated with a huge variety of other substances. These will cause serious problems if they are released into rivers or the sea because:

▶ Sewage contains large amounts of organic material, and decomposers in the water break it down. This requires lots of oxygen so deoxygenation of water occurs and fish and other animals die.

▶ Sewage contains large amounts of minerals particularly phosphates and nitrates so algae and other plants grow very rapidly (this is **eutrophication**). When the plants die, decomposers break them down, so the water becomes deoxygenated and animals die.

▶ The water becomes cloudy, and less light can penetrate. This affects plants because there is less light for photosynthesis and animals because gills and feeding mechanisms can become clogged.

How does sewage treatment occur?

Modern sewage disposal uses **decomposers** (bacteria and fungi) and potozoa to remove organic matter and minerals from sewage effluent. The clean water that remains can then be returned to rivers.

Sewage treatment is in four main stages:

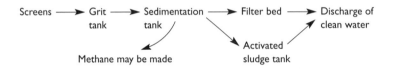

Fig. 8.21

Stage 1: **Screens** remove sticks, paper, rags, plastic, etc.

Stage 2: **Grit tank** – rate of flow is reduced by baffles, so grit and stones sink. These can be cleaned and returned to the environment.

Stage 3: **Sedimentation tanks** (usually several) – sewage remains still in tanks and faeces sink to form **sludge**. This may be
 (i) dried to form fertiliser,
 (ii) dumped at sea,
 (iii) digested by bacteria to form methane gas (anaerobic digestion) – this can be a valuable fuel.
 Liquid effluent goes on for further treatment.

Stage 4: There are two alternative methods which can be used at this stage depending on the amount of effluent to be treated and the time available:
 (a) **Activated sludge tank**
 Liquid effluent is pumped into a large tank and a 'starter culture' of decomposers is added. Oxygen is bubbled through the tank or the effluent is pumped into the air to aerate it. The decomposers feed on the organic matter and minerals, and clean water is released.
 (b) **Filter bed**
 The tank is full of gravel and stones (clinker). Around each stone is a slimy layer of bacteria, fungi and protozoa. A sprinkler arm trickles the liquid effluent down through the bed. Decomposers feed on the organic matter and minerals and clean water is released. Many invertebrates, e.g. worms/insects also live in the bed.

 The sludge obtained in Stage 3 of the process can be used to make methane (**biogas**) by anaerobic digestion. See p. 317 for details of this process.

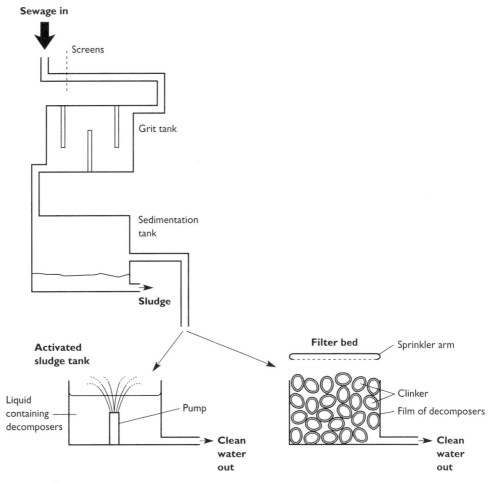

Fig. 8.22 Sewage treatment

Genetic engineering

See p. 202 for details of the techniques of genetic engineering.

Genetic engineering is the transfer of DNA from one organism (the **donor**) to another organism (the **recipient**) so the recipient acquires new characteristics.

Currently there are many cases of successful products made by genetic engineering and many which still at a research or development stage.

In medicine

▶ Production of **insulin** by genetically engineered bacteria. The insulin can be used to treat diabetics.
▶ Production of **human growth hormone** by genetically engineered bacteria.
▶ Tests for **genetic diseases**, e.g. cystic fibrosis using recombinant DNA technology.
▶ Tests for **infectious diseases**, e.g. AIDS, using recombinant DNA technology.
▶ Production of **monoclonal antibodies** by hybridoma cells which can be used to:
  (a) identify people who are carriers (heterozygous) for some genetic diseases;
  (b) identify tumour cells at any early stage of development;
  (c) target anti-cancer drugs on tumour cells.
▶ Production of genetically engineered fruits and vegetables which contain antigens, so they act as **vaccines**.
▶ Production of transgenic animals for use in **organ transplants**.

In agriculture

▶ To develop plants which are suited to particular growing conditions, e.g. can grow at cooler temperatures than normal.
▶ To develop crops which are **disease resistant**, so yields will be increased.
▶ To develop crops which are **herbicide resistant** so fields can be sprayed and crops will not be affected.

▷ To transfer genes for **nitrogen fixation** to plants so that nitrogenous fertilizers would not need to be used.

▷ To develop cattle with a **high meat-to-fat ratio** which grow quickly.

▷ To develop cows which produce **low cholesterol milk** or milk containing antibodies.

▷ To develop animals which are **disease resistant**.

In food production

▷ To develop crops which have a **long shelf-life**, e.g. tomatoes.

▷ To develop genetically engineered **rennet** which is used in cheese making.

Other uses

▷ Production of **enzymes** for use in industrial processes by genetically modified microbes.

▷ Production of new strains of yeast which are more efficient at **fermentation**, for use in gasohol and alcohol production.

▷ Genetic fingerprinting using recombinant DNA techniques – this is analysis of an individual's unique DNA pattern, allowing very accurate identification to take place.

REVISION ACTIVITY 8 It is sometimes necessary for members of a family to prove that they are related. One way in which scientists can help is by 'DNA fingerprinting'.

(a) What is the function of DNA in a cell?

(b) In a 'DNA fingerprinting' test cells were taken from the mother, the husband and the child. The cells were broken open and DNA fragments were extracted. The DNA fragments in each sample were separated into a column of bands, called a DNA fingerprint. The diagram below shows a DNA fingerprint of each member of the family. The bands have been numbered to help you answer the questions which follow.

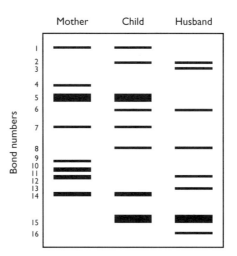

Fig. 8.23 DNA fingerprints

(i) Which of the bands in the child's DNA fingerprint are in exactly the same position as the bands in the mother's DNA fingerprint?

(ii) Explain why some of the bands in the mother's DNA fingerprint are absent from the child's DNA fingerprint.

(iii) The bands in the child's DNA fingerprint which are absent from the mother's DNA fingerprint must have been inherited from the child's natural father. Does the husband's DNA fingerprint show that he is the child's father? Explain your answer.

(c) DNA fingerprinting can be used to prove paternity (whether a man is the father of a child). Give three other uses of genetic finger-printing.

▷ **Movement and support**

You should also read pp. 55–57 about movement in Section 4.1.

Key points

▷ movement is one of the characteristics of living things – all organisms can move at least part of themselves;

▷ many animals have a skeleton to help support the body, and to aid movement;

▷ vertebrates have an internal skeleton with a backbone – invertebrates may have a hydrostatic skeleton (based on fluid) or a tough external covering called an exoskeleton;

▷ wherever two or more bones meet, a joint occurs. There are different types of joints with different ranges of movement;

▷ muscles can contract to pull bones closer together. Muscles always work in pairs, which are called antagonistic pairs;

▷ locomotion is the movement of a whole organism from place to place. Animals are adapted for a particular type of locomotion, e.g. swimming, running, flying, depending on the environment they live in;

▷ a tropism is a growth movement in plants, towards or away from a particular stimulus. Tropisms depend on the production of hormones.

Vertebrate skeletons

All vertebrates have an internal skeleton made of bone or cartilage.
The skeleton has three main functions:

1. to support the body (against the force of gravity);
2. to protect some internal organs;
3. the bones act as levers to make movement more efficient.

The Human skeleton

'Look at the diagram of a skeleton on p. 55.'

There are five main parts to the human skeleton:

1. the skull
2. the vertebral column
3. the limb girdles
    (a) shoulder (pectoral) girdle
    (b) hip (pelvic) girdle
4. rib cage and sternum
5. limbs

Aquatic and terrestrial vertebrates

When animals live in water, the water is able to support some of their weight. This means that their skeleton does not have to support their whole body weight, so we can see three important differences between the two types of skeletons:

1. Aquatic animals grow much bigger. The biggest living animal is the blue whale, which can grow to 100,000 kg. It can do this because the water supports some of its body weight.
2. The bones of an aquatic animal do not have to bear as much weight, so they are not as thick and strong as the bones of terrestrial animals. Elephants can grow to weigh about 6,500 kg, and they have very thick and heavy bones. Think about now much bigger a whale's bones would have to be if it lived on land.
3. Almost all terrestrial vertebrates walk on land supported by limbs; this means that their limbs must support their body weight. They have strong limb bones and limb girdles to transmit forces from the vertebral column.

Aquatic vertebrates swim through the water, so they do need strong limb bones to support their weight. They use their limb bones as paddles or flippers to propel them through water. Some aquatic vertebrates, e.g. seals, walruses, sea lions, come out of the water to rest on land. They are not very mobile, and cannot move far because their skeletons are not well adapted for life on land.

(a)   (b)

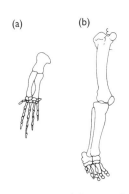

Fig. 8.24 Limb bones of (a) whale (b) elephant

Invertebrate skeletons

Invertebrates do not have an internal skeleton made of bone. There are two main types of invertebrate skeletons:

1. **Hydrostatic skeleton**, e.g. slugs or earthworms. This is simply a cylinder of fluid surrounded by two layers of muscle (circular and longitudinal). The two types of muscle are antagonistic to each other..

When the circular muscle contracts, that part of the body becomes longer and thinner. When the longitudinal muscle contracts, that part of the body becomes shorter and fatter. Waves of contraction pass along the animal, propelling it forwards.

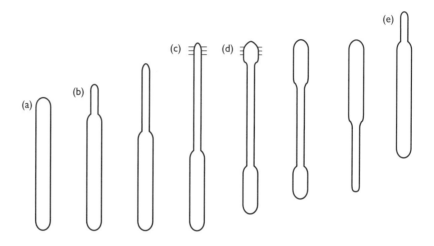

(a) Earthworm at rest.

(b) Circular muscles at front of earth worm contract, so this region becomes long and thin.

(c) Bristles are extended to anchor front end.

(d) Lonitudinal muscles in the middle of the earthworm contract, to pull back end forward.

(e) Process is repeated.

Fig. 8.25 Locomotion in earthworms

2. **Exoskeleton**, e.g. insects, crustaceans. This is a system of tough tubes and plates covering the outside of the animal's body like a suit of armour. There are thinner regions where two parts of the skeleton meet – these are the joints. Muscles are attached to the inside of the skeleton, and contract to move it.

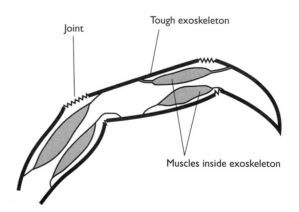

Fig. 8.26 Exoskeleton: insect leg

Structure of bones

If a typical bone is sawn in half, we can see that there are several distinct regions.

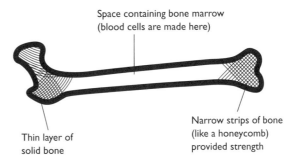

Fig. 8.27 Inside a typical bone (femur)

▷ **compact bone** – a tough layer of solid bone forming an outer covering;
▷ **spongy bone** – thinner strips of bone which are strong, but light;
▷ **bone marrow cavity** – inside some bones, where blood cells are made;
▷ **cartilage** – which covers the ends of bones where they form a joint.

Bone is a living material with three main constituents:

▷ **bone cells** – these make the bone and remain alive inside it. They allow the bone to grow, to repair itself if broken and to become stronger in response to activity.
▷ **minerals** – mainly calcium phosphate and calcium carbonate. These make the bone hard, so that it can resist compression and carry body weight.
▷ **protein fibres** – mainly collagen. These strengthen the bone, making it less likely to snap or crumble under pressure.

Joints

A joint occurs wherever two or more bones meet. There are different types of joints, with different ranges of movement.

The main types of joint found in the body are:

▷ fixed joint: no movement possible, e.g. between bones of the skull;
▷ gliding joint: bones slide over each other, e.g. between wrist bones and ankle bones;
▷ hinge joints: movement is in one plane only, due to the shape of the bones, e.g. elbow, knee;
▷ ball and socket joint: movement in all directions, due to the shape of the bones, e.g. hip, shoulder.

Inside a joint

Hinge joints and ball and socket joints are called **synovial joints** because they contain synovial fluid to reduce friction. They are stabilised by ligaments which are strong (have high tensile strength) but are slightly elastic. The articular surfaces of the bone are covered by cartilage which is strong and very smooth; it is not completely rigid so it can act as a shock absorber.

'Look at a diagram of a synovial joint on p. 56.'

The human elbow joint

This is a hinge joint which is operated by two muscles, the **biceps** and **triceps**.

'It is easy to remember how the muscles work: Biceps Bends the joint when it contracts.'

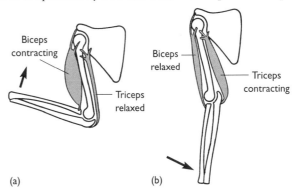

Fig. 8.28   (a)   (b)

The biceps is a **flexor muscle** because it bends (flexes) the joint.
The triceps is an **extensor** muscle because it extends (straightens) the joint.

Mark the following statements true or false.

(a)   The ribcage protects the spinal cord.

(b)   A hinge joint allows movement in every direction.

(c)   Biceps is a flexor muscle.

(d)   Tendons are elastic.

(e)   Ligaments are elastic.

(f)   Cartilage reduces friction inside a joint.

(g)   All joints are movable.

(h)   Bones contains living cells.

(i)   Earthworms have an exoskeleton.

(j)   Wasps have an exoskeleton.

(k)   Tendons attach muscles to bones.

Locomotion in animals

Locomotion means that the whole organism moves to get from place to place. It is important because it allows animals to:

▶   find food
▶   find a mate
▶   seek shelter
▶   colonise new areas
▶   escape from predators.

Animals have different methods of locomotion, depending on where they live. Most animals are **adapted** for one type of locomotion.

Pentadactyl limb and locomotion

Vertebrates, apart from fish, have a **pentadactyl limb pattern** (sometimes called a pendactyl limb pattern). This means that the arrangement of bones is basically similar in all vertebrate limbs.

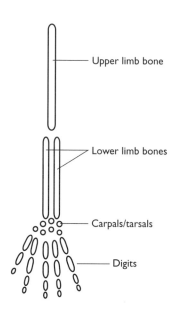

Fig. 8.29 Pentadactyl limb pattern

There is

one upper limb bone,
two lower limb bones,
several carpels (wrist or ankle bones),
five digits, made up of metacarpals and phalanges.

The actual structure depends on the use of the limbs,

e.g. in **birds** – the forelimb is used for flight,
     in **bats** – the forelimb is used for flight,
     in **horses** – the forelimb is used for running,
     in **moles** – the forelimb is used for digging.

Locomotion through the air (birds only)
Adaptations for flight
Birds which fly have several important adaptions:

▷   **Light bones** to retain strength but reduce mass. This occurs because bones are almost hollow with supporting bony struts inside (like a honeycomb structure).
▷   **Large sternum and keel** for attachment of flight muscles.
▷   **Feathers** to provide a large, surface area in contact with the air, but at minimum mass. Feathers have barbs which lock together to provide a continuous, strong surface in contact with the air.
▷   **Streamlined body shape** to reduce air resistance.

Remember:
Other animals can also fly, e.g. insects, bats, but have different adaptations. This section is only concerned with **birds**.

Principles of flight
There are two important features of the wing which allow flight to occur:

1.   shape of the wing;
2.   movement of the wing.

1. **Shape**

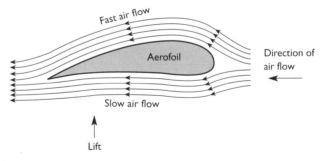

Fig. 8.30 Aerofoil

If you look at a wing in cross-section, it is an **aerofoil** shape. When air passes over it, it generates **lift**.

2. **Movement of the wing**
The wing moves up and down (flapping) or remains stationary (gliding). When a bird moves upwards, flapping flight is needed. The **down stroke** is the power stroke: feathers provide a strong surface to push against the air and forces the bird forwards and upwards. The **upstroke** is the recovery stroke; feathers rotate so that air can pass between them and the wing can easily be moved back to its original position.

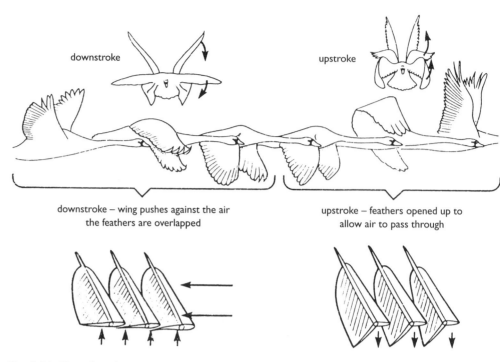

downstroke

upstroke

downstroke – wing pushes against the air
the feathers are overlapped

upstroke – feathers opened up to
allow air to pass through

Fig. 8.31 How the wing moves

Locomotion through water (fish only)
Adaptations for swimming
Fish have several important adaptations for moving through water:

▷ **streamlined body shape** to reduce water resistance;
▷ **smooth slippery scales** to reduce water resistance;
▷ **fins** to reduce unwanted movement (yawing, pitching and rolling) and to change direction of movement;

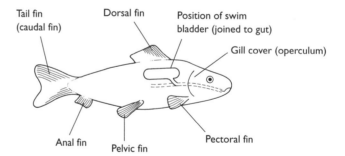

Tail fin
(caudal fin)

Dorsal fin

Position of swim
bladder (joined to gut)

Gill cover (operculum)

Anal fin

Pelvic fin

Pectoral fin

Fig. 8.32 Positions of fins

▷ **muscle blocks** arranged in a zig-zag pattern around the vertebral column to produce wave-like swimming movements;
▷ **swim bladder** to provide buoyancy, so that the fish can change its depth position in the water.

Remember:
Other animals can also move in water, e.g. *Euglena*, *Amoeba*, *Paramecium*, mayfly nymphs, etc., but they have different adaptations.

Principles of movement through water
How the fish moves through water depends on three things:

1. Contraction of muscles
The muscles blocks are arranged in a zig-zag pattern around the vertebral column. They contract in sequence to produce a wave-like motion, so the body bends from side to side. This propels the fish forwards in the water.

2. **Fins**

Fins have two functions:

(a)   to prevent unwanted movements,

e.g. rolling: prevented by dorsal and anal fins
     pitching: prevented by pectoral and pelvic fins
     yawing: prevented by dorsal and anal fins

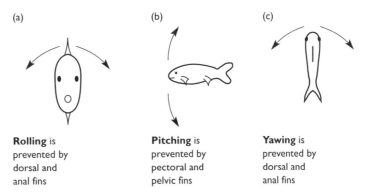

(a)	(b)	(c)
Rolling is prevented by dorsal and anal fins	**Pitching** is prevented by pectoral and pelvic fins	**Yawing** is prevented by dorsal and anal fins

Fig. 8.33 (a) Rolling (b) Pitching (c) Yawing

(b)   to cause changes in direction, allowing controlled movements upwards and downwards, left and right.

3. **Swim bladder**

This is a gas filled space (usually air filled) inside the fish's body. The fish can adjust the amount of gas in it to change its density so that it exactly matches the density of the water. In this way it can remain motionless without floating or sinking and can move more easily through the water. If the fish wants to change its depth, it can change the amount of gas in the swim bladder; this helps to resist damage to the body by water pressure.

Tropisms

A tropism is a growth movement of a plant in response to a stimulus.

Phototropism is growth in response to light. Shoots are **positively phototropic** – they grow towards light. This is beneficial because they have more light for photosynthesis. Roots are **negatively phototropic** – they grow away from light.

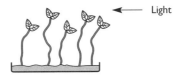

Light

Fig. 8.34 Shoots are positively phototropic

Geotropism is growth in response to gravity. Shoots are negatively geotropic – they grow away from the force of gravity (upwards). Roots are positively geotropic, they grow towards the force of gravity (downwards).

Tropisms are controlled by the distribution of a plant hormone called **auxin**. It is produced at the shoot tip and the root tip. If it is distributed evenly, then growth occurs evenly. If it is distributed unevenly, growth occurs unevenly and that part of the plant bends.

Phototropism
▷   Auxin is made in the shoot tip.
▷   Auxin collects on the side of the shoot away from the light.
▷   It causes cells on this side to grow **faster** (elongation) so the shoot curves towards the light.

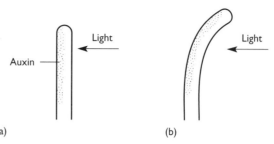

Fig. 8.35 Role of auxin in phototropism (a) auxin collects on the side of the shoot away from the light, (b) cells here elongate, so the shoot bends.

Geotropism
▷ Auxin is made in the root tip.
▷ Auxin collects in the lower side of the horizontal root.
▷ It causes cells on this side to grow more **slowly** so the root curves downwards (towards gravity).

'Notice the different effects of auxin in the root and the shoot. In the shoot it makes the cells grow faster, in the root it makes them grow more slowly.'

Fig. 8.36 Role of auxin in geotropism (a) auxin collects on the lower side of a horizontal root (b) cells here grow slowly, so root bends

Experiments with tropisms
There are two main types of experiments:

1. **Altering the stimulus,** e.g. providing light from one direction only, or removing the effects of gravity with a clinostat.
   (a) light

REVISION ACTIVITY 10

Predict how these seedlings will grow.

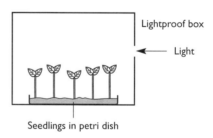

Fig. 8.37

(b) gravity

A clinostat slowly revolves, so it removes the effects of gravity. A bean seedling pinned to a clinostat for 4–5 days will develop a horizontal root, because auxin is evenly distributed in the root as it revolves.

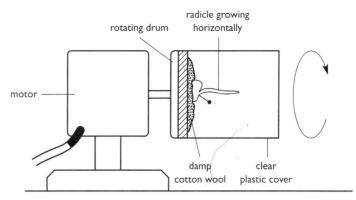

Fig. 8.38 Clinostat

2. **Experimenting on the root or shoot tip**
Remember, auxin is made in root and shoot tips, and light is detected at the tips.

REVISION ACTIVITY 10   State what will happen in each of these experiments.

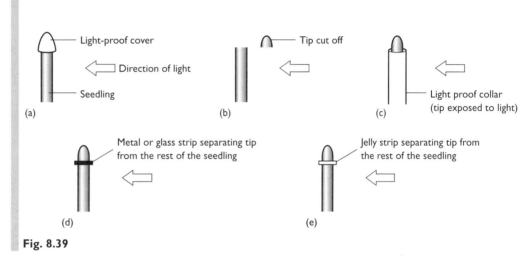

Fig. 8.39

SOLUTIONS TO REVISION ACTIVTIES

S1   (a)
Table 8.6

Features	Bacteria	Viruses	Fungi	Protoctists
are unicellular	✓	✗	S	✓
have a cell wall	✓	✗	✓	S
have a proper nucleus	✗	✗	✓	✓
have cytoplasm	✓	✗	✓	✓
have organelles	✗	✗	✓	✓
reproduce asexually	✓	✗	✓	✓
reproduce sexually	✗	✗	✓	✓
are useful to humans	S	✗	✓	✓
are harmful to humans	S	✓	S	S
are killed by antibiotics	✓	✗	✗	✗

(b)   Viruses, bacteria, yeasts, algae

S2   **bacteria:** slime capsule, decomposer, bacillus
       viruses: capsid, polyhedral, envelope, replicate, AIDS
       fungi: mould, sporangium, hyphae, decomposer, mycelium, chitin
       protoctists: malaria, chloroplasts

S3   (a)

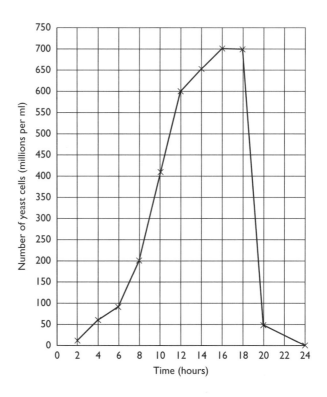

Fig. 8.40

   (b)   (i)   140 million per ml
         (ii)   11 hours
        (iii)   6 hours (6–12 hours)

   (c)   Population becomes constant in size (stationary phase) then decreases due to:
       ▶   lack of nutrients of oxygen,
       ▶   build up of waste products.

   (d)   30–40°C

S4   (a)   If the middle of frozen food is still frozen it may not heat up properly when the food is cooked. Bacteria may remain alive in this part of the food and cause food poisoning.

   (b)   If food is stored in a warm place, the numbers of bacteria increase very rapidly.

   (c)   When frozen foods defrosts, it warms up and the numbers of bacteria on it increase rapidly. If it is frozen and defrosted **again** the numbers of bacteria can be dangerously high.

   (d)   Bread contains more water than biscuits – biscuits are too dry for decomposers to work properly.

   (e)   Irradiated food may contain dangerous toxins even though all the bacteria have been killed.

S5   (a)   Malaria is a serious disease caused by a microbe called **Plasmodium** which is a type of **protoctist**. If a person is bitten by an infected female **mosquito**, the pathogens enters the blood stream. It multiples in **red blood** cells and **liver** cells. After a few days the infected cells burst open releasing more **Plasmodium** and toxins. The toxins cause a fever, and the person feels very ill. More cells can be infected and this cycle is repeated over and over again. A person with malaria may suffer from anaemia because so many **red blood** cells have burst. The mosquito acts as a **vector** because it carries the pathogen from one person to another.

(b) (i) use mosquito nets, mosquito repellant, insecticides;

(ii) kill them with insecticide, drain swamps/ponds where they breed, introduce predators to eat more of them, e.g. fish eat mosquito larvae in ponds.

(c) Antibiotics kill bacteria. Malaria is caused by a protoctist, not a bacterium.

S6 (a) (i) bacteria – TB, whooping cough, salmonella, cholera

viruses – flu, measles, AIDS, polio, hepatitis B

protoctist – malaria

fungi – athlete's foot, thrush

(ii) TB, whooping cough, salmonella, cholera, i.e. bacterial diseases.

(b) (i) **antibodies** are chemicals made by white blood cells in the body,

antigens are marker proteins on the surface of the cells.

(ii) **antibiotics** kill bacteria inside the body when they are taken as medicine,

disinfectants are strong chemicals used to kill microbes outside the body, e.g. on worksurfaces, drains.

(iii) **B-lymphocytes** make antibodies to kill pathogens,

T-lymphocytes kill cells infected by viruses.

(iv) **active immunity** occurs when a person makes antibodies,

passive immunity occurs when a person is given ready-made antibodies, e.g. in anti-serum.

(v) **innate immunity** is the defence mechanisms which are always present to prevent disease, e.g. skin, acid in stomach,

acquired immunity is the ability to make antibodies to kill a particular pathogen.

S7 (a) Yeast feed on sugar.

(b) The flask would explode if the gas could not escape.

(c) Fermentation occurs faster at warm temperatures (because it is an enzyme-controlled reaction).

(d) Other micro-organisms could kill the yeast or spoil the product.

S8 (a) protein synthesis; using the base code.

(b) (i) 1,5,7,14

(ii) When meiosis occurs, only half of the chromosomes are passed on to the egg or sperm – the rest will not be present. So only half the mother's bands are present.

(iii) Yes; some of the child's bands (2,6,8,15) are not from the mother; all have come from the husband; all the bands in the child are from mother/husband.

(c) ▷ To link a suspect to crime, e.g. blood found at scene of crime.

▷ To solve cases where babies are mixed up in hospitals at birth.

▷ To identify a person charged with rape (if the police have some of the sperm/semen).

▷ To identify individuals (everyone's DNA is different).

S9 (a) False   (f) True

(b) False   (g) False

(c) True   (h) True

(d) False   (i) False

(e) True   (j) True

                   (k) True

S10 The plants will curve towards the light.

S11 (a) The seedling will not bend; the tip is covered by light, so it cannot detect light.

(b) The seedling will not bend; the tip is removed, so no auxin is produced.

(c) The seedling will bend towards the light; the tip is intact and uncovered so phototropism proceeds as normal.

(d) The seedling will not bend; the tip detects light and produces auxin, but the auxin cannot travel away from the tip due to the impermeable barrier.

(e) The seedling will bend towards the light; the tip detects light and makes auxin, and the auxin diffuses through the jelly.

> ## EXAMINATION QUESTIONS

▷ **Question 1** The diagram (Fig. 8.41) shows a fermenter used to produce penicillin in large quantities from the fungus *Penicillium*.

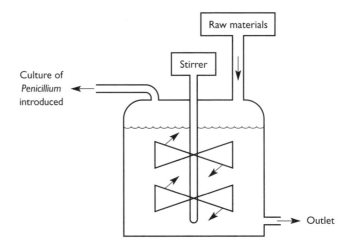

Fig. 8.41

(a) (i) State **two** raw materials which *Penicillium* needs and explain why the fungus needs them. *(4)*

(ii) Suggest why the mixture is stirred continuously. *(1)*

(b) The graph shows the production of penicillin by the fungus.

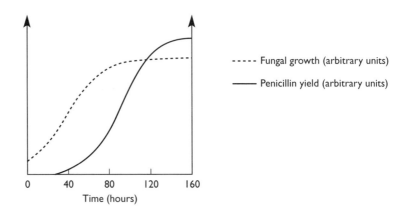

Fig. 8.42

(i) After how many hours does *Penicillium* start to produce penicillin? *(1)*

(ii) Suggest a reason for the decrease in the rate of growth of Penicillium after 80 hours. *(1)*

(c) State how the fungus is separated from the penicillin at the end of production. *(1)*

(WJEC)

▷ **Question 2** 'Quick-chicks' a modern factory farm, can produce thousands of oven-ready chickens in nine weeks from one 'hen house'. The diagrams below show the main stages in producing oven-ready chickens. To check for *Salmonella* bacteria, samples were taken from the hen house floor and from the chickens at each stage. The number of *Salmonella* bacteria in each sample was recorded.

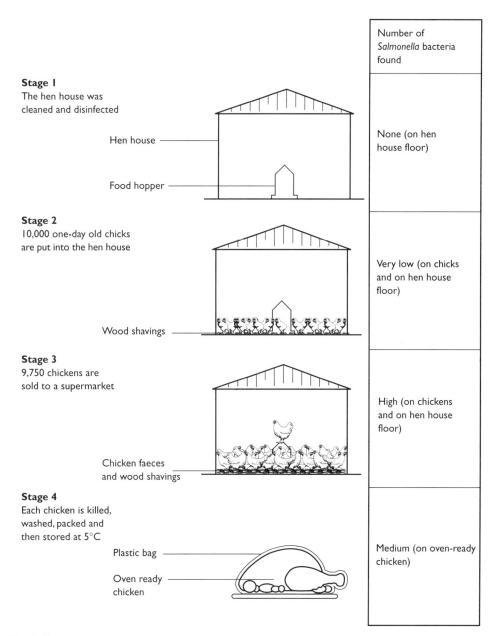

Fig. 8.43

(a) Why were no *Salmonella* bacteria found in samples taken from the hen house floor during stage 1? *(1)*

(b) Suggest how the *Salmonella* bacteria reached the hen house by stage 2. *(2)*

(c) (i) In which part of a chicken do *Salmonella* bacteria live? *(1)*
   (ii) During which stage did the *Salmonella* bacteria spread most effectively from chicken to chicken?
   Give a reason for your answer. *(2)*

(d) Suggest why there were only 9,750 chickens by stage 3. *(2)*

(e) Why had the numbers of *Salmonella* bacteria decreased by the end of stage 4? *(2)*

(f) Give two advantages of keeping an oven-ready chicken in a plastic bag during storage. *(1)*

(g)   A customer buys a 'Quick-chick' chicken from a supermarket.   *(2)*
   (i)   Suggest **one** condition which would increase the number of *Salmonella* bacteria in the chicken.   *(1)*
   (ii)   How could the customer make sure that all the *Salmonella* bacteria were killed before eating the chicken?   *(1)*
   (iii)   A family ate chicken meat containing a high number of *Salmonella* bacteria. Suggest one effect this may have on the family.

(LONDON)

▷ **Question 3**   Yoghurt is made from milk.

(a)   Write a word equation for the process involved.   *(2)*

(b)   The flow diagram below shows the stages in the manufacture of fruit yoghurt.

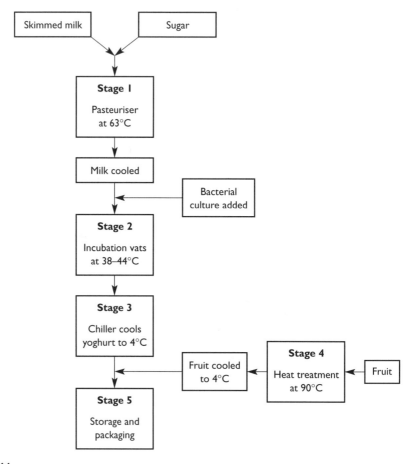

Fig. 8.44

Explain the importance of stages 1,2 and 4.
Stage 1   *(2)*
Stage 2   *(2)*
Stage 4   *(2)*

(c)   A dairy farmer sold milk to be made into yoghurt. The milk could not be used because it contained small amounts of an antibiotic.
Explain why milk containing antibiotic cannot be used to make yoghurt.   *(2)*

(LONDON)

▷ **Question 4**   (a)   Table 8.7 lists different types of foods and the organisms which are used to make them. One example has been done for you. Complete the table.

Table 8.7

Food	Micro organism involved in the production of food
wine	yeast
cheese	
yoghurt	
bread	
vinegar	
beer	

(5)

(b) Food can be preserved in different ways.
   (i) Briefly explain how food is preserved by canning. *(4)*
   (ii) Name **two** other ways in which food can be preserved. *(2)*

(c) Read the information given below. Using this information and your knowledge of biology answer questions (c) (i) to (iv).

> Many supermarkets now sell food containing single-cell protein, SCP. Many of the processes for manufacturing SCP use wastes as their starting material. They can therefore help to solve local pollution problems as well as providing valuable food. One example uses flour waste from the flour industries to grow a fungus called *Fusarium*. The fungus is grown, harvested and processed to make fibres which are pressed together to make a material called mycoprotein. The texture is made to resemble meat chunks and can be flavoured to taste like chicken or beef. It is used to make pies and other products and is sold under the name of Quorn™. The mycoprotein has a high protein and fibre content but no cholesterol.

   (i) Why is the mycoprotein sometimes called a single-cell protein? *(1)*
   (ii) Describe one way that SCP manufacture can solve a pollution problem. *(2)*
   (iii) Why is the fact that mycoprotein has no cholesterol a strong selling point for this protein source? *(2)*
   (iv) Which component of mycoprotein may help to prevent bowel disease?

(MEG)

▷ **Question 5**   The diagram (Fig 8.45) shows a fermenter which is used to make vinegar.

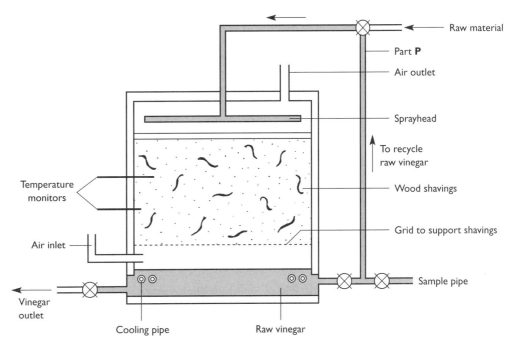

Fig. 8.45

(a) (i) What is the purpose of the wood shavings in the fermenter?   *(2)*
    (ii) What substance is used as a raw material in the manufacture of vinegar?   *(1)*

(b) Part P of the fermenter is used to increase the production of vinegar. Explain how this works.   *(2)*

(c) Explain why blocking the air outlet would reduce the amount of vinegar produced.   *(2)*

(d) Why is it important to monitor the temperature inside the fermenter?   *(2)*

(LONDON)

▷ **Question 6** (a) Families living in rural areas of China have used biogas generators for many years. The generators are tanks made from soil and a weak cement mixture which sometimes allows the tanks to crack. The tanks are buried to reduce heat loss. Every few weeks, manure and household wastes are added to the tanks which need to be quite large. Methane is collected through pipes from the tanks. The fermented material is rich in nitrogen and is used as a fertiliser. About twice a year the tanks are cleaned but a little of the fermented material is always left at the bottom of the tank when new waste is added.

(i) State and explain **one advantage** and **one disadvantage** of using this type of biogas generator.

Advantage   _____   *(1)*

Explanation   _____   *(1)*

Disadvantage   _____   *(1)*

Explanation   _____   *(1)*

(ii) Explain why some fermented material should be left in the tank when it is cleaned out.

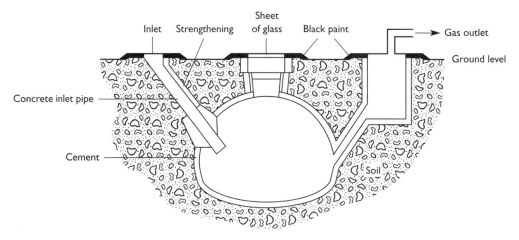

Fig. 8.46

(b) The design of the biogas generator shown in the diagram (Fig. 8.46) makes the temperature inside the tank 10°C higher than the old type of tank. As a result, the new generator produces methane at a faster rate than in the older design. The tank is also smaller than the older design. Technologists think that the new type of generator will be more popular and because of its small size will be possible to use in towns.

(i) Explain how the tank could increase the temperature inside it.   *(2)*

(ii) State why a higher temperature inside the new tank could improve its efficiency.   *(2)*

(iii) Above a certain temperature methane is not produced. Give an explanation for this.   *(2)*

(WJEC)

▷ **Question 7**   Some students investigated the production of alcohol from sugars by yeast. They used solutions of the same concentration of four different sugars, **P, Q, R** and **S**. For each sugar they set up the apparatus as in diagram **A**. The length of the bubble of carbon dioxide shown in the diagram **B** was measured every five minutes for each apparatus. The temperature was kept at 25°C. The amount of carbon dioxide indicates the amount of alcohol produced.

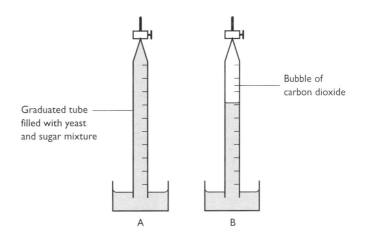

Fig. 8.47

Table 8.8 below shows the results of the investigation.

Table 8.8

Mixture	Length of CO_2 bubble at five minute intervals (cm)						
	5 mins	10 mins	15 mins	20 mins	25 mins	30 mins	35 mins
Yeast + Sugar P	3.0	10.0	17.0	26.0	35.0	38.0	40.0
Yeast + Sugar Q	0.5	1.0	1.5	2.0	2.0	2.0	2.0
Yeast + Sugar R	0.5	1.0	1.0	1.5	1.5	1.5	1.5
Yeast + Sugar S	4.0	11.0	19.0	27.0	36.0	40.0	42.0
Yeast + Water	0.5	0.5	0.5	1.0	1.0	1.0	1.0

(a) (i)   Why was the yeast and water mixture included in the experiment?   *(1)*
     (ii)   Which sugar produces most alcohol?   *(1)*
     (iii) Why was it important that the tubes were **completely** filled with yeast and sugar mixture at the start of the experiment?   *(1)*
     (iv)   Why did the rate of production of carbon dioxide slow down after a time?   *(1)*

(b)   Suggest **two** ways in which the rate of alcohol production could have been increased.
    (2)

(c)   Yeast lives naturally on fruit. Some of the sugars (P, Q, R and S) came from animals. Suggest which of these sugars came from animals. Give a reason for your answer.   *(2)*
    (LONDON)

▷ **Question 8**   Malaria is a disease which kills many people in tropical parts of the world. The female *Anopheles* mosquito acts as a vector for the disease.

(a)   What is meant by the term 'vector'?   *(2)*

(b)   The diagram below shows the life cycle of the *Anopheles* mosquito.

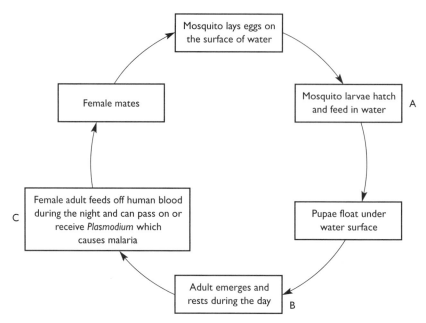

Fig. 8.48

Explain how the disease could be controlled at points A, B and C on the diagram.

A _____ *(2)*

B _____ *(2)*

C _____ *(2)*

(c) Malaria can be controlled by the use of drugs.

The effectiveness of two drugs, **X** and **Y**, was investigated using people working in a cocoa plantation. The people were divided into three groups of equal numbers.

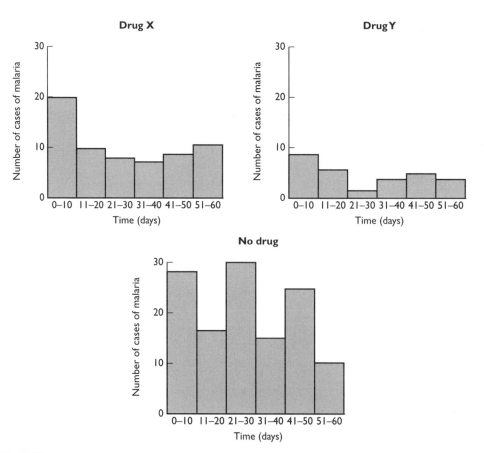

Fig. 8.49

Group 1 was given a daily dose of drug **X**.
Group 2 was given a daily dose of drug **Y**.
Group 3 was not given either of the drugs.

Over a period of two months, the number of cases of malaria in each of these groups was recorded. The histogram (Fig. 8.49) show the results.

(i)   State **two** precautions which should be taken when choosing the people in each group.   *(2)*
(ii) Why was Group 3 used?   *(1)*
(iii) State **one** conclusion which can be drawn about the efficiency of drugs X and Y.
                                                                                          (1)
(iv) Suggest one way in which the number of cases of malaria could be further reduced using only these drugs.   *(1)*

(LONDON)

ANSWERS TO EXAMINATION QUESTIONS

▷ **Question 1**   (a) (i)   **oxygen** is needed for respiration,
                              sugars are needed to provide energy by respiration,
                              minerals, e.g. nitrates are needed to make protein.
                        (ii) it is stirred to mix the fungus and the nutrients, and so that the fungus will not sink to the bottom.

            (b) (i)   30 hours
                 (ii) lack of food/build up of waste products

            (c) The fungus is separated out by filtration, then the penicillin is purified

▷ **Question 2**   (a) It had been cleaned and disinfected, so the bacteria were all killed.

            (b) Some chicks were infected by *Salmonella* before being introduced to the hen house.

            (c) (i)   They live in the gut, (1) but are also found on the outside of the body, e.g. feet and feathers. (1)
                 (ii) Stage 2 (1)

                 At the start of stage two, there were low levels of bacteria.
                 By the end of Stage 2, there were high levels (on the floor and on chickens). They have spread because:
                 ▶ chickens are packed into a small space; (1)
                 ▶ they are standing in faeces containing bacteria. (1)

            (d) Some had died, (1) e.g. due to trampling, fighting, infection, lack of food. (1)

            (e) Chickens have been washed, and had the gut removed. Both of these processes would remove bacteria. (1)

            (f) If it is kept in a plastic bag
                 1. Any bacteria on it will not contaminate other foods. (1)
                 2. No new bacteria can get onto it.

            (g) (i)   Storing it in a warm place. (1)
                 (ii) Cook it thoroughly. (1)
                 (iii) Sickness/diarrhoea/high temperature/stomach ache.

▷ **Question 3**   (a) lactose ⟶ lactic acid + energy
                          (1)   (1)

            (b) **Stage 1** – pasteurisation kills microbes in milk, (1) this prevents disease and prevents other microbes affecting the process. (1)
                 Stage 2 – incubation allows the bacteria to grow fast. (1), it is the optimum temperature (1) They will convert lactose to lactic acid efficiently, so pH will fall, and milk proteins will cause solidification. (1)

Stage 4 – heat treatment sterilises fruit, killing microbes. (1)
This prevents the yoghurt being contaminated, and prevents possible food poisoning. (1)

(c) The antibiotics will kill the bacteria which convert lactose to lactic acid, (1) so the whole process would not work. (1)
(Note: some people are allergic to antibiotics) (1)

▷ **Question 4** (a) cheese – bacteria
yoghurt – bacteria
bread – yeast
vinegar – bacteria
beer – yeast

(b) (i) **Canning**. Food is cooked inside the can (without the lid sealed on) and air is driven out, before the lid is sealed on. (1)
Cooking kills microbes; (1) sealing the can prevents entry of more microbes. (1)
The can is air-tight. (1)
(ii) Freezing, drying, pickling, salting, sugaring, vacuum packing, irradiation, pasteurisation.

(c) (i) Because it comes from single-celled organisms, e.g. yeasts or algae.
(ii) It uses plant waste as a raw material, (1) so there is less waste to be burned or dumped in land-fill sites. This reduces air or land pollution. (1)
(iii) Cholesterol is linked to heart disease, (1) so a low-cholesterol food is a healthy food. (1)
(iv) Fibre from the fungal cell walls. (1)

▷ **Question 5** (a) (i) Bacteria live on the surface of wood shavings, (1) this improves air circulation in the fermenter, (1) and keeps bacteria in contact with air and ethanol. (1)
(ii) ethanol

(b) Fluid is recycled/returned to the fermenter, (1) to make sure all ethanol has been converted to vinegar. (1)

(c) The bacteria need oxygen (1) for respiration.

(d) Bacteria work best at a warm temperature, (1)
if it is too cold, they work slowly, (1)
if it is too hot, they are denatured. (1)

▷ **Question 6** (a) (i) Advantage: useful fuel is made from a waste product.
Explanation: methane can be used for heating and lighting.
Advantage: it is cheap to make.
Explanation: the raw material is free (biodegradable waste) and there are no running costs.
Disadvantage: it could be dangerous.
Explanation: methane is a flammable gas, so it is important that it does not explode.
Disadvantage: it would smell unpleasant.
Explanation: some gases will escape during the decay process, e.g. when the inlet/outlet is opened.
(ii) It contains bacteria which break down waste, (1) so it will start to break down the next batch of waste as soon as the waste is added. (1) It is a starter culture. (1)

(b) (i) Temperature is raised because:
▷ black paint reduces heat loss by radiation; (1)
▷ thick walls reduce heat loss by conduction; (1)
▷ glass is a good insulator. (1)
(ii) Enzymes work faster at warmer temperatures, (1)
a 10°C rise in temperature will double the rate, (1)
so biogas is produced more quickly. (1)

(iii) Enzymes are denatured, (1) so they no longer work at all, (1) and waste is not broken down. (1)

▷ **Question 7**   (a)   (i) It is a control, to show that sugar is needed to make carbon dioxide.
(ii) **S** (because it has the highest fermentation rate).
(iii) So there was no air present (process must be anaerobic); also so the tubes could be compared.
(iv) Lack of sugar, or build up of ethanol poisons yeast.

(b)   increase the temperature slightly, (1) add more sugar, (1) add more yeast.

(c)   **Q** and **R** came from animals. (1)
Not much carbon dioxide was produced, (1) because yeast enzymes could not break down those sugars. (1)

▷ **Question 8**   (a)   An organism which carries disease from one individual to another (1) without suffering from the disease. (1)

(b)   **A**: add fish to the water to eat eggs or larvae, (1)
drain wet areas, or cover tanks, etc. (1)
spray water with insecticide. (1)
B: add oil or detergent to water surface to stop pupae breathing and prevent adults emerging, (1)
C: use insecticide to kill adults. (1)
use mosquito net or repellent to prevent being bitten, (1)
use insecticide to kill adult. (1)

(c)   (i) They should be the same age.
They should be healthy, i.e. not have other diseases.
They should be outside for the same length of time.
They should all have an equal risk, e.g. all use insect repellent, or none do, etc.   *(2)*
(ii) Group 3 is a control, so you can assess the effectiveness of the drugs. (1)
(iii) Both are effective, but Y works better than X. (1)
(iv) Give a mixture of both drugs. (1)
Give higher doses of both drugs. (1)

▷ **STUDENT'S ANSWER WITH EXAMINER'S COMMENTS**

Some students investigated the increase in the volume of bread dough.

Equal amounts of identical dough were placed in three separate syringes. Each syringe was connected to a set of apparatus as shown in the diagram below.

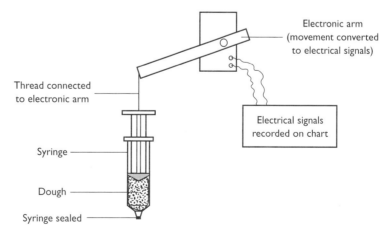

Fig. 8.50

Each syringe was placed in a water bath set at a different temperature (25°C, 35°C and 45°C).

(continued)

The graph below shows the changes in volume of the dough at each temperature.

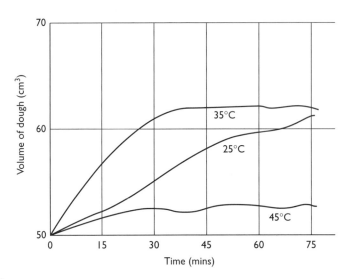

Fig. 8.51

(a) Why did the volume of the dough increase at all three temperatures

'Correct' ——————▶ *yeast was making carbon dioxide* ✓   *(1)*

(b) Explain the shape of the graph for the dough kept at 35°C and at 45°C.

35°C

'The key to this question
is **explain**.' ——————▶ *a lot of carbon dioxide is made at first, then it levels off.*   *(2)*

'This is not an **explanation**
of the graph. Respiration
is rapid at first, because
the yeast is at its
optimum temperature
(enzymes work well). It
levels off due to lack of
sugar, or build up of
waste products.'

45°C

less carbon dioxide is made. It is too hot for respiration to occur properly ✓   *(2)*

(c) In certain conditions, yeast and sugar will produce alcohol.
     What are these conditions?

'Enzymes controlling
respiration have been
denatured by the high
temperature.'

if there is no oxygen. ✓   *(1)*

(d) The alcohol in wine turns to vinegar very quickly after a bottle has been
     opened, leaving the wine with a sour taste.
     Wine sold in special boxes keeps for much longer.

The diagram below show a wine bottle and a wine box, before and after opening.

'Yes, when conditions are
anaerobic.'

Bottle

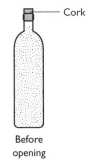

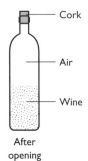

(continued)

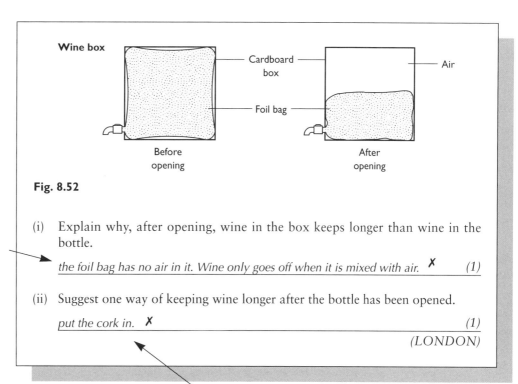

Fig. 8.52

'This student has not mentioned the bacteria which changed wine into vinegar. The bacteria need air. The wine box has no air in it, and it does not allow the bacteria to get in.'

(i) Explain why, after opening, wine in the box keeps longer than wine in the bottle.

the foil bag has no air in it. Wine only goes off when it is mixed with air. ✗   (1)

(ii) Suggest one way of keeping wine longer after the bottle has been opened.

put the cork in. ✗   (1)

(LONDON)

'This would not stop the wine going off because there is still air in the bottle, you could remove the air with a vacuum pump.'

SUMMARY

Micro-organisms

▷ There are four main types of micro-organisms: bacteria, viruses, fungi and protoctists (protozoa).

▷ Micro-organisms may be helpful to humans, e.g. used in food production, harmful to humans, e.g. cause diseases in humans (or in animals or plants humans depend on), or may have little effect on humans.
   Micro-organisms which cause disease are known as pathogens.
   Micro-organisms (or other living things) which live in or on a living organism and cause it harm are known as parasites.

▷ Bacteria are single-celled organisms about a thousandth of a millimeter in diameter.
   Their shape varies according to their type, e.g. spherical, rod-shaped, helical.
   They have a single chromosome made of DNA but no proper nucleus, and their cytoplasm is surrounded by a cell wall.
   They reproduce by binary fission (a simple form of asexual reproduction).
   Some bacteria are pathogens, e.g. causing salmonella, cholera, TB.
   Some bacteria are useful, e.g. in manufacture of yoghurt, cheese, vinegar.
   Many bacteria have little effect on humans.

▷ Viruses are much smaller than bacteria, and only multiply inside the cells of living organisms.
   They have a very simple structure: a small piece of nucleic acid (RNA or DNA) surrounded by a protein coat (the capsid), and possibly an outer envelope.
   Viruses do not have a nucleus or cytoplasm, and they do not carry out the basic life processes, e.g. feeding, respiration, excretion, etc.
   They replicate (copy themselves) inside a host cell, and usually kill the host cell when they are released.
   All viruses are parasites, and all viruses are pathogenic to their host. Some viruses cause disease in humans, e.g. measles, flu, AIDS, hepatitis.

▷ Fungi are bigger than bacteria, and may be single celled, e.g. yeasts, or multi-cellular, e.g. moulds, mushrooms.
   Fungi have a proper nucleus and cytoplasm, and cells are surrounded by a cell wall.
   Multi-cellular fungi consist of a mycelium made up of branched hyphae and reproduce by releasing spores.
   Unicellular fungi are spherical or oval, and reproduce by budding (simple asexual reproduction) or by sexual reproduction.
   Some fungi are pathogens, e.g. causing athlete's foot, and many plant diseases.
   Some fungi are useful, e.g. in baking and brewing, in the manufacture of antibiotics, as a food source.
   Many fungi have little effect on humans.

SUMMARY CONT.

▷ Protoctists (protozoa) are single-celled, simple organisms.

   Some are similar to plants (algae), and are very important as producers in food chains. Others are similar to animal cells, e.g. Amoeba, and feed on organic material. They have a nucleus and cytoplasm, and some have a cellulose cell wall.

   Some protoctists are pathogens, e.g. causing malaria and a type of dysentery.

   Some protoctists are useful, e.g. as a food source for humans or animals.

   Most protoctists have little effect on humans.

▷ Bacteria and fungi can be grown in the lab on petri dishes containing nutrient agar, or in vessels called fermenters.

   The culture medium must contain carbohydrate and minerals, and some microbes need vitamins or protein in addition to this.

   Conditions for growth must be carefully controlled, e.g. optimum temperature, pH and air supply, to get maximum yield.

▷ Viruses can only survive inside living cells, so they are difficult to grow in the laboratory.

▷ Protoctists can be grown in fermenters: some will need light in order to photosynthesise.

▷ Aseptic technique is very important when handling microbes. This prevents contamination of the microbes you are growing with other organisms, and prevents contamination of the laboratory environment.

Micro-organisms and disease

▷ Not all diseases are caused by microbes: some are genetic, e.g. cystic fibrosis, some are environmental, e.g. lung cancer, some are degenerative, e.g. arthritis, some are dietary, e.g. scurvy.

▷ Pathogenic bacteria can enter the body in food and water, they can be breathed in, or be transferred by direct contact.

▷ Antibiotics damage bacterial cells walls, and will kill bacteria. They are ineffective against viruses, fungi or protoctists.

▷ Some bacterial infections can be avoided by careful food handling and storage and by good personal hygiene. Proper cooking will kill bacteria in food, and disinfectants will kill bacteria in the home environment.

▷ Pathogenic viruses can enter the body in food or water but they are usually breathed in, or transferred by direct contact. They will invade cells and replicate inside them, causing tissue damage when they are released.

▷ Viruses can only be treated with anti-viral drugs, and some of these have serious side effects. Many viral infections can be avoided by immunisation (vaccination).

▷ Pathogenic fungi are normally transferred by direct contact. Infections can be treated with anti-fungal drugs.

▷ Pathogenic protoctists may enter the body through contaminated food or water, or may be spread by an animal vector, e.g. malaria is spread by mosquitoes.

▷ The human body has several defence mechanisms to combat pathogens including:

   (a)   phagocytic white blood cells which engulf pathogens;

   (b)   antibodies made by lymphocytes.

      These mechanisms (a) and (b) are called natural immunity.

      Immunisation (vaccination) can improve the body's response to infection. This is called acquired immunity.

Biotechnology

This is the use of micro-organisms to make products useful to humans, or to carry out complex processes. Examples of biotechnology include food production, sewage treatment, production of enzymes, fuels and pharmaceutical products, e.g. antibiotics, hormones, vitamins and vaccines.

▷ Yeasts (fungi) respire anaerobically if they are grown without oxygen.

   glucose ——————⟶ energy + carbon dioxide + ethanol

▷ This reaction (sometimes called fermentation) is very important for brewing and baking.

▷ Many fungi will produce antibiotics, e.g. penicillin: these are chemicals which slow the growth of bacteria or even kill them. If fungi are grown in fermenters, in the right conditions, large amounts of antibiotics can be obtained.

▷ Some fungi can be used to make human or animal foods (mycoprotein), e.g. moulds grown in a fermenter are processed to make 'Quorn'. This is high in protein and fibre, and low in cholesterol and fat.

▷ Some bacteria (called lactic acid bacteria) can convert lactose (a type of sugar found in milk) into lactic acid. This is the basis for yoghurt production, and is also important in the manufacture of cheese.

▷ Some bacteria convert alcohol into vinegar when there is oxygen present. These are called acetic acid bacteria.

▷ Many bacteria and fungi are used to manufacture enzymes. The enzymes can be used in biological washing powders, in food processing, e.g. as flour improvers, as meat tenderizers, in confectionery production, in baby foods (to 'pre-digest' food) and in brewing.

SUMMARY CONT.

▷ Some bacteria can be used to convert plant waste, e.g. sugar cane waste, into ethanol for use as fuel. This is known as gasohol, and can be mixed with petrol for use in cars.

▷ Some bacteria can be used to convert domestic waste, e.g. human and animal faeces, biodegradable rubbish, into methane gas for use as fuel. This is known as biogas, and can be used for heating, to work machinery, etc.

▷ Some bacteria and fungi are very important in sewage treatment. They are decomposers, and they break down organic material in urine and faeces to form carbon dioxide and water.

▷ Bacteria and fungi can be changed by genetic engineering to produce human hormones, e.g. insulin, growth hormones, or to make vaccines.

▷ Domestic plants and animals can be changed by genetic engineering to produce products containing vaccines,
    e.g. milk which provides immunity from diseases,
    potatoes/bananas which provide immunity from disease.

Movement and support

Animals have a skeleton which helps to support the body and is used in movement. In vertebrates this is an internal skeleton, made of bone or cartilage. In invertebrates the skeleton may be an external covering, e.g. in insects, crustaceans, or may be a core of fluid, e.g. hydrostatic skeleton of earthworms.

▷ Bones are made of minerals and protein, and contain living bone cells. They are strong, and resist compression. They act as levers when they are moved by muscles. Cartilage covers the joint surfaces to reduce friction. Ligaments stabilise joints.

▷ Muscles can contract to move bones. They are attached to bones by tendons (these cannot change in length), so when muscles contract, bones are pulled closer together. Muscles always work in pairs (antagonistic pairs), e.g. biceps and triceps, which have opposite effects.

▷ Animals are adapted for locomotion in a particular habitat. Many vertebrates have a pentadactyl limb pattern, but the detailed structure depends on the function of the limb,
    e.g. in birds, forelimbs are adapted as wings for flight
       in the mole, forelimbs are adapted as strong legs for digging.

▷ Birds have strong, light bones to reduce body mass for flight. Wings provide an aerofoil shape, and feathers provide a very large surface area with minimum mass. Birds have large breast muscles to move the wings for flapping flight.

▷ Fish are a streamlined shape, and scales reduce friction to allow efficient movement. Paired fins reduce pitching, and allow the animal to change direction. Median fins reduce yawing and rolling (side to side movement). Muscle blocks arranged in a zig-zag pattern around the vertebral column produce a wave-like movement along the length of the body, and many fish have a swim bladder for buoyancy.

▷ Some protoctists can move through water by beating cilia or flagella, or can change shape to creep across the substrate.

▷ Plant movements are called tropisms – a tropism is a growth movement in response to a stimulus,
    e.g. shoots grow towards light: this is phototropism
       roots grow downwards (stimulus is gravity: this is geotropism).
    Tropisms depend on production of hormones, e.g. auxin by the root or shoot tip.